MOSTLY ON THE EDGE

THE EDGE

KARL HESS

An Autobiography

Edited by Karl Hess Jr.

 **Prometheus Books**

59 John Glenn Drive
Amherst, New York 14228-2197

Published 1999 by Prometheus Books

03 02 01 00 99   5 4 3 2 1

Library of Congress Cataloging-in-Publication Data

Hess, Karl, 1923–1994
    Mostly on the edge, an autobiography / edited by Karl Hess, Jr.
       p.   cm.
    Includes bibliographical references.
    ISBN 1–57392–687–6 (cloth : alk. paper)
    1. Hess, Karl, 1923–1994. 2. Social reformers—United States—Biography.
3. Journalists—United States—Biography. 4. Libertarians—United States—
Biography. I. Hess, Karl, 1947–   . II. Title.
HV28.H439A3   1999
303.48'4'092—dc21
[B]   98–55751
                                          CIP

Printed in the United States of America on acid-free paper

Contents

Preface

Mostly on the Edge is the autobiography of Karl Hess. It is the story of a man whose life touched many of the compelling events of twentieth-century America.

Karl was on the edge of political power, working for the national committee of the Republican Party and writing as senior speechwriter for Sen. Barry M. Goldwater in his 1964 presidential bid. He was on the edge of great events, first as a journalist, next as an anti-Communist, and finally as a voice in the advance of libertarian thought. He was on the cultural edge, immersing himself in the social changes that transformed America in the years during and after the Vietnam War. He was on the edge of ideology, moving from a youthful socialism to an ardent Republicanism to a vocal New Leftism to a peaceful and personal anarchism. He was on the edge of the future, speaking of the promise of technology and speaking out for the education of children. He was on the edge of ideas, championing a politics of place that is today changing the political landscape of America. Most of all, he was on the edge of the great American pursuit of happiness. And he found it, on the edge of the Opequon Creek, in the Eastern Panhandle of West Virginia among family, friends, and neighbors.

Mostly on the Edge speaks for itself; it needs no prefatory explanation to reveal what meanings and messages lie hidden or revealed in its passages. But there is one essential feature of the autobiography that the reader should understand. It was not completed by the time of Karl's death.

Karl set his mind to writing his life story in January 1988. What little progress he made that year came to a screeching halt when he suffered a near-fatal aortic dissection after a speaking engagement in Hartford, Connecticut. Already physically worn down by a weakened heart, his recovery was slow, preventing him from making any substantial progress on his autobiography for almost two years.

By 1990, his energy had rebounded as much as it ever would in the four years that remained of his life. He was able to start, in earnest, the writing of *Mostly on the Edge*. Progress, however, was slow, interrupted by recurring bouts of congestive heart failure and repeated visits to the University of Virginia hospital. Nonetheless, almost half of the book was either completed or partially sketched by the time of his heart transplant in the summer of 1992.

Karl never fully recovered from the aftereffects of the heart transplant. His body was wracked with continuous pain up to his death on April 22, 1994. Yet amidst that pain, he managed to complete or sketch out an additional third of the manuscript. Sadly, he was unable to complete the book before his death.

Completing what my father began became a labor of love for me. He helped immensely by leaving behind outlines, several versions of individual chapters, and a wealth of notes and letters. At first, of course, the project seemed daunting; how could an unfinished autobiography be finished and still remain an autobiography? But, as I reviewed the chapters he had written and the thousands of pages of recent letters and notes, I realized that the completed autobiography lay within my hands. All I had to do was to follow his outline and to pick and choose among his voluminous correspondence the remaining pieces to the finished work that is now *Mostly on the Edge*.

Chapters 1–14 were either completed or close to completion by the time of my father's death. Several of the chapters required intensive editing, much of which was provided by Catherine Murray. A few of the chapters required degrees of rewriting or the insertion of additional materials from notes, letters, and, in the cases of chapters 7 and 9, written accounts (fully explained and italicized in the text) from two of Karl's closest friends, Ralph de Toledano and Bill Lewis.

Chapters 15–20 presented a much greater challenge, for they were largely incomplete. Letters and notes provided a starting point to finishing them, but what made their completion possible were the nearly twenty hours of taped autobiographical interviews of Karl conducted by Charles Murray. Charles met my father for the first time in the spring of 1990. As their friendship quickened and became closer, Charles suggested that they turn their long hours of conversations into recorded discussions of my father's life. They did just that, assembling fourteen tapes of autobiographical reflections from April to August 1990.

With interview transcripts in hand and a mountain of correspondence that for most people would be a lifetime literary achievement, I launched into the completion of the final chapters. Much of the organization, of course, is mine. It was determined by what I felt to be the issues and events most important to my father, the small hints he left behind in outline notes, and by the various written and verbal materials I was able to retrieve from his letters, essays, and tapes. In all of this, Therese Hess assisted with ideas, dates, critical events, and editing. Her help was invaluable in the final chapters, for no one knew these latter years of my father's life better than she. However, the piecing together of my father's writings and the refining of many of his incomplete statements and thoughts into more polished prose were my responsibilities alone. In every instance, the content and most of the words are his; I have simply filled in the missing spaces to provide a flowing text.

There are occasions in the book where I have had to speak directly, in my own words. Those instances are noted. Because of conspicuous gaps or missing years or missing ideas in the manuscript, I have been forced to fill in the holes with written excerpts from several of my father's past essays. All excerpts—and there are only a handful at that—are prefaced by an editor's note to explain why I have included them, and inserted as subtext to set them apart from the flow of the main text.

The reader will also see that each chapter is prefaced by an italicized quote, poem, or brief essay. I learned from my father's notes that he had planned to preface his chapters with various sayings from a list of quotations he had compiled over the years. I have used several of those quotations. However, I have also taken the liberty to insert a different class of prefatory materials. In the chapters that he did not fully complete, I have relied on one excerpt, two poems, and an essay by or about my father to serve as introductions. Chapter 17 is prefaced by a brief excerpt from his writings; chapter 18 is prefaced by a poem written by him on his favorite topic, West Virginia; chapter 19 is prefaced by Karl and Therese's wedding poem; and chapter 20 is prefaced by a wonderfully kind and gentle commentary written about my father by columnist James Kilpatrick.

I have relied on other devices to ensure that my father's autobiography is as complete a statement of his life as is possible. A partial bibliography of his more recent works is included at the end of the book and several of what I believe are his most important short writings are reprinted in their entirety. Photographs taken from various periods of his life are presented in the text. These materials, I hope, will help fill in the holes of an unfinished manuscript left by my father's death.

I have also appended a chronology to the start of the book to serve as a temporal guide to readers as they march along the course of my father's life. If there is a weakness in *Mostly on the Edge,* it is the lack of defining dates and a clear sense of the progression of time. That, however, is how my father thought and lived. To have inserted a more definite time boundary to the phases of his life would have violated his own free-wheeling sense of time and, in the process, robbed *Mostly on the Edge* of its power and spontaneity. To quote my father,

> Since this seems a good place for confessions, I must confess also that it was only recently that I learned the number sequence of the months, having depended too much on calendars in the past to be bothered with it. Therese's insistence that this was simply a way to get her to tell me which month was number nine, convinced me that I had better set the matter straight. Still, I cheat a bit, having a numerical list of the months beside my computer.

and . . .

> The times and places of my life are a bit dim in my memory. I never was very good at remembering dates, anyway. But the moods and what I now perceive as the meaning of almost seventy years of interesting life are very sharp in my mind. This is not a chronology of a life. It is, simply, a life.

Mostly on the Edge is just that: simply a life. But it is a very remarkable life, one whose dynamic character helps to explain why two celebrated men from opposing ends of the American political landscape—

Charles Murray of the American Enterprise Institute and Marcus Raskin of the Institute for Policy Studies—could hold my father in such esteem, have him as a close friend, and write such generous forewords to his book.

There are others, of course, who have written harsh words about my father and his past. Freedom of Information materials gathered from the FBI, IRS, and CIA reveal an almost paranoid fear on the part of these agencies for my father's proclaimed anarchism and for his belief in the sanctity of the individual and the competency of men and women everywhere, individually and in their neighborhoods, communities, and associations, to govern themselves in peace and in charity.

My father was a gentle anarchist. He shared Thomas Jefferson's unshakable faith in the power of reason and he embraced the kindly and conscionable individualism of Henry David Thoreau. But he went one step further. He mixed reason and individualism, and from the alchemy of the two he discovered the ethics of being a good neighbor, a good friend, and a good lover. It may seem like a simple message, and my father would be the first to say how simple it is. But the lesson of living mostly on the edge is that the simplest and most important things in life are often the most difficult to find and the most challenging to comprehend.

Karl Hess Jr.

Foreword

by Charles Murray

In November 1989 my family and I moved to a little town in western Maryland. Locating us on her map, a friend called with the good news that I was only about twenty miles away from Karl and Therese Hess, and had to meet them. A few weeks later, our friend—Joan Kennedy Taylor—brought us together for dinner at the Yellow Brick Bank restaurant in Shepherdstown, West Virginia.

By the end of 1989, Karl was frail to the point of ethereal. His beard was sparse, his color dreadful, his movements slow. He was also absolutely captivating. By the end of the evening he had become one of my favorite people, and sympathy had nothing to do with it. He was just one hell of a fellow, wise and funny and phenomenally charming.

How to describe it? The nineteenth-century novelist William Dean Howells once said that, marvelous as Mark Twain's writing was, his conversation was better yet. The same might be said of Karl Hess. In the book that follows, you are about to read authentic Hess—I can hear his voice in the words—but, oh, what you missed if you never had the opportunity to sit down and talk with him.

He was the very opposite of the ideologue. He did not hold forth. There were no long monologues, no dicta handed down. He listened a lot, even to people with whom he wholly disagreed. He was not just patient, but listened with authentic consideration, open to learning from anyone.

A conversation with Karl might head off in any direction, but you could be fairly certain that at some point in the evening at least one of the things you thought of as a settled issue would be called into question. Take the issue of natural rights, for example, a cornerstone of thinking for many libertarians. No one was more passionately for freedom than Karl. No one was more adamantly opposed to the government's use of force. But Karl was not persuaded that human freedom was grounded in natural rights. "Natural rights" was an abstract concept, and Karl, deeply suspicious of abstractions, considered it to be wrongheaded and irrelevant to his defense of freedom.

Or at least that's what he thought when I knew him. Never have I met a man who was engaged so continually in thinking his way through life, or who was so undefensive about the ways in which he changed his mind. Karl's two most well-publicized acts were his refusal to pay federal taxes and his move to West Virginia to live by barter. In his last years, I got the impression that he looked on both of these acts as he might look on the admirable but impulsive doings of a beloved younger brother. There was a period of time when he actually did get along without using much cash, and actually did trade his welding services for the goods and services of his neighbors. But when a visitor would ask him about his original ambition to remove himself from the cash economy, he would say "You can't live by barter!" and laugh and laugh. As for his defiance of the IRS—well, maybe it served a purpose, he hoped. But he also recognized how costly it had been for him and particularly for Therese. Pragmatically, Karl wasn't sure that the gain had been worth the cost—a realization that Karl could reach without any sense of renouncing his younger self.

Pragmatism may seem an odd word to use about a man whose politics were so exotic, but it fits. Karl brought a matter-of-fact realism to his conversations that was sometimes almost brutal. We were talking once about abortion, that most vexed of contemporary moral issues. After listening to my tortured "on the one hand . . . on the other hand," dancing around the question of when a fertilized egg becomes a human being, Karl said, "Well, if you leave it alone it's sure not going to turn out to be a nanny-goat." Karl said he thought of abortions as potentially justifiable homicides. You can't duck the fact that a human being has been killed. But sometimes homicide is justifiable. Just make sure you can justify it. It took Karl maybe forty-five seconds to deliver himself of this stance toward abortion. I have forgotten nearly every other conversation I have had on the subject, but not the one with him, and those few sentences have pretty much determined my own attitude ever since.

Karl did that on many topics, and for many people besides me. That is one way of thinking about his legacy. Many people who write about public policy have had their minds changed by Karl Hess.

But Karl himself would not be impressed by this argument. He would be the first to say that it really doesn't make any difference whether he influenced other thinkers and writers. History will turn out the way it turns out for reasons that have nothing to do with grand historical figures or with the greatest political philosophers, let alone with today's ink-stained wretches writing op-ed pieces and position papers. Tools determine history, Karl said. He liked nothing more than leading you through some series of political events from the past and then asking you how much Henry VIII or Napoleon—or Locke or Jefferson, for that matter—had to do with the channels history had cut, compared with the role of new tools that were arriving on the scene.

Few have died at a time when their analyses were being more dramatically vindicated. The modem and the personal computer are archetypal Hessian tools, eroding centralized authority and giving individuals previously unimaginable power and autonomy. Karl saw that the state must stand by and let its hegemony crumble not because Karl Hess or anybody else said the state *ought* to let it happen, but because the new tools were irretrievably beyond the control of the state. Everything the state does in its struggle to control the cyberworld has to be implemented through the very technology it wants to regulate, and the effervescence of that technology is antithetical to everything that the state holds dear. The image of plodding government bureaucrats trying to keep up with teenage hackers delighted Karl.

Karl's true achievement is not measured by his influence on events nor even by his influence on the thinking of his friends about specific policy issues, but by his influence as a teacher about the largest questions. He was profoundly right about how human beings are meant to live together—cooperatively, affectionately, respectfully, with no need for institutions of power except to deprive us of the first use of force. Politically impractical today? Perhaps.

Idealistic? No. Karl taught those of us lucky enough to know him to think about human society and its possibilities in more dimensions, with more colors, and with more humanity than we had dreamt of in any mechanistic, by-the-numbers policy analysis.

The day that I remember best—one of those rare days when you recognize at the time that the way you see the world has been altered—was when I took Karl to the Antietam battlefield, which he had never visited despite living only a dozen miles away. First we stopped in Shepherdstown to pick up some doughnuts. I pulled the car up in front of the bakery at a No Parking sign, intending to be back within a few minutes while Karl waited in the car. As I was about to turn off the engine, I could sense Karl's uneasiness. In a kind of epiphany, I suddenly knew exactly what was the matter. I pulled out and drove down the street to a legal parking spot. Karl quietly said something about wanting to respect the agreements his neighbors had made.

His words were not literally meant. Shepherdstown was not Karl's hometown and the people who decided to put up the No Parking sign were not his neighbors. But the No Parking sign was the kind of law that Karl, the anarchist, not only could live with but insisted on living with— a law made on a small scale by people who are trying to get along. Can a good libertarian, let alone a good anarchist, come back with a dozen excellent reasons why even small communities are dangerous given the power of the state? Absolutely. I believe in many of those reasons myself; as did Karl, who often advanced them when engaged in debate about ideas. But Karl and I were not engaged in a debate about ideas that morning. We were buying doughnuts. Was it a good idea, for the harmony and well-being of *that* town, in *that* situation, for us—real people, not abstractions—to observe the No Parking sign instead of flouting it? Yes. And that truth is every bit as profound as the larger truths of liberty that Karl argued so well.

We went on to Sharpsburg. As we toured the battlefield I told Karl tales of the individual heroism that had occurred on that ground. Karl was as sentimental as any man I ever met, and he especially loved stories about exceptional courage or devotion. The stories I told were just that, and I would not have been surprised to have seen tears in Karl's eyes. But I saw no tears. He listened, and he was moved, but not as moved as I had expected him to be.

It was Karl's second lesson for me that day. This time he brought me face to face with the true meaning of the cliché that "ideas have consequences." Ideas do indeed have consequences for external events, but they also have consequences for our most heartfelt ways of responding to the world. For Karl, the evil of the state sending men to their deaths was so great that, even 130 years removed, it kept him from taking the enormous pleasure he loved to take from men doing heroic deeds.

I suppose an intellectual could write a journal article deconstructing the things I learned that day, for the lessons from the bakery and the battlefield are in many ways mutually inconsistent, even contradictory. But Karl never suffered from the hobgoblin of small minds. He never suffered from a small mind, period. Karl's chosen study was how life works, and how it ought to work, for human beings. In the pursuit of that vocation, Karl did not reach conclusions. He apprehended truths.

Charles Murray is the Bradley Fellow at the American Enterprise Institute. He is the author of Losing Ground: American Social Policy 1950–1980, In Pursuit: Of Happiness and Good Government, *and (with Richard J. Herrnstein)* The Bell Curve: Intelligence and Class Structure in American Life.

Foreword

by Marcus Raskin

Karl Hess always had time. He had time for one of my children, Noah, whom he had made wonderful sculptures with and for. He had time for scientific experiments of an immediate practical and beneficial nature whether with the raising of fish or the ordering of architectural space in new ways. And he had time for writing, for seeking to rebuild a decaying neighborhood. He had time to discuss, to suffer the inexperienced, the hopeless, and the eager wondering student. He even had time to advise the high and the mighty. He had time to develop a loving relationship with his omnicompetent wife, Therese, and his gifted sons, Karl junior and Eric. He had time to wonder and search. And he had time to be reborn in another setting which he came to shape.

From each of these relationships and activities we begin to glimpse the character of a man—noble, steadfast, and wise; timeless in his qualities and in our memories. But Hess understood that he lived in time that for him was limited. He knew that his task was that of finding ways to bring together freedom and responsibility to others. Hess's task—his life project—was a search for the integration of one's head and heart, and in some cases the hand, so that each works with the other. To put this in existential terms, Hess meant for the person's body and mind to become an integrated project that manifests itself in loving and caring for an object which he made or about which he cares.

19

The object may be an idea, a thing, or nature understood and used in new ways. Above all, he must recognize the dignity of the human other. In other words, the person as integrated project is fulfilled in the recognition of others, their being, their thingness, their subjectness, and their personhood. This sense of self leads to the person's journey in the world. The person of nobility seeks to act in ways which allow and encourage fellow human beings a similar life. He may do this through political and social movements, commitment to ideals which invariably are the cause for disappointment when applied in practice, an exemplary life which others emulate, or a scientific and artistic life in which discoveries and methods that are followed open new understandings that are meant to stimulate and broaden our meanings of freedom and responsibilities in and to the world. It may mean refining traditions in that subtle way which transforms their meanings for modern situations. Such work is not reactionary but reconstructive. This was the work of a free man whom I admired, learned from, and loved.

Karl Hess searched for those relationships which he hoped would allow him to be simultaneously free and responsible. At different times, acting for and against ideologies which promised him the way that linked tradition and change, liberty and practicing equality, peace and dignity, boundaries and free expression, Hess knew that he had to be disappointed. He looked for the social helix (or was it elixir?) in the damnedest places, believing that life was a continuing experiment which nevertheless had rigorous social rules. They were not impenetrable but they were there. Hess spent much of his life seeking rules that were comfortable if not impenetrable. This took him in many directions, each of which made him a commentator on the directions taken by the rest of us who were less prone to experiment, more willing to suspend political disbelief for the future, and unable to see how what we were made the common day-to-day reality around us. He was a realist in the sense that he would not shake responsibility for his actions. He knew that each action he took was a choice which defined him and the rest of us. He made this reality for himself and the rest of us.

In the twentieth century the search for freedom and responsibility has taken men and women in many directions. I first came to know Hess after the Goldwater presidential campaign. His political ideas were never foolish because they started from ideas about and in reality. The abstract ideal lived with him in day-to-day reality. Consequently, he saw life and politics in a multidimensional way and he saw the need to borrow and integrate from the best of all ideologies which sought to bring freedom and responsibility together. Once he discovered this quality in himself he saw it necessary to move out of the Right, first into the Left and then into an independent place that saw politics, wrongly in my view, as somewhat of a distraction from the real work of the world. He believed that science was an exercise in honesty and in this it was a great social invention of the modern world and the human spirit. On the other hand, he saw the Right as tied to state power and the presumption of state rights, ideas he rejected in his heart. After all, why should the state have rights? It already had power. Only the people either as individuals or as a collectivity, that is primarily voluntary associations, could have rights.

Hess was a man of enormous talents, a presence whether speaking or in silence, a truly modern man, an autodidact who did not feel that any body of knowledge was beyond him. He believed that any skill could be learned and should be passed on. There should be no administrative barriers such as accreditation or certification in order to learn those skills. Nevertheless, Hess believed there were the rules of the craftsman to reflect on and then accept.

Hess was an entrepreneur who eschewed profit. In other words, he was a commentator, critic, and social entrepreneur for the community. There was a Thomist-like quality to him which believed that individual profit could leak out of the community as a whole and therefore the community as a whole would suffer.

Perhaps it is more pertinent to compare him to our Founding Fathers—especially Benjamin Franklin who experimented, learned from others, and found the necessary words which would tend to win people over in discussions. He was a rhetorician and pamphleteer. But, like Franklin, he did not specialize in the dogmatics of debate, or the angry rhetoric which helped to destroy reasonable discourse. He left such activities of pulling and tearing to others whom I suspect he disdained. But he was less worldly than Franklin, who saw part of his task as turning a thing of nature or an invention into an interest-bearing instrument. I doubt if anyone could accuse Hess of being that sort of entrepreneur. He lacked the "competitive gene" and so envy was not one of his traits.

Perhaps it is not surprising that he was free of envy for he knew, like Machiavelli, that fortune in its various meanings as much as anything else dictated success or failure for any person. While human beings made history, it was not necessarily their choice as to the type of history they made. Those who tried to make history with grand schemes did so on the backs of others. Such people angered Hess and caused him to draw back from the large, the sweeping, and the social organization based on unearned hierarchic roles and command.

Such views had consequences. It meant that he did not try to score points against adversaries for opportunistic reasons, or look to be invited to fashionable parties and places, whether Left, Center, or Right, or be concerned with wealth. He was someone whom the state had to keep an eye on, whether through the tax collector or some other social control agencies. Because he was not envious he lacked an important element of the capitalist spirit, that of applying the code of exploitation to others. Indeed, his belief was that if governments and large corporate structures are to be avoided and exploitation to not dominate social and economic life, it is necessary to organize consensual social relations for any specific set of activities. This consensual base was predicated on human affection and need; never self-interest as it has come to be used. But he was not a utopian or pollyanna about people. More often than not I suspect that he had his fingers crossed in hope because he had seen perversity and distortion which the broken dreams and exploitive ideologies of the twentieth century had visited on humanity. Like the Tolstoyan character Levin, but far more honestly and with no resources, he withdrew from the urban life to rebuild in a rural village setting.

There was another characteristic which came through so strongly even when he espoused republican virtues. He held capitalism in deep disdain, especially corporations and individuals who bankrolled the Republican Party not out of conviction for any ideas they might have held about individual liberty, however lightly, but because they intended to use the state to protect their pile of accumulation and add to it. It was clear that he could not survive long in a corporate culture which held no place open for the individualist. But he had also seen the character of the state, its bureaucratic violence, and its sheer organized dumbness which stunted creativity and the entrepreneurial. So here was this modern-day man who perhaps was patterning himself after Thoreau; a man who believed in self-reliance, who was committed to the search for honesty, who analyzed his past but was never captured by it, who intended to find those points of moral solidity in a world where every pillar about him was made of salt that swayed and fell to the ground, often poisoning the earth. Where was he to turn?

At first he turned to the New Left and for a time saw how its emphasis on the small, on consensual face-to-face arrangements, on an antistatist and anticorporate mentality, on the madness of war and imperialism, on the dignity of all people could be his intellectual and ideological home. But theoretical conclusions were never enough for Hess. He faulted the Left for not learning how to build and sustain projects so that they would be more than marginal and transient activities. There was another deficit which he could not overlook in the New Left. Like others before them, whether Left or Right (the Center assumes that it *is* history), those smitten with ideology dared to say that they not only rode the crest of history but that they represented the forces of history.

There was a seminar at the Institute for Policy Studies which I think did more to cause him to reconsider who and where he was than any other single event. A young activist scholar dared to say that he was speaking for the "forces of history" much the way others on the Right now assert that "democratic capitalism" is the end point of history. Hess blanched and often returned to that moment in discussions with me, wondering how anyone could speak as if he or she knew and spoke for history and the future. He could not abide the certitude of answers known only through intuition or revelation.

He left IPS to start again, away from the city he knew so well. At first I thought he decided to be an exile or perhaps a Cincinnatus who would leave the city but plough near the road in case a call came from Washington. Hess would have thought this very naive, for he left, in his mind, to take up citizenship and become rooted in American life in ways he previously had not experienced.

So, now human time has ended for the physical Hess. But we have his writings, his thoughts, our memories of him which changed and reshaped our lives. We have his life as an important searchlight to come to ourselves.

Marcus Raskin is a professor in the graduate program of public policy at George Washington University and cofounder of the Institute for Policy Studies. He is the author of numerous books on public policy, politics, international affairs, and political theory including Being and Doing, The Common Good, Politics of National Security, *and* Visions and Revisions.

Life Chronology of Karl Hess

May 25, 1923	Born
1924–1928	Childhood in the Philippines
1929–1938	School in Washington, D.C.; graduates Alice Deal Junior High
1937	Summer at the Washington, D.C., morgue
1938–1939	First employment at WOL and Mutual Broadcasting
1940–1941	Reporter at *Washington Star*
1941–1942	Reporter at *Alexandria Gazette*
1942–1944	Reporter at *Washington Times-Herald*
1944	Father, Carl Hess Jr., executed by Japanese
1944–1945	Reporter at *Washington News*
1945	Marries Yvonne Cahoon
1945–1947	Editor of *Aviation News* (now *Aviation Week*)
July 22, 1947	First son, Karl Hess IV, born
1947–1949	Religion editor at *Pathfinder* magazine
1949–1950	Writer for Republican National Committee
1950–1954	Press editor, *Newsweek*
1954–1956	Freelance writer for United Features Syndicate, Spadea Syndicate, *American Mercury, National Review, Congressional Digest,* and *Collier's Yearbook;* editor for the anti-Communist newsletter *Counterattack,* and the *Freeman* magazine

1955	Active in prepublication effort for *National Review*
1957–1958	Editorial director of *Fisherman* magazine, Middletown, Ohio
1958–1961	Vice President of Public Relations at Champion Papers and special assistant to president Reuben Robertson Jr.
July 29, 1960	Second son, Eric Callan Hess, born
Summer 1960	Writes the Republican Party National Platform with Chuck Percy
1961–1962	Executive editor of the *Washington World*
1962–1964	Director of Special Projects at the American Enterprise Institute
1964	Cowriter of the Republican Party Platform
1964	Chief speechwriter for Barry Goldwater in presidential campaign
1965	Start of twenty-four-year period of exclusive freelance writing
1965	Divorce from Yvonne Hess
1966–1969	Part-time motorcycle racer
1967	*In a Cause That Will Triumph* published
1967–1968	Welds sculpture in Rhodesia
1968–1970	Joins the Institute for Policy Studies
1968	Graduates from Bell Vocational School; starts K-D Welding Company; sets up welding and sculpting studio on Capitol Hill
March 1969	"Death of Politics" (named by *Playboy* best essay of the decade)
August 1969	Attends pivotal YAF convention in St. Louis
1969–1970	Coeditor with Andy Kopkind of *The REpress*
1970–1973	Dues-paying member of the International Workers of the World union
January 27, 1971	Marries Therese Machotka
1974	Starts Community Technology
1975–1976	Member of faculty of Goddard College's Social Ecology Institute
1976	Apartment robbed in July; moves to West Virginia
1976–1977	Builds West Virginia house
September 1976	Starts West Virginia Appropriate Technology Group
1976–1981	Member, Board of Directors of The Fund for Investigative Journalism

1977–1981	Matched with Larry Lawson, in Big Brother/Big Sister Program
1978–1979	Member of West Virginia Academy of Science
1978–1980	Member of Appropriate Technology Task Force, Office of Technology Assessment, U.S. Congress and Member of West Virginia Governor's Advisory Committee on Appropriate Technology
Fall 1978	Mother dies
1979–1983	Artist in Residence, University of Illinois, Champaign-Urbana
1980–1985	Furniture refinishing and sales at the Eastern Market, Washington, D.C.
1980	"Radical in Residence" at Warren Wilson College, Swannanoa, North Carolina
1981–1985	Editor of *Survival Tomorrow* newsletter, Kephart Communications
1981	Academy Award for 1980 short documentary, *Toward Liberty*
1982	Member of first board of directors, Eastern Panhandle Literacy Volunteers; certified literacy tutor
1983	Keynote speaker at National Conference of Literacy Volunteers of America
1985	Recipient of "Future of Freedom Award"
1985	Aortic valve replaced at Georgetown Medical Center, Washington, D.C.
1986–1989	Editor of the *Libertarian Party News*
1986	Recipient of the Phoenix Award of the Society for Individual Liberty
July 1988	Aortic dissection while speaking in Hartford, Connecticut
July 22, 1990	Grandson Patrick Carnell Hess born
1990	Recipient of the "Freedom Torch Award" of the International Society for Individual Liberty
1991	First recipient of the Thomas S. Szasz Award for "Outstanding Contributions to the Cause of Civil Liberties"
August 1992	Heart transplant
April 22, 1994	Death of Karl Hess

Acknowledgments

Mostly on the Edge is a product of many people. Two, in particular, made it all possible: Robert D. Kephart and Andrea Millen Rich. They provided the unwavering support and gentle nudging needed to see the book to completion. On my father's behalf, I say thank you for the friendship and love you shared with him over the years.

I also extend very special thanks to Charles and Catherine Murray. Catherine honed the rough edges of the first half of the book, and for that I am deeply thankful. I am also thankful to Charles for the help and companionship he extended to my father in his final years. Without the hours of taped conversations between them I am doubtful the manuscript could ever have been completed. Again, on my father's behalf, thank you for being such generous people and such constant friends.

I am also indebted to Charles Murray and Marcus Raskin for the moving tributes they offered to my father in their respective forewords. Your words will not be forgotten.

I am also grateful to Bill Lewis and Ralph de Toledano for taking the time to record their remembrances about my father's life. The two of you were special friends who knew my father as few did. Without your contributions *Mostly on the Edge* would be lacking its most magical edge. Thank you so very much.

I also want to thank Melvin Peck for the many hours he spent doing the homestead chores that my father could not do by virtue of his declining health. Each acre you mowed—and you mowed hundreds, I know—gave my father the freedom to write one more page in his life's story.

More than just thanks is due to Therese Hess, the love of my father's life. She and I collaborated closely in the book's completion, and I know that more than a few tears were shed as she spent countless hours editing the manuscript and sharing dates, anecdotes, and personal stories with me. The good things in life never die, Therese. He will be with us forever.

Finally, I must say the thanks that properly should have come in my father's own words. Over a hundred of his friends and associates joined together in 1990 to establish a Friends of Karl fund. Monies from that trust helped support my father during the final years of his life and provided the space and time he needed to write *Mostly on the Edge.* To each of you, I dedicate this book.

Alan S. Abrams, Gary Alexander, "Anonymous" (Sacramento), Anita Anderson, A.S.H.E. Affiliated Medical Clinic, Sara Baase, John A. Baden, Bernard Baltic, Ralph "Sonny" and Sharon Barger, Richard Barnet, Sara Base, Naudeen Beek, Henrik Bejke, James U. Blanchard III, Karl Blasius, Walter Block, William R. Bock, Bill Bonner, R.W. Bradford, Eric and Beth Brewer, Martin C. Buchanan, "R. C.," Edwin Camerlo, James M. Camillo, Peter Cappello, Doug Casey, William Casey, Castle Enterprises, Ed Clark, George Clowes, Barry Conner, Richard Cooper, Ed Crane Jr., James Dale Davidson, Wainwright Dawson, Adrian Day, Carolyn and Everett De Jager, Stephen A. Dunlap, Thomas Dunlavey, Charles V. Eimermann, M. E. Elrod, Robert Falk, John Finerty, J. R. Fitzgerald, Roberta Floden, D. M. Fowle, Jean M. Frissell, Marshall Fritz, James Gallagher, Sonia and Marvin Garret, David Gilson, Barry M. Goldwater, Stan and Minette Golomb, John Gould, Edgar Gunther, Charles E. Haden, Henry E. and Jean Haller, Anthony Hargis, Claude Hendricks, Henry-Madison Company, J. "Lucky" Hilderman, George von Hilsheimer, Ron Holland, Kim Hood, I & O Publishing, IFPF, Robert D. Ing Sr., International Travel Consultants, Thomas Kilday Janus, Ray M. Kaloustian, Erika M. Kaye, Russell and Barbara Kerkman, William S. Kerr, Charles Koch Charitable Foundation, Glen Kowack, David J. Kramer, Dennis E. Kurk, Terri Langlois, Mary L. Lehmann, Mike and Mary Lenker, Libertarian Party of

Anchorage, W. R. Lloyd Jr., Spencer H. and Emalie MacCallum, Mackay Society, Toin K. Mahi, Lenna Mahoney, Ezio Murio Maiolini, Robert A. Markley, Richard and Marilyn Maybury, Wesley G. McCain, John McFalls, John L. McKnight, Roy Miller, Michael John Moran, David C. Morris, Christiane Munkholm, Charles Murray and Catherine Cox, Victor Neiderhoffer, Ian Nimmons, Don Y. Northam, Earl O'Brient, Michael R. O'Mara, Ross Overbeek, Paladin Enterprises, Inc., Tom G. Palmer, Donald M. Parrish Jr., Steven Pencall, Jim Penick, Ted Nicholas Peterson, Thomas Phillips, Charles "Chuck" Pike, John Pochek, G. G. Produ (Hilderman), John A. Pugsley, Jerry E. Purnelle, R. C., Steve Rabinowitz, William and Judy Redpath, Dale R. and Katherine L. Reed, Grace E. Reed, Kenton Riggs, David and Mary Roffers, Daniel Rosenthal, Thomas Scott Ross, David Justin Ross, Richard S. Roth, Murray and Joann Rothbard, Richard L. Rubin, Rick Rule, David Sacks, Douglas L. Saunders, Warren F. Schwartz Jr., Thomas M. Sellke, Butler Shaffer, Mark Skousen, William Statler and Leona Mahoney, Mark A. Sullivan, Randolph and Dianne Szabla, Timothy L. and Zelma J. Talley, Joan Kennedy Taylor, Paul Terhorst, James A. Turbett, Philip M. Tusbitt Jr., Charles G. Ullery, Roberto Veitia, Petro Vlahos, Rosa Maria Ward, William C. White, Carl Whitson, Peter Wilson, and Millard Zeisberg.

Mostly on the Edge

Mostly on the Edge
Karl made his Stand
Liberty over Popularity
Evolution over Security
Principle over Power
Merit over Uniformity
Virtue over Vanity
Spontaneity over Control
Communication over Pedantry
Community over Nationalism
Freedom over Tyranny
Morality over Religion
Charity over Pseudo-Christianity
Truth over Expediency
Risk over Complacency
Autonomy over Authority
Life over Surrender

John Gould
June 1994

1

Overview

A man who is about to tell the truth should keep one foot in the stirrup.
—Old Mongolian saying

I have participated in most of the major cultural and political-social movements of our time, excepting only one. I am not now, nor have I ever been, a liberal.

I'm a classical laissez-faire liberal, but not your modern, mainstream, big-government liberal. Heaven forbid. I have made some sensational mistakes but not that one.

My work was always close to power, visible in the center of things, sometimes influential, but mostly on the edge.

With all the moving, seeking, and experimentation, however, I don't honestly feel that my basic ethics and concept of self have changed much at all. I remained throughout it all, mainly a product of my mother's influence.

I was very briefly a teenage idealistic socialist. I was a born and then born-again Catholic, deeply involved in the religion of politics and the politics of religion.

My closest friend in my early teens, while my mother worked as a switchboard operator, was the son of a multimillionaire. But then, I was too, except that my mother had left him, with no alimony and no regrets, to make her own way as a low-wage, hardworking, single mother.

35

My mother taught me to read, encouraged me to think, and put up with my every romantic or rational seizure from atheism to hedonism, from incredibly stuffy affectations to those of a zoot-suiter (the early equivalent of a beatnik). She also encouraged me to leave school, which I finally did at age fifteen, having developed an effective technique for avoiding the compulsory school laws.

In my teens, I was a researcher for a popular radio quiz show, news editor of a Washington radio station, city editor of a suburban daily, and reporter and rewriteman for the old *Washington Times-Herald*, which was as close to being a true Front Page extravaganza as could be imagined.

Also, as a teenager, I was an autopsy assistant at the District of Columbia Morgue. There I learned a good deal about the delicate mortality of the human condition.

I learned a lot about the differences between men and women by being, first, in a typically suburban marriage dominated by corporate ambitions. It was immensely unfair and even hurtful to a fine woman. I learned how abrasive and yet how inevitable the women's movement was. And, finally, I married the best friend I have ever had or expect to have.

I was news editor of McGraw-Hill's *Aviation News* magazine (where I committed a tiny act of espionage on behalf of a friend at the British Embassy), then went on to be religion editor at *Pathfinder* magazine, a rural newsweekly with, for those times, a huge circulation. My religion editorship was only slightly encumbered by the fact that I really didn't have any idea, at the time, of what Protestants were. I learned.

I worked for the Republican National Committee during the Dewey campaign, and went from there to an associate editorship at *Newsweek,* where I was part of a distinctive conservative minority on a firmly liberal staff. I also edited the first nationally circulated anti-Communist newsletter.

I was in on the old Right and the beginnings of neo-conservatism— helping to start *National Review* with Bill Buckley, working with people like Max Eastman and Frank Chodorov. I was there as the old Right was overcome by the cold war militarism of the conservatives.

I was part of the extreme Right, having worked with some truly radical right-wingers such as Russell Maguire, owner of the Thompson Submachine Gun Company and a prominent anti-Semite. I recall another prominent anti-Semite whose luxurious New York apartment entrance hall was lined with beautiful cabinets inside of which, door by door, were displayed the entire history of the *Protocols of the Elders of Zion* and vignettes from the conspiracy to take over the wealth of the Dead Sea for Israeli interests.

I worked with H. L. Hunt in Dallas and found him to be a man of incredible gullibility but with great charm and wit when he was out on the land and not out on some mighty crusade.

Then I was part of the corporate Right, not only working as assistant to the president of Champion International but also traveling the country with an active and successful union-busting consulting group.

I worked closely with Joe McCarthy.

During the same period, before Castro's triumph in Cuba, I smuggled guns and munitions to anti-Batista factions.

In the same militant mood, I tried to convince the great gangster, Frank Costello, that he should arrange the mugging of Communist couriers.

In a more passive, literary mood I ghosted books for a Presbyterian minister, an early conservationist, a congressman from Missouri, a future secretary of defense, an American counterintelligence agent, a man who had been held in both Soviet and Nazi concentration camps, and the scion of a distinguished Mafia family who, among other distinctions, had helped his mother shoot his father's mistress.

For a time I worked at the American Petroleum Institute.

I worked at the American Enterprise Institute, then the most respected of conservative think tanks, where I was instrumental in hiring Jeane Kirkpatrick who, of course, went on to greater glory. About the same time I and Ralph de Toledano, a syndicated columnist and a longtime friend, edited *The Conservative Papers* for Mel Laird, then a powerful conservative congressman and, later, secretary of defense. We were, because of our collaboration, influential in introducing Henry Kissinger to the power center of the Republican Party.

Prior to the 1960 and 1964 Republican presidential campaigns, I was chief writer for the party's national platform.

Then there was the Goldwater campaign, which featured Ronald Reagan in his incarnation as a major conservative speechmaker and the full-fledged emergence of the New Conservatism. As chief speechwriter for the Goldwater campaign, my research assistants were such future luminaries as Richard V. Allen, a hotspur of the Nixon Security Council; David Abshire, who became ambassador to NATO; the jurist Robert Bork; and the now Chief Supreme Court Justice William Rehnquist. A future Attorney General, Richard Kleindienst, offered me a woman as a gift during the presidential campaign.

After the 1964 campaign, there was the development on the Right of a classical liberal undercurrent (anarchic, libertarian, individualistic) which was highlighted by a deep split in Young Americans for Freedom—a split for which I was the master of ceremonies.

And when, postcampaign, Goldwater intimates were pretty much purged from the party, I learned a trade, welding, and made a living at it even while ghostwriting a syndicated column for Senator Goldwater.

Separated from my first wife, I lived on a boat, near Washington, with a young lady who introduced me to hallucinogenic drugs.

Concurrently, the New Left was developing. It was initially defined by the Port Huron Statement, a thorough indictment of modern liberalism and imperialism. It seemed to promise an anti-imperialistic, isolationist foreign policy reminiscent of the rhetoric of the late Sen. Robert Taft, encouraging trade among all nations even while it discouraged militarism and nationalism, and presaging the emerging libertarianism of dissident Republicans.

My article, "The Death of Politics," which appeared in the March 1969 issue of *Playboy* magazine, has been credited with being an important rallying point for libertarians.

I was very active on the libertarian side of the New Left, even being asked to represent that viewpoint at the major New Left think tank, the Institute for Policy Studies. I also joined the anarchist trade union, Industrial Workers of the World, a mostly ceremonial membership by the late '60s, but one which taught me, sadly enough, that even anarchists can become terribly bureaucratic. Neither they nor anyone else on the New Left cared much about material world economics, preferring to hold glowing opinions and make unfulfillable promises.

I protested the war in Vietnam—a war which I had once vigorously supported until getting hold of something like early versions of the Pentagon Papers. Heroes fought it in the field while idiots far away contrived its strange strategies. My wife, Therese, and I both spent time in jail.

I worked with the Black Panthers, realizing that this group, almost alone among black militants, was decentralist and antistatist at the neighborhood level. Its national newspaper, unfortunately, was edited by Marxist-Leninists, thus giving rise to a major, unfortunate misrepresentation of the group. And the Panthers, like most of the New Left, were under the tragic illusion that shouting revolutionary slogans actually was revolution.

My work on the New Left was noticeable enough to draw the attention of the House Internal Security Committee (formerly the House Committee on Un-American Activities, with which I had actively cooperated for a number of years in the '50s); the FBI, with which I had also cooperated; and the CIA, with which I had never had a chance to cooperate. One result was the active attention of three separate informers who spent some time with me. Two decided I was not as dangerous as the agencies that had dispatched them. The third was said to be working for the CIA, which seems to inculcate a sterner loyalty in its associates.

Then came the counterculture, alternative technology, and urban homesteading, Mother Earthing, and trying to re-create a barter economy.

I also raced motorcycles. For a time, a motorcycle was also my only means of regular street transportation. I joined a strange motorcycle gang in which I was the only person without a Ph.D.

I met and greatly enjoyed the company of people who called themselves anarchists. The most influential one of them, Murray Rothbard, became a good friend and a continuing factor in my life, though he later moved into the fringe of the Republican Party best described as Paleo-Conservative.

It was during these years that I took one of the most rash, and perhaps counterproductive, actions of all: a forthright, voluntary public refusal to pay taxes to the Internal Revenue Service. I injudiciously wrote the IRS a letter about it rather than just seeking relief through tax cheating, apparently the more respectable way of doing it. As an IRS agent insightfully noted in his 1971 *intelligence* report of my flagrant indiscretion, "[Mr. Hess's] open defiance of Internal Revenue Laws makes him more of a criminal than one who would conceal these facts." On the lighter side, the same agent described Therese, my wife of very visible Czech origin, as "a woman of Spanish descent."

Refusing to pay taxes is not a laughing matter, however. It has cost me a mint of money, left me pretty much destitute, and caused a terrible amount of trouble for my family and for other friends.

The IRS, which makes up its own rules as it goes along, appears to be an unstoppable national police force. Apparently, the president and the Congress are so afraid of IRS agents and tactics that they are unwilling to make the "revenooers" obey such simple precepts of our law as the presumption of innocence until proven guilty by a jury of peers.

And I married Therese Machotka, my dearest friend and greatest love. It was one of the most important things that I have *ever* done—along with siring two wonderful sons in my earlier marriage.

Together, Therese and I operated an experiment in urban neighborhood self-sufficiency which drew the attention of both *Science* magazine and the television show *60 Minutes.* It was also the basis for a documentary film, *Toward Liberty,* which won an Academy Award.

During the same time, I became a fairly good metal sculptor, with *Time* magazine covering one of my shows. I did a piece of monument sculpture for the archives building in Salisbury, (then) Rhodesia, where I developed a deep love for that troubled country. When I began working with the Black Panthers, my sculpture was removed. Sad. I still loved the country. There was still a lot to talk about.

I am, as I write this, back to my roots as a classical liberal—a libertarian—and until recently I even edited the national newspaper of the Libertarian Party. I have written a book for young people about capitalism, and have renewed enthusiasm and respect for entrepreneurs. Because of my intractable situation with the IRS, Therese has become our breadwinner. My own writing is for the show-off pleasure of it. I am what might be called a rural yuppie, doing all of my work, since the onset of a disabling heart condition, by telecommuting, on my wife's computer and via modem.

I can now see high technology as truly an alternative technology. Once I felt that alternative technology meant going backward to more primitive times and simpler tools. No more.

I have gone in and out of recognizing the value and the accomplishments of the free market and of capitalism and the failure and dehumanizing characteristics of state socialism whether majoritarian or totalitarian. The free market, which stands above and beyond but can include capitalism and even voluntary collectivism, I now feel holds the practical key to solving most of our problems—ecological and economic.

I have been deeply concerned by environmental issues, and still am, but I am no less concerned that there is a strain of pure fascist socialism and a foundation of antihuman hatred in parts of the environmental movement. I remain convinced, as I have been throughout my winding way, that the individual or voluntaristic community ownership of property is an essential element of a free, peaceful, and prosperous society.

This autobiography maps the path that brought me to today (1994). I am convinced that where I am, in ideas and even in physical location (in

West Virginia), is where I was always headed and is where I will remain. Unless, of course, I have substantial reason to change my mind!

I am not, you might gather from that last observation, any longer an ideologue. I do not seek to change the world. I would no more trust myself the task of telling others how to live than I trust any of the people who have chosen that as their profession or avocation.

To paraphrase the most marvelous Marx of all (Groucho) in his comment on country clubs, I would not want to be a member of a world society that let me tell it how to run itself. Nor can I think of another human being, past, present, or future, whom I would trust with the job.

Sometimes, in view of my odd life, I hope that I'm not simply crazy.

Most people seem to come to terms with their personality fairly early. Many have an ideological armature that holds them erect, even rigid. Most sew on some sort of cultural cloak so you can identify them quickly: conservative, liberal, ethnic activist or victim, butcher, baker, candlestick maker, prude, rake, gent, lady. Think of someone. Doesn't a label like that pop into mind? Think of them again. Don't you usually think that you know what sort of person you're thinking about? If you're thinking about me, forget it. I'm now seventy years old and I have never—except for brief periods—been able to suppress the raging inconsistencies in my mind between being a fairly ordinary, conservative sort of person, and a good-enough neighbor, or being an overaged hippie with a touchy-feely concern for people and a hedonistic appreciation of good dope and sex, or being a beamed-up high-tech barbarian spaced-out on machines and programs and possibilities.

There is a core that holds me together but it's not big or fancy and most of the people I know would find it infantile. It probably is. I know that I've never grown up. That's another craziness. I'm old enough in years, why not old enough in stolid character?

My core is just that I try not to betray my friends (I don't have any idea what I'd do under hypnotic drugs or torture). I am madly (take that literally if you wish) in love with Therese Machotka. My sons and my very closest friends mean more to me than humanity or society. I try not to tell lies (but I have trouble with concepts of truth). I try to write short and simple sentences, most of the time. After that, I swear, I can't think of anything in my life that is firm, unalterable, or even crucially important.

Of all the things a person can be that sound crazy, anarchist must rank way up near the top. Yet I do believe that I am one. But most of the anarchists I know would disagree because of what they would consider my unalloyed capitalist view of property ownership: If I don't own it, someone else will. There's no way to have property that isn't owned unless it's also undiscovered. And you get property by using it and having your neighbors agree that it's yours—except, of course, there's no real private property anymore because you have to pay rent (taxes) to the government on all of it, from income to land, and you get to keep it only so long as you do. Communal property? Sure. The members of the commune own it no matter how loudly they protest that NOBODY should own anything.

Am I religious? Do I believe in anything? I believe that there is no God. But I know that's just an opinion. Believers have a different opinion. They call it faith. It can be a very strong opinion. Some people even conduct their lives in certain ways because of it. Most people just talk about it. I have faith in a few other things. Sharp edges cut cleaner than dull ones. Foot-wide, quarter-inch, cold-rolled steel weighs a bit more than ten pounds per linear foot. Gravity works. So do airplanes. Most men like the Three Stooges. Many women don't.

I have tried to accept my life in much this way. It hasn't been a glorious or golden life. It's been my life. I have enjoyed just about every second of it, have contemplated ending it only a couple of times—which I bet is par for the human course—and now, against some really impressive odds, I'd be pleased to have it go on and on.

It has been a life lived in a space between fame and ordinariness that is actually rather rare, with most people being one place or the other and with me schlepping back and forth from one side to the other.

I have been well known. I have generally been just ordinary. Some famous people who know me seem to think that I'm some sort of beatnik who *could* have been respectable. Some ordinary people who know me are shocked or bewildered, but most often just amused, when they find out that I've done famous stuff like being interviewed by Barbara Walters. I take it all in good humor and, in good humor, savor living mostly on the edge.

2

Amelia

Do not follow where the path may lead. Go, instead, where there is no path, and leave a trail.

—Anonymous

I was born, a cannibal twin, on May 25, 1923. My womb-mate did not survive, because I had, literally, absorbed some of his fetal substance—not on purpose, you understand.

At any rate, Icky Herman, as my kids later on delighted in calling him, didn't make it. I did—with such extra parts as sequences of three teeth where only two were supposed to be. This caused a certain amount of dental confusion and cost but I never blamed old Ick for it. Being a cannibal twin is such a good story that I would have gladly paid for the privilege by putting up with damn near any other spare part that could be easily concealed when not needed.

When I got to reading philosophy and even thinking about it (at an age early enough to cause immense difficulty in grade school), I ranged back and forth between Viking hubris—in my rage to survive, I had devastated my very first opponent—and a delicate sensitivity—Icky had been my brother, after all, and perhaps he should be honored for his sacrificial role in my survival.

To tell the truth, the Viking stuff has persisted and the idea of sacrifice has slid nearly off the end of my agenda of genuine concerns. I have no remorse, I have no guilt, and if I profited at old Ick's expense it is just this: confidence in myself and certainty of what I do best. I can write a speech as well as anyone, and I can tell you within a word or two when the applause will begin and when it will end. I am quietly arrogant—not boastfully so—and I can't imagine my life any other way. Beside which, I doubt whether for even a millisecond old Ick ever had a choice about getting out of my way. He was simply not a competent fetus. A bad start to be sure.

So much for the mystery of birth. I was out and alive. Old Ick was out and gelatinous. Where Old Ick and I were born, or ejected, was in Washington, D.C.

My mother, the first woman I truly loved, was twenty-three at our birth. She was beautiful, by even Hollywood standards, extraordinarily smart although not a high school graduate, and the matrimonial prize of my lusty father, a Spanish-German-Filipino gent named Carl Jr. Actually, he wasn't a Filipino back then, but an American. Living in the Philippines up to and during the Second World War, he dropped his American citizenship and became a citizen of the Philippines to gain release from a prison camp where he and other Americans had been placed by the temporarily victorious Japanese troops.

That practical view of patriotism was his finest nongenetic gift to me. I understand that there should be a strong genetic inheritance but, after you get to know my mother better, you may agree that Daddy genes would be a pitiful match for GaGa genes.

Everybody called her GaGa after my oldest son called her that during his infancy. Since then I think of her with that name, though when I was young, she insisted that her name was, always and only, Mother. I am stuffed to overflowing with GaGa genes. I have detected scarcely any Carl Jr. genes. I even changed my name to Karl to rather formalize the position. My father has always seemed an anecdote in, not a deep influence on, my life.

Recently, however, a dear friend pointed to something that I recognize in myself but which, he observed, was evident in my father. We are both romantics. My father was romantic in the sensuous sense. But we both, now that I am brought to think of it, are romantics in the Viennese waltz, honor at dawn, marines on Mount Suribachi, galloping off into the sunset sort of romanticism.

I was, for romantic instance, the only member of the staff who actually thought that Senator Goldwater was going to win the 1964 election. My father, for an even more impressive instance, lost his life because of a smart-ass response to one of the last Japanese patrols sweeping through Manila on the last day of the occupation. What happened was that my father was playing poker in the German Club in Manila when the last Japanese patrol swept through that part of the city, rousting people as they went from building to building. A Japanese soldier, I have been told, gestured for my father to get up from his seat. His response was to tell the soldier that he was holding an extraordinarily good hand and did not want to move. The soldier had him whisked off to the nearby Masonic temple where he was beheaded. Losing your head for a gesture is surely big-time, even if terminal, romanticism.

Losing—or changing—your first name because you don't feel it fits you is another matter. Young people, perhaps all people, must have doubts somewhere along the line about their first names. A first name preference is like a love preference, often inexplicable. My own preference was based on a sort of linear concept. C as in Carl seemed too soft and curled up. K as in Karl seemed, because of those uncompromised straight lines, much stronger and more in keeping with my own self-image of independence and freethinking.

Just think of the differences first names can make and how important they are in reinforcing self and public images. Billy Buckley? Charles Chan? Don Trump? Herb Hoover? Tommy Aquinas? Mother Terry?

When GaGa and Carl Jr. got married the earth really did move. After my birth they departed for the paternal home in the Philippines, via Japan, where they arrived just after the great September 1923 earthquake which registered 8.3 on the Richter scale, and killed 200,000 people. I was four months old at the time and, cuddled and protected by a fine nanny, didn't experience a moment of discomfort. Since I was also, obviously, hard to impress with adult-scale cataclysms, that entire historic event remains for me nothing but the series of snapshots my father took of shattered buildings and windrows of bodies.

I do not pretend to remember anything of those early years but GaGa was an indefatigable storyteller and she made me feel as though I could remember everything. The home to which GaGa, Carl Jr., and I were headed was the domain—literally the domain—of Amelia Simon, my paternal grandmother, and her second husband, Carl Hess Sr. My grandfather was a stockbroker and, so far as I could learn, specialized solely in being rich. (My father was rich too, but he also was a tennis champion in the Philippines. Fortunately for me, he came to Washington, D.C., on a playing tour, had his picture taken at the portrait shop where GaGa worked, asked her out that evening for dinner, and on the next day proposed to her. Romantic to the core.)

But Amelia!

First there was her lingual bias. She considered English-speaking people to be a race somewhat inferior to the Spanish upper class to which she belonged and from which she had emigrated to the Philippines with her first husband for a little colonial diversion—unhappily ended by his death but soon renewed with a German emigré, my grandfather. True to her conviction, she refused ever to speak English.

Then there was her almost religious devotion to gold as a medium of exchange. Today such devotees are called hard money advocates. But what a pale and scrawny bunch they seem compared to Amelia. She just plain *liked* gold. She didn't dress her fancy up with complex economic theory. Compared directly as visual experiences, paper money looks fragile, light, and is whimsically decorated with the symbols of politics, not the sort of hefty values that Amelia appreciated. Gold is solid, heavy, wanted, and valued everywhere. So, Amelia kept her part of the family fortune in gold bullion. Her husband, being out in the world, dealt in paper.

Finally, there was her conviction that servants needed to be whipped just a tad when they failed to perform satisfactorily. It is possible that Amelia never made a very cutting distinction between slaves and servants. Alas, it is not clear that servants and other employees made the distinction very clearly in their own minds—at least not back in those days.

This particular conviction did seem to cause anger in some quarters. Once, my mother was awakened suddenly late at night by the thud of a knife slamming into the backboard of the bed in which she was sleeping. The knife, it was assumed, had been meant for Amelia, who (I was told) was impressed only by the incompetence of the knife thrower. And since she took the thrower to be other than a native of Spain, the incident supported her prejudices about the lesser races. Ultimately Amelia's enthusiasm for harsh discipline was blunted and, finally, ended by the local police force.

Mother's arrival in Domain Amelia was marked by what seems to me to be a thoroughly American indiscretion. Mother went to look at the kitchen. Looking at kitchens is both an American habit and a democratic one, I think. At any rate, when Amelia discovered that a member of the family had been in the kitchen, she summoned Mother for an immediate lesson in aristocratic behavior. Never, she admonished, would Mother (Mrs. Carl Hess Jr.) ever set foot in the kitchen again. She, Amelia, had never been in it and she could see no reason for any other family member to be there either.

There was slight variation on this theme when later my uncle married a native person, a Filipino, from a well-to-do and respected family connected somehow to the Bank of the Philippines. From the moment of that marriage, Amelia insisted that my uncle forego sitting at the family table for meals. He and his *native* wife were to eat with the servants, who, also, were *natives.*

Mother told me that after these two kitchen episodes she suspected that things just weren't going to work out.

Amelia was, I am sure, exactly the sort of Spaniard whose earlier connivance with the Catholic friar missionaries made revolt inevitable in the Philippines. As much as I am saddened by thinking of having to make the choice, I feel fairly sure that my mother and I would have taken the side of Emiliano Aguinaldo in that long, bloody revolt.

It was not Amelia's lordly ways which did in my parents' marriage, however. Rather, it was infidelity. My father had an eye and a thigh for ladies, native or otherwise.

Later, we discovered through his will that he had sired, and would acknowledge, as many as sixteen children by various women in and around Manila and Baguio, where our summer home was located. Baguio is now popularly referred to as "a resort city" and, despite its devastation in a 1990 earthquake, bids to remain a resort open to one and all. When we summered there, I am told, it was a refuge for the very rich, rather like much of the beachfront at Malibu.

Whether there are any social advantages in transforming a haven for the rich into an amusement for anyone with the temporary means to enjoy it, is the sort of interesting question that has been getting me into ideological trouble over the years. Frankly, I do not see any objection at all to a sequestered place for the very rich. This is said to make me a conservative. On the other hand, I do not see any objection at all to people in the poorest neighborhood getting together to make their place interesting and then sequestering it. There is no need, in my view, for everyone, everywhere, to be traipsing through everyone else's neighborhood. If the folk in the neighborhood, rich or poor, want to be open and friendly, fine. If they want to be closed off and surly, fine. Their preference should not, of course, be reinforced by laws imposing an idiosyncratic viewpoint on anyone or everyone else.

A *voluntarily* segregated neighborhood seems proper to me. An involuntarily integrated continent does not. Eric Hoffer, the long-shoreman-philosopher, once said that racial problems in America would subside only when white people wanted to move into the neighborhoods of black people. He did not, of course, mean gentrification. He meant voluntary desegregation. Compared to the racial tensions we have today, after decades of continental, indiscriminate integration, the slower course of voluntarism strikes some as reactionary and yet, it seems to me, it is something that should have been and still should be considered.

All of that makes me a classical liberal. We liberal-conservatives often are called libertarians, and libertarians in turn often are called anarchists. But back to the Philippines.

My father's infidelities, which were apparent to Mother, did not and would not end. It was certainly true then that the high-spirited Latin temper was gender-biased in the extreme. Men, rich or poor, had and were expected to have mistresses. Women had disgraces.

Mother decided to leave. No divorce. No property settlement. She just bundled me up and off we went, back to Washington, D.C., where her then-unmarried brother, working in Washington for U.S. Steel, had a house ample enough for all of us, including my maternal grandmother, Lucretia Lay Snyder.

Our arrival back in America was marked by some rather stringent circumstances. Mother had no money. She had no special skills. She was a single mother.

But, in Mother's often-stated view, such details were no excuse for not living a dignified and satisfying life. Which is exactly what she contrived to make happen.

3

Mother

It is necessary to try to surpass one's self always; this occupation ought to last as long as life.

—Queen Christiana

Mother's chief activity when we moved into my uncle's house was to find a job. Since her total armory of skills consisted of the ability to speak standard English quite clearly, it was obvious that communications would be her game, and communications it was. She took a job as a switchboard operator, first in an office setting, later in an upscale apartment building.

She also taught me how to read. How? By reading to me constantly from infancy on and, when I could speak, having me follow along as she read aloud, with pauses to explain letter sounds. Then she read *with* me. Then she argued with me about *what* we had read. And I read so much, from H. G. Wells's *Outline of History* to rousing adventures such as *Captan Blood* and *The Three Musketeers*. I loved it. Most kids would if given the chance.

Today I am part of a volunteer program to teach adult illiterates how to read. Not one of my students has acknowledged being read to as a child. Literacy, like many problems, is not so huge and intractable when you think of it in terms of what little children learn or fail to learn and, particularly, when you think of it in terms of a child and a mother rather than all children and all mothers, mere social statistics.

I cannot help contrasting my mother with the many single mothers who constitute so much of the welfare rolls today. If they attended merely to the basic skills which my mother had—standard English, legible handwriting, and clear, straight talk—they would be so much better off than as perpetual wards of the welfare bureaucracy. They would, among other things, be more employable than they are now.

Ah, but my eagerness to preach gets ahead of the story. Yet I am so impressed by my mother that the urge is irresistible. Just one more lapse. It may seem here and elsewhere that I am quite willing to "blame the victim" as the current social slogan goes. That's true. I do. I watched my mother throughout her life take full responsibility for everything she did, whether she could be considered a victim or not.

Certainly she was a victim of the role-casting of women prior to the Second World War. Her role had sent her to a Catholic seminary and imbued her with the notion that she must marry, have children, and not pretend to do man's work. Yet she simply refused to be a victim. She did what she could, as she could, without complaint and without excuse. Why not blame the victims? They are, by and large, volunteers, accepting their victimhood as a grisly badge of honor rather than as a blight on their lives.

There are signs that this is changing. I hope so. We need more people like Mother, less victimhood, fewer sullen resentments, less sequestration into cultural cul de sacs or ghettos.

Freedom, to Mother, was simply being human to the hilt: being absolutely responsible for your own choices in life, questioning authority, being honest in all dealings with others.

I never, her entire life long, saw her defer or bow to any other person because of that person's status or authority. I never heard her express a feeling of guilt for anything she had done. Apology, openly and without qualms, but never any guilt. Regrets for some things undone; never guilt. Nor, since the time that I could argue reasonably and, if necessary, make my own way away from home, did she ever pull maternal rank on me.

I did, with her tacit blessing, anything and everything that I could be personally responsible for.

There were times when she spiked the process a bit. Once when I was riding my tricycle in the small backyard of my uncle's row house on Twentieth Street in Washington, my mother warned me not to ride too close to the three steps that led to the alley. I objected that there was no danger and proceeded to ride even closer to make my point. She didn't stop me, she didn't say a word; she just watched as the rear wheel of my tricycle skirted and then slipped off the edge. I fell down the steps in a tumble of metal and flesh, reaping from my bravado a few minor bruises, a moment of sheer terror, and a new dimension of respect for Mother's admonitions. She imposed no other rule on tricycle riding except that I understand the hazards as clearly as possible. Thumpo. I certainly did.

When, in my early teens, I got riotously drunk, she let the nausea and the hangover rather than haranguing make all of the arguments necessary to sober me up and keep me that way. When, also in my early teens, I asked her advice with regard to the bedding of a sweetheart, she told me about the implied and demanding contracts of parenthood and not one word about morality. For me, as for virtually any young person you will meet, the morals would have deferred to the hormones but the financial obligations would not. I was impressed.

I suppose, come to think of it, that my mother was a great and gifted teacher and that all of her lessons were about being absolutely and uncompromisingly an individual. When, as many parents do, she derided statements that began with, "Aw, but all the other kids are doing it," she did it in a way that left no mistake: Not only did she not care about what the other kids were doing, she also did not give a fig for what the entire rest of the human race was doing. She said there was only one of her and only one of me on the planet and that the rest of the people on earth would have to take care of themselves since she was too busy taking care of her-self—and would I please do the same!

On other occasions she used what, it seems to me, was her most pow-erful intellectual, tutelary tool: a steadfast refusal ever to answer a ques-tion, no matter how innocuous, if I could be goaded or led into finding the answer for myself. As a result, we spent a considerable amount of our time walking to and from the Mount Pleasant branch of the public library. I hasten to add, for those posed to accuse me of arrant and immoral use of state-owned facilities, that she also was a devoted customer of the many rental libraries which abounded in those days.

We had to go to many places for answers, of course. I would ask her what time it was and she would say, "Let us go to a clock." Then I'd learn to tell the time. I would point quizzically to a person, or some part thereof, and she would show me Gray's *Anatomy* and say, "You figure it out."

We'd read books and read books. She taught me how to read so she wouldn't have to answer questions.

I once asked her what her first name was and she shuffled me off to the Bureau of Vital Statistics where she taught me to look up birth certificates. When I discovered, by checking my own birth certificate (Mother having been born in New York City), that her name was Thelma, she asked me to ignore that and to remember that her name, insofar as I was concerned thank you, should be Mother. That was fine. Thelma?

We spent time, also, at the army's then crazy-quilt medical museum seeking answers to various intestinal and glandular inquiries. Leaning in one corner was the immense, dried penis of a whale. In various bottles just sitting along the shelves there were hearts, livers, fingers, toes, entry wounds from various unpleasant foreign adventures, leprous horrors, and just about everything else a sensation-sensitive young person could want. I am amazed to this day that the museum was not the foremost attraction in town for young people, particularly of the sorts who today seem to relish the phony chainsawing of sensational movies. The real stuff is far more interesting and even more scary.

In addition, Mother supplied an amazingly varied group of male friends and lovers of whom I could ask questions on subjects ranging from oxidation (a chemical engineer) to navigation (a rear admiral) to internal combustion (an auto mechanic) to geography (a bus driver) to ballistics (a virtually professional hunter). I suppose that Mother could have been called promiscuous by the standards of that day. Now she would be seen as merely liberated.

And always, we read together, discussed things together, listened to music (some of it she played herself on the piano), and walked about observing the natural history, architecture, and social mores of a great city. Mother told me it was a shame that so many people walking on the same streets kept their eyes focused on the pathway without seeing the great concrete forest around them.

She was particularly interested in looking up. The roofs of buildings, she taught me, often go unobserved although they present remarkable sights, with odd upper windows, parapets, bulges, indentations, decays, friezes, crenelations, and, every wonderful now and then, a roof repairman standing there like a hero, right on the edge of disaster, nonchalantly doing his job.

When I was very young, Mother left me at my uncle's house when she went to work, in the care of my grandmother. Grandmother's idea of discipline was that if it did not kill you, it was okay. When I was older, about four, Mother began taking me to work with her. I would sit under the switchboard that she operated at 2101 Connecticut Avenue, just about the swankiest, best address in town. I was there mainly so that we could talk to one another; also she would read to me. And in the apartment building I could meet other children, all rich, and their adult parents, even richer. But since I also got to meet and spend time with the janitorial staff, one of whom became my closest grown-up friend, my social development was properly broad even by today's exacting standards. Among the non-janitorial grown-ups who took a shine to me were the Borahs, Senator and Mrs.—he the famed opponent of the League of Nations, she the magical lady who used to take me to the movies.

Interrupting some of this, for a time, was my rash and uninformed decision to go to school. My mother objected strenuously, feeling that the time I was spending sitting underneath the switchboard—both of us always with a book—was more useful. But what did I know? I was curious about school. So off I went, to the Oyster Elementary School, a school not for bivalves, but for the kids who lived in what was then one of the toniest neighborhoods in Washington.

I do not recall that it was either interesting or dull. My memory is almost a blank about it. I do know that I managed not to learn the alphabet in proper sequence. One of my delights then, and now, was to look things up in the dictionary by roaming through it section by section until coming to the desired letter. I am still unable to open a dictionary and just look up a word. Whatever page it opens to is where I find myself transfixed by all of the fascinating words I do not know.

But it was the library that was, and remains, my most beloved school.

Because of it, I never graduated from high school; I didn't need to. I chose instead, with my mother's blessing, to spend my learning days reading books at home, at work, and, of course, at the neighborhood library. In any case, I had my diploma from Deal Junior High, and I couldn't imagine what use an additional piece of paper would be. Since those dropout days, I have lectured at dozens of colleges with the distinction of never having attended one as a student. Wherever I lecture, though, I always manage to spend some time in the library.

When I did go to school, it seemed to be the mission of professional educators to teach rambunctious young minds to suppress curiosity, to shut up, to not ask questions, to become orderly and obedient citizens of the national state. They didn't even like local history back in those days—the late '20s and early '30s. The nation was the object of respect, not the people in it.

The schools in those days were there to *teach.* The library, then and now, was there to encourage you to *learn,* and to *think.* The difference is striking. When children are taught out of standard curricula and along inflexible lesson plan lines, their minds are being fenced in, filled with someone else's idea of what is important; they are actually discouraged from thinking. When children are encouraged to learn, to strike out beyond the rigid schedules, their minds are being opened, they are beginning to think and not just react. Thinking should be the great goal of education, in my view.

The very best teachers try to encourage thinking while at the same time passing along some of the shared culture that has brought us along as a continental people. Some try to inspire respect for local traditions and for local people who deserve it.

The library is like a great open frontier into which a child may plunge like an intellectual Daniel Boone, running this trail, tracking that one, climbing trees, looking around, pitching camp, lighting campfires, fending off hostile ignorance, staking out great new territories, blazing trails, stalking information, cooking it, eating it, glorying in the greatest adventure that a human being can have: the adventure of discovery through the supreme human ability, the ability to think, to imagine things with words and with other images.

I look at children in the library these days and I know that they have a vast advantage over other kids, no matter what their grades are in school. The kids in the library are providing for themselves exactly the sort of education that will make all the difference in the years ahead. The kids in the library are beginning to think for themselves, to learn about the ways in which information can be searched and assessed. They are practicing some sort of self-discipline just by being there.

In the years ahead, I think, the greatest rewards will go to people who do practice self-discipline, who think for themselves, who take responsibility, who take risks, who don't have to be ordered around.

People are concerned today about the growing gap between those who do a lot and have a lot and those who do less and have less. I believe that gap will be with us, perhaps, forever. And I believe that you can get a glimpse of who is going to be on which side of that gap simply by looking at the libraries. The kids you see in the library, by and large, have a far brighter future than the kids on the street corners or the ones mindlessly huddled all day and night in front of TV sets. I think that everybody knows this but that most people are reluctant to talk about it. They may wish that some miracle will occur so that everyone can be prosperous and happy without anybody exerting themselves very much—certainly without having to spend time thinking about anything.

The street corners and TV rooms are for the wishful thinkers, the people who will continue to fall farther and farther behind. Exceptions? Of course. Some of the TV kids are going to become tomorrow's Spielbergs or even tomorrow's Crays, Jobs, or Wozniaks. But, generally, the libraries are for the self-starters, the thinkers, the adventurers, the people who compose the music, make the science, design the stuff, keep cracking through the walls of ignorance.

The library is one of the most exciting places in any town or community. Inherently. But given an excited and exciting librarian (not just someone who knows the Dewey decimal system), it becomes a showcase, a virtual disco of discovery.

I remember several summers at our library in Martinsburg, West Virginia, where kids are taken pretty seriously, teaching logic to a gang of third and fourth graders. They loved the arguing. They loved the discovery. They loved the thinking. So did I.

A bunch of kids together can be a community of inquiry. Where is there a better place to encourage such a community than in a library? The old idea of libraries as simply places to store books and to parcel them out surely has fallen to the more productive idea that libraries should be the idea centers of a community, vital and alive with activities, all the sorts of activities that involve the development of the mind. Movies, debates, concerts—all of those things and so much more are now the appropriate activities of a library, large or small. The library was once thought by some to be the most important university of all. In the age of information it could be that once again. For me, it never stopped.

I also remember spending a day in one of our wonderful carousel libraries down in the southern part of West Virginia. (Carousel libraries—small, octagonal, inexpensive, prefabricated structures—were placed throughout the state in the 1980s, in poor, rural counties which, until then, had no library facilities at all.) I was there as a writer, just to talk to people about anything that might interest them and that I might know about.

People of all ages came in throughout the day. We all learned from each other. What an exciting day!

You can even look ahead to what might be another phase of library development: an infomobile, electronically linked to major databases so that as it traveled from one town to the next it could provide customized information for the customized questions of individuals. It is impossible, of course, for books to be as up to date on things as electronic databases. The infomobile might also double as a culturemobile by providing showings of films or television shows that might not otherwise be available. Many of those shows would be about our very own state and its people. The West Virginia Film Commission is renowned throughout the country for its collection of films generally and for its collection of films about West Virginia in particular.

Such an innovation, or any similar innovation—for example, elementary schools encouraging reasoning—would do more for the future of this state and for the well-being of the people in it than any number of such look-to-the-past developments as bringing in big factories owned by Japanese, Germans, Saudi Arabians, or Floridians. I know that this line of thinking runs right up against the powerful political reality in which it is to the advantage of some to keep many West Virginians (for instance) as ignorant as possible, and as low paid as possible. But the future has a way of coming along no matter what a few people might want. The library can be the staging area for a better tomorrow.

The library should be the toolshed of innovation, the fueling area for the leaps of fancy and flights of imagination which have altogether replaced brute force and muscle power as the main ingredients of a peaceful and prosperous future.

Library: I love you.

From Oyster Elementary, I went to fifth grade at another nearby school, the John Quincy Adams School, just on the edge of the neighborhood in which we lived and where my mother worked.

I do remember several things about John Quincy Adams. One is Mrs. Deming, whom I remember as a fine teacher: She did not laugh when I had to confess to her that although I had read H. G. Wells's *Outline of History* before going to school, I still did not have the alphabet down pat.

Another confession—this time, to a significant theft. On one of my trips to the Mt. Pleasant branch of the public library, I sneak-thieved a copy of the Modern Library edition of Euclid's *Elements*. I still have it. I wonder now and then whether I should return it. Perhaps now I will have to. I was involved in three other thefts, later on. One was foolish bravado. One was obnoxious joyriding. One was purely ideological.

The foolish one was when a friend and I came across a large power shovel with an operable ignition switch (we always called them steam shovels even though the steam engine had long since disappeared in construction work). This was on upper Sixteenth Street, then just developing as an upper-middle-class neighborhood. We drove the shovel down the street for several blocks, parked it discreetly at the curb, and fled.

The obnoxious one was stealing a car just in order to have the forbidden pleasure of driving. I was thirteen as I recall.

The ideological one was the most foolish of all—something which no longer surprises me since I've come to believe that ideology itself is a foolishness of opinion gone global and commanding. What happened was that, during the sixties, there was a good deal of talk in the left-wing circles where I traveled for a time about the virtue of stealing from giant corporations.

The terribly shallow rationale for the position was pure vengeance, getting back at the rich people, the politics of envy which persists to this day. And so, in the company of my then-girlfriend, I stole a pair of work gloves from the local Sears store. Stupid. Shoplifting is shoplifting. It is not noble. It does not effect social change. People who do it at the outset as a gesture cannot be curbed from doing it later on as a warped idea of doing work. I stopped because my mother's voice kept whispering in my mind that what I had done was ignoble, foolish, and actually would hurt some innocent people by comprising part of the cost of doing business without any productive return.

There was a fourth theft but since it was signally unsuccessful, I don't regret it too much. It involved me and the son of a vice president of the phone company. We escaped being sent to reform school not because of the position of my friend's father but because of the sentimental memory of one of the arresting officers, who had lived in the Philippines and actually knew of and respected my father's family.

The incident was a raid on the chemical laboratories of the Department of Agriculture. My friend and I both had chemical labs in our rooms but wanted to increase their productive capacity. So, like General Motors seeking one more subsidy for *its* productive increases, we turned to the government for an increase in ours.

Both of us wore knickers and had cut off the bottoms of the pockets to enable the knickers to be used as sorts of saddlebags for loot. By the time an alert guard caught us, we had managed to pilfer a handheld spectroscope, various items of chemical glassware, and eleven pounds of mercury.

My mother's outrage at this shabby little adventure was great. I felt diminished and ashamed. And until the ideology and the glove business, I never even thought of doing it again. I became, from that moment on (and in spite of the temporary ideology madness), much more thoughtful about the meaning of property. Even though I still see a vast difference between so-called public property—purchased or commandeered through the force of government taxation or confiscation—and actual private property, I have come to feel that stealing anything is just an invitation to a very bad habit. It could turn you into a politician.

When, at fifteen, I finally decided to quit my various childish ways, and school, and go to work at a radio station—I had been offered a job by a resident in the apartment house which my mother was now managing—my mother had only one concern. She wondered how I was going to manage to escape school without arousing a swarm of truant officers. My successful plan, which she applauded, was to register at every school in town and then, one by one, transfer, transfer, transfer. For all I know, the paperwork is still being processed some half-century later.

Some final words on lessons my mother taught me. Once, while abroad on one of our long weekend walks through the city, we took an excursion through the lobby of one of the most fashionable hotels in Washington. Because I was shabbily, if neatly, dressed, I expressed a sense of reluctance to be seen there and a desire to get out. We were in the geographic center of the great lobby when my embarrassment overcame me. Mother, taking no care to whisper, there and then lectured me socratically about the source of my discomfort.

"Do you feel that what these people [grand sweep of the arm] think is of any importance to you?

"Do you feel that you are inferior to these people because you are dressed differently from them?

"If you were standing here stark naked would you not be just as fine a person as though you had on a tuxedo?

"Do you think that your clothes are more important than you are?"

My embarrassment, at least at the moment, did not disappear. But I have never forgotten the lesson or the penetrating significance of the questions. I've been trying to live up to the answers, which my mother inspired, ever since.

Without ever having heard the term so far as I know, my mother raised me to be a classical liberal. And in every job, or political or social cause in which I have been involved since 1938, when I turned fifteen and went to work, it has been my libertarian urge, mother-taught, that has kept me reasonably sane, self-esteeming, and secure enough to live my life on my own terms and not on someone else's ideological or managerial leash.

Mother was a convinced Taft-type Republican and was greatly offended by FDR. I grew up agreeing with her. I understand this to be a subtle leash in itself. But it was her concept of personal responsibility, rather than any specific political view, that proved over the long run to be the most powerful part of her influence.

Wherever I worked until the odd years of the late sixties and the seventies, I was the house conservative. There was even a stylistic dimension when I was very young. I greatly enjoyed carrying an umbrella, and was quite neat and tidy in dress, very polite in action.

Civility was a standard for anyone of good character and the lack of it could not be excused, in my mother's view, by poverty or any other social condition, or even by outrage. I do not believe she would have cursed even at FDR had she had the chance.

There is also the matter of what George Bernard Shaw called "verbal class distinction." In everything that I've done, from working with the Black Panthers to being a commercial welder, the lack of a regional accent and the use of really standard English pronunciations of the sort you used to learn in drama school, has helped to keep me out of trouble. I can recall being in a swanky department store, during my hippie days. The clerk whom I approached for a purchase was obviously suspicious because of my appearance. But when I spoke, he seemed immensely relieved. I suppose he felt that no one could speak with such modulation and pronunciation and still be a bad guy. Could it be? No. I recall that members of the Nazi SS were said to have all gone to war with copies of classic literature in their packs. They probably spoke upper-class German as well.

I have never had much difficulty in taking both sides of the old nature versus nurture question. That marvelous woman is part of my genetic makeup and just as powerfully the nurturer of my character.

But how did Mother get the way that she was so that she could help me become the way that I am?

I honestly don't know.

Her family, genteel and once well off, had come upon very hard times by the time she was in high school. Then she dropped out of high school. Then she married. Then there was a baby. Then years of work. Then a second marriage, widowhood, and life alone on a small pension.

While she was waiting for the ambulance to take her to the hospital where she died of a heart ailment, she wrote a series of notes. They did not try to pass along profound last words. They just asked that her newspaper subscription be cancelled, that the laundryman be informed there would be no need for a pickup, and that the eggman be told Mother would need no more. Things like that, throughout the house. And then the last note. In her portable typewriter, carefully stored on the floor of the entryway closet along with her boots and umbrella, was a small piece of paper stuck to the platen. "Karl, I love you. GaGa." I cry often when I think of those notes. But then I think of the walks and the talks. . . .

4

Adolescence

I came to the place of my birth, and cried, "The friends of my youth, where are they?" And echo answered, "Where are they?"

—Arab saying

I was a teenager only briefly, if my memory is correct.

That memory business is significant, of course, when writing an autobiography. I have never kept a journal of my activities nor have I kept many records of any sort. Living aboard a small boat for several years, for instance, made it impossible to find space for keeping files and such. It would have been prudent, I suppose, to have deposited things with an archivally-minded friend or a university, but only recently have I been much good at looking ahead—and now looking ahead is part of the process of looking back. Odd.

And so here we are, stuck with my memory and impressions rather than with formal records, memos, and diaries.

But there is a perspective from which, thinking about my lifetime as I have been, I am amazed. Think of it: When I was growing up there was no television. No FM radio. No credit cards. No photocopying machines. No faxes. No computers. Living together was called "shacking up." Gays were queers. Blacks were Negroes or colored. There were, sadly, niggers as well. The five-and-ten cent stores offered things that cost five and ten cents. There was plenty of marijuana around but only musicians were said to smoke it. Gasoline was about a dime a gallon. A new car could be bought for $600. My dream as a teenager was to have a job someday that paid a kingly $100 a week, plenty to support a marriage and family.

I do not recall the exact date on which I became a teenager, although I have no reason to believe that it did not take place at the accustomed time, my thirteenth birthday. I do know that it was all over with just two years later, when I went to work full-time.

Music was an important part of my teenagery, just as it is for teenagers today. Music is an important part of my seniority, also, with only a little updating from the earlier years.

Glenn Miller was the clear favorite for me and for my friends, in pop music. *Moonlight Serenade* and *Tuxedo Junction* recall themselves as the virtual musical signature of the times. Benny Goodman's *Sing, Sing, Sing* probably was the single most effective recording, with the Goodman-Ziggy Elman *And the Angels Sing* not far behind.

The major discovery, however, was classical music. Mother loved light opera and we listened to whatever was available on the radio; we didn't have a record player for a long time. Then I heard the *Scheherazade Suite*. It was the first record I ever bought and possibly the only one I ever have, literally, worn out. My ardent proselytizing of it among my friends made a good number of converts and, before too long, the Goodman and Miller bands and the band (oops, orchestra) of Arturo Toscanini vied for play time in the basement where we met.

The basement was in the home of Dr. and Mrs. Schafer on the edge of what is now called the Adams-Morgan area in Washington, D.C. Dr. (of Philosophy) Schafer was an inspiring drinker and full-time arguer. Mrs. Schafer was a landlady, renting out rooms in the upper floors of her capacious house while reserving a large unfinished room in the basement for her children from an earlier marriage, the brothers Robert and Roy Lyman Neuhauser and their sister, Cissie.

Roy Lyman, known far and wide as Neudy, was no peer although he was just about my age, maybe a year or two older. Neudy, after some serious thought, proclaimed himself God and, in a moment of regal benevolence, even appointed me as co-God for an indefinite term.

Neudy was not suffering from some divine dementia. Quite the opposite. He, we, all were atheists, having undergone night after night of arguments with Dr. Schafer regarding the possibilities of God and being absolutely unable to come up with any notions that held water, holy or otherwise. I do recall that our arguments held a lot of beer and, when the saved-up allowances permitted, sloe gin (a substance which tended to produce drunkenness, ribald hilarity, and the recitation of poetry for the rest of the evening).

Being a Roman Catholic by birth rite, I was familiar with Cardinal Newman's rather candid assertion that since there was no irrefutable rational reason to believe in God, either you believed or you didn't. It was a matter of faith. That seemed fair enough. So, I didn't.

My own atheism had begun to form shortly after my First Communion, shaped from doubts, lack of faith, and the painful observation that in the upper-middle-class church, St. Thomas, where my family were parishioners, black people (they were colored people back then) were obviously unwelcome. If I had not had so many colored friends, I cannot say that the treatment of colored people at St. Thomas would have bothered me at all. But I did, because of Mother's work as a switchboard operator, where she was pretty much just another hired hand, like the janitors. And so the segregation at St. Thomas did bother me, at just the time when all of my other doubts about mysticism were colliding with a growing respect for the material world.

The nonbelieving basement bunch centered around Neudy and his stepfather. I orbited in the firmament around them, along with Dwight Martin, later a foreign correspondent for *Time* magazine; Neudy's younger brother, Robert; Norborne Thomas Nelson Robinson the Third, later publisher of the *Congressional Digest*; Chandler Brossard, who became an early-on beat novelist; Eggy Eggleston, who died, as did Neudy, in the Second World War; and several others who, although so important then, have slipped from memory now.

One of Dwight's great moments came when the Claude Rains version of *The Invisible Man* was released. In that movie, the only way the poor old Invisible Man could be visible was to wrap his body in bandages. He made quite a sight, frightening to most who saw the film. Capitalizing on this, Dwight would wrap his entire upper body in bandages, hide behind a hedge, and then leap out when a hapless walker passed his way. The risk of causing serious cardiac damage was never a consideration for Dwight or for any of the rest of us who cheered him on in what seemed Halloween epitomized. I cannot be surprised at the thoughtlessness of teenagers today. Perhaps, for some, it is some sort of degradation of the ethical sense. Perhaps, as with Dwight, it is simply thoughtlessness, no thinking about consequences, just doing something dramatic.

Cissie, Neudy's older sister, often visited the basement with her boyfriend, Herb. She was, in my view then, the most beautiful woman in the world, he the most handsome man. Being in love, however, was not a principal project for any of us. Getting laid was a seemingly impossible dream in those relatively prim and proper days. Masturbation was a constant exercise but we never discussed it, except in jokes about the two kinds of people on earth, those who did masturbate, and those who lied about it. I do not recall that it ever occurred to us that girls might do it. Why should they? At any rate, the merest invitation to any one of us by any girl at all would have had us untrousered and standing at the ready for their and our pleasure. Teenagers today can be no more horny than we were then. And we survived our celibacy all right. Has that changed? Would a teenager today simply die if virginal past thirteen or fourteen?

Everyone was under the impression that Neudy had lost his virginity but no one could say when or with whom. It was an article of faith.

Our sex substitutes were argument and music.

I have long since despaired of making too much sense out of Spinoza and Schopenhauer, although I am currently reacquainting myself with the latter. Nietzsche still haunts me also, but most of the things we argued about in the basement are as indistinct as the cobwebs in the corners there, brilliant when the lights were on, gone in the dimness. If our interminable arguing about philosophy did nothing else for us, it made us very, very good readers in order to press our cases against one another. These days, I understand that is a major accomplishment and still a desirable one.

It strikes me now that we were pretty culturally literate in those early teen years. I do not believe that simply knowing there once was a man named Spinoza amounts to a hill of cultural beans. I do believe that early practice in careful reading of his work or anything of the sort is infinitely useful and enlightening and even ennobling. The process of reading, of thinking about what was read, is the essential value. Remembering what you read is incidental, in my view. I would prefer a companion who is brightly literate, but perhaps not widely read, to a person with full cultural literacy credentials who can tell you what any number of old crocks thought but has no interesting thoughts of his own.

I recall a truly interesting movie critic, Tom Donnelly, on the *Washington Daily News*, where I worked at the outset of the Second World

War. I learned a stunning lesson about cultural literacy from Tom. It was his sly practice to bring up a novel or play of some fame and then ask whether those around him remembered the memorable part where such and such did this or that. I have been present perhaps a dozen times when he did this. Not once did anyone, including me, say "No, I can't remember that at all." Instead, everyone just nodded like a library owl, wisely attesting to his cultural literacy. After the first time this happened when I could not, for the life of me, recall what Tom was talking about, I undertook to read the text in question. To my irritation and then my delight, I realized that he had simply made up something, tossed it pearl-like before the swine, and then probably chalked up another mark in his book of human foolishness. Although I never intruded on his little game by asking questions, I never again listened to anybody else say something that I was expected to understand, but didn't, without asking questions. I am sure this has exposed my own cultural illiteracy on a number of occasions.

How many people know the names and titles but have no real familiarity with the text? Plenty. But by the glib standards of the popular cultural-literacy books they are culturally literate. What they really are, are good cocktail-time Trivial Pursuit players. You have to dig a good deal beneath their cultural literacy to find whether they are, in addition, well-read, thoughtful, imaginative, and the sort of people you'd want driving the getaway car.

Neudy was not only the strongest of our bunch, casually able to wrestle or even swat any one of us into submission, he also was the smartest in a special way. I had a fairly decent home chemical laboratory and enjoyed experimenting in it. What I did was more poetic than scientific, just a pinch of this and a pinch of that. Neudy had no laboratory. He did all of his experimenting in his mind. One such experiment resulted in a simple method for synthesizing methanol, all done in a notebook. Checking it, at the time, it seemed to make great sense. Certainly it was more than I had come up with in my slapdash lab.

The difference between an engineering and a scientific approach to things should have been apparent to me then, but was not until much later. The engineering approach—pretty much what I was doing in my lab— was just to find something that worked, whether you understood why or not. Neudy's way was more the way of a scientist: theorizing, then finding out whether the theory could be attached to some material reality, could be repeated, and so forth. Neudy became a captain in the chemical warfare service in the Second World War. His funeral, at Arlington, was the only one of the sort I ever attended.

One of the practical outcomes of my practical approach to chemical engineering was that I supplied explosives to the basement bunch. Simple gunpowder was highly favored for most activities, such as informal fireworks. More sophisticated munitions using such things as picric acid were favored for making huge booms under the wheels of the trolley cars that passed through the neighborhood. Some of the mixtures were so delightfully sensitive that, when packed in a keyhole and permitted to dry, they would produce a stunning pop when someone attempted to insert a key.

One serious error reduced my zeal for explosions drastically. I had got hold of some phosphorus which I badly mishandled, causing it to explode and propel a red hot dollop of the stuff onto my right hand at the top joint of the index finger, peeling back the skin and making an absolutely terrible-looking wound. Its scar is still vaguely visible.

There was, in the building that my mother managed and where I had my lab, a drugstore. In those benighted days, druggists could be helpful without prescriptions. This one, Dr. Schwartz, knowing the nature of the wound, was able to neutralize the corrosive effect of the phosphorus, ease the pain, and get the curative process started. At another time he actually took several stitches to close a wound. I have no idea whether this was legally sanctioned and certainly didn't care. Later I came to care about such things very much, believing that any law which would prevent helpful activity is an abomination. Perhaps my entire later position opposing licensing of any sort began with my wounds way back then and the skillful care of Dr. Schwartz.

Dr. Schwartz and the physician Abe Blajwas, who lived in the same building and became our family doctor, raised another question.

It was not surprising that Roy Lyman Neuhauser, Neudy, was conscious of his German heritage. In the late thirties he was aggressively so, enthusiastically hurrahing Hitler's rise to power and, particularly, his anti-Semitism, without appreciation of how lethal that bigotry was becoming. Viewed from a very youthful perspective, at that particular time, the Nazi movement was a romantic one. The uniforms were terrific. The arrogance was inspiring. And the idea of hating Jews seemed so very justified. They were bankers. They were rich. They were sly. They also were the pharmacist Schwartz and the doctor Blajwas.

My mother, deeply disturbed by my rantings about Hitler, asked Dr.

Blajwas to have a heart-to-heart talk with me. He was one of the kindest and most patient persons I've ever known. He pointed out to me, with irresistible logic, that if I were going to hate Jews, I would have to hate him. He also asked me to consider the history and the culture of Judaism. One suggestion was to listen to a radio program called *The Eternal Light* which celebrated Jewish history and culture. Mother and I listened to it every week. Dr. Blajwas gave me books about Judaism. He gave me the chance to think.

Anti-Semitism was the popular bigotry of my youth, just as anti-black racism was for many young Southerners. But the young Southerners had grown up in a racist culture. It permeated everything in their lives. Anti-Semitism for me was not pervasive. It was not taught from birth on. It certainly wasn't encouraged by my mother, whose only long-lasting bias was the one against Franklin Delano Roosevelt. (And, no, she never called him Rosenfeld!)

My anti-Semitism had two foundations, both dumb.

One was my own appearance. Thanks in part to a bang here and a bump there, I acquired a nose which my mother insisted on calling Roman but which to me looked very much like the caricatures of Jews that popped up even in the popular press during the thirties. She later told me that my paternal grandfather was half-Jewish. At any rate, my fledgling anti-Semitism was a sort of preemptive strike against anyone's thinking me Jewish. Then there was the Neuhauser fascination with Hitler. The combination was irresistible until Dr. Blajwas got hold of me and convinced me to *think* about such things instead of indulging in my own extemporaneous dramatizing. You can hardly thank a person too much for such good, friendly advice.

I came out of it wanting to *be* Jewish and to begin to understand about Hitler what was so obvious to millions of other Americans. Neudy and I both enlisted immediately after Pearl Harbor. My history of tropical diseases, when ferreted out by the people in the Eighth Armored Division, where I was in training, got me quickly discharged.

In sharp contrast to my rowdy local friends was someone I met while in grade school, Ned Mitchell, later to become a heavy-duty banking official. He, in turn, had a friend named James Scott Appleby, who went to a private school. Ned thought we should meet, and he and I waited outside Appleby's school one day. Down the street came Scott's black limousine, chauffeured by one Charles Counts.

Although I had been taken to the movies by the wife of a famous U.S. senator (Borah), and although my mother worked the switchboard at the poshest apartment house in Washington, and although my father was a millionaire (with no fiscal effect on my life), I had never had any close relationship with a really rich person. Scott's family was rich. The Appleby house was just a block from the British Embassy and, although a bit smaller, was actually larger than some of the other embassies on Embassy Row. I have no idea of the source of the family's wealth. My mother had told me that it was impolite to inquire about anyone's income. I did gather, however, that the senior Appleby had started poor, somewhere in the South, and ended up rich. Railroads seemed to be involved.

At any rate, I was treated to the almost daily thrill of being picked up by the chauffeured limousine, either outside school or at the apartment house where we lived and which my mother managed after leaving her job on the switchboard. Interestingly, the middle-class apartment building, the Valley Vista, was just a block from the upper-class apartment house where she had operated the switchboard. Yet, by leaving the upper-class setting, she had definitely upped her own financial and social status.

My own movement up the scale was wholly vicarious, through my rich new (and soon very close) friend Scott. The panoply of his wealth included two chauffeurs and three limousines so that Mr. Appleby, Mrs. Appleby, or Scott would never be without transport. The third limousine, if needed, was driven by one of the household staff, which included at least one butler and a flock of maids and cooks. All of the help, except the principle chauffeur, Charles Counts, were what we then called colored.

As with every activity I can remember, with the exception of public school, I learned a good deal from the friendship with Scott. I learned, for instance, how to play chess. Scott's father taught me. He was just a wonderful caricature of a Southern success. Mr. Appleby was fairly short, and a bit overweight, which caused him, when at home and doing such things as playing chess with me, to loosen his belt, undo the top of his fly, and sag gently. His wife, on the other hand, was thin and far from laid-back. She seemed to have taken to wealth as a form of sin which she could overcome by sheer moral righteousness. Not that this meant she was in any way offended by wealth. It was, I surmised, just that she felt if she seemed to be enjoying it someone might suspect that she had not always had it. She seemed to tolerate riches, never truly enjoying or displaying them. I do not know what her relationship was with her husband. It seemed a bit distant, if anything. I do recall that her relationship with her son was as fine an employment of guilt as ever I have encountered. Whenever Scott seemed on the verge of disappointing her in any way, wanting to do anything that she didn't want him to, she would rein him in simply by threatening to have a heart attack if he continued on the disapproved path. Had we known more about the cardiac system, Scott might have better resisted. As it was, he tolerated the reins rather than risk the possible manslaughter of his mother.

I learned more than chess in that house. I learned a good deal about lust. Scott and I both daydreamed hotly about sex with one of the servants, a tall, wonderfully pleasant woman named Tol. Scott even got up the nerve at one point to ask her if she would dally with us. Fortunately, she had a sense of humor and just laughed him out of the request without reporting it to his mother. That would have been just enough, I'm sure, to make her forbid Scott ever to see me again. I don't think she ever did fully appreciate how her son and the son of an apartment house manager could be such good friends. Mr. Appleby didn't seem to think a thing about it, except that I often made an interested, if not accomplished, chess companion.

Unable to lose our virginity in the traditional way, Scott and I delved deeply into what was then politely called self-abuse. If there was a cavity in anything we would try a thrust or two into it. If there was lubricant available we would slather into it. Egg whites were the worst choice although it did give some insight into the manufacture of meringues.

If it could be done, we did it—or at least we tried to do it in our headlong, headstrong ways. We had a love affair with life; we suffered neither fear nor prudence in its pursuit. Our antics harmed no one, at least not then; they only quickened an entrepreneurial spirit to step beyond convention and test the unknown. Scott, however, went a step too far as an adult. On a drunken lark and for God knows what reason, he drank a bottle of Old English Leather, lapsed into a coma, and died some years later. I would visit his bedside on occasion, wondering when he would open his eyes and, with a devilish grin, credit it all to a cosmic joke.

There was one other association with the rich and/or powerful that my mother arranged for me at great financial sacrifice. It was not worth it. The enterprise was to get me enrolled in Mrs. Shippen's Dancing School, where all the proper kids of all the proper parents went to learn the protocols of the formal balls and other gatherings in which they would spend so much of their lives. Everybody was so incredibly polite and indrawn, masked, that it was a real bore and lasted, for me, just a few months. I have learned, from others who attended, that some of the young men there actually pulled practical jokes and bedeviled the young ladies. Alas, they would probably all turn out to be undersecretaries while the most serious of the dancers would be Cabinet officers, renowned lawyers or lobbyists, or legislators, or bank presidents.

Much more valuable than Mrs. Shippen's, in terms of civilizing me, were the monthly dinners that Mother and I had together in downtown Washington after attending a movie at Keith's Theater, just across the street from the Treasury. First, I learned a great deal about the pleasures of conversation, as Mother and I discussed movies and much else. Then, in our favorite restaurant, which was Chinese, I learned about the possibilities of foods well beyond milk shakes and grilled cheese sandwiches. Those were my favorites at the fine soda fountain in the Peoples Drug Store just across the street from my uncle's neighborhood theater.

My first job, when I was fifteen, was with the Mutual Broadcasting System, in the newsroom of the affiliate in Washington, WOL. It was a fateful job and fateful decision. I had to choose between the Massachusetts Institute of Technology—where I had just been admitted, in the absence of a high school degree, to study chemical engineering—and the life of a scribbler. It was immediately apparent to me that writing was more fun than even chemistry. And so I dropped my romantic notions of engineering (the heroic feats of the mind, the heroism of a Howard Rouark in *The Fountainhead*) and picked up a pencil, pad, and my first typewriter. I have been atoning for that decision ever since.

I was hired at WOL strictly on whom I knew rather than what. Resident in the building that Mother managed, a fairly fashionable apartment house on the southern edge of Rock Creek Park in northwest Washington, was Walter Compton, just about the hottest property at Mutual in those days. He had more time on air as a news commentator than anyone else in the network. And he was host of a very popular quiz program, *Double or Nothing*. My work was constant and fascinating: editing wire copy, adding research items, and putting it all together in a timed script for Walter to read in the splendid baritone voice with which he had been genetically blessed. I also researched questions and answers for the quiz show.

One of my jobs was watching the teletype news printers for important bulletins (signaled, in those days, by a series of bell clangings from the teletype itself). Since I would rather hang around the newsroom than anyplace else, I always happily volunteered to stand by the machines at night, on weekends, whenever I could.

There was a notable bell clanging when German troops marched into Austria "to preserve order" and to set the stage for the Second World War. One of the people whom I was asked to notify when something special was on the teletype was Mutual's most conservative and widely respected commentator, Fulton Lewis Jr. I called Fulton Lewis shyly and apologized for bothering him at home. He was gracious. Don't worry, he said grandly, you were correct to call. "But it's just a local incident, believe me."

I lasted just about a year on the job at Mutual.

One day I was dispatched to pick up the actress Faye Emerson at the Washington airport. Through some minor misbehavior in traffic, I was stopped by a policeman who asked to see my driver's license. Being fifteen, I didn't have one. Only the influence of the Mutual Broadcasting System got me released. But the discovery that they were depending on a fifteen-year-old to edit news shows and provide questions for a quiz show, as well as pick up actresses, unstrung their patience and I was out.

I was unemployed for a day. There was an ad for a reporter at the *Alexandria* (Virginia) *Gazette,* which I answered. Fortunately, my sixteenth birthday was close enough that I could stop being fifteen during the job interview with some confidence. The managing editor, Thomas Moore McBride, actually didn't care how old I was. He wanted to know whether I could write and observe. I convinced him on both points. I've been a writer and an observer ever since.

The Second World War came along while I was at the *Gazette.* I was as eager as anyone to get into the military. That was, it may be recalled with interest, the last of the popular wars.

Old enough to enlist, I did. But not without some special privilege. The police chief in Alexandria, with whom I dealt regularly as a reporter, had a brother who was a major stationed at Fort Knox, the home of the Armored Cavalry. I expressed enthusiasm about tanks, and the cop chief suggested that I contact his brother. The brother assured me that if I could just make it down to Fort Knox, he would see that I got into a tank unit. Off I went, by bus.

Major Butler, my host, invited me to stay at his home on the base and escorted me to the enlistment office. He also suggested that I might want to be assigned quickly to the Officer Candidate Program. That sounded fine to me but, first, there was an orientation period with the Demonstration Regiment of the Eighth Armored Division.

Fort Knox, at that time, was a truly idiosyncratic place. Moving from the regular cavalry to the armored cavalry, as the tank corps was first called, many officers insisted on retaining their horse cavalry appurtenances. It was not unusual to see an officer mounting his tank with riding boots and—so help me—spurs! Ah, tradition.

The first demonstration in my orientation was in no way romantic, traditional, or even heroic. It was bloody and scary. A tank had been brought back from the fighting in the African desert where the Germans had first used their deadly handheld rocket launcher, the counterpart of what became the bazooka on our side.

The tank had been pierced by a rocket. Unable to go entirely through, the projectile had spent its remaining energy whirling around inside the tank like a gigantic and crazed reamer. The result placed before our recruit eyes was a tank whose interior seemed painted red and abraded almost smooth.

We also learned that a tank, if ignited by even conventional gunfire, would become an instant oven, and that, mercifully, the people inside would die within a matter of seconds. That was nice to know.

It was not these matters, however, that moved me out of the armored forces and back into civilian life. What got me was a small lie or two that I had included in my enlistment papers. I had not confessed to having had numerous tropical diseases when I was in the Philippines. My evasions were exposed when I became quite ill and was diagnosed as having some sort of residual malaria attack. It was explained to me that the perjury on my medical record was technically a court-martial offense. Imagine going to the slammer for trying too hard to get into the service. At any rate, Major Butler intervened and got me simply discharged. I forget the classification of the discharge but I was out and very saddened by the fact. Throughout the war I felt terribly guilty about not being at the battlefront.

From Fort Knox I got a lift into Louisville where I could catch a bus back to the Washington area. Being thirsty and hungry, and having very little money, I decided to get a quart of milk at a store near the bus station. Outside, I opened it and discovered to my horror that it was buttermilk, one of the most noxious of all liquids. There was enough sadness, with that and with leaving Fort Knox, to make the entire trip home an absolutely miserable journey. I was convinced, then, that the only honorable professions for a person were those of priest, poet, or warrior.

It was clear to me now that journalism (which I hoped would count as a subset of poetry) was my only path. I had, of course, begun to think about that while at the *Alexandria Gazette*. But there had been a possible diversion before that.

Earlier, I had gotten involved with The Drama. First there were the Blackfriars Guild players at Catholic University, where Father Gilbert Hartke turned a college outreach program into one of the most renowned of all little theater groups. I played the young George Gibbs in Thornton Wilder's *Our Town* and then, on the basis of that, was accepted at a private drama school, King-Smith, where I could work for my tuition by writing one-act exercises for the students. The writing experience was invaluable and enjoyable.

My only bad moment as a thespian came when I was a ballet dancer. As part of the enlargement of our horizons, the splendid but not yet fully famous Martha Graham came to lead us through the heady abandon of one of her modern dance pieces. The trouble, for me, was that it was to be danced barefoot—"modern" apparently referring to something other than the treatment of one's feet, which, I was convinced, should always be shod when out in public. At any rate, I went along with it for a while but then determined that the discomfort of being barefoot just wasn't worth the otherwise uplifting experience. And so, during one exercise, I just shuffled right offstage, put on my shoes, and strode out into the less arty world of journalism.

5

The Morgue

All human things are subject to decay,
And when fate summons, monarchs must obey.
                    —John Dryden, "Mac Flecknoe"

A significant part of my education took place at the morgue of the District of Columbia. Getting to the morgue was instructive in itself. It involved the omnipresent interconnection of death with sexuality and virtually everything else human. The connection was clear and commanding in what I experienced later of business organization, academic research, and politics.

The coroner of the District of Columbia, when this whole thing commenced, was a Dr. Rosenburg, who had taken a fancy to the older sister of my friend and schoolmate Toby Wood. He invited Toby and me as chaperones on a visit to the doctor's bachelor apartment in a hotel directly behind the *Washington Times-Herald* (a newspaper for which I would be a reporter several years later).

Charming fellow, Dr. Rosenburg. And, to a couple of teenagers, virtually magic. On the insides of the several closet doors in the living room of his suite he had hung eight-by-eleven glossy photos of the most traumatic injuries which had brought corpses to his official attention at the morgue.

I suppose that nowadays, the corpses would have to be referred to as clients. At any rate, the corpses, or pieces thereof, made a truly grisly display which may or may not have had an erotic effect on Toby's sister but which certainly had an exciting effect on Toby and me. We both intended to be scientists or engineers or something like that, and looking at the parts of people seemed as stimulating to that urge as looking at the parts of a mechanical device or an earthworm. I wonder whether our curiosity about the corpses was in any way similar to the impulse that drives so many teenagers these days to flock into the chainsaw sort of horror movies. I do not like those movies at all, but I certainly did like the insides of Dr. Rosenburg's closet doors.

So evident was our enthusiasm for Dr. Rosenburg's work that he graciously invited us to spend as much time as we wanted at the morgue. Since Toby had a much more serious view of formal education than I, he had to decline in order to attend school regularly. I was already in the last stages of my tolerance of schooling. The morgue became my daily volunteer work. That could have made me, I suppose, the first morgue candy striper. There should be more. What a grand time it was! I was fourteen.

Let me, first, introduce you to the two full-time, and animate, morgue residents who became my mentors as I became their mascot. The senior member of the pair was, as I recall, named Charley. The younger had a name which I forget but a lifestyle which I vividly recall.

Let's call the latter Rod. He lived on a very small boat anchored just behind and partly under the morgue, which at that time was perched on and overhung a stretch of the dock along Washington's now-fashionable waterfront. It was shabby and romantic back then, when the morgue, the oyster boats and questionable craft of all sorts, and the harbor police and fire station lined the docks. Not too far away, around a turn in the Potomac, where it is joined by the Anacostia River, were the docks at which many years later, an exile from big-time politics, I would live on a houseboat.

Charley, if you insisted on giving him a job description, was the janitor of the morgue. Rod was the caretaker and watchman. Both had extraordinary talents.

According to every coroner's office doctor to whom I spoke, Charley had the best rough diagnostic ability of anyone at the morgue. He had seen so many corpses and he recalled so many autopsies that he could just look at the incomers and give a very good guess as to what had done them in. Some of the causes were far too subtle for that, of course, but when it came to the regular stuff, Charley had a distinguished and renowned record for accuracy.

Rod was apparently designed to serve as the full-time attendant of a penis. When we came to work every morning, it was our custom to count the condoms swimming lazily along the sides of the Rodcraft. These days, of course, those floaters (or white herrings as many called them) would be counted as outrageous pollution. In those days they were merely counted, with admiration and envy. I was never invited to share the sexual wealth that Rod seemed to have accumulated, but I was invited to share the diagnostic wealth that Charley had accumulated; and although the details have had little practical value in my later life, they did set me to thinking and trying to practice habits of careful observation which have been useful.

The general educational value of working at the morgue flowed from two activities. First there was the menial chore to which I was initially assigned as the kid volunteer. I drove along with Charley each morning as he went to the local hospitals to pick up the latest crop of remains. It was quite easy to lose respect for the remains while working on the meat wagon. It was such an odd and ancient truck that the driver had a seat but everyone else had to sit on the floor in the body of the truck. Since I was everyone else, I got myself well seated when the day's work commenced. It got crowded sometimes shortly thereafter. When it was, I had to sit on a corpse since they had first dibs on the floor, naturally.

"Remains" is such a fine and accurate word for what we picked up. The humans had gone. The remains remained. The life was gone. The meat remained. It took only a trip or two to convince me that the connection between the remains and the former resident had absolutely vanished. These were the remains of former humans. Not human remains. There was nothing human about them. A sculptor could have constructed them out of clever plastic.

I believe that we have caused ourselves a good deal of useless misery and fostered a lot of unfortunate sentimentality by having come to regard the remains of people as almost as important as the people themselves. It must be similar to believing that flags are more than pieces of cloth or that sacramental wafers are more than dough. Living humans thus endow non-living objects with qualities of animation. Such zealous opinions may have enormous value to their holders. What a kindness it would be if they would only abstain from pressing their beliefs on everyone else.

What anguish is occasioned by an open-coffin funeral, for instance. People who should now have only a memory of the dead person are forced to have an actual physical encounter with something that looks like the person and, thus, stirs all of the immediate sorrow that they might have felt beside a deathbed. Why do people so dishonor the dead that they must gape at the remains of them, weeping and agonized, rather than just remembering them?

When my mother died, in a suburban Maryland hospital, I was unable to get in from West Virginia in time to see her corpse in the hospital morgue. I probably would not have looked at it under any circumstance. Later, at the funeral home, I had a second chance to view what remained of this most amazing woman. I couldn't. She had moved from life into my memory, where she remains lively and loved.

I have no idea how I would have reacted had she shown up at the morgue as a candidate for autopsy.

When I have described an autopsy to some people, they have recoiled, thinking that I am being coldly, even sacrilegiously, detached from my own and the dead's humanity. But the dead have no humanity. The dead are humans departed, gone. The bodies remain. The remains, the remains. To respect the dead, the morgue made me see, we should learn to cast off respect for the remains lest we become too thoughtlessly unaware of conscious, glorious life while fixating on lifeless meatiness.

Losing respect for the remains did stimulate in me a strong and abiding respect for life itself. Seeing how little was left after life had gone was impressive. Even so, the contrast gave rise later on to a new and perplexing question having to do with life even while it *is* apparently there. Are there breathing bodies, human bodies, which are nonetheless no longer truly alive? The question is asked more and more in the case of people in comas with flat brain lines who can be kept breathing or receive nourishment only with mechanical assistance. It is an obvious question to ask with regard to so-called brainstem babies, those born without brains, literally, but with only enough of the upper brainstem to maintain respiration.

My feeling is that the flatliners and the brainstemmers are not living human beings. They are respiring remains, much like Scott Appleby was despite my yearning for him to be otherwise. The question should be widely discussed. It's important. A too-casual answer could give rise to horrible mischief by politicians who could misuse euthanasia in the same way they once misused their power to commit misfits to mental institutions or jails. A too-casual answer in the other direction could continue the perpetuation of agonizing bare-life—torturing families, endlessly eating up resources that could better serve the more vibrantly alive, the people we look at day by day and understand that they *are* alive. The machine-dependent coma-locked, on the other hand, are a mysterious life form, breathing but only because of their mating to a machine patiently pumping nutrition into their bodies or pumping oxygen into their lungs.

Recently, I asked my doctor what he thought of so-called living wills, the documents which attempt to preclude subjecting a person to indefinite life-support activities without any observable medical benefit. We agreed that neither of us would want to have our body kept alive after our brain had ceased to function. Yet, my doctor told me, our view is not at all popular in local medical and hospital circles. Even nurses (who usually strike me as the most sensible people) oppose the view that life-support systems should be withdrawn at *any* point. They must be defining life as mere circulation of fluid. If the body is still slightly pink and warm, that must be seen as life. What endless mischief there is in such a view. What endless agony of expense, what shackling to misery!

It was with the clearly dead, gone, departed, often disassembled that I spent my time at the morgue. The only time that there was any serious doubt about this status came when a young woman was brought in and filed away in one of the refrigerated drawers in the rear of the morgue. Charley quickly diagnosed suicide from the burned streaks stretching downward from the corners of the woman's mouth. Bichloride of mercury, he opined.

Later in the day, however, there was a terrifying series of thumps from the drawer of the supposed suicide. We are none of us too far from our primitive heritage at such a time. Everyone fled the building. Regrouping, and resuming our modernity, we went back in, opened the drawer, and discovered the supposedly dead woman gaspingly eager to get out.

There was a simulation of this sort of thing on another occasion when we attempted to identify a murder victim who had been stowed for a few days in a trunk at the Washington train station. The woman was placed in an airtight, copper coffin with a glass viewing plate over her face. Anyone who was missing anyone or who had any reason to think he might recognize the remains was invited to take a look. The procedure went smoothly enough most of the time. When it didn't, the results were dramatic.

The morgue's ancient cooling system, the machinery that cooled the storage drawers, depended upon a very large compressor which was controlled by a thermostat. When it switched on, its large flywheel was activated by an electrical motor which, along with all of the gears and mechanisms that made up the entire cooling system, created a booming, clanking, mechanically huffing and puffing extravaganza of sudden noise.

When the machine was on, people coming in to look at the corpse in the copper coffin just accepted the noise as background din. When it was off, the viewing area was nicely quiet. But when there were people looking into the coffin and the machine came on, the sudden shock of it all, every single time, sent the viewers scuttling out at flank speed. After the experience with the not-dead nonsuicide, there was little temptation to feel superior to the scuttlers.

Now let us look at the autopsies themselves, and at what your morgue candy striper did during them. You will immediately recognize that such an informal role would be impossible in our neat, formalized, regulated, modern day. You may wonder, as I certainly do, whether it wouldn't be a good idea to let willing young people have more hands-on experience with such things.

The purpose of an autopsy is to establish the cause of death when there is no death certificate issued by an attending physician. Roughly, this means that anyone who dies on the street, or out in the fields, or at home, or after or during an assault or murder, has to come to the coroner for an intimate, ultimate inspection.

The inspection begins at the top. The brain has to come out. It can yield a good deal of information (though think of how much more information it could have yielded while part of a living organism). To get the brain out, the skull has to be sawed open. This involves a long cut across the top of the head from ear to ear. When this is done, the scalp is pulled away from the skull, down across the face, making a mask of tissue stretching down across the nose and almost to the mouth. It is one of the strangest sights I have ever seen.

That done, the sawing begins. I'm sure that there are wonderful power tools to do it now. Back then a surgical hacksaw was the tool. Sawing carefully to avoid slicing into the brain itself, we made a long cut just above the pulled-down scalp and then a cut up the sides of the skull and across it so that a sort of quarter section of the bone could be pulled off, permitting access to the brain which was then pulled out and made available to the coroner. I got to do the cutting and sawing. The coroner, a certified professional, got to yank the brain.

Portions of the brain were then sliced into microscopically viewable sections to detect any mischief that might be revealed there. There were no thoughts, no dreams, no poems or songs, just the sort of thing which, if laid in a butcher's tray, might be savored by someone seeking the ingredients for an exotic dish.

The empty brain cavity was itself of interest. I was bowled over to learn that the scent of alcoholic beverages can be detected in such aromatic detail that you can know whether the person, if he had been drinking before death, was drinking beer or whiskey. The doctor who introduced me to this wonder did it simply by saying, "Here, sonny, smell this" while pointing inside the brain cavity. My only hesitation at the time was that the ashes from the mentholated cigarette he was smoking might fall down my neck while I sniffed. Was that just fourteen-year-old bravado or prudence? I do not know.

The same assistant coroner who introduced me to the sniff test also gave me a dramatic demonstration of the toughness of the human skull. It was his delight, showing off for the admiring teenager, to elevate the skull of a remnant and then let it slap, kaboom, back onto the dissecting table with a great thud. Wonder of wonders, just as he said, you just couldn't seem to be able to bust one of those things. When alive, it seems easy.

After the brainwork came the gooey stuff. This meant a cut from the neck down to the navel and then other cuts across the top of that out toward the shoulders and across from the lower part to the sides of the body. The skin area thus outlined was then pulled to the side, one flap to the right, one to the left. Next, the ribs and the sternum had to be sawed through and removed. This permitted dissecting out all of the internal organs, including the lungs, intestines, and stomach, to parse all of their information about what the late person had been eating or drinking or whether he or she had been afflicted by some possibly fatal disease or penetrated by a knife or bullet. The heart, of course, could yield up its own evidence of failure. All of the organs were taken out and inspected by the coroner. I got to do the cutting and the removing, under careful and very instructive supervision.

After the disembowelment, all of the organs were randomly placed back in the chest and abdominal cavity, the ribs were laid back on, and the hide was stitched back together.

I was permitted to do the stitching when things weren't too rushed. There are two things about the stitching that I don't imagine I'll ever forget. One is the snapping sound that the needle made as it popped through the skin for each stitch. The other is the terrible difference between cutting and then stitching the remains of fat people compared to lean ones. The hide of the fat is underlaid by a thick, yellowish layer of, what else, fat. The lean are just that, lean—skin and muscle. When I grew quite fat myself at one time, I recalled the yellow layers of fat that I had often sliced through. It was an incentive to get back into shape. Perhaps diet clinics should think about the potentially instructive value of autopsy visits.

One of the very first autopsies where I was permitted to scalp and cut involved a fellow who had been just about bisected by a shotgun blast during the commission of a robbery. It fell to me to have to locate and remove every single one of the offending shotgun pellets while the attending coroner carefully noted the locations. As was occasionally the case, the death of this inept felon finally was ascribed to traumatic heart failure when none of the pellets was found to have caused the death by itself or in combination with its companions. I was most intrigued by the fact that death itself comes in such carefully compartmentalized packets.

The least workable bunch of remains that passed our way were those of an unfortunate fellow who had slipped into a large pipe being used to transport gravel from the bed of the Potomac to the area being filled in to form what is now National Airport. (I believe that the area actually was called Gravelly Point.) When the man emerged from the other end of the pipe, along with a substantial amount of gravel, he had been abraded nearly to gravel himself. What could be recovered was dutifully brought to us at the morgue. I can't recall that there was anything that could be done except to groan over the guy's truly bad luck or carelessness and make the not-too-rash assumption that death was due to disassembly or whatever the medical term for that might be. I wonder whether the CIA, noting that it all happened at an airport site, would call it terminal disassembly?

The morgue experience bred in me a firm determination that when I die, I be cremated as rapidly as possible, consigning myself as neatly as possible to the memory of those who knew me. I do not want to be a corpse. I would not want to be a corpse that breathes, either; thus, I have signed a so-called living will urging my beloved wife and sons to make sure that when the brain line goes flat, the remains will be permitted to cool without intervention from machines dripping and drooling into and over something which no longer can care. If there is to be weeping, I want it to be for the loss of *me*, not pity for the lingering package.

6

Scribbler

Another damned, thick, square book! Always scribble, scribble, scribble! Eh! Mr. Gibbon?
—William Henry, duke of Gloucester, upon receiving from
Edward Gibbon volume 2 of the *Decline and Fall of the Roman Empire*

Although the teenage business didn't last long, nor the business in the morgue, the scribbling business, making a living by writing about things, has gone on my entire life. There is a secret to whatever success I have had in this field. When pressed, I can write a simple declarative sentence. This has given me an advantage over many college graduates of English and journalism courses. Even in the new journalism of meandering beginnings or gonzo personalism, the writers of complete sentences seem to hang on better than most. There is little advantage to being illiterate in the business of journalism. The differences between many small-town newspapers and more highly regarded ones boil down to the difference between semiliterate and literate staff writers.

Too often the level of reporting is quite low and it seems to me that semiliterate staff writers, with absolutely no editorial oversight, are the reason. A person who has not come to know and respect the internal logic of an English sentence is likely not only to write sloppy prose but also to skip information which, to a more literate person, would scream for attention. If a person is satisfied with an incomplete or muddled sentence, that same person may be satisfied with gobbledygook, half-baked answers from public officials where the level of literacy often seems even lower than among ordinary journalists.

If the great investigative journalists of our time had not been bird-dog serious about running their questions through to a satisfactory and full answer, we would all be the poorer.

I recall that Seymour Hersh, one of the great ones, broke the My Lai 4 massacre story because of that sort of dogged insistence on asking just one more, and then one more, question. The information that led him to the massacre story was available to virtually every other journalist in America, certainly to all who had access to the AP news service. His great scoop developed this way:

At the time, I was a fellow at the Institute for Policy Studies. An associate, Judy Coburn, came across a one-paragraph Associated Press wire-service dispatch saying that a Lt. Calley was going to go on trial for allegedly having killed civilians at My Lai 4 village in Vietnam. She passed the clipping along to Hersh. He, among the dozens, if not hundreds, of other journalists who saw the same item, decided to follow through, even before the trial, asking more and more questions. When he broke the details of what came to be known as the My Lai 4 massacre, it was regarded as one of the scoops of the decade.

Hersh writes fairly uncomplicated, clear prose. He asks uncomplicated but demanding questions. He is not satisfied with official answers that leave any points hanging. He is rude, crude, and insistent, and never awed by authority. He is, therefore, a fine investigative journalist.

The finest prose stylist in the business, I think, is John McPhee, a frequent contributor to the *New Yorker* magazine. There are no loose sentences in his work. No loose thoughts. Nothing but clarity and wonder at what he sees. He doesn't cover the politically charged matters that Hersh does. But what he covers, he covers with unequaled simplicity and depth. He is able to make any reportage fascinating because he ferrets out all of the details of the situation, whether it be the ecology of Alaska or the workings of a restaurant.

An old friend, John Holt, once said that the most revolutionary act a writer can perform is to write clearly. Sadly, as standards of English composition slip toward extinction, it is becoming more radical, revolutionary, and rare every day.

During the period of his greatest creativity, Dr. Gonzo himself, Hunter Thompson, wrote a bit more lyrically than logically but, as do many poets, managed to drive home what I still regard as the most penetrating exposures of political sham ever written (*Fear and Loathing on the Campaign Trail*). Later he seemed to lose close attachment to any order in sentence or structure and regrettably became a sideshow attraction rather than the Rabelaisian balloon popper he once had been.

For many newspapermen of my generation, H. L. Mencken was the model. He remains so, for me, for his irreverent attitude toward the pompous and the powerful.

"Question authority" is my guiding slogan. In order to question authority properly, you must be prepared to act the simpleton. No odd phrase or technical cant should pass the journalist without being questioned. Among other things, this means that the journalist must ask dumb questions such as "What do you mean by victory?" or exactly what is a fungible asset, or a sortie, or a human personnel asset, or how does the Federal Reserve System control interest rates, or what is U.S. foreign policy, or what's an energy policy, or why don't many children know how to read by the third grade?

While I was covering the Pentagon for the large-circulation rural newsweekly magazine, *Pathfinder,* I was amazed to discover that some of the regular reporters on the beat actually interviewed each other to produce feature stories said to have emanated from "knowledgeable sources." At military press conferences I cannot recall many reporters asking follow-up questions to flesh out answers replete with official jargon and little else.

In many papers, legal phrases usually are reported as though everybody is familiar with them. Inexcusable. Exactly what is second-degree sexual assault? Is there a difference between judges recusing themselves from cases or just excusing themselves? What is the crime of "uttering"?

It's a sad practice and simply encourages sloppy thinking among the readers, not to mention the reporters. People begin to accept mysterious words as having meanings which, although they do not know them, are assumed to be "official" and thus do not need to be questioned. The words become more like music. Some sound grim, some sound exuberant, some sound tense, and so forth. They have tones, threatening or soothing, but not meaning.

Perhaps my first job in journalism, at Radio WOL in Washington doing research for a quiz show, helped develop my own enthusiasm for answers. To this day, I find nothing more exciting than beginning with a question and tracking it through records, files, clippings, books, anything, to hunt down an answer that finally does not raise even more questions. At the same time, it is prudent to be aware, when you have found such an answer, that it is satisfying simply because you do not know enough to ask yet another question. Uncertainty and doubt are healthy companions for any intellectual activity. The problem with ideology, for example, is that it turns off the mechanisms of uncertainty and doubt.

I have come to feel that ideology is an addiction to be avoided more earnestly than any narcotic drug. I have known people as helplessly dependent upon an ideology as any drug addict upon a chemical substance. Withdrawing from drugs is an act of will. Withdrawing from an ideology seems like an act of self-destruction, since these addicts have made loyalty to the ideology and antagonism to contrary ideologies their central identifying characteristics. The person must form his own personality from his own cognitive processes without the fabrications of ideological tailors; but the recovering addict feels naked and lost. There is nothing handier than ideology to keep you from the task of inventing your own personality, character, and ethics. Yet there is nothing, in my view, more essential to taking advantage of being human than to engage in exactly those enterprises.

As bad as timidity in questioning is the tendency for reporters to attach themselves to some government unit and become, in effect, ex officio members of it. A reporter assigned to a special beat faces a choice: to become closely and sympathetically allied with the people being covered or to maintain a distant or even adversarial relationship. Choose the former and there are always good chances of being on the inside for scoops—at the sufferance of the people being covered, of course. Choose the latter and there is constant hard work. Part of that work, however, is developing clandestine associations with disgruntled, or conscience stricken, or just deeply honest people in the area being covered. From such sources develop true scoops and not programmed leaks.

The specialized beats that I covered gave me a chance to try both choices. In covering the police department, for several papers, I chose to be as cooperative as possible. There was a good reason. The police, way back then, in the late '30s and early '40s, seemed clearly to be the good guys, fighting the bad guys. Why not be on their side?

There was a point when that changed. The head of Washington's vice squad at one time was a truly repulsive officer, an actual sadist whose delight in physically abusing prisoners was well known but never mentioned, though most policemen disliked him as much as did the reporters.

Finally, when some hapless prisoner attempted legal action against the man's brutality, I was able to write about it and convince the city editor that it was a worthwhile story. That was all it took to end the sadist's career. No bells and whistles, just an early retirement. I'm not sure, despite the unpopularity of the vice squad boss, that I ever again was trusted as much by the other cops. But then, I didn't stay on that beat too long anyway. It was, generally, a beginner's assignment, and I was rising fairly rapidly.

Even before covering police headquarters in Washington, for the *Washington Times-Herald*, I worked for the *Alexandria* (Virginia) *Gazette,* my first newspaper journalism experience, though a small-time and small-town one. I was hired on as the reporter. That's right: *the* reporter.

There were two editors and one reporter. One of the editors was the boss editor, whose main assignment seemed to be to attend town functions and make friends for the paper. The other, my late but longtime dear friend Thomas Moore McBride, had the job of actually putting the paper together, laying it out, copyreading it, and staying alert to potential stories for the reporter to cover.

One of the first stories to which I was assigned was the crash of a military training plane in a wooded area near Alexandria. Thanks to Tom's attentiveness to his police radio and my readiness to take off immediately in the company car, I actually got to the crash site before the rescue people, the military, or the police.

There is something about a demolished airplane, and bodies demolished within it, that is so very sad. There was no fire, no noise, just the shaded quiet of a forest. And a crumpled mass of metal, like tin cans crushed by a giant. And a redness-like clumsily applied paint over most of it. As I stood at the wreckage, something flopped down from it. It appeared to be an aviator's leather helmet. But it was perfectly shaped, as though a head might still be in it. Actually, there was only part of a head, the top part, neatly sheared off.

That was when the sadness really struck me. I had been taking flying lessons and knew the exuberance of flying on a good clear day such as this one. The people in the military plane must have felt that. And then something happened. And it was all over with. Life was gone. Flight was gone. All gone. All sad.

The *Washington Times-Herald* was my first big-time journalism experience. I went there after the *Alexandria Gazette* and my brief association with the Eighth Armored Division.

Let me introduce you to the cast of this newspaper. I say cast because working at the *Times-Herald* was as much like being in a stage play as being on a newspaper. It was *The Front Page* come to life:

William Perry Flythe Jr., second-generation newspaperman. His father had been a star of the Hearst papers, renowned in newspaper legend for having got the scoop on the killing of Pancho Villa; allegedly, Flythe Sr. was drunk at the only telegraph available in Parral where the deed was done—or else 100 miles away at Chihuahua where General Pershing had harried the bandit revolutionary. Whichever, his legend was bright.

Actually, Billy's best story about his father was set in the more cosmopolitan precincts of Mexico City, where Billy's father had been assigned, with few onerous duties, as a reward for his great scoop on Pancho Villa. The house where the Flythes lived was next to the house of a Mexican general of renowned, bilious temperament. For some reason, the senior Flythe decided that the general needed slaughtering and so, one fine day, he picked up his revolver and strode with deadly intent toward the general's house.

Billy said that he felt orphanhood bowling down upon him. What match would his bibulous papa be for the bilious general? Within a few minutes, the sounds of gunshots rolled like doom from the roof garden of the general's house, where the officer was known to spend a good deal of his leisure time. Billy was now sure that he was an orphan, and ran as fast as he could over to the general's house and up to the roof.

There, each seated in a lounge chair, were the father and the Federalista. Each had a pistol. They were shooting at empty whisky bottles ranged along the edge of the roof.

A large pistol, a 9mm Mauser, that lovely model with its magazine in front of the trigger guard, played an important role in a more contemporaneous adventure of Bill Jr. Billy, who had an inexhaustible talent for becoming romantically involved with very goofy ladies, found himself unable to extract himself from the coils of one. He wanted out. She wanted the heavens to split and mountains to tumble before that would happen.

Unimpressed by such ardor, and fairly sure that his wife was hot on the scent of the liaison, Billy devised a fine way out. He began to fill his inamorata's head with suggestive tales of his involvement with the Irish

Republican Army, then seen by many as a heroic bunch of freedom fighters. When he felt that it had all sunk in sufficiently, he cued me to come bursting into the lady's apartment, my 9mm Mauser at the flourish. I was there, for the IRA, to take the deviant Flythe away to face his superiors. What a role! My year or so in drama school had left me a dedicated ham. At any rate, the young lady, tearfully, let her lover go, did not call the police, and vanished into the past tense of Billy's libido.

Another pistol, a Smith & Wesson .38, nearly played another role in Billy's tempestuous love life. His wife, Alice, the child of real IRA soldiers and said to have been smuggled over here from Ireland in a trunk, was a woman of great and violent temper, given to shredding Billy's clothes and tossing them out the window upon any new evidence of his infidelity. Billy's wardrobe was accordingly sparse.

His idea for the pistol was elegant. He would leave it in a place where Alice could find it in one of her rages, or simply when drunk. He was depending on her to pick it up, take a shot or two at him, and miss—or, at least, not inflict a fatal wound. Then the outraged Billy would have her jugged for assault or, even better, attempted murder. Nothing came of the plan, as well thought out as it was. Neither of them was ever quite sober enough. Finally Billy and Alice divorced and Billy married an heiress.

Another character in the *Times-Herald* cast: Augustus (Gus) Miller. It is true that not every journalist could have the J-gene of a Billy Flythe, but you might think that some teeny tiny background or interest in the subject would be helpful. Not so. Gus Miller was a physical therapist who had, literally, just wandered into the *Times-Herald* during one of its loonier moments of employment expansion. Someone, probably with a degree in personnel assessment (P. Ass.), hired Miller onto the crew as, of all things, night city editor. The paper was a morning one, with its largest editions going to press around midnight. It was these crucial editions that Miller was to preside over in regard to all local news.

And preside he did. No detail was too small to escape Miller's squint-eyed attention. He was probably twice as old as anyone else on the city staff, even as old as the copyreaders who, sitting at a semicircular table beside the city desk, looked like a squad of ancient monks illuminating manuscripts. Actually, their job was to clean up the spelling and grammar in stories and put headlines on in accordance with a vague makeup plan that someone had put together.

There was Miller's file cabinet. Although it did hold some papers, mostly it held everything else that Miller felt needed to be alphabetically stored. A friend of mine left a pair of gloves in the city room. I did not hesitate before finding them in Miller's file cabinet, under G. It also was where he kept his honey which, from his experience as a physical therapist, he had come to regard as a perfect high-energy food. Any reporter about to dash forth on an assignment that might be hectic (murder, arson, suicide, for instance) was asked first to step over to Miller's desk and receive a tablespoonful of honey for quick and vital energy.

Miller also had a great talent for writing overnight memos which were often far better than the incidents to which they referred. These memos were left for the day staff and were intended to apprise them of unfinished business from the late-night side and to alert them to upcoming developments. A classic, which I recall vividly, was in regard to the murder of someone whose body was shoved from a car speeding past Union Station. Miller's overnight memo said, "Be alert. Murders like this usually come in threes. The next one may be a young debutante." Perhaps it was the honey overenergizing his mind.

That same murder involved me in a curious pursuit. Someone had noted several of the numbers of the license tag of the speeding, body-dispensing car. Our alert managing editor, Ray Helgeson, fairly new from Chicago (the traditional training ground for newspaper eccentrics), got hold of the numbers and quickly had the police headquarters reporter look up permutations of them.

Then he assigned me to go to the houses of people owning cars with license tags matching the partial numbers from the fleeing vehicle. I was to ask them where they'd been that night. It was past midnight. Fortunately, I never found anyone who could have been involved. After I'd been screamed at and had doors slammed in my face a few times, and after I'd checked out a few auto hoods to see if any were still hot, I got to thinking that Helgeson had, deliberately and with no apparent concern, sent me on an assignment which, if successful, would have found me, at one or two o'clock in the morning, face to face with a killer. I suppose that in his own crazy way he felt this would be just one hell of a good story for *someone* to tell.

Probably Helgeson's career high came on a Christmas Eve. He fired one of the staff. When someone asked him why, of all times, he'd chosen this day to fire the guy, Helgeson replied, "Well, look, it was Christmas Eve, it was snowing, the guy had a sick kid at home, his wife was about to leave him. Christ. I just couldn't resist it." He hired him back the next day.

Helgeson had an insatiable curiosity as shown by his hope that I could interview the Union Station murderer. Once, convinced that a person listed as dead from natural causes had actually been murdered, he sent two husky reporters to the grave and had them dig up the body, then take it for an independent autopsy. Alas, it showed no signs of foul play.

Then there was blind Tom. Here was a fellow whose background was in bookkeeping and whose eyes had gone so bad that he wore half-inch-thick lenses in his glasses. By some stroke of luck, he had a highly placed friend on the *Times-Herald* who managed to have him hired as a reporter. He was one of the best. He looked so disheveled and so sad, squinting though those bottle-bottom lenses, that the people he interviewed probably felt sorry for him. At any rate, he could worm more information out of people than anyone else on the staff. Also, his bookkeeping background meant that he was perfectly content to spend entire days looking through ledgers to track down a discrepancy here, a discrepancy there. It all adds up.

One curious bit of language sticks in my mind. In those days it was customary to identify African Americans as "colored." I don't know when the practice ended but surely it was not before the Second World War; even during that war, the identification of "colored troops" was familiar. Now, the curiosity. These days if someone wrote that someone else was colored, the skies would rage, the earth, and many garments, would be rent. The proper usage has become "people of color."

I understand that people of color can be black, brown, reddish, yellowish, or what have you, sweeping African Americans into a new melting-pot world in which there just are people of color and people of all-colors, white people. But what in the world, I wonder, is the difference between calling someone colored or a person of color? Since there seems no sensible explanation in terms of ordinary language, I have come to believe that the only reason lies in just not wanting to use a phrasing that was popular prior to the civil rights movement. Fair enough.

But there is an even stranger usage regarding Jews, a reverse sort of situation. For a time it seemed proper only to refer to Jews as "members of the Jewish faith," or something like that. The stark term "Jew" just wouldn't do. Jews themselves, it seems to me, put an end to that wimpy circumlocution after fighting their way into possession of a homeland and establishing the state of Israel. I don't think that any Jew today would resent being called a Jew or feel that a speaker was being sweetly sensitive by referring to them as "members of the Jewish faith."

And I wonder, is the supposed sensitivity of referring to people of color, rather than to a colored person, a symptom of something along the same lines, an insecurity about words with internal and historic integrity, such as "Negro" and "colored"? "Negro," which originally, as I understand it, referred to the Sudanese people of the area now called Ethiopia, came to refer to all black Africans. In a way it is the equivalent of Jew. A Negro. A Jew. A person of color. A member of the Jewish faith. People should insist on being called whatever *they* want. And there is good reason, I know, why "black" eclipsed the pre-civil rights appellations of Negro and colored, and why African American is today on the ascent. But it seems to me that the more direct and simple the name, the more pride and security it reflects.

But since nobody really asked about all that, let me return to more practical matters.

As was expected of reporters in those days, just about everyone on the staff drank to excess as often as they could. I did not, not because of any puritan instinct but because when I got drunk, I vomited. I became, therefore, a sort of designated driver for the rest of the staff, spending at least part of every night hauling someone home or at least stacking them in some part of the newspaper building where they could sleep it off safely.

The occasion for liquid sin was most convenient; as a matter of fact, it was just around the corner on the second floor, above a retail store. It was called the Printers Club. It opened at midnight and, like a vampire, fled to closing at dawn. There were some printers who frequented it but mainly it was reporters who kept the place noisy with argumentation, complaining, boasting, lying, and with bodies falling, sliding, seeping, oozing, crumpling, collapsing, and otherwise becoming briefly unconscious just enough to restore them for the next day's assault upon the world of corruption which made for the best reading then and now.

Some truly dedicated drinkers hardly ever made it as far as the Printers Club. Zeke Hearin, for instance. He had discovered that Scotch whiskey and milk mixed very well. He was a rewriteman, as I was too after putting in my time as a reporter. This meant taking information by phone, from reporters in the field, and then turning it into nicely phrased stories.

The Scotch-milk discovery meant that Zeke could sit at his typewriter sipping on milk laced with hidden Scotch so as to be just about liquor lunatic by the end of the shift. Actually, the drunker he got, the more poetic he got, and some of his rewrites by early morning had a good deal more imagery than information in them.

Later, during the Second World War, Zeke was in the merchant marine, including the perilous run to and from Murmansk. During that period I got many postcards from him, from many parts of the world. Every one said, "Ah, there, Mr. Hess." Nothing more.

It was at the *Times-Herald*, also, that I learned how whores obtained their photo-illustrated calling (calling girl?) cards. And also it was where I ran into the remarkable Jones twins.

First, the twins. Both were photographers and later became justly famed as war correspondents, in Korea, and then as television executives. They were such identical twins that no one could tell them apart. One worked for the *Times-Herald* while the other one worked at the *Washington Post*, but no one ever really knew which Jones was on hand in either city room. No one really cared. They were both fine photographers.

They also gave rise to stories which probably still are being told by elderly ladies who will never forget their long-ago interminable sexual encounters with a young man named Jones. Fact of the matter was that when one Jones had begun the encounter and climaxed a time or two, he would profess the need to step out for cigarettes, whiskey, or to take a picture. Shortly thereafter the other Jones would arrive, identically dressed, and ready for action. This would go on all night. No wonder that Jones fellow became a legend.

Now for the calling cards. These pieces of highly personal identification, decorated with photos of the young lady doing what she did professionally, were taken by the night-shift photographers in the studio of the *Times-Herald*. It was, so far as I could tell, a virtual monopoly. Usually the photographers themselves posed with the ladies, getting for free what less fortunate johns were paying for around the corner in Franklin Park. After a particularly busy evening of this desirable moonlighting, there would be a shortage of photographers able to rise to the occasion. It was at such a time that the photo editor, the redoubtable Garvin Tankersly, would forsake his desk, descend to the studio, and show all involved what a truly dedicated satyrmaniac can do when called upon. He never failed in the task so far as any of those who tried to keep count could tell.

The romantic notion that a newspaperman worth his bourbon would be fired from many jobs as the result of natural reportorial cantankerousness was popular while I was at the *Times-Herald*. It just could be that the *Times-Herald* was the last of the "Front Page" sort of paper.

At any rate, I got fired from it.

The lever for my removal was the nightclub column of the news-paper, an assignment that rewritemen shared seriatim. It was an inter-esting column since it was almost entirely fictional, reflecting what the writer thought should be happening at local nightspots. Actual reporting would have required leaving the Printers Club for the inferior entertain-ment of public bars.

It was my pleasure, whenever I had the chore, to make sure that our city editor always was mentioned and always in the same words: "Seen trading witticisms with the other customers at Kavakos Bar and Grill was *Times-Herald* city editor Augustus Miller." Kavakos was a notoriously brawly and ribald spa.

After the first instance, Miller asked that I stop. He asked me after the second. On the occasion of the third he said that I would be fired if I did it again. On the occasion of the fourth he apparently did something about it, although I never heard about it officially.

Coming in to work the next night, I was met by our Newspaper Guild representative, another rewriteman named Harry Gabbet. He asked whether I wanted to fight my dismissal. Since it was the first I had heard of the event, I asked the most sensible question that I could: "How much severance pay?" It was enough to tell him that under no circumstances was he to seek justice. Take the cash and let the credit go, as the poet sings.

Gabbet was famed much more for a great invention than for his union activity. One slow night, he wrote an endearing, entirely fictional story about some people in the suburbs who had spotted the tracks of an unfa-miliar creature. Gabbet said that a quick check with the Smithsonian Insti-tution had verified that the tracks were, in fact, those of the Bovalipus Snal-ligaster, a medium-sized but determined little mammal thought to have become extinct some years back. Harry carried on his delicate little lessons in natural history for months before wearying of the game. No editor ever questioned him closely on the matter. It was too fine a little story.

After speaking to Gabbet in the hallway of the *Times-Herald* on the evening of my firing, I wandered two blocks north to the offices of the town's tabloid Scripps-Howard newspaper, the *Washington Daily News*, where I was hired immediately.

Along with the fact that both the novelist Robert Ruark and the mag-nificent war correspondent Ernie Pyle were briefly on the premises, the most memorable thing about the *News* was a very tall, very muscular pho-tographer who had once talked an entire line of young secretaries into sitting along the edge of a bomber at a nearby airbase. He had also convinced them that they should doff their underpants and hoist their skirts. It was to boost the morale of our fighting men. It must have boosted a lot more than that. What a picture. What a cunning argument.

It became clear to me that men and women both are likely to do things in order to be photographed that they would never do publicly otherwise. I suppose that this could be called the *Playboy* phenomenon except that it seems to operate powerfully even without the payment of *Playboy's* generous modeling fees, or any fees at all.

There is an extension of this phenomenon that amazes me even more. When people who have just lost a loved one are asked to supply a picture of the departed they most often *do* it. It is a constant chore for reporters to ask for the loan of photos just as it is one of the most unpleasant of constant chores to ask a person in the midst of shock over a loss to tell you all about the person just killed. Still more amazing is the way that the bereaved put up with the clutter and confusion of television interviews—as though the press has an undeniable right to poke and pry into their most anguished thoughts and remembrances.

What a sad thing it is that the press often is criticized for trying to pry out government secrets and shame. I consider it one of the most useful occupations, one which all free men would applaud, as did Jefferson. Yet the press is rarely criticized for intruding on small personal tragedies and feeding on the anguish of people who feel defenseless against the demands of the famous, bigger-than-life folk in television. It is this latter intrusion that seems indecent to me and altogether indefensible by any argument about the public having the right to know. The public should be edified when corruption is reported among the rulers. It should be ashamed when someone's moment of agony is thrown before them like a morsel before animals. As a newspaperman, I do not recall any part of the job that I really didn't relish—except asking for those sad little photos. I disliked it then. I dislike the memory of it now. I abhor the television version of it whenever some pretty TV personality asks those ugly questions about "Was your son a good boy?" or "Where was he driving when the truck hit him?"

True to custom, I was fired from the *Washington Daily News* for another smart-assed gesture, another thumbing of the nose at authority. But this time it was owing to a much more distinguished level of foolishness than my dismissal from the *Times-Herald*. I was fired from the *Washington Daily News* because of Franklin Delano Roosevelt.

Let me put my relationship to the president into some perspective. It was not a personal relationship—although I did go swimming in his White House pool a time or two thanks to the kindness of FDR's naval aide, who dated my mother for a time. Otherwise the relationship was purely ideological. It seemed to me then and it seems to me now that FDR, an overpowering nationalist and populist forging a grand alliance of the discontented, the dispossessed, and the angry, brought the country to a nationalist fervor similar to the national fervors that brought national socialism to Germany and fascism to Italy and to Spain.

Did I think that FDR was a fascist? No. I believed that he was what he appeared to be: an American aristocrat with a sense of national service that emboldened him to think he could, in effect, conscript the nation into a benign collectivism of self-sacrifice and pie-in-the-sky national glory. It was the Second World War, I believe, that derailed the dream of a generally individualistic nation.

I could see no place for the individual in the Rooseveltian dreams. There were places only for what could be seen as the New American Man, a sturdy workingman ready to plug away at whatever loony scheme the politicians proposed so long as it "soaked the rich" and cherished the savings of widows and orphans. Some widows and orphans and many trade union members did well, it was said, during that era—under the frightening icon of a blue eagle that looked like a patch from a German uniform. The cost in inflation remained hidden for years. The cost in suppressing small business and entrepreneurial risk taking was hidden also, under the veil of attempts to make the economy rational.

The two most highly regarded of all presidents seem to be Abraham Lincoln and FDR. I have little regard for Lincoln in his bloody war to keep the union intact (why not two Americas *de jure* instead of, as we still have, *de facto*?). I have little regard for Roosevelt's march toward federal power at a brisk parade step. Since then, no serving president (and only one aspirant to the presidency, Barry Goldwater) has given much more than lip service to calling off the parade.

Until Lincoln, liberty, not democracy, was the *national* zeal. Democracy was a *local* process moderating liberty and civilizing it. At worst, of course, it was a way of privileging some and oppressing others; but, because it was so localist in nature, the scale of oppression and violence was smaller and spottier and even escapable. Slavery, a product of neither democracy nor liberty, was a baleful inhibition to either. Had Lincoln not had nationalist ambitions, however, the local processes of democracy—which already were arising as rebellions prior to the war at Harpers Ferry and in the abolitionist underground—could have brought liberty.

As it happened, the War Between the States, our bloodiest enterprise as a nation, stamped out the possibilities for local liberty and localistic de Tocquevillian self-rule by establishing for the first time a truly effective *national* democracy. A centralized state alien to anything Thomas Jefferson had imagined on his Monticello hilltop arose from the ashes of war with a sound and fury "like a firebell in the night." It set into motion a windstorm that would cut relentlessly at the foundations of personal liberty and community democracy, doing as it has for more than a century the bidding of its administrators.

My mother's attitude toward FDR did nothing to moderate my views. She was so opposed to his policies, his demeanor, to everything about him, that when she moved to a suburb of Washington late in her life she nearly refused to buy a house she liked because it was just a block from Roosevelt Street. She would not complete the deal for the house until she had been given a signed document from the county commission averring that the street was named for Theodore and not Franklin.

(Speaking of glory-bully nationalists, however, Theodore was quite an operator on his own. Among other things he came up with the idea of making nature a monument to the state. More than any president before or after, he aggrandized the national forest system and made bureaucracy the kingpin of the once wild and self-governing West.)

At any rate, when FDR died I did not weep a tear nor rend a garment. I did drink a fair amount, right up to my get-sick level. Consequently, I was feeling pretty miserable although still not tearful the following morning when, before dawn, an editor at the *News* asked me to come in and start writing obituary encomiums for the late, great departed. I refused because of my celebratory hangover.

Thus, in 1945, a revered president died, a nation wept and wailed, and I got fired again.

7

Journalist

I find the great thing in this world is not so much where we stand as in what direction we are moving.

—Oliver Wendell Holmes

After being fired from the *Washington Daily News*, I was quickly transported from the blood and guts of daily newspapering to the more tidy, corporate world of modern magazine journalism.

The trip began just a few blocks north of the *News* building at the offices of *Pathfinder* magazine, then the second largest newsweekly in the land, reaching more than a million readers—not as many as *Time* but more than the then fairly new *Newsweek. Pathfinder* was a magazine intended for a rural audience. It was published by the Farm Journal group headquartered in Philadelphia.

I recall its managing editor, Don McNeil, and its editor in chief, Wheeler McMillen, with constant admiration. McNeil hired me for a reason that strikes me as greatly more sensible than whether I had ever been to journalism school, or any school for that matter. He asked me to look up a word for him in the office dictionary. I went to the book, opened it, and, as has happened to me just about every time I ever have opened a dictionary, got diverted to a word of which I had never heard—but *not* the word McNeil had asked about. The diversion must have been obvious

99

because it brought us into a discussion of curiosity. To McNeil, curiosity was the key to journalism. I couldn't have agreed more. By the time we had hashed that subject over thoroughly, I was hired—to be the magazine's religion editor!

The fact that I was an atheist didn't strike me as a handicap. The real handicap turned out to be that I had been raised a Roman Catholic and, so help me, had only a very vague notion of what Protestant churches were. They were just the places where all those other people went. Had it not been for curiosity, the religion section of *Pathfinder* would have been an endless celebration of Latin American religious holidays, arguments in the Vatican, and the latest attempts by half the Catholic episcopacy to roll history back past the Council of Trent while the other half wanted to roll it ahead to a reconciliation with Marxism.

As it was, I went to worship at my own church, the public library, and soon I could tell you as much about the emerging tensions in the Southern Baptist Conference, the liturgical movement among Lutherans, and the difference between the full immersionists and the dunkers and dippers and the sprinklers as I could earlier have told you about the difference between venial and cardinal sin.

My chief gratitude to the editor in chief, Wheeler McMillen—who was always the epitome of what my mother would have called a perfect gentleman—was for introducing me to Felix Morley and his nearly classical liberal view of the American Constitution. It was not until later, when I had occasion to work with James Jackson Kilpatrick, that I met an even hardier defender of the political ideal that the Constitution represents—an ideal, I surmised, to which only a rare few paid attention and even fewer appreciated.

McMillen was, even at the late date of the end-of-the-forties postwar recovery years, what can only be termed a premature anti-Communist. I worked for him before that crucial period when many outstanding liberals finally gave up all hope of reconciliation with Stalinist Communism. It was at the time when attacks against Communists in America were often viewed as merely veils for anti-union, antiblack, retrogressive social policies. Hollywood was at full howl on the subject. So were many journalists, some of them merely repulsed by the heavy-handed inquisitions of the House Un-American Activities Committee (HUAC), and others among them personally committed to a socialist political agenda which (so they grotesquely persisted in believing) required that they not attack

Communism. Anti-Communism was assumed to be right-wing and anti-liberal. Anti-anti-Communism was modish and among journalists almost mandatory.

The number of overtly anti-Communist journalists was so small that I can remember most of them without notes even at this date: George Sokolsky, Ralph de Toledano, Tony Smith, Jack Kilpatrick, Vic Lasky, Victor Riesel, James Burnham, Bill Buckley, Max Eastman, John Chamberlain, Frank Chodorov, H. L. Mencken, Felix Morley, Westbrook Pegler, and, eventually, me.

My own anti-Communist journalism was Wheeler McMillen's idea: a regular column on international Communism, in *Pathfinder.*

The anti-Communist journalists of the time were so few and so embattled by the anti-antis that they naturally formed a network of support and information sharing. In addition, they had two strong official allies, supporters, and sharers of information: the Federal Bureau of Investigation, through one of its assistant directors, Deke DeLoach; and HUAC, through its research director, Ben Mandel. Not bad sources. And prolific.

My anti-Communism was forged out of my mother's determined individualism and my own brief association, as a fourteen-year-old, with the Socialist Party and with a local pro-Communist bookstore. Still regretting my thankfully brief association with anti-Semitism, it seemed an atoning act to look for association with some polar opposite. Communism seemed the most obvious pole. The Communist bookstore was the most available point of association and, since no one seemed anxious to go out of their way to recruit me into the Party, the only available one.

The bookstore was loaded with the usual library from International Publishers, pamphlets straight off Soviet presses, and that most rousing publication, the *Daily Worker*, perhaps half of whose circulation was paid for by Washington police and various federal investigative agencies. The bookstore was loaded also with the word "socialism," and in my blissful ignorance of what any of it really meant, I soon lumped the two, with Communism being the militant phase and socialism being the work-within-the-system phase, as with Norman Thomas's Socialist Party of America.

I joined the Socialist Party as soon as I could find a meeting. My mother, patient as always with my adventures, just asked me questions about what I hoped to accomplish with this new association—and made sure that I read Westbrook Pegler, the archconservative anti-Rooseveltian columnist, every day.

Mother's view of Communism was highly colored by her view of FDR. It was FDR's accommodations with the Soviet Union, prior to the Hitler-Stalin pact, that convinced her there must be something terribly wrong with Communism. Why else would Roosevelt cozy up to it? She was also convinced that Roosevelt was a socialist. She went into political raptures when the Socialist Party announced that the Democrats (read FDR) had passed so much of their program that they had little left for which to campaign.

But it took something even more convincing for me to make a break with socialism, just a few weeks after forming my tie with it. I attended a Socialist Party meeting.

Just about halfway through the meeting, with socialist pie filling the skies and raking the heavens, I had this nearly religious revelation: What it all really added up to was the idea that, "If everyone in the world could just be made to think as I do and behave as I do, then there would be no war, no famine, no injustice, no poverty." The statement was even made that we could settle for nothing less than Utopia. Socialist Utopia, of course. The Utopia of the philosopher princes.

The Communist bookstore wasn't much better. It had offered nothing to excite me in the long run except for Lenin's *State and Revolution*, which I had interpreted as very antagonistic to state central authority and, in simple extrapolation, pointedly anti-Rooseveltian—and anti-Utopian Socialist. Yet there was after all one other thing that tugged at my imagination: stirring, strident, bigger-than-life music—the music that the Communists dredged out of the Spanish Civil War (all those great and rousing fighting songs— how could a youthful romantic not be a Communist or at least an anti-Franco partisan) and the early resistance to Hitler anthems ("Die Moorsoldaten").

There was no way around it; the songs of the Spanish Civil War were the most exciting political happenings of the day. Who could listen to them without being stirred by emotional waves of heroism and elevated to lofty heights of idealism? I certainly couldn't. And the songs were on the right side, the Republican side, the side that happened also to be Communist. Maybe it all was inevitable; it was part of my weaning on *The Three Musketeers* and Sabatini, it was part of my genetic inheritance from my soon-to-be beheaded father, it was part of my mother's standing up on her own to an indifferent world, and, I suppose, it was later part of the reason for my profound admiration for Goldwater. Strange: Spanish Civil War, a beheading, a liberated woman, and Barry Goldwater.

Oh, well. I wasn't invited to become a Communist and I quit the Socialists after that first meeting. Where was a young fellow to go then for compatible politics? The Republican Party, of course.

Think about it. The Republicans were radical then. They had the best notions of what I had hoped to find in socialism, but they didn't have the obsession with power. Small businessmen, not big business, made up the party's core. It represented the only strong anti-imperialist political position. Anti-imperialist? Republicans? Uh-huh. But Republicans were not smart enough to call it that. They let it be labeled isolationism, as though they wanted the United States to sneak off the world stage, slam the doors, and bolt the windows. The underlying Republican argument, that we should trade with everyone but not interfere with or intervene in their internal politics, was lost behind that unattractive label. Isolationism. Brrr. But I decided not to be put off by labels.

Back, then, to the anti-Communist network of which I immediately became a part.

Think of the situation. It was all so very different from today, when journalists become specialists in some part of social or political interest. Where will they get their information? Unless they are backed by their employer to spend virtually unlimited time digging out stuff (the way the *Washington Post* supported Carl Bernstein and Robert Woodward and the *New York Times* came to support Seymour Hirsh; or the way the *Des Moines Register* supported the reporter who really should be honored as the real pioneer of modern investigative journalism, Clark Mollenhoff), unless they are so backed—and few are—then they have to get their information from people placed within the area of interest that they cover. They get their best information from "sources." Sources are just people in government or private offices who have access to scandalous information.

The reporter doesn't dig out the news. The reporter digs out the source, cultivates the source, then listens to what the source has to say, evaluates it, and, if it seems okay, repeats it.

There undoubtedly will be reporters who will greet any information about the FBI or HUAC feeding information to journalists as the most heretical straying from news purity. Nonsense. The defense reporters are given tons of material by their sources in the Pentagon. Even most of the economics reporters have to depend on their buddies at the Federal Reserve or Treasury for the contents of their little bites of TV time or page-one exclusives.

So here we have the FBI and HUAC, awash in information about the Communist conspiracy (alas, that's right, *conspiracy*), and here is a little handful of reporters who agree that it's a conspiracy and a menace. Of course they get together. Of course they form a symbiotic relationship. Of course the reporters report what the sources say. Of course the sources seek out the reporters they think will listen.

Does anyone actually believe that Ralph Nader has never been slipped a secret memo by a disgruntled source or that there are no people at the Environmental Protection Agency or the Food and Drug Administration who do not seek to whisper juicy things in his ears? Is it really possible that he gets information without sources? How? Might he rifle the safes of greedy corporate officials late at night? Of course not. Nader, like most people in the business of gathering and disseminating information, is mainly a middleman. He passes along what others originate.

Even under the Freedom of Information Act, it is difficult and usually impossible for a reporter to get to the raw files from which to reconstruct the balance sheet of some infamy or another. The business of government and the business of business is, to every extent the participants can make it, a closed book. Our freedom is blessed when anger or corruption in high places looks to protect itself or relieve a guilty conscience by leaking the good stuff to a reporter. Just think of what happens when someone tries to do this in full public view, when someone tries to be a heroic and public whistle blower. Despite every effort to protect such brave folk, they usually end up losing a lot, banished from jobs, shuffled off into obscure places, and so forth.

It is usually when the dogs start fighting among themselves in some elevated kennel that we the people get some of the inside dope. Despite which, I bless with what journalistic prayerfulness I can muster those few tough-minded reporters and their capitalist sponsors who do take the time endlessly to sift through files, through accounting ledgers, through garbage if necessary, to get at some hitherto unrevealed sinning in either the private or the public world.

I admit it freely: I never was one of those. I was like most reporters, most journalists. I took my information from sources and, when I was a full-time anti-Communist columnist, those sources were, mainly, the FBI and the House Un-American Activities Committee.

There again, just think about it. How in the world could any journalist be able to report that such-and-such a person held Communist Party membership card number such-and-such? Did they rifle the Party's safe? Did they pick someone's pocket? Of course not. Someone sent them a photostat.

The FBI always sent their info in the classic plain brown envelopes, unmarked and unidentifiable. The envelopes would come hot and heavy when a suspected Communist was figuring in some running news story. HUAC, and its avuncular research director, Ben Mandel, did their info sharing at a much more dependable, close-up, and, in my view, a much more reassuring manner. Ben would just talk to you, let you look at a file or two, and then steer you away from or toward foolish or good questions to ask during interviews.

Even when I became the subject of and not the favored recipient of HUAC (later renamed the House Internal Security Committee) and FBI information, I found the personal touch of the committee more pleasant and a good deal easier to deal with than the remote stare and curious errors of the FBI. That time came during my association with the New Left, discussed later on.

As pleasurable as things were at *Pathfinder,* writing the anti-Communist column and being an enthusiastic part of an embattled minority, the need to make more money to support a wife and, in 1947, a son urged me into more traditional, less ideological, journalism.

The magazine journalism trip continued from the *Pathfinder* building, just off 14th Street at Massachusetts Avenue, southward several blocks to the National Press Building at 14th and F Streets, and the offices of a McGraw-Hill publication then called *Aviation News* (later to become *Aviation Week*, in keeping with the this-or-that *Week* titles of the company's other technical magazines). I was hired as news editor since I was familiar with airplanes, knew how to fly, and always had been a machinery lover.

It was at *Aviation News* that I learned how easy it is to be treasonous. It may be recalled that some poor schmuck recently was given a horrendous jail sentence for passing along information to one of this country's most loyal, if occasionally annoying, allies, Israel. My tiny treasonous act involved another of our unshakable allies, Great Britain.

One of the friends I made soon after taking the aviation magazine job was a Royal Air Force officer stationed at the British Embassy. When Chuck Yaeger burst through the sound barrier in the X-1 aircraft it was officially a high secret. But *Aviation News* got hold of all the details and was preparing to print them in an upcoming issue. In order to do my friend at the embassy a favor, I phoned him immediately with the details, giving him several days' advantage over most people in Washington, supersonic-wise. I assume that some bureaucrat with a vibrating blue pencil would have delighted in sticking it to me on some charge. They certainly tried to make *Aviation News* feel like a menace to society for that scoop, as well as for the dozens of others the magazine pulled off right under the eyes of the Pentagon's security police. It was always our perhaps naive notion that the KGB had at least as much money, time, and energy as we did at *Aviation Week* to spend on acquiring exactly the same information.

One of the magazine's scoops, the photo of a hitherto secret combat aircraft, came when a staffer saw it taped to the front of one of the pedal carts that delivered mail in the Pentagon. But most of the magazine's scoops came from, you might know, "sources"—particularly sources inside the aviation industry itself, where the chance to advertise some secret military advance could lead to a healthy boost in stock values.

Having read all of John LeCarre's work, I assume there is some loony logic that prevents our intelligence people from behaving as though Israel and Great Britain and the editors, for instance, of the Janes reference manuals, or magazines like *Aviation Week*, are actually decent people and on our side. But I say, if you couldn't trust Margaret Thatcher, who in the name of all that is politically holy *could* you trust? Secrecy for any but the most immediate reasons of protecting troop movements or exotic chemical formulas is bad business for a society that wants to be a free society. If liberty is worth dying for, it surely should be worth inconve-niencing a few bureaucrats for.

Even assuming that every member of the press is a rotten apple, dead set on destroying all of our institutions and plunging us straight into chaos, I still would have to hold with Thomas Jefferson on the subject of liberty. The press is a small annoyance to put up with compared to the state of affairs in a society where bureaucrats have an impenetrable shield behind which to hide their every act, their every fall from grace.

It is easy to despise the arrogance of the press, particularly the TV phalanxes of pretty faces and profoundly ordinary minds. The point is that these folk are highly paid entertainers. The real reporters are far too scruffy a lot to be allowed on TV prime time. The same goes for cantan-kerous commentators. Imagine H. L. Mencken walking into a network personnel office.

And what are your qualifications, Mr. Mencken?

Well, I've written a highly regarded multivolume discourse on the American language, and I presume that language and TV still might have a remote association.

That makes you sound like an old curmudgeon, Mr. Mencken.

Precisely.

Well, to be perfectly frank, Mr. Mencken, you really don't have the sort of physical presence we have come to expect from our prime-time people.

On the other hand, I daresay that I look a hell of a lot more like most of the audience than any of the slickers you're hiring these days. I also drink a lot of beer and good whiskey. And I've been a working newspaperman my entire adult life.

Oh, well, you see, Mr. Mencken, we regard that as a technically narrow specialization. It takes a lot more than that to handle yourself in front of a camera.

I thank you for the warning and I bid you a fond farewell. There are some advantages to being dead, after all.

8

Big-Time Journalist

Ah, ye knights of the pen! May honour be your shield, and truth tip your lances! Be gentle to all gentle people. Be modest to women. Be tender to children. And as for the Ogre Humbug, out sword, and have at him.
— Thackeray, *Roundabout Papers*

During the years that I worked full time as a journalist in Washington, I also freelanced as a writer of speeches for politicians, as did just about everyone I knew. Sometimes it was as a volunteer, for politicians with whom I shared prejudices—such as anti-Communism, for example. I made another part of my living as a ghostwriter of books, a practice that I carried on for years and half a dozen published manuscripts.

Ghostwriting had its challenges. It forced me into a more passive, literary mood. It also introduced me to people and subjects far afield from the small and intimate circles of American anti-Communism. The very first book I ghosted was a really interesting one on comparative religion done for a Presbyterian minister while I was religion editor at *Pathfinder.* After that, I ghosted *Crime without Punishment*, the story of an American counterintelligence agent who had been in both Soviet and Nazi concentration camps.

Next, I entered the environmental fray even before environmentalism was a household word. *Big Dam Foolishness* was, to the best of my knowledge, the first book to expose the fiscal and environmental insanity of damming America's major rivers. From dams I plunged directly into nature writing, authoring the "Nature and Science" volume for *The Bookshelf for Boys and Girls*, giving my childhood fascination and fantasy with chemistry, chemicals, and combustion a much safer outlet. My interest in water and natural science never really waned. A quarter-century later I wrote "The Water Crisis" for *Gallery* magazine.

From nature I jumped to organized crime, where I ghosted the autobiography—*Unless They Kill Me First*—of a high-level mobster, Vincent Siciliano. A scion of a well-known Mafia family, Vincent held the distinction of (among other things) having helped his mother shoot his father's mistress. Less flashy ghosting projects included books for a congressman from Missouri (Tom Curtis) and a future secretary of defense (Mel Laird), and a few shorter pieces for such figures as the shah of Iran, Richard Nixon, and the Black Panthers.

But the hard-prosed political writing was the most exciting. Imagine being in your early twenties (when I first began ghosting) and putting words into the mouths of famous people, political celebrities, hard chargers, all of the kind who provide charisma and cannot be expected also to provide thoughtful or quotable prose. The feeling of behind-the-scenes power that all of this engenders is just part of the overall feeling of superiority and the pride of inside knowledge that is an ordinary part of Washington journalistic egoism.

Let us look at this egoism more closely. Remember, most Washington journalists are synapses in a tissue-maze of gossip that happens to be about nationally recognizable people and purposes. They rub shoulders with people of supposed power and on much different terms from, for instance, reporters who associate with entertainment superstars. Reporters covering entertainers are, by and large, servile hacks, basking in the light of stars and not about to turn off the light by being uppity. That's one end of the spectrum. At the other end are the malicious tabloid gossipers who are quite happy to trade the high of being seen with stars for the high salaries of papers that pay them for nasty stuff rather than sycophancy.

The relationship of Washington reporters to friendly sources (their own stars) is rarely servile or superior. It is more collegial. The official folk do the talking. The reporters and columnists do the interpreting, the popularizing, the choral praising. Sometimes, still, they do the ghostwriting, even though most officials in Washington today have their resident ghosts who are just jealous enough of their own power to fend off even the most friendly offer for help from an outsider.

In Hollywood, one could never mistake the star and the servant journalist. In Washington, columnists of the stature of Mary McGrory, George Will, Robert Novak, and Charles Krauthammer may be seen as virtual peers of the stars in whose light they bask.

Mary McGrory has for years been a virtual spokeslady for the Democratic National Committee. Novak obviously is close to military, CIA, Justice, Treasury, and State Department hardliners in the modern conservative mode. George Will, although the intellectual superior of most of the people about whom he writes, still must settle for crumbs of information from the tables of the mighty for those times when he isn't writing about himself.

Krauthammer, who seems to be closely involved with the rising intellectual aristocracy in the Pentagon, strikes me as far and away the brightest mind of the big-name columnists. But the closer he gets to revelations about complex bureaucratic statistics and arrangements, the closer you know he has had to get to someone who will always be just a bit farther inside the power structure than a columnist ever could be.

The relationship of ordinary reporters to sources may not be nearly as commanding as that of the columnists but it is as collegial. When I covered the Pentagon, I spent more time with a colonel who was my closest source than I did with any of my personal friends. I felt as though I were simply another officer, in mufti. Having a colonel rather than a general as a source is not always a sign of deficient ambition, by the way; a colonel can be at least as useful. But the point is that it is difficult, if not actually impossible, to cover a government agency without being drawn into some sort of friendly insider's collegiality with someone or some faction.

I suppose that the closest thing to a truly unconnected journalist ever to work in Washington was I. F. Stone—"Izzy"—whose newsletter, a must-read resource for most other journalists, was the result of his pack-rat habit of keeping, filing, and indexing so much Washington data, gossip, and statistics that he could make howling great stories about political contradictions, bold-faced budget lies, and so forth. Izzy did not roam the corridors of power or cultivate mighty friends. He just kept magnificent files.

Short of that terrifically demanding sort of journalism, what can a person do to appear to be ahead of the pack in Washington? In my experience it is fairly simple, involving access to a small but potent battery of information. The reporter who reads, fairly regularly, the *Economist,* the *Wall Street*

Journal, the *New York Times,* the *Washington Post,* the *Los Angeles Times,* the *Baltimore Sun,* and MIT's *Technology Review,* and can afford to do computer-based searches and to subscribe to a couple of newsletters in his field of choice, will know about as much of what's going on as most congressmen and senators and even Cabinet-level officials. One helpful shortcut is to get hold of any of the CIA's daily summaries of overseas broadcasts and news stories. For that matter, just watching CNN throughout the day keeps some ordinary folk about as well informed as most reporters.

But that is a digression from where my career headed when I started writing political speeches.

By the time of Gov. Thomas E. Dewey's second run for the presidency against Franklin Delano Roosevelt, I was asked by Jim Selvage, of the then-famed Selvage and Lee public relations agency, to write some speech material for the candidate. I accepted the offer, went to work, and quickly discovered that political speechwriting was easy, natural, and fun. The agency and the Republican National Committee liked what I wrote and asked for more. I was good at it, and not by accident.

When I was fifteen I already knew the rules of propaganda writing; in fact, I was one of the better propaganda writers around. I had observed what works, in part because I had read a lot of speeches and, in part, because I had read so many boring political platforms and knew, by painful study, what not to write. I knew that speeches, to be good and to work, didn't need a facade of elaboration, flourishes, and long, involved sentences that serve only to show off scholarly pretensions. My rules of good speechwriting—which served me through one presidential campaign and three Republican administrations—were simple: write short sentences; use Anglo-Saxon words, not Latin-rooted ones; and stick to a single idea, and make that idea memorable. I learned quickly that people remember only one thing from a speech—not two, and certainly not three.

Attuned naturally to speechwriting, and being a journalist by trade, I suppose I was fated to become a scribe for politicians. In those days, politicians rarely employed staff speechwriters; they depended on journalists such as myself to spin their messages into something pleasant to the ear and something that could easily be consumed by the mind.

In any case, scribbling for Dewey was a fine assignment. Mother was pleased, as can be imagined. My wife, also a Republican and at the time rotogravure editor of the *Washington Star,* was pleased as well with the extra work.

It wasn't what I did so much as whom I got to know in the process that made a big difference in my life. The work was okay. The acquaintance was life changing. One official of the Republican National Committee, Robert Humphreys, had close friendships with people at *Newsweek* magazine, where he had been national affairs editor. And *Newsweek* needed a new press editor. It took just one phone call to get me an appointment with the features, or "back of the book," editor, Frank Callan Norris. It took about a fifteen-minute interview and, lo, I was hired.

Let me explain the press editor situation. At that time there was a regular section of the magazine covering what was going on in print journalism around the world. (There is still such coverage but not on so regular a basis.) Consider the odd situation of such an editor on a major news magazine. There was a science section and a science editor. But there were not other scientifically literate people on the magazine, usually. The music editor knew vastly more about music than anyone else on the staff. The drama editor saw more plays. The book editor read more books. And so on. But print journalism was a different matter. Everyone on the staff was an expert on just that one subject: the press. Everyone was completely immersed in its skills, business, gossip, friendships.

One consequence was that press editors were not renowned for longevity in the position. With so many experts parsing every sentence, criticism of the coverage was constant. Until I got it, the longest anyone had held the job at *Newsweek*, I believe, was three years. I made it to four when internal politics and the convenient return of the publisher's son (who needed a good job and, wouldn't you know it, picked the press section) ended my streak.

My four years' experience with the group journalism of a modern news magazine was instructive if not inspiring. It was also a balancing act for my growing anti-Communist views; I was part of a distinct minority on a definitely liberal staff.

After being hired at *Newsweek*, I was stunned to discover that I was expected to start work as soon as possible. That day, if possible. Next week absolutely. It was not so much the scary prospect of having so quickly to take on a major, high-visibility journalism job that was overpowering and intimidating; it was the truly frightening reality of having to move from the relative serenity of Washington, and a suburban apartment, to the whirly-gig world of mid-Manhattan. But, determined to get started as quickly as possible, I took a room at a sleazy hotel just up Broadway from the *Newsweek* Building which, then, was right on Times Square.

Scared? To my socks!

The room where I was to spend the next several weeks, until my wife found some place for us to live, had no window. It was, I surmised, some sort of closet that had been fashioned into a bedroom as the hotel hit the skids. To shuttle between that wretched room and a strange new world and job left me, every evening, desperately trying to get to sleep as early as possible and not break down into tremors and tears of sheer terror. I have been very close to death since that time but I have never been as frightened.

It didn't last too long. The job was preoccupying, the staff was full of brilliant and eccentric people, and I had a researcher, Jay Brennan, who had served the previous press editor and knew how the magazine worked. And then there was Frank Norris, the editor in charge of all of the departments of the magazine except the national and foreign sections.

Frank Norris was the most inspiring editor with whom I have ever worked. It was his ambition that stories written by his people should always include some poetic phrase that would make a powerful impression and point. One example: a music review in which the song "Begin the Beguine" was described as the sort of music you would hear "way down the beach." If you know the song, and particularly the Artie Shaw rendition of it, you will understand how brilliantly correct is that simple phrase.

He also had another editorial concept that struck me as brilliant. Science, he felt, should be written about in plain, even casual terms. Sport, he insisted, should be written about as one of the human race's most serious enterprises. For all I know, it was that Norrisian concept that led to the superb writings of Red Barber and, later, Tom Boswell, and the very serious writing about baseball by George Will—who grants the Chicago Cubs no less stature in the history of man than Western civilization itself.

Way, way back, when I was at the *Washington News*, a series of unfortunate situations drained the paper of all its regular sportswriters. I was dispatched to the first major league game I ever had attended. Someone handed me a strange black book with absolutely undecipherable diagrams and data lines. I believe it is called a box score. Anyway, I watched the game with great interest. It involved the old Washington Senators and was played at the now-vanished Griffith Stadium.

When the game was over, even though I was not absolutely sure who had won, I realized that I'd have to write *something* about it. In those far-away days, out-of-town reporters on such an assignment wrote their stories right there in the press box. They always made carbon copies, rashly throwing away the actual carbon paper. I retrieved a bunch of the carbons, which can be read fairly easily, and went back to the *News* and wrote a story good enough to put me briefly in danger of permanent assignment to sports. Still, it didn't take much to convince the sports editor that the story was, in fact, a fluke, and that my knowledge of sports did not include expertise in anything but fencing. (I had waved the old epee, foil, and saber for several years at a local Salle de Armes. Also, I did make it into the semifinals of the Mid-Atlantic amateur tennis championships when I was thirteen or fourteen, but that just meant I could play tennis, not that I knew anything about it as a subject.)

So, back to *Newsweek*.

The way a newsmagazine operates was, to me, revealing. Although it cannot be denied that any set of facts can be tilted to reflect a political, ideological, or social bias, it also cannot be denied that in terms of assuring that the facts have a basis in reality, the newsmagazine checking technique is quite good.

It is the job of each writer's researcher to take the first draft of each story and to check it, word by word, for factual accuracy. Nothing is taken for granted. If the story is about Thomas T. Thomas, the writer must provide convincing evidence that the name is accurate (confirmation in a standard reference, a phone number to call if the person is newsworthy but not hitherto famous, several consistent references to the person in the *New York Times* or the *Wall Street Journal*). Lacking evidence, the researcher must go to the trouble of figuring out a way to find independent confirmation. If there is a statistic used, it must also be verifiable—perhaps through the source quoted as providing it, or through a standard reference, such as the various Janes manuals (Should that have an apostrophe? The researcher will check.) and the specialized compendiums (Is that an accurate word for this? The researcher will check.) of military and naval hardware.

If a quote is taken from an interview, the interviewer is expected to have decipherable notes or, better, a tape recording. If the quotation is potentially sensational there will be considerable discussion about calling the source for a confirmation. Even if that is impracticable, the insistence on checking it all out and the discussion itself is usually enough to dampen the enthusiasm of an interviewer for making up a remark.

Each word of a story, literally, is dotted or otherwise marked to indicate that there is some better source for it than just everybody's memory or casual knowledge. While the newsmagazine does have unlimited freedom to slant stories by selective presentation of topics or facts, there is little or no freedom just to make up stuff out of whole cloth.

I wrote one article for the *National Enquirer,* on a congressional report which provided some basis for questioning some federally declared minimum daily requirements of nutrients. Believe it or not, the editors there were as cranky as the researchers at *Newsweek* in insisting on verification of facts in the story. Each part of the story quoting from the hearing, for instance, had to be accompanied by the actual hearing document (not a photocopy) containing the quotation.

How this squares with the apparent lack of serious verification in the *Enquirer's* sensational stories about entertainment stars is beyond me. As to the really weird stories in the grocery-store tabloids, it is instructive to read the passing attributions of sources which, time after time, turn out to be newspapers in remote corners of the earth.

But on some stories, I can testify that at least one of the tabloids is pretty darn fussy. They also pay extraordinarily well.

I tried to add my own checking procedure, beyond the required verification by a researcher. I told the people in the typing pool, where the edited stories went for final clean copies, that if they actually read any of my stories as they retyped them, I'd appreciate their calling me directly if a sentence didn't make sense to them. If they couldn't understand it, it was my view, neither could thousands of others of the magazine's readers. I made it my adage and guide that clear writing was indeed a writer's most revolutionary action.

Another digression. In the world of business, where I briefly lived (as the assistant to the president of a truly huge multinational corporation), the dictum was that the safest action a writer can take is to write foggily. Underlings won't dare question it. Higher executives just ask that you clean it up a bit, or else they shrug it off, assuming that someone must know what the hell you mean. Back in the late '50s, the preferred grammatical voice in a corporation was the passive rather than the active ("It is recommended" rather than "I recommend"). Pinning oneself down with a straightforward sentence did not leave sufficient wiggle room.

It is my understanding that many corporations today, as they rediscover the relationship between clear thinking and profits, are encouraging clear, crisp writing. Hurray.

But the business world came later in my career. When I was fired from *Newsweek** in favor of the publisher's son, I moved from the high-visibility, actually envied world of newsmagazine journalism, into the gloriously darker areas of straight-out ideological journalism. First, how-

---

*[Editor's note: Ralph de Toledano, journalist, syndicated columnist, and political analyst of the post-World War II years, was Karl's close friend and trusted colleague. They met at *Newsweek* and forged strong ideological bonds between them in the rising storm over Communism. What follows is a brief sampling of the events at *Newsweek* as recalled and written by de Toledano.]

Karl came to *Newsweek* as press editor, a job of some hazard since everyone on any publication thinks he is the real expert on the printed medium. He introduced himself to me on his first day on staff to let me know that he shared my views on Communism, the media, and the general state of the world and the *res publica*. He realized the vulnerability of our position, even on a magazine which leaned to conservatism, the Republican Party, and anti-Communism—if only because much of the working staff was militantly liberal.

We talked and played a lot in those first years at *Newsweek*—and we were serious, too, as we contemplated our crumbling times. The magazine was giving me a fairly free hand in those days, writing on the important political stories. Karl was writing the best press section the magazine had before or since. Previous press editors had devoted themselves to the gossip of the trade and to the convolutions of its corporate structure. Karl, as much as he was allowed, set this kind of news in the context of the times and its ideological underpinning. (One of those who read Karl's stories and approved of them was Whittaker Chambers, a friend who later stood by Karl as he was politically knifed by some of *Newsweek's* editors.)

Karl was a political and fiscal conservative, and a fighting anti-Communist. He had a hunger for adventure which jarred the stuffy sensibilities of *Newsweek*. For example, Karl sought me out one day, sparkling with excitement, to tell me that he had been invited by Taiwanese officials to take part in one of their coastal raids on Communist China. "Look, Karl," I told him, "you don't look Chinese and you don't speak Chinese. If you get separated from the raiding party or it runs into trouble and disperses, you'll be finished. The Chinese know where to hide, but what will you do?"

Karl wouldn't listen. "But, oh, what a great story," he insisted. "Anyway, I've accepted. Of course, I'll have to get *Newsweek's* permission." He did not get it—not because *Newsweek* was worried about his safety, but because if he were captured the State Department would make trouble for the magazine.

There were lighter moments at *Newsweek*, too. The science editor, George Boehm, was a mathematical whiz with screwball tendencies, but he and Karl got along very well. The music editor was a six-foot-tall Texan, built like a longshoreman but unmistakable in her sex. Her idea of covering music was to telephone Rudolf Bing at the Metropolitan Opera and call him four-letter words, with an occasional ten-letter expletive thrown in. The music editor got hundreds of records for review—typically 78s which she locked away in a metal cabinet until she could get them to her apartment.

Staffers tried every possible way to get her to share this bounty, but with no success. Karl and George decided to do something about it. Showing up at 3 A.M. and wearing

ever, more digression—a whole chapter's worth, this time—on the period I spent as a gun shooter and a gun runner.

---

cotton gloves for the dramatic effect, they managed to open the cabinet and take a substantial number of records.

The maintenance men responded to the music editor's loud complaints by giving her a heavy lock to put on the cabinet. Karl and George bought a similar lock and at 3 A.M., a few nights later, sawed off the old lock, helped themselves, and put the new lock on the cabinet. The music editor's outraged cries could be heard on *Newsweek's* two floors when the second lock had to be sawed off.

A plainclothes cop from the neighborhood precinct was called. He looked at the cabinet, shook his head, and advised the music editor that she should put a metal bar across the cabinet doors. On their third raid, Karl and George removed the back of the cabinet, took what they wanted and replaced the backing. Now it became a mystery as to how the "thieves" had gotten into the cabinet. A puzzled music editor raged again, but no one on the magazine really cared.

She was advised that just maybe if she gave away a few records, the raids would end. When, out of frustration, she began leaving the cabinet unlocked, the raids stopped.

What finished Karl at *Newsweek* was the McCarthy imbroglio. I had introduced Karl to Joe McCarthy. I was doing the *Newsweek* stories on Joe and also giving him such advice as he would take. Karl was a 100 percent partisan for McCarthy and did one or two stories exposing the falsity and dishonesty of the press's coverage. I was appearing on radio and TV programs confounding McCarthy's enemies. *Newsweek* was not entirely happy about this, but Malcolm Muir Sr.—the publisher—was not sure which way the coin would fall, so he said nothing to either of us.

The trap was sprung when Karl and I signed—along with a long list of McCarthy adherents—a full-page ad defending the senator against press and political slander. My name appeared without affiliation, but Karl signed his as *Newsweek's* press editor. That tore it. Karl was called in—though not a word was said to me—and told that he had compromised his objectivity as press editor and embarrassed the magazine. Karl was allowed to continue his work for some time, though a black cloud hung over his head while the top editors tried to think of a way to ease him out, without political repercussions. No one had the courage to simply say, "You're fired."

Finally, Frank Norris, the back-of-the-book editor and Karl's immediate superior, was told to give Karl his notice. Norris refused flatly. The top editors dithered for a while, and then the editor in chief, who was secretly on Karl's side but did not have the gumption to defend him, called Karl in and gave him the news. Karl left quietly, going to work for a brief time with John Chamberlain on the soon-to-fold magazine, the *Freeman*.

9

Gun Shooter, Gunrunner

Come you back to Mandalay,
Where the old Flotilla lay;
Can't you 'ear their paddles chun-
kin' from Rangoon to Mandalay?
On the road to Mandalay,
Where the flyin'-fishes play,
An' the dawn comes up like thun-
der outer China 'crost the Bay!
— Rudyard Kipling, "Mandalay"

Guns and I have been close friends all my life. When I was very young, one of my mother's boyfriends—a dedicated hunter— schooled me in firearms safety and use, and ignited in my soul a respect for guns and a passion for shooting and outdoor sport that would last a lifetime. Guns were special; for me, they combined the beauty of machinery (rarely in my life have I seen a piece of machinery I didn't love) and the romanticism of American history.

While still in school, I built an air-rifle target range in the apartment house that my mother managed. By age fifteen I had my own rifle and handgun, had killed my first deer, and had given my mother her very own rifle for a Christmas gift. While at *Newsweek* I became a licensed gunsmith and signed up as a life member in the National Rifle Association. Since then, I have shot in dozens of revolver and shotgun matches, and even set one small record in combat pistol accuracy at the prestigious Campfire Club of America, an upper-class sportsman club north of New York City.

My passion for shooting has infected my sons, too. Each began shooting with a trimmed-down .22 caliber rifle before the age of ten, and both have remained avid shooters ever since. The younger, Eric, has proceeded to world-class status in big-bore rifle shooting; while he was getting his master's degree there, he was captain of the rifle team at the University of Virginia.

A condition for captainhood at the university was to be enrolled in the Reserve Officers Training Corps. Eric did well there, earning ROTC's "cadet of the year" honors. When he called me in near panic over the upcoming ceremony, I reassured him that he would perform well in the awards presentation, outfitted as he would be in his full parade dress. I also told him he should be pleased by the honor—one takes honors where one finds them—and that he should not worry about the rather different relationships with the military elsewhere in the family. His brother, Karl, was a conscientious objector. His father was an antiwar protester who had been jailed for his activities during the Vietnam War.

Eric came close to a career in the Marine Corps; he had been offered an officership at their splendid sniper school. I was never less than proud of him. I was also confident that he would have substantial doubts about his ability to give a full day's work for a full day's wages in the Marine Corps. On his first deer-hunting trip, he had come face-to-face with a dilemma. The deer was in his sights. And here was a young man used to shooting at targets one thousand yards away! So he couldn't miss. He also couldn't squeeze the trigger. An unlikely Marine, eh? But, I swear, I was no more or less impressed by his failure to kill the deer than I was by his thoughts of joining the Marine Corps.

He would have been a fine Marine. He *is* a fine soil hydrologist. I would call him apolitical; his contemplation of a career in the Marine Corps was not stimulated by patriotic zeal so much as sheer ballistic enthusiasm. His older brother, who started target shooting when he was five, is an outstanding range ecologist, and the author of a book on the Western rangelands that strikes me as just about in the de Tocqueville class. He was an anarchist in college and, in his forties now (and a Ph.D. no less), is a free-market champion of local and individual autonomy.

What little I gave my sons in the way of passion for guns and the outdoors took shape in the formative years of the early 1950s while I was at *Newsweek.* After my brief residency in the rundown New York hotel, my wife and son joined me in the Empire State and we settled in the suburban village of Dobbs Ferry. There I met Bill Lewis*—Hondo as I called him

---

*[Editor's note. Bill Lewis, now living in Canaan, New York, recalls the *Gunsmoke* years. They were the side moments wedged in between the demands of *Newsweek* and the rising chorus of anti-Communism. They were the flip side of the '50s, the eye of the hurricane where shelter from a world gone insane still seemed possible and desirable.]

Karl and I met as neighbors in Dobbs Ferry, New York, after the war in the early '50s. We were two outdoor spirits restive under the constraints of weekend responsibilities and seeking escape from suburban life by subtle ruse or outright lie:

"Are you going to clean the basement this morning as you promised?"

"Ah, no—Karl and I are going to check out some property . . ."

"Check out, huh. Probably need shotguns for that checking out."

Before other duties called, we would be cruising north in my 1936 Nash coupe, with Free Wheeling and Rumble Seat, sometimes with our young lads, more often not, shaking off the mantle of city life for field, stream, bog, or mountain, outfitted by L. L. Bean and Herter's, armed by Browning or Winchester, or, if the season dictated, Payne rods and Abercrombie flies.

If it happened to be Saturday, all conversation would halt between 12:30 and 1:00 P.M. Rerun time on CBS. We flicked on the ancient coffee-grinder radio to *Gunsmoke,* and the original Matt Dillon transported us west of the Mississippi. We became self-styled anachronisms, belonging with Coulter, Bridger, or Wes Hardin, but certainly not with *Newsweek* or the ad agency in New York City where I spent my weekdays. We gave ourselves western names on these excursions: Hondo, Wes, Matt, and Wyatt. And they stuck with us.

By late Saturday afternoon we would be in the Taconic Range checking for late hatches in trout pools that forever remained secret, or, after the leaves turned, we would be further north in the Berkshires or Adirondacks, to be outwitted by woodcock, grouse, and pheasant.

A born Westerner, I was hunting and fishing as a youngster. Karl got a late start, but as with all of his pursuits, he took to the natural world with enthusiasm, study, and joy. It wasn't long before he was giving me pointers. Pissed me off sometimes. Once he damned near blew my foot off with an old pump shotgun as he threw a shell into the chamber. We didn't listen to *Gunsmoke* on that Saturday. Instead, we went out and bought an over and under Browning. We gave the old pump the deep six.

When Karl hit his first grouse with the new Browning, I said to him, "Better than hunting Communists, isn't it ?"

"If you're speaking of the larder, yes; Communists make poor table food," was his reply.

Fear of attack by the Soviets made for lively conversation in the '50s, real enough for some people in the East to build bomb shelters and stock up on canned goods. Karl and I compromised and built a club shelter in my basement. We called it the Dobbs Ferry Rod and Gun Club. Male members only, please. That offended my eleven-year-old daughter. She was adamant: "I'm joining and I don't care what you say."

(and Matt as he labeled me). We spent the *Newsweek* years (at least week-ends and vacations) shooting, hunting, camping, and listening to *Gun-smoke*. He was my closest friend; he was, in our bravado vernacular, my smelliest, nastiest, hairiest, orneriest, bestiest friend.

My enthusiasm for killing deer, rabbits, squirrels, and game birds waned as I got older. I switched to killing fish, first with a fly rod and flies with Hondo, and then later with a crossbow of sorts, powered by surgical tubing, that was a standard weapon of skin diving.

Skin diving was wonderful. Below the ocean surface lay a world that

---

"Only if you become an honorary boy," said Karl.

"Forget it," said my daughter.

It was a fine club, with good-smelling creels, wet waders, bloody game bags, Hoppe's gun solvent—which Karl wanted me to market as a deodorant: "A dab under the arm takes you back to the farm"—and boots. Ah, the boots: elk-hide tops from L. L. Bean that could be resoled after you wore out the rubber bottoms. Our wives detested this smelly retreat and wouldn't come near it.

My son was very fond of Karl. Karl listened to children, showed interest in what they had to say and do. One afternoon while my wife and I were gone, and John was under the supervision of a neighbor, Karl got a tearful call.

"Mr. Hess ?"

"Yeah, John."

"Would you come over and skin my alligator?" His eight-inch pet had expired and he needed taxidermy work in a hurry. Karl rang the bell and told the house sitter, "I'm here to skin the boy's alligator." It was an expert job, done in the presence of a suspicious neighbor, with one of Herter's fine skinning knives. The skin was carefully mounted on a pine board, and to this day, forty years later, it remains one of my son's prize possessions.

Karl said in later years, "I have been asked to do a lot of things, but only once did anyone every ask me to skin his 'gator."

For many years I have had in my library a book that Karl gave me titled *Woodsmoke*. It is filled with native American lore. One item in it that took our fancy was how to make the Perfect Walking Stick. These were the instructions: tie a simple overhand knot in a small sapling, say a willow, and return in ten or fifteen years to a knot that has become a thick serviceable handle. Well, we tied knots in saplings all over the state. "See there," we would say to our kids, "remember this spot. We'll come back in a few years and you will have yourself a neat cane." I am seventy-five years old and I am still looking. Never found one. I could use it, though. The trails have gotten steeper in the Berkshires where I live.

I have since given *Woodsmoke* to Karl's oldest son. But I still keep a child's book that he gave me one Christmas. Its title is *Outdoor Stories for Indoor Folk*. Written on the fly-leaf is this continuing message:

"For Hondo. So, when the woman talk gets too much for you, you can read this and think of us menfolk out in the bush, folkin."

It is signed, "Matt."

was different, shocking, surprising, sometimes dangerous, but almost always beautiful. And the sounds are as impressive as the sights—the bovine gruntings of large horseshoe crabs, the sharp crack of an evasive fish's fins and body as it crashes into action to get away from the monstrous diver chasing it.

The sights remain dominant, however: The sheer horror of running, mask to fish eye, into a sea robin, arguably the ugliest of all fish, looking like the Freddy Krueger of the sea world; and the vertiginous blow to the mind when diving across a plain and then suddenly over and past a steep and sheer underwater cliff. The earthling notion that you must hurtle down that steepness is as powerful as if some force had just popped you over the edge of the Grand Canyon. But on you swim. Incredible. The near panic, like the middle of a bad dream, when pursuing some quarry you suddenly find yourself over a weed bed that stretches as far you can see in every direction, making it impossible to orient yourself.

There is also the mind game that the imagination plays upon you when you look around over that yellowish jungle, brilliantly sunlit at about twenty to thirty feet of depth. You suddenly realize that there are multitudes of odd things in that jungle, unseen, possibly hostile, possibly ugly to the point of offensiveness.

My enthusiasm for skin diving centered on Long Island Sound. On the ocean side, the favored range was from Shinnecock Inlet north to Montauk Point. On the Sound side it was Orient Point down to Greenport.

There was one problem with my enthusiasm for skin diving: I could not swim. But with flippers, I found it convenient to go anywhere on or under the surface. Still, I remember one awkward moment. My diving friends and I were walking (without flippers on) from one sandbar to another in what seemed to be shallow water in the Shinnecock area. We were each carrying a load of equipment for the weekend's sport. I stepped into a hole of perhaps ten feet in depth. Down I went, then bobbed back up to the surface, shouting for assistance.

Now, I had not told my friends about my aquatic disability. They assumed I was being my usual clownish self and went on their way. With considerable thrashing and lunging, I did manage to get across the hole and to a more hospitable chunk of the earth's surface. I did not drop any of the equipment—because of determination or paralysis, I do not know which. In any case, the skin diving lasted for as long as I was at *Newsweek.*

When I finally returned to the hunting of mammals, it was in later years, in what was still called Rhodesia, and I used a tranquilizer gun and dart to bag an elephant. It was an interesting hunt and it happened in the winter of 1967–1968.

I was in Rhodesia for a season, with my old and dear friend Wainwright Dawson, one-time organizer of orientation and training sessions for incoming Republican congressmen and their principal aides. He was the inspiration for a plan in which I would do a piece of metal sculpture for the Rhodesian government. This was all prior to the transformation of Rhodesia into Zimbabwe. When I was there, Zimbabwe referred only to a bunch of ancient ruins.

Living in Salisbury, I became acquainted with Arthur Jones, then a fairly well-known wildlife photographer, later to become wealthy and renowned as the inventor of Nautilus exercise equipment. Arthur, who drove around Salisbury in a galleon-sized Cadillac with Texas license tags, had just learned to fly a helicopter and asked whether I would like to accompany him on a flight to the Tuli Circle, across the Limpopo River on the northern border of South Africa. The project included darting an elephant to illustrate the technique commonly used in the relocation of elephants known to be ravaging local farmlands.

Fortunately, as a pilot myself, I had developed an unshakable (although altogether mystical) faith that no aircraft could ever do anything nasty if I were within reach of the controls. This confidence was useful in the elephant hunt because Arthur had not fully developed chopper skills. His hovering was unsteady at best, and was accompanied by shouted denunciations of the equipment, the technology, the flight training school, and the Communist conspiracy.

But the trip was a wonder. Africa, of course, has some of the most wonderful landscapes on earth. Southern Africa, in turn, has most of the grandest. And I was able to see some seven hundred miles of the best of *that,* from a helicopter without doors, flying just above treetop height. Arthur, whose personality struck me as perfect for a gunship pilot, had developed some proficiency in the treetop style of flight. Thank goodness.

When we finally landed in South Africa we went to visit our contact for the venture, a local game warden. He was a Boer. He was big. He was friendly in a bearlike way. He put me in mind of the folly of going out of your way to engage such a person, or others like him, in combat. With him, we visited some farms in the area for the latest news on elephants.

I had always thought of thatched huts as necessarily small and hospitable only to people who had little contact with up-to-date appliances. The first farmhouse we visited was a round thatched structure, its roof a several-foot-thick layering of boughs and leaves. The house was about fifty feet in diameter, with a floor space greater than that of a tract house, or even most farmhouses, in North America. Inside, it was palatial and humming and shining with the latest conveniences.

I had also visited the thatched homes of other Africans, in Rhodesia: the brightly decorated but quite compact round houses, rondevals, in Shona settlements. The exterior decoration was, typically, a circling of abstract designs running all around the house. Inside, the clay walls came down to a ledge which could be used as a storage platform or a seat, running around the interior from each side of the entranceway. The thatched roof was pierced in the middle by a hole to permit smoke from interior cooking fires to escape, rather like the opening at the top of an American Indian tepee. Most beautiful, to me, was the Shona version of cookware: a group of gourdlike pottery cooking vessels which could be nested one inside the other and were usually kept on the seating ledge. The rondevals were a lovely sight from the outside and impressive on the inside because of the Shona habit of scrubbing them down each day with cattle urine, leaving the dirt floor, the seat, and the walls leathery and dark almost like Cordovan.

It was clear to me that I would prefer to live in the larger thatched house of the farmer. But it also was clear to me that the Shona who stayed in their settlements and in their rondevals were living a more pacific and seemingly pleasant life than kin who had chosen to go off to Salisbury to work as servants, live in cement blockhouses, and begin the agitation for a black majoritarianism.

A digression within a digression: At that time, prior to the majoritarian triumph, Rhodesia was practicing a form of racial separation which seemed to me far more reasonable and productive than the shuttle-apartheid of South Africa. By shuttle-apartheid, I mean that in South Africa black Africans poured into the towns and cities each day to do work, and then had to shuttle back home afterward to townships and shantytowns where plotting against white Africans must have been predictably stimulating. In Rhodesia there were segregation *and* integration. Some areas, both in cities and out in the countryside, were for Euro-Africans only. Some were for black Africans only (Euro-Africans being prohibited from trading or even entering there). Some areas were mixed, open to anyone who wanted to live there, European or whatever. It would be naive to suppose that the separation was fair, that the choice lands were not being withheld for Euro-African occupancy, but there were advantages over the South African system.

The disadvantage of the shuttle-apartheid, it seemed to me, was that it enforced segregation cruelly with no compensation whatsoever. The Rhodesian plan offered, in the segregated lands, a way to preserve an ancient culture. In the mixed lands it offered a way for people to get to know each other and to be neighbors. In the Euro-African areas the great failure, it seemed to me, was the very widespread employment of servants who typically would leave their segregated, acculturated home areas and come to town for the promise of "a better life." To live as a servant, in urban poverty, in a barrackslike cement-block house, rather than back home in a rondeval struck me as a choice that could be sensible only if coupled with a hot desire to take advantage of whatever educational opportunities might be found in an urban area. The fact of the matter was that a major part of the entire Rhodesian national budget was devoted to schools in the all-black African areas.

No matter what else, the Rhodesian plan seemed to offer the possibility of slowly accreting civility. Indeed, this seems to have been the case, since Rhodesia gave in to black African majoritarianism in relative peace and with relative stability subsequently—at least as compared to other black African majoritarian nations, created out of violence and sheer hatred.

At any rate, I came to love Rhodesia, the Shona villages and villagers, the black African craftsmen with whom I worked while fabricating my metal sculpture, the Euro-African Rhodesians who were so hospitable, so sturdy of character, candid of outlook, and, in my view, absolutely decent people—all living in what I came to believe to be the most beautiful landscape on earth, excepting perhaps only Hawaii. (As for the sturdy character of a population, I would put Iceland or most small towns in the United States as close equivalents.)

So impressed was I by Rhodesia that I bought a few acres of land in an upland area. After I finished the sculpture, which I will describe in a later chapter, it was installed outside the National Archives building and remained there until several years later when altogether misleading reports of my work with the Black Panthers caused the government to pull the thing down. Sigh.

But none of that gets my elephant shot, does it?

Having been told of a herd nearby, Arthur and I returned to the skies and whirled off. And there they were. Elephants and giraffes, seen from near helicopter range, are magnificent. The downward slanting angle of sight amplifies the great, gangly ballet of the running giraffes and the stately bulk of the elephants as they move in a haste that is nonetheless dignified. We saw the giraffes first. Then the elephants in a family-sized group.

We had only four tranquilizer darts and the sun was getting low. My job was to edge out into a shooting posture with my feet on the skids of the helicopter. The camera that would record the scene for the footage Arthur needed was fixed just behind me and could pick up both my shooting and its effect on the elephant. It almost didn't have anything to record. My first three shots were complete misses as we skimmed over the running elephants.

I had only one dart left. We swung around and skimmed up over the largest of the elephants, Arthur cursing everything and suggesting that I might be a Communist. Ready. Aim. Fire. It was as fine a shot as could be wished. The dart flew as if laser-guided precisely into the right side of the elephant's gray, mountainous ass.

The tranquilizer took just a few moments to begin taking effect, and Arthur kept us swinging in tight circles to see it all happen. First, the elephant acted drunk, staggering like an ocean liner with a careless skipper at the helm. Then he seemed tired and leaned up against a tree which was a bit taller than the elephant—better than ten feet tall at the shoulder when we measured him later. Slowly, as the elephant succumbed to the tranquilizer, he leaned more and more heavily against the tree and, majestically, the tree gave way under the weight, then fell uprooted to the ground with its guest asleep upon it.

That was our signal to land and get the old boy back on his feet. There were plenty of empty patches for landing in the scrub where we had done the deed. In a moment Arthur was at the elephant's ear ready to inject an antidote into the ear's huge veins. I asked for a moment alone with my elephant, not to muse, but to carve my initials delicately into one of his tusks. I have hoped ever since that no piece of ivory with a little "kh" on it ever will end up in some unfriendly hands.

Then I recovered the fateful dart, Arthur injected the elephant with the tranquilizer's antidote, and I assumed we would beat a hasty retreat. Not at all, Arthur reassured me. Wait. We'll be safe, even just a few feet away. So we stayed to watch the elephant jiggle his head, get groggily to his knees, then stand fully upright. After one supercilious glance at Arthur and me, and with a few steps into a mahpani thicket, he just disappeared, from sight and from sound. How can anything that huge move so quietly? A Stealth elephant no less. What a day!

My interest in guns—even if only narrowed to a harmless propeller of darts—did not stop with the hunting of game and the pursuit of sport. Well before I toppled my elephant on the South African veld, I had already put my sights on toppling the Cuban dictator, Fulgencio Batista.

It was in the early 1950s, and it happened this way. Ralph de Toledano, my dearest and closest friend at *Newsweek*, and an unrepentant Red-baiter to this very day, asked whether I had any interest in helping *someone* overthrow Batista. Of course I did.

Ralph had been contacted by Carlos Hevia, Naval Academy-trained engineer, Bacardi executive, and a former president of Cuba. Hevia wanted guns and napalm for supporters anxious to get Batista out of power. At that time, serious anti-Communists agreed that Batista was moving closer and closer to the Soviet Union for support of his increasingly unpopular regime. An agreement to let the Russians build a submarine base in Cuba was the big concern of the time.

Hevia spoke to Ralph and informed him, "We are planning an invasion of Cuba. My organization is pro-U.S., pro-democracy, and we have substantial anti-Castro support in Cuba. What we want is a newspaperman of standing, a *norteamericano,* who can speak Spanish and who will go in with us [on the invasion] and give the world the story. This is very secret and you must give me your word of honor that you will keep that secret, whether you accept or not."

Well, Ralph shared the secret with me, knowing my interest in stopping Batista. I packed my bags, flew to Miami, tracked down Hevia, and offered my services. He accepted. My job was to secure weapons and munitions for the rebellion.

I began by shopping for small arms. I decided the best bargain in rifles for Hevia and his troops would be the Johnson semiautomatic, a finely designed weapon that got lost in the shuffle of the U.S. Army as it shifted from the magnificent Springfield Model 03-A3 to the superslick Garand. But there were plenty of Johnsons around and at good prices. I arranged with my friendly local gun dealer in Westchester County, where we lived, to buy them in bulk quantities; my excuse was that I was reselling them to hunting lodges in the Far West. Made sense.

I stored some of the weapons in my garage at Dobbs Ferry. In fact, one of my favorite photographs of all time was taken through the open garage door. It shows row after row of Johnson rifles stacked across the garage. And in the midst of them is young Karl's little red tricycle.

To make sure I had sufficient weaponry—just in case Hevia wanted more—I asked around for serious arms dealers. One dealer, with posh offices in a posh office building near Wall Street, was named Sonny. My visit with him was just a glimpse of what must be an altogether engrossing commerce. He was so matter-of-fact. The Israelis were letting go of a bunch of good mortars. There were also attack aircraft and medium bombers available at several places in Africa. Hand grenades here, machine guns there. For a gun lover it gave rise to almost hallucinogenic fantasies.

I was authorized to purchase nothing beyond the rifles, but I assured Sonny I would put my new friends in touch with him for any further needs. Nice fellow. How I would have loved to say casually, "Oh well, let's have a dozen of those mortars, a couple of bazookas, and a dozen or two of these submachineguns. Charge it."

Getting the napalm actually proved easier than getting the guns. Writing on *Newsweek* letterhead, I got in touch with the manufacturer, Dow Chemical. Describing myself truthfully as a dedicated experimenter, I told them I wanted to burn off a modest acreage of scrub and weeds quickly for replanting, and that I thought napalm might do the job. No problem. A huge barrel of the saponifying agent that is the base of napalm soon joined the tricycle and the rifles in the garage.

Unfortunately, the napalm powder did not come with any instructions and, it seemed to me, it would not be prudent to bother Dow about the matter. I knew a good chemist, however, at the Shell Laboratories in St. Louis. And in fact he had exactly the information I wanted. He wrote the instructions out for me in a pleasant letter which ended with ". . . and then run like hell."

Still there was a problem. I had to get the instructions translated accurately into Spanish. Here, I called upon a friend at the restaurant workers' union headquarters on Eighth Avenue, just a block from what was then the best chili joint in the universe. He got one of his Spanish-speaking friends to do the job and, after a translation back by another union friend to make sure that the delicate business was not sloppily or incorrectly stated, the Hevia revolution had its napalm.

One additional task still remained for me. Dr. Hevia or someone on his staff prepared a flyer to be dropped over Havana; my job was to get thousands of the things printed and then to drop them onto the streets of Cuba's capital city. Although my own pilot's license had lapsed, I had a friend whose main occupation was repossessing automobiles but whose pilot's license was up-to-date and squeaky clean. Dr. Hevia forked over a small bale of cash money and off we went to Miami to rent a plane and dump the pamphlets. The only glitch in the venture I recall was that, in my excitement, I hurled the first batch of pamphlets from the plane without cutting the strings binding them together. Thus, our aerial bombardment of Havana consisted initially of a heavy bundle of papers, not a gentle rain of persuasion. Nobody, as my younger son keeps reminding me, is perfect. I know, I know.

The Hevia coup might have succeeded, replacing Batista with a pro-American and halting Fidel Castro's march through the hills to Havana (a far more successful route than by light aircraft as it turned out), except for one small problem: the State Department got wind of the plot. Everything we were doing violated the Neutrality Act. But as I quickly learned, if you violate that or any other national security rule in an approved sort of way, you have little to worry about. The late Whittaker Chambers, then a close confidant of many in the FBI, was able to tell me exactly where I had been and what I had been doing during my gunrunning days.

Hevia and his associates were arrested, tried, and thrown into prison. I was more fortunate. Some months later, two FBI agents visited Ralph and asked about my ties to Hevia. According to Ralph, the interview went as follows:

"Do you know Karl Hess?" Ralph confessed that he did.

"We understand that he had something to do with Carlos Hevia and that invasion group. What do you know about it?"

Ralph responded shyly with a question: "Why should he want to get involved? He's been in the shop every day, as far as I know."

"Well, he's made a hell of a lot of long-distance calls to Miami," one special agent said.

"He's probably got a girlfriend down there," Ralph answered.

Apparently that was enough. The agents left and my brief flirtation with war and rebellion came to a grinding halt. My other anti-Communist efforts, with perhaps an exception or two, took more conventional forms.*

---

*[Editor's note. Karl's passion for guns had a more philosophical side. In quieter moments he wrote on the importance of guns to a free society. Below is an excerpt from his April 1957 essay, "Should You Own a Gun?" published in the *American Mercury*.]

When intellectuals meet to effuse over the "battle for men's minds," they often speak of the great "thinkers" who brought the "idea" of freedom to our own country. The American Revolution becomes, in their reconstruction of it, a solemn procession of lofty-browed men smiting the British and their mercenaries with lightning bolts of philosophy. To be sure, it *was* the "idea" of freedom that inflamed the colonies against a foreign ruler. But it was the long rifle, lovingly bored at Pennsylvania forges, and skillfully carried into the central woodlands, that *brought* freedom to America. It was the same rifle, improved with a percussion lock, that created our southern border, at the Alamo and at San Jacinto. And, if the Emancipation Proclamation was written with a pen it was sealed with a Spencer carbine.

And so the intellectual effusions are clearly wrong. Freedom is never thought into existence. It is fought into existence. And that is the way it is kept—by men with the arms to protect their prize.

Today it is the same. When, some time ago, the enslaved East Germans briefly rioted against the Red overlords, they threw a few bricks, made some classic pictures of defiance, and then lapsed back into an unarmed slavery. In Hungary it was different. There were guns there. If there had been more there might even have been, at the end of the fighting, freedom. There was the *urge* to freedom—there weren't enough guns.

Is it imaginable, for another instance, that the Russian people would forever submit to the central tyranny of the world if there were arms easily and commonly available?

The question of freedom, therefore, when stripped to its steel center, is just this: Who has the guns? There is nothing exclusive about the *idea* of freedom. Presumably it can arise anywhere, anytime. But it runs into the grim question: Who has the guns? If everyone has them, then a ballot becomes not only possible but inevitable. If only a few have them, a dictatorship becomes as tempting and as inexorable. . . .

What, then, of the question with which we began? Should you own a gun? At the very least there would seem to be no reason why you shouldn't. And, looked at seriously, there may be emphatic reasons why you *should.* The reasons may sound melodramatic in a land of virtual milk and honey and, more importantly, a land of laws such as ours. But, in a world balanced on an atomic razor's edge, nothing really is melodramatic.

Here are the reasons. First there is the crime and safety angle. Crime rates do *not* go down when the citizenry is disarmed. They go up. Firearms safety, too, is not aided by a disarmed citizenry. If there are to be guns anywhere in the land there also is the responsibility of a general familiarity with them.

Next there is the angle of national defense. Nations such as Switzerland and Finland have relied for years on an armed and gun-wise citizenry as their first line of defense. Finnish marksmen, ordinary men trained as civilians to shoot straight, held off hordes of Russians for three months in 1939. (As a result of that resistance, as a matter of fact, the Soviet began training *its* civilians as marksmen—*but not letting them keep their arms.*) Swiss citizens traditionally keep rifles in their homes and always are prepared to mobilize into a defense corps. And Swiss citizens have remained free for many, many years.

Finally, there is the matter of the *sort* of freedom for which America stands. It is a freedom of individual men. It is a freedom of individual responsibility and individual rights. It abhors the collective, effete "safeties" of older, tired nations in which the people must be "protected" from themselves. It is a freedom which, if it ever came to it, would be fought for on every single American doorstep. It is the sort of freedom of which Winston Churchill spoke when he referred to fighting on the beaches and by the hedgerows. It is precisely the sort of freedom which, having been abolished so far as guns go in Britain, made a sort of mockery, really, of what Churchill was saying to a disarmed nation.

It is the sort of freedom which, based upon an ideal and an urge, was born in gunfire, preserved in gunfire, and which is, even today, maintained by a ready strength of arms. Upon those ready arms, too, rests the freedom of hundreds of millions elsewhere.

So, when the intellectuals speak glibly of the nature of American freedom—which they often transform into a docile, unprotected thing—it might be wise to recall what really happened when that freedom was born. It was not born amid dignified debates and ivory-tower ponderings. Dr. William Gordon has recorded how it began—at Bunker Hill. The colonists, he reported, were poorly armed, "but," he went on in explaining their victory, "they are almost all marksmen." That's how it began. That's how it can continue—and prevail.

10

Anti-Communist

There will never be a really free and enlightened State until the State comes to recognize the individual as the higher and independent power, from which all its own power and authority are derived, and treats him accordingly.

—Henry David Thoreau

In the '50s, opposition to the policies of the Soviet Union drew ridicule and phalanx opposition from intellectuals, journalists, entertainers— most public figures of any sort. It still offends me to recall it. As people began to come to their senses about the Soviet issue, they began to call people like me premature anti-Communists and sometimes to forgive us for our impetuousness. But that took quite awhile. No wonder we sometimes grew extremely cranky on the subject and even became (dreaded phobic foaming at the mouth) *extremists* on the subject.

How could anyone *not* be extremist on the subject? There was the evidence of the purge trials, the testimony made public even as they were conducted. There was the undisputed evidence of a murderous secret police operating around the world and making even the darkest accusations against the CIA seem like misdemeanors. Joseph Stalin was a bloody murderer. The campaign of starvation waged against the small farmers of the Ukraine was as monstrous as the Nazi Holocaust. And on and on and on. The horror is not that there were some Americans who were too harsh in their attacks against Stalinist terrorism. The horror is that there were some Americans who actually deluded themselves that the blood-soaked Bolshevik regime presaged a desirable future, not just for Russians but for the entire world.

There is still a good deal of moaning and groaning in some quarters about the horrors of McCarthyism and the lives that the junior senator from Wisconsin is said to have ruined by recklessly charging people with Communist membership or sympathies. If only there could be some commensurate moaning and groaning about the literally millions of innocents killed by Stalinist terrorism in the same period. Only when Nikita Khrushchev made it acceptable to denounce Stalin did the moaners and groaners start clucking and twittering about the twentieth century's most brutal regime and empire. Yet even to this day you would think that the McCarthy brouhaha in Hollywood ranked even with the tyranny in the Soviet Union.

A recent book on the horrors of McCarthyism shuddered at the fact that there were 227 resignations from the State Department from 1953 to 1955, the peak years of the Wisconsin senator's reign of terror. Two hundred twenty-seven resignations from a staff of thousands, even if each had been directly linked to McCarthyite charges (which is of course unlikely), is not a pogrom.

McCarthy was often ill-tempered, often not sober, often rash in his individual judgments—but he was not, ultimately, wrong. There *was* a Communist menace. He helped create the atmosphere in which important parts of it could be exposed. The same could be said of the House Un-American Activities Committee (HUAC), although in fact it dealt more in the sort of tactics that became known as McCarthyism than did McCarthy himself. HUAC's hearings on Hollywood, for example, never gave any impression other than that the people who took refuge in the Fifth Amendment when asked about Communist connections were full-fledged agents of the Soviet Union. Most, of course, were just simpleminded political hicks romantically identifying themselves as martyrs in the cause of the greater good of mankind. They deserved ridicule, but not to be dignified with the sinister implications in which the House Committee dealt.

Their successors who bleat and bleed sympathetically with every anti-American crusade on the planet are not agents of a foreign power, either. They are simply agents of their own inexplicable hatred of the country in which they have achieved the success that gives them any audience at all. My impression is that things are becoming more and more difficult for the America haters as more people around the earth come to see America not as the great devil but as the great promise and their deliverer. If only everyone who had flourished under capitalism could bring themselves to imagine that others might want to try it also!

Among all the goofy positions I have taken in my life, hatred of America has not been included. I have been critical of this or that part of it, of course. I have disliked the government greatly, but always in the knowledge that the government was not the country.

To love, reflexively, all who hate America—as I have known many people to do—is enormously silly, or enormously wrongheaded, or even enormously vicious, a form of political or ideological fanaticism. Where else on the face of the earth would these unthinking critics want to live? Where else would they meet with America's own tolerance of their own dissent? Certainly not in any of the past or present socialist or Communist nations which the complainers seem to adore and yet manage (and have managed) to avoid living in.

Particularly galling are the rich ones. I have known rich denouncers of America both Left and Right. At least the right-wing ones are so typically wound up in Zionist conspiracy theories that even the liberal press knows better than to give them much more than the horse's laugh they so richly deserve. The left-wing ones present a more troubling picture. They back the most destructive causes with money they have earned or inherited through exactly the system they profess to despise. I don't know one of them, however, who has simply given up the riches and gone to work, impoverished, for their cause. They are listened to because they are rich. They are rich because they live in America. What a circle of craziness.

Joe McCarthy, as I knew him, was more like Huey Long than like Torquemada. The real, ideological anti-Communist in his family was his wife, Jean, whose orthodox Catholicism made of anti-Communism a divine crusade. For Joe McCarthy it seemed to me to be somewhat less than that—more a way to get attention, something he had just come across, something that worked. But however shallow his anti-Communism, the fact that he was willing to go so far in raising anti-Red hell attracted to him just about all of the relatively few anti-Communist journalists.

Ralph de Toledano, then at *Newsweek*, was pretty much the pointman and recruiter. Bill Buckley was as helpful as he could be in trying to keep McCarthy's Gaelic enthusiasms from running away with his facts. (To his credit, William F. Buckley Jr. defended McCarthyism at a time when to do so was equivalent to departure from the human race. As I look back upon his career, I realize that Buckley has probably championed more unpopular causes than even the ACLU.)

I was mostly on the edge of McCarthyism, in transition at the time from the envied world of newsmagazine journalism to the less-envied and darker world of straight-out ideological journalism. Being a professional conservative, however, the transition to professional anti-Communist was easy. I wrote speeches for McCarthy—something for which I was well-prepared by the fact that I had, for several years, written the column for *Pathfinder* magazine on the Communist conspiracy and menace. None of the speeches I wrote was very sensational, but all of them were as factually solid as I could make them.

In that respect there always was the help of the FBI through its informal networking with anti-Communists. That networking was managed by an assistant director of the bureau named Deke DeLoach, from whose office poured an endless stream of plain envelopes with deep background on the Communist affiliations of people in the public eye.

Forrest Davis, a contributor to the *Saturday Evening Post*, was the major author of McCarthy's sensational attack against Gen. George C. Marshall—an attack that showed how McCarthy did get carried away. George Marshall did a number of things and took a number of positions that displeased many anti-Communists, but these were not then and never could be an excuse for branding the man a conscious tool of the Communist conspiracy. If every American who took a position shared by the Politburo had been a conscious tool of conspiracy, then it would have been all up with us long ago. In fact, some of the positions held by Americans *were* inspired by contact with people eventually identified as Soviet agents—but this did not make them witting members of a conspiracy. McCarthy went too far when he said that it did, though he was absolutely right in his larger point—that there was a Red menace here at home; that there were Communist agents at work.

Does anyone now doubt it?

Premature anti-Communists were, by and large, also prematurely correct.

There is a trend, as this is being written, to call the Politically Correct movement on campus a kind of left-wing McCarthyism. It is nothing of the sort. The PC form of slander, intimidation, and intolerance takes any expressed opinion that is not PC and turns it into a manifestation of racism, sexism, even Eurocentrism—a new crime unearthed by the politically sensitive, as though an entire European legacy of science and logic is now to be disowned in favor of a more fashionable cultural tradition.

McCarthyism did not savage people because of their cultural practices or heritages. It did attack people who had actively supported some Soviet-line activity by marching, signing a petition, or making a significant public statement. That is quite different from calling a black scholar a self-hating Negro, for example, because he cares less for politics in poetry than for literary merit.

On the other hand, even as the PC movement closes in on universities from the Left, there is a wind blowing more subtly from the opposite direction. As the columnist Thomas W. Hazlett has written, "The only time you'll see Jesse Helms in the same zip code with the Bill of Rights is at an NRA convention." The constant attacks against CBS by the group called Accuracy in Media are another example of PC on the Right. Of course much of television news reporting is full of liberal bias. By all means the public's attention should be called to it. But the charges should be confined to the inaccuracies and errors; there is no point in impugning the motives of media figures who are merely reflecting the anticapitalist climate of the age.

Today's PC attacks whether from Left or from Right bear little substantive resemblance to McCarthyism. There was more substance to attacking Communists' influence on unions, for example, than there is in the elaborate speech codes being wrangled over on college campuses now. And that brings me to a small, and presumably anti-Communist, anti-union effort with which I was briefly involved.

The principal in the effort was a management consultant named Nathan Schefferman. Available to any corporation who could pay his substantial fees to dampen union organizing efforts, Schefferman realized that there were two powerful forces which he could turn against union activities. One was the distaste that women working in the home must feel for the disruptions a union could bring to their lives—strikes, no paychecks, instability. The other force was anti-Communism. Even then, in the '50s, most production workers were patriotic and largely opposed to Communism and even socialism. Most were Democrats. My involvement with Schefferman centered on the anti-Communist angle, although personally I felt that the woman-at-home opposition would be the most effective.

Hearing that I was a freelance writer and an anti-Communist, Schef-ferman hired me to go on a cross-country trip with his crew of anti-union activists or specialists. The plan was to stop at the factories of certain of his customers facing a union vote and to discourage a pro-union vote by any means we could think of. One of the crew was a handsome fellow whose role was to make contact with women, either in the plant or at home, and discuss with them the grave disruptive possibilities of a pro-union vote. Another crew member was a sort of bully-bodyguard, since this could be a dangerous venture. And then there was Nathan Schef-ferman himself.

Schefferman was a round sort of person and not at all given to small talk, which worked out well since we were traveling the country in a large Cadillac with the top down. Among other things, he could not stand polite niceties such as saying hello or how are you when you reached him by phone. Waste of time. Rather like the famously impatient Flo Ziegfeld, he would not even look at a memo that was more than a paragraph long. Ziegfeld was said to have observed that if you couldn't get your big idea onto the back of his calling card, you probably weren't clear on the matter. Schefferman permitted a bit more space, but not much.

My part of the show was to write pamphlets or handouts as we went along, exposing any known Communist Party or Communist-line associ-ation of anyone involved in a local organizing effort. Local management supplied as much information as they could, and I carried a good deal of information of my own.

It was a wild, hectic trip, with little rest and a lot of windswept riding, alleviated by Schefferman's insistence on stopping "for a little dairy" whenever we were near anything that looked like a delicatessen. I have no idea, from way back here in time, whether we deterred any union onslaught. I do understand, however, that it was in the long run an unnec-essary business, since the unions themselves have managed, without much outside help, to make themselves inessential to a majority of Amer-ican working people.

I do feel that our attacks on the pro-Communist activities of a few union officials were a dangerous diversion from what should have been our chief complaint against the unions, as they began to emphasize work rules even above pay raises. Union-management agreements on slow-down, Luddite work rules have, according to some industrial analysts, reduced the productivity of American workers by half. Even so, of course,

American workers remain the most productive, in terms of work finished per hour, of any workers on earth. Imagine what those same workers could be doing—and probably will be doing—when they are freed from restrictive union-management work agreements.

Religion always played an important role in the opposition to Communism, even as it played an important role in its support.

The most powerful religious influence on anti-Communists, it seemed to me, came from Catholicism and, in particular, from the Communist-turned-Christian mystic, Whittaker Chambers. His book, *Witness,* made the fundamental distinction that Communism represents the ideal of man without God. Anti-Communists, in this view, represented the great remnant of those who insisted on the concept of man with God. The idea seemed so powerful to me at the time that I tried to reject my own atheism and to get back to church. If that was what it took to oppose Communism at its roots, then that was what I must attempt.

It was a miserable attempt and wholly wrongheaded I now see. Human-centered materialism, man without God, does not mean a slide toward Communism at all. What could be called a humanocentric view of things is just pro-human, not pro-Communist and not anti-Christian. You certainly don't have to be against something just because you don't belong to it or believe in it.

At any rate, I sought the counseling of priests and earnestly studied to regain my lost Catholicism, even prayed for the gift of faith before realizing that I simply don't have it and couldn't pretend that I did.

Meantime, of course, there were prominent Christian clergymen doing their best to defend Communism, seeing in it a revival of primitive Christianity itself, ensnared by the notion that Communism actually had something to do with common sharing rather than tyrannical power and top-down authority. Some religious people remain thus deluded to this day, joining in clerical attacks (by the Catholic Council of Bishops, for instance) against capitalism.

I believe that Chambers was precisely correct in identifying perfervid Communism as a new sort of religion, even if godless. I believe that, like religion, Communism became for many of its adherents an item of such powerful faith that every enormity could be justified. Christianity too, of course, had its crusades and pogroms. But there was a difference: Christianity has flourished for centuries without thinking it had to suppress the human desires for accomplishment and for creature comfort. Communism finally collapsed because it did try to suppress those desires, leaving its people impoverished, both materially and morally.

Perhaps now, the argument can rest where it always belonged, not with the difference between man with and man without God, but in the difference between humans free to explore, invent, create and those who are kept from the same pursuits by authoritarian rules. The actual struggle is the one between capitalism, the ownership of property and enterprises by individuals, and collectivism, with its various projections of ownership by all or ownership by no one—except, of course, by the State.

This notion became a very important one later on when I worked with Senator Goldwater and is even more significant today as some environmentalists ruminate over the idea of the earth without humans.

The most organized, large-scale anti-Communist activity in which I was involved professionally—with McCarthy, I was a volunteer—was writing regularly for *Counterattack*, the first major anti-Communist newsletter. Founded by three former agents of the FBI, *Counterattack* was backed with funding, as I understood it, from such corporations as Sears.

Its founders also spun off such a notable and serious think tank as the National Security Council. The council's dedication of its headquarters at Paris, Virginia, was certainly suggestive of friendly connections with the military and intelligence elite. Members of the Joint Chiefs of Staff, highly placed CIA and FBI operatives, and anti-Communist senators and congressmen all showed up, some ferried to the event in military helicopters.

My job, which brought me into *Counterattack's* Wall Street offices once a week, was wonderfully convenient. My former wife and I had moved from Dobbs Ferry to go farther north, close to Sing Sing, to Jefferson Valley where I was making a living as a freelance writer. What I did at *Counterattack* was to write each week's issue based upon material mailed to me by the publisher, Art Cullen, and then visit the office once a week to finalize the form each issue would take.

Counterattack was, in effect, a huge file cabinet. Each day, researchers under Art Cullen's direction would scan every Communist or Communist-line publication in the land. Every name in every story, in every advertisement, or every announcement of an event was added to the file and cross-indexed by where it had appeared and when. *Counterattack's* stock-in-trade was to take the events of the week, extract from them people who took any part of the current Soviet line, and then publish their entire background of support for or involvement in the activities of Soviet-line groups.

One week "John Doe" would be reported with well-known Communist connections and the next week "John Jones" would be listed a fellow traveler. At the same time, John this or John that would be reported as signing a Red petition in the *Daily Worker*. I suppose the information was useful to someone; certainly, signing a petition in the *Daily Worker* raised real questions about a person's common sense, if not his or her sanity. And, as I felt at the time, it probably made such individuals prime candidates for being drummed out of thoughtful society.

The publication did not, as McCarthy was said to, assume that every one of those people were conscious agents of the Communist conspiracy. But as a famous name was plunked down and then followed by the citation of a dozen or so affiliations with Soviet-line groups or joint public statements, the impact could be devastating.

Also, *Counterattack* would do background searches regarding anyone—say, a potential employee. The practice was roundly condemned as blacklisting, or redlisting. There were, at the same time, groups involved in keeping track of people who had ever supported the Ku Klux Klan. I cannot recall any outrage at that as being Klan-listing or redneck listing. The simple fact was that some companies did not want to hire anyone with a record of Communist sympathies—or anyone with Klan sympathies either, for that matter. Why should the former part of that prejudice seem so baleful, the latter so sensible? Even the trade unions, finally, had to be as prejudiced against the Communist-liners as they were against the Klanners.

Counterattack's major transgression, however, was to issue a special publication listing all of the Soviet-line signings, joinings, marchings, and so forth of people prominent in entertainment. It was called *Red Channels*. To be sure, the editors made it plain that a person who signed a lot of Soviet-line petitions or joined a lot of Soviet-line-following groups was probably a follower of the Soviet line. It did not seem to me then or now that a person who thus signed, joined, marched, and petitioned should be ashamed of what he was doing. There were perfectly innocent reasons for following the Soviet line on a number of issues. What *Red Channels* pointed out, however, was that these folks were pushing some Soviet policy at just the time when the Soviet Union could best benefit from it.

The activities of the so-called front organizations were not innocent and they were not detached; they were purposeful and inspired. I do not believe that *Counterattack* falsely maligned people. It just made them responsible for their actions.

One sad situation that I can recall from my *Counterattack* days involved the German playwright Bertolt Brecht. He was a perennial favorite for our exposures, having been involved in hard-line Communist activities for much of his life. I can recall putting together story after story detailing his Communist and Communist-line activities. He lived the latter part of his life in East Germany and, when he died, it was revealed that he was in great disfavor with the ruling Communists. Brecht had, in fact, left a treasury of writing critical of them, though not critical of his earlier Communist dreams.

Counterattack was not in a position to make as much of Brecht's opposition to at least a part of the Communist empire as it had been to expose every detail of his support of that empire. For the really hard-line anti-Communists, no small progress away from Communism or fellow traveling would suffice. People were expected to flatly denounce the Soviet Union and Communism and everything associated with it—or continue to be suspected of pro-Communist sympathies.

One very widely read columnist of the time, one of the few hard-line anti-Communists with a large audience, managed to turn the recantation of Communist-line activities into a substantial cottage industry. When a Hollywood executive was eager to clear this or that star of suspicion of being a Communist, the columnist George Sokolsky would listen to evidence of the star's recantation of past mischief, and either write an exculpatory column himself or get someone else in the small anti-Communist old boys' network to do one. I had been told that Sokolsky charged only a comparatively modest fee for his advice in these matters.

If there was a communications director for the old boys' network of anti-Communists it would have to be Jack Clements, director of public relations for the Hearst group of newspapers and periodicals. Uncle Jack, as most called him, kept everybody who was writing anti-Communist material in touch with each other. He was able to provide part-time, get-on-your-feet work for any of them who fell on hard times, as many did. His contacts among anti-Communist groups in Europe were said to be formidable. His contact with the Catholic Church, through his close friend Cardinal Spellman, was intimate and effective.

At one point Jack Clements managed the sale of the venerable *American Mercury* magazine—once edited by H. L. Mencken—to J. Russell Maguire, the owner of, among other things, the company that manufactured the Thompson submachine gun. Maguire's ownership turned the magazine from a generally conservative publication to a specifically anti-Communist one. It developed an idiosyncratic style that seemed at first just odd to me; but later, when I got to know the new owner better, I saw in it a heavy-handed anti-Semitism. The style was to run in parentheses any Jewish-sounding family name of significant Communists: "Trotsky (Bronstein)," for instance. This mechanism for demonstrating that many early Communists were Jews delighted Maguire but left me unimpressed.

One of the other things that Maguire wanted to do was to revive the *Dearborn Independent*, the wildly anti-Jewish newspaper backed by Henry Ford. His agenda seemed clear. Jews and Communists had become pretty much the same thing in his mind. The anti-Communism of the *Mercury*, which of course I supported, would from then on be tottering dangerously on the verge of old-fashioned, know-nothing anti-Semitism. I stuck it out, writing for the magazine a good deal longer than I should have; when I did leave, it was without having forestalled the magazine's slide into anti-Semitic sleaze. Like many of my friends, I was willing to put up with a good deal of insanity to have *any* outlet for anti-Communist journalism.

Anti-Semitism on the Right. Yes, there was some there, and I assume there still is. Yet I do not honestly believe that it is any more prevalent on the Right than, for instance, on the black-power Left. The anti-Jewish attitude of many black fellows at the Institute for Policy Studies, where I eventually worked, was obvious, even though there were as many Jewish as African-American fellows at IPS. Black fellows found it easy to believe ancient myths about the control of Jewish bankers over the financial institutions which they believed were oppressing African Americans. The anti-Jewish ranting of such figures as the minister Louis Farrakhan and even the more subtle antagonism of the Reverend Jessie Jackson fed this.

One of these days, the violence-prone white supremacy groups are likely to discover that hating blacks is a detriment to their hating Jews. I can imagine an easy accommodation in which the white groups and black groups agree formally, as they already do informally, to absolutely oppose race mixing and join in attacking Jews.

I must admit, however, that there were anti-Jewish manifestations on the Right that were downright zany. I was asked to visit with a very rich right-winger at his mansionlike apartment in midtown Manhattan. He walked me down a hallway lined with magnificent oaken cabinet doors. Inside each of the doors there was an illustration of some Jewish perfidy, centering mainly on Zionism—which, my host explained, was merely a cover for Jewish control of the vast mineral deposits of the Dead Sea. My host, incidentally, was Jewish. It was Zionism that exercised him.

Today hatred for Jews animates those violent groups (neo-Nazis, the National Alliance, skinheads, and such) which are always characterized as being far rightists or right-wing extremists. This wing-ism is an absurdity. The so-called Far Left, the Marxist-Leninist collectivist left, is not one inch more or less collectivist than the race-obsessed violent right wing. Both "wings" believe in the absolute subordination of the individual to a collectivist ideology, a theology of political perfectionism.

One of my favorite of all *Doonesbury* cartoons points to the tolerant liberalism of spirit that is America's finest heritage. In the cartoon, the director of a local Communist Vietnamese reeducation center is phoning his superior. *Reeducation officer*: "There's a young man enrolled in my class who is a very slow learner. I think he should be transferred to a more intensive program. *Superior*: "Now, Comrade, you know that's impossible! Why, all of our re-education centers are dangerously overcrowded and understaffed as it is." *Reeducation officer*: "Yes, sir, but this is an especially difficult case. The man's got a Ph.D. in political science.... Yes, sir ... I've got him staying after class now for remedial Marxism! But it doesn't seem to be helping any." *Superior*: "What did he write his dissertation on?" *Reeducation officer*: "Jeffersonian democracy." *Superior*: "Have you tried shooting him?"

It was the absolutism of Communism that repelled me, the lack of any tolerance for individual differences. It is the same absolutism in religionists, politicians, mystics, and other brands of believers that repels me still.

It really wasn't until Bill Buckley's *National Review* got underway that informed anti-Communism and responsible overall editorial policy became assured in a mass-circulation magazine. On the Left, the same virtue was displayed by the *Reporter* magazine, one of whose most sturdily anti-Communist writers, Meg Greenfield, is now editor of the editorial page of the *Washington Post*. She is still an unyielding but never hysterical analyst of Communist tyranny and expansionism. I had one date with Meg back when she was writing for the *Reporter*. I was enthralled by her then, in person. I remain enthralled at a distance of miles and years. Great journalist.

The smallest and surely the most odd anti-Communist effort in which I was involved was with James Burnham, the gifted and very farsighted author of *The Managerial Revolution* and, as was I, a founding contributor to Bill Buckley's *National Review.* Burnham and I got the idea that it would be useful if some profit-seeking expert from the ranks of organized crime would do a little moonlighting as a hijacker of Communist Party operating funds.

It was our conceit that, with our many contacts, we could get information about the routes and routines of Communist money-carrying couriers. Armed with this data, an expert criminal should be able to do the hijacking job neatly—and patriotically. Later I would discover that many members of organized crime groups, for one of whom I ghosted a book, are indeed very patriotic; they are not at all attracted to any notions of a classless society or letting the government own or control everything, or any other socialist idea.

Whom should we approach for our brilliant and practical scheme? Start at the top, of course. We were near the top of our trade, so why not go directly to the top of *their* trade? We decided that Frank Costello, lauded in the press as the boss of bosses in organized crime, was our man. Perhaps we were naive in assuming that this was even a possibility. Mr. Costello did not have a listed phone number or even an address, but he did have an attorney, duly noted in the press. We went to see him.

Without shame we proceeded to tell this very distinguished attorney of our Grand Plan for dealing a severe blow to the Red menace. How embarrassing it is now to remember his incredulous look and his patient explanation, as though tutoring a couple of morons, that Mr. Costello was a respected businessman, that all of the press and congressional-hearing furor was a sort of civic hallucination, and that he understood our deep concern for our country, a concern deeply shared by Mr. Costello, but . . .

Of all the people who hired me to be their house anti-Communist, the most interesting was, beyond a doubt, H. L. Hunt, the billionaire Texas oil wildcatter, reputed in the '50s to be the richest man in America. H. L. was large, ungainly, and rough of speech and movement—a delight to be with when the focus was not politics. I spent some time with him on his various ranches and found him to be a very funny fellow, a wonderful teller of tall Texas tales, and just the sort you'd like to go fishing with.

He did have a few quirks. Packard automobiles, for instance. He felt that driving a Packard was such a sign of deep-rooted ignorance as to require immediate remedial action. He fired one fine geologist for just such a sin.

H. L.'s own taste in automobiles was rather hard to divine. One morning, he told the first female employee he met coming into the office that his old car (a Pontiac) had worn out and would she please get him another one. Back then, in Texas, "car" often was taken to be synonymous with Cadillac. So, she went out and bought him a Cadillac. Next day, having driven the new car home and then back to the office in downtown Dallas, he told the next first female employee he met to please get him a smaller car instead of that great big one someone bought for him the other day. A bit of quick research indicated the wisdom of another Pontiac. It was bought and parked in Hunt's space. Later in the week, someone timidly asked him where the Cadillac might be found. Oh, he replied, I parked it out there someplace—indicating with a sweep of his hand the entire state of Texas.

Hunt was an absolute pushover for people who could nourish his growing concern about Communism. Come up with a new Red conspiracy theory, or propose a new way to shine the light on Communist agents, and Hunt was ready to shovel out the money. His not-so-subtle way of supporting Joe McCarthy, for instance, was to make surefire losing bets with him on sporting events. Hunt himself was said to be spending about $5,000 a day on gambling. But after all, gambling had been his original skill. That's how he won his first oil leases.

Hunt's absolutely worst choice of causes to support, I believe, was the one which resulted in his signing his name to a book which proposed that voting rights be apportioned according to personal wealth. The richer you were, the more votes you'd get. How Hunt could fall for that one is beyond me. He understood that his own personal wealth was, as they joked at the Petroleum Club, "all tied up in cash." Really wealthy people, he knew full well, were people like the Rockefellers and DuPonts—and the former family, he judged, was not much different from the Lenin or Stalin family. He remarked to me once, after a visit to the Rockefellers' Chase Manhattan Bank, "They made me wait in the outside office just like anybody else." It should have discouraged his support of a wealth-based democracy, but it didn't.

Hunt's obsession with Communism caused him to miss a chance to become the richest, possibly the most practical member of the counterculture. At one point, as the owner of immense numbers of rural properties, he thought of starting practical farming centers where young people could live and work together and learn commonsense farming. The counterculture's fervid back-to-the-land enthusiasm could have been thus leavened by some practical knowledge. One of his children, a daughter as I recall, argued against the farming idea. It was her notion that it would do precious little good to teach young people to farm if their future was about to be blighted by the Red menace.

Neither she, nor any others that I recall on the anti-Communist Right, really seemed to have any deep feeling for the power of the American idea, of the inspiring power of its prosperity, of the potential for unashamedly showing off how much of America was living a life that would seem to most of the world magnificent. Hatred of Communism dampened love of the American idea and reality—the very ideas which now have toppled collectivism just about everywhere, the ideas which always have found more people wanting to emigrate to America than to any other place on earth.

Hunt did have an instinct for the positive which, if it had animated his anti-Communist zeal, could have made a great difference. One indication was a magazine which I designed for him. Entitled *Facts Forum,* it took the thoroughly sensible view that if you line up in a straightforward way the collectivist versus the capitalist arguments on any matter, the commonsense superiority of the capitalist views will be obvious. Neither the magazine nor the idea got very far in a publishing world where the fad then, and for years, was to shoot down anything smacking of capitalism on sight (except the publishing business, of course).

At one point, wanting to see more advertising in the magazine, Hunt suggested a page or two of ads from the various oil-well drilling equipment and service companies that he owned. When I indicated that such a spread might seem self-serving, he came up with a headline that strikes me now as an example of the proper enthusiasm of a man who had won his first big oil leases in a poker game and never for a moment doubted that America was the land of the most golden opportunity. He wanted the pages of the oil-well drilling ads to be headlined, "Now *You* Can Be an Oilman."

I used to argue some with Hunt about the content of the magazine, but he had an argument-ending question for which I could never find a convincing answer. He would say, and not in an unkindly way, "If you're so smart, why aren't you rich?"

I know the answer now. It's simply because I have never offered the products which in a free market would make me rich. I am not unhappy about that, however. I have lived very much the way I have wanted to and have done the things I wanted to do. I just made a choice. I'm responsible for it. Society didn't do it. The system didn't do it. The system, in fact, made it all possible.

What collectivist society could even come close?

11

Businessman

*Thou hast most traitorously corrupted the youth of the realm in erecting
a grammar school; and whereas, before, our forefathers had no other
books but the score and the tally, thou hast caused printing to be used;
and, contrary to the king, his crown, and dignity, thou hast built a
paper-mill.*

—William Shakespeare, *King Henry IV*

It's no wonder that capitalism has become a confused and confusing
concept in America. Working for a major corporation in the late '50s
and early '60s certainly confused me.

My path to Champion Papers—a papermaking, fiber and wood products conglomerate nested in the middle of the Fortune 500—was cir-
cuitous. In 1957, while I was freelancing in Jefferson Valley and visiting
Manhattan once a week, I met an accomplished angler, skeet shooter, and
entrepreneur named Frederic Dodge. He had just convinced some people
in Hamilton, Ohio, to upgrade a little magazine they owned—the *Midwest Fisherman*—into an English-style gentleman's angling magazine.
And he was looking for an editor. We liked each other, and when he
learned that I enjoyed fishing, and was a camper, canoeist, and shooter,
the editorial direction of the *Fisherman* (its new name) was mine. It was
time to pack up our Jefferson Valley stuff and move it, along with my

149

wife and son, to Hamilton. I speak of moving the stuff and the family—as if they were so much furniture—because that pretty well sums up the attitude of the corporate culture I would soon be entering.

But not quite yet. From the first issue of the magazine until its last, only a year later, we were successful in creating a well-illustrated, slick magazine that included the usual I-caught-something-special-halfway-around-the-world stories but also good fishing fiction, gourmet fish cookery, and detailed, meticulous assessments of both places to fish and the equipment to do it with. The major owner of the *Fisherman* was Dwight Thomson, one of the nephews of the founder of Champion Papers and then a vice president of the corporation. Thomson was lavishly generous in subsidizing the magazine and it actually began to break even when a substantial increase in mailing rates did the whole thing in.

I was not left high and dry in Butler County, Ohio, however. Dwight Thomson's cousin, Reuben Robertson Jr., was the son of Champion's founder and its president. And Robertson was looking for an assistant who could write speeches, oversee the corporation's product and management image, and advise on public relations. Seeming to fit the bill, I was hired.

It was at Champion Papers where I learned that the skill of modern management is simply manipulating people, not producing goods. It is said that you manipulate people in order to produce goods, but I believe that managers manipulate people in order to enhance their own power and that the production of goods is quite incidental to that project. Champion's management philosophy was not nearly so brazen, though in practice it deviated little.

The man actually running the show there was an in-house consultant named Charley Kluss. Peter Drucker was our visiting consultant. Whizzes both, yet they had what seemed to me curious ideas.

Kluss was convinced that a proper industrial manager would be a manager not of processes but of people. Drucker once said that I had an unfortunate "craft bias" because I was so interested in the way paper was made and in how it could be made better. I was always spending time out in the mill and was therefore biased toward production techniques rather than management. Kluss was in steamy agreement, always wanting to get me off the shop floor and back to the typewriter while I insisted that I could write better speeches for a papermaker if I knew how to make paper.

It was not until I read Tracy Kidder's book *The Soul of a New*

Machine that I fully understood what had so troubled me in the Kluss formulations of tight, hierarchical, manipulative management. In Kidder's recounting of the birth of a new computer, the best, most creative sort of managers were the ones who did everything they could to encourage the independence of designers and engineers and everyone else in a project, to protect them from bureaucratic time wasting, to let them get on with the work for which they had been hired.

Kluss and Drucker only reinforced my dawning realization that people do *not* need managing. People involved in the production process know more about it than any of the managers, and if left alone can do a much better job. In every instance I know of where workers have been given the freedom to organize and manage their own work, they have produced more and better products, absenteeism has gone down, and perceived satisfaction has gone up.

There are some managerial functions that may be useful, such as coordinating supplies or getting things to a certain place on time, but this is just another form of work and not an outstanding job. It requires no more skill than working on a lathe or turning pulp into 3 × 5 note cards. I have never believed that because a person is keeping tabs on the toilet paper that they should also keep tabs on the fate of Western civilization. But as I learned at Champion, few managers who are production oriented—whose goal is really to work with other people to get things done—ever scale the heights of promotion. It seemed then that the most highly paid people did abstract, manipulative work; they simply said yes and no to staff proposals.

There was another big area of disagreement between myself and Champion's consultants: the free flow of information. I was on the side of letting it all hang out, of spreading information like fertilizer. Kluss was more of a mind to put it in carefully edited newsletters; he often would argue for hours, even days, over a single word, as though language could be made to deceive all of the people all of the time.

When it came to the president's message in the corporation's annual report, our efforts took on the somber, ponderous weight of a wartime battle plan. I can recall hours spent worrying over single words in the president's statement. One definite oddity in the annual report (and in many of the president's speeches, again carefully and lengthily edited by Kluss) was that a man who always defended free enterprise in theory would at the same time condemn competition as the cause of corporate woes. I am sure that were he alive today he would be an ardent protectionist. So much for free enterprise in the world of quasi-capitalism.

The whole annual report was an excruciating exercise in clever language. I don't know for whom such reports are written, actually. For serious investors, the balance sheets tell all that they need to know. No amount of gobbledygook or sweet talk can ameliorate the bad ones, or add to the good ones. Yet we spent such long hours over our descriptions of corporate activity—particularly over elaborate, so-carefully worded excuses for any company shortcomings.

At one time the people operating Champion's Canton, North Carolina, papermaking plant (the company's original operation) understood the power of actions as opposed to clever words in persuading people of Champion's vitality. Many years ago they decided to pay all hourly-wage workers with silver dollars on certain given paydays. Now silver dollars are just physically more impressive than either paper bills or checks, and an employee walking away with a bag of them felt well and truly paid. In addition, as the stream of silver began to flow through their stores, every merchant in Canton could see vividly how important Champion was to all of them, to their families, to all of Canton.

But in Ohio, we word-wrestled. There was a whole literature written for our employees, too. The person in an organization who holds a monopoly on information has serious power. It is a way to have organizational clout without doing anything else. This surely was a way of life around Champion. The substitute for a free flow of information was a stream of carefully worded official memos, notices, bulletin board statements, newsletters, and, of course, excerpts from the president's speeches reprinted in the company's magazine—which I supervised, being convinced at that time that employees could be inspired to do better work, to be more loyal, to vote against unions, by a house organ that pictured them and featured them as part of a single happy family with homesites in Ohio, Texas, and North Carolina.

I think that idea has been fully and happily discredited. I became convinced that house organs generally do not do what they are supposed to do: wean the readers away from their real communities and their families and put them at suck on The Corporation. This failure is a good thing. Blind obedience and loyalty strike me as costly luxuries these days. The days of the numb assembly line are gone or going. Tools are now getting smarter and smarter. The people who use them must get smarter too. Employees at all levels need to be thinking people, able to respond to swift changes or emergencies, able to think things through without being told, like idiots, to do this and do that upon signal. Employees deserve to be treated as serious people and as thoughtful people. If they are not, they should be fired. There is little room in modern industry or invention or business for sluggards, empty heads, the mentally deficient even if over-muscled. All that has passed.

Of course, the same thing is true for the executive suites. I suggested at one time that it would be a useful thing to list the salaries of all white-collar workers, executives and all. Put the lists on all of the bulletin boards, was my naive notion. Why be ashamed of salaries? If people were worth their pay, they should be confident enough to let it be known. If they really thought their salaries would cause turmoil, then perhaps they should take less, down to the point where they wouldn't mind exposing them.

Talk about your lead balloons!

The gauge of excellence at Champion, then, was not so much a person's work performance as his personality and loyalty to the corporation. Personality was felt to be a good indicator of whether the manager could inspire—read manipulate—people; loyalty was valued as a virtue in itself. And it had to be loyalty on a par with Gordon Liddy's, when he declared he would be willing to stand on a street corner and be assassinated by a CIA colleague if it would help the sitting government. Champion did not administer quite such a stringent test of loyalty, but its insistence upon utter commitment to the company was nonetheless fanatical. The corporation had to precede in importance all other relationships, including families.

One result was the almost ritual scheduling of important meetings on Sundays. Saturday wouldn't do because a person not at work on Saturday as a matter of course was figured to have the potential of a field hand, not an executive. And so Sunday. *Not* to be called to a meeting on Sunday was a mark of corporate inferiority. Ambitious people dreaded not being called for Sunday work. Clearly, I was not ambitious. I was invited to only about half of the Sunday meetings during my tenure, and even tried to figure out ways of avoiding the ones to which I had been summoned. No executive me, alas.

Yet I remember so well one of the meetings that I did attend. The assistant treasurer of the corporation arrived a few minutes late, all sweaty with apologies. His son, he explained, had most inconveniently broken his leg, and he'd had to drop him off at the hospital before coming to the meeting. Most of the other attendees beamed with approval. No one even mentioned the son or asked about his condition. I sensed then that I was in a very screwed-up world.

But all my experiences were teaching me an important lesson about the sort of management which, should it continue, could turn this country into a productive slum. Fortunately it seems to be vanishing, thanks in good part to our dear friend, the personal computer. Computers may succeed in reversing the bad course management has followed since the time of that wretched efficiency expert, Frederick W. Taylor. I have read that one of Taylor's great discoveries was how to ensure that a shop foreman would know more than his work crew: Make the crew know less. Regardless of his other contributions to what came to be known as either scientific or modern management, he certainly scored a bull's-eye on that one. In any case, computers are helping us all to know more.

An executive whom I have come to admire, even if only at a distance, is Seymour Cray, whose supercomputers remain a jewel in our techno-industrial crown. A friend who had, on consecutive days, visited an old-line computer company and then Cray, near Milwaukee, Wisconsin, had this to say about the difference.

At the older company, he said, "People seemed always to be walking around with their heads down, and they could tell you something only about the particular part of a project on which they were working. There was no lively interest in anything else going on. You didn't get the idea that projects were even related. At Cray, everybody seemed bright eyed and bushy tailed and even the janitor could tell you things about what was going on and why."

There was a time when the creation of data-processing departments brought a good deal of the information problem to the fore. The data-processing people resisted, literally to their departments' deaths, the idea of letting individual managers have personal computers, networked to share information throughout the organization. The urge for information— which animated the hackers who birthed the computer age and still keep it young and healthy—won out, of course. I feel the urge for information freedom always will win out. Besides which, it is greatly more productive to encourage workers to share information rather than to hoard it.

During my short career in the business world, perhaps my only really innovative and useful work was to make use of the corporation's resources to attack Communism.

Coated papers were an important part of the company's wares; because they are the perfect palettes for fine printing, there always was a demand for samples. It was my notion that instead of just handing out random samples we could put our premier papers together in a large, glossy magazine. The subject: Communism. The title of the finished project was *The Protracted Conflict*, based upon the ancient Asian strategy of wearing down an enemy by constant, small acts of attrition rather than by frontal assaults. Our purpose was to show that was exactly what was going on internationally, as Communist troops or their surrogates nibbled up the small Baltic states, then some in Africa, then some in Latin America, and so on. The Indo-Chinese war, though it featured some spectacular frontal assaults as well, was clearly informed by that strategy of protracted conflict.

I wrote the text for the publication along with my friend James Burnham. The graphic design was by Noel Martin, then working at the Cincinnati Museum of Art.

The publication was extraordinarily popular and perhaps even influenced some paper purchases. It also brought me back to the attention of people in Washington. One of the groups that I consulted for help in preparing the magazine, at the University of Pennsylvania, included Col. William Kintner, who was also very influential at the Pentagon.

Our publication so impressed Colonel Kintner that he asked Champion to loan me to a Pentagon task force on military branch libraries—the libraries where ordinary soldiers would go for information. There was not nearly enough information on Communism, of course, and especially not much on Communist political tactics such as the idea of protracted conflict. Reporting directly to the secretary of defense, our task force made specific recommendations about titles for the military libraries and, by extension, for educating soldiers about Communist strategies, social, political, and military.

My loan to the government was not confined to that one assignment. Later, I was loaned to the White House to put together a plan to assist Republican candidates for the U.S. House of Representatives. At that time, during the Eisenhower administration, congressional candidates were really second-class citizens. There always seemed to be plenty of money for Senate candidates. Presidential campaigns just had to whistle to get tons of money. Congressional candidates struggled. Congressional races are no longer so neglected today, and even presidential candidates understand the importance of helping their partisans in their races for the House.

While I worked on this assignment, I shared an office with Stephen Hess, now a renowned political sage. Our names gave the switchboard some trouble, but not for long. The White House switchboard was, and no doubt still is, the most effective communications mode ever devised by humans. There never seemed to be a time when they could not get in touch with anyone, anywhere in the world. Even where there were no phones.

One day I was taking a break for some fishing aboard the cabin cruiser of another White House assistant, Doug Price. A helicopter appeared, hovered over the boat, and gave us a message by bullhorn. Back to work we went.

Perhaps the most seductive part of working at the White House, even as a temp, was the deference of transportation companies and the availability of White House limousines. I can recall at least one flight, booked from the White House, where the plane dutifully delayed takeoff for about twenty minutes, awaiting my arrival. As soon as I was finally ushered aboard the plane, it departed from the gate. The irritated but avid curiosity of a full planeload of delayed passengers evokes a sly, foolish sense of self-importance. (I could not understand why John Sununu, the Bush administration's traveling wise guy, did not appreciate how very much more arrogant he could be by flying commercial and always arriving a few minutes late.) The wait-for-power gambit works just as well for trains. Not for taxis, however. Most taxi drivers are far too thoroughgoing capitalists to let pomp and circumstance get in the way of honest profit. But then they probably never will have the temptation. Official limousines are far too plentiful.

Those limousines taught me another powerful lesson. No wonder official people have overblown views of their self-importance. How, for instance, can a president keep his head on straight when people, even friends, actually call him "Mister President"? When on every formal occasion he is introduced to the waiting folk by a military band playing "Hail to the Chief"? And the limousine has to play an important part in all of this egoflation. Enthroned in the living-room comforts of a limousine, you cruise ordinary streets in an extraordinary manner. No meter watching for the godlings. No cursing the traffic. No worry about whether some old, familiar clunk or clank in the engine will suddenly turn into a stall. No worries, except the worries appropriate to the upward bound. Can you make your point perfectly to someone whom you want to say yes to your proposition? Are the flip charts perfect? Has the other side gotten to him first?

The subject matter of the concerns of people in Washington is so far removed from ordinary concerns and comprehension (never saving a person, always saving people) that the limousine adds a wonderful extra dimension of insulation. There you are, zooming along as fast as a superbly skilled driver can go. Looking through the windows, as you move, the unofficial people on the sidewalks seem stroboscopically frozen, just about motionless. They are the slow, the waiting masses. You are the moving, the fast master.

The higher up in politics you go, the more apparent this effect. Congressmen still must spend a good deal of time with constituents, even the grungy ones. Senators don't. Cabinet members don't. Secrecy and pomp, like limousines, move the movers farther and farther away from the ordinary concerns of unofficial people.

All of this being loaned out to the Pentagon and to the White House eventually led to my writing two Republican Party platforms and to signing on with my only enduring political hero, Barry Goldwater. It did not, however, prevent my being eased out of Champion in one of the most interesting package deals I have ever heard of. It began with another one of those mistakes that I would have continued to make throughout a corporate career: the mistake of trusting that people were more interested in good work than in personal advancement.

The design of our anti-Communist publication, *Protracted Conflict*, was so great that Noel became the corporation's consultant on publications. Together, he and I designed the new company logo, and wrote up a complete corporate image program. That, in turn, was so good that a newly hired vice president for, believe it or not, corporate image, convinced Noel and me that our work was too important to be trusted to just an ordinary presentation to the board of directors. He would break the ground for us and make the presentation himself. We were dumb and delighted. That was the last thing that Noel and I ever heard about our program, except that it had been enthusiastically adopted and that the new vice president had become the virtual god of imagery.

At about the same time, Lew Thomson, another vice president of the corporation, and another heir of the founder, was put on the list to be moved into some other field of work. Reuben Robertson had been killed in an auto accident and there no longer was any pressure to keep kin at work. The new president was Karl Bendetson who, in his most notable previous management career, in the World War II army, had been in charge of rounding up and putting into prison camps the Japanese population of America. More recently, Bendetson had been managing the Champion manufacturing plant on Buffalo Bayou, outside of Houston. He was Kluss's man and, in fact, probably the best choice that could have been made at the time.

My help was enlisted in an effort to convince Lew Thomson that a wonderful world of opportunity awaited him outside of the corporation. Lew and I had worked together on the beginning of the corporate image project, we had worked together on some graphic arts exhibits, and we had become good friends. What, I was asked, did I think would encourage Lew to leave? The idea of owning and running a newspaper, I knew, had great appeal to Lew. Would I be interested in joining him on such a venture? Well, come to think of it, I would—particularly in view of my obvious ineptitude at corporate matters.

And so Lew and I left the company, voluntarily, like a couple of hicks being slickered into some big city fellow's game. I set out to find a newspaper we could buy. Lew moved to Potomac, Maryland, bought a beautiful house and a boat for cruising the Potomac River, got horses for the kids, and waited to become a publisher. Despite earnest effort and the help of major newspaper brokers, however, nothing appropriate came to light. Lew, not so happy about all that, took over a lithographic plate manufacturing company which another Champion executive was anxious to see sold.

Again there was the moving of furniture and family, now expanded by the birth of our son Eric. Back to Washington. And back to full-time ideological combat in the trenches of the Right, and then, in what was seen as a strange reversal, on the ramparts of the New Left.

12

Platformer

It is a tale told by an idiot, full of sound and fury, signifying nothing.
—William Shakespeare, *Macbeth*

While at Champion Papers, I was loaned to the Republican Party to be the chief writer for the 1960 presidential campaign platform. To accord with law, my partisan work had to be on my own time. The corporation generously gave me some extra vacation leave—compensation, in theory, for all of the overtime that I had worked.

The people in charge of the platform committee were Charles Percy of Illinois, president of Bell and Howell, and Gabriel Hauge, Harvard economist and investment banker.

The formulation of the platform began some weeks before any formal meetings of the platform committee were scheduled. The formal hearings, I was to observe, were a public spectacle, an ego-stroking exercise for delegates to the convention.

The first and defining part of the process was directed through the White House. All members of the Cabinet were ordered to submit their notions of what the ideal platform plank would be in their own area of authority. Staff in all of those departments cranked up wish lists; those lists were vetted by top staffers and the secretary and then sent on to me and my own bosses at the White House, chiefly Bryce Harlow and Ed McCabe, of whom more will be said later.

The truth of the matter is that all of the work of all of those Cabinet people and staffs ended up being merely suggestive. It was Harlow and McCabe who made the final decisions; even before the Cabinet memos arrived, they knew roughly what should go into the platform.

Harlow and McCabe would present me with comments or memos, sometimes just conversational notes, and my job was to put it all into clear language—except where evasive language was deemed to be more prudent. Evasive language usually meant substituting a glowing phrase for a specific statement: something like "assure a decent standard of living for all Americans" rather than "raise taxes to subsidize the poor." Understandable choice. The object of a platform is not to establish an agenda for an administration. It is to placate all factions in the party and to sound good on the evening news. It also is to assure that any reasonably potential presidential candidate can live with the document.

The reasonably potential candidates in this instance were Richard Nixon and Nelson Rockefeller, and they had direct influence on the platform work through staff members assigned directly to work with Chuck Percy, Bryce Harlow, Ed McCabe, and, eventually, me.

What a bunch. Chuck Percy is the most consciously careful, and most conscientiously upwardly mobile, person I ever have met. The story was that as a young man he had sorted through American businesses until he found one controlled by a single, strong person where he could rise without competition from built-in successors, such as founders' children or protégés. Bell and Howell, where he began as a sales trainee in 1938, was just right.

When he headed up the Republican platform committee he was president of Bell and Howell and had improved the company's performance considerably. He was not just a driven man, he also was a bright and talented executive. More lately, of course, he has been a senator from Illinois.

Ed McCabe is a senior partner in a distinguished Washington law firm. I have worked with him in many political ventures. He is the most unflappable person I have ever met. The tendency of most people I have known in politics is to bristle at every insult, glow with every compliment. Not good enough. McCabe's great ability was to make everybody around him stop and, in effect, count to ten and think about whatever it was that had just happened. It should be a very simple ability, one which could be codified into that marvelous bumper-sticker phrase about putting your mind into gear before running your mouth; but it is surprisingly rare. And it is a very important ability. Few things can get a politician into more trouble than an uncontrollable urge to snap back at every criticism. As Ed always pointed out, it rarely is absolutely necessary to respond at all, much less to respond hastily.

His advice along those lines was richly rewarding later, during the Goldwater campaign, when Pennsylvania's Governor Scranton issued a diatribe denunciation of Senator Goldwater. The immediate reaction of just about everyone was to slash back immediately. McCabe convinced us to wait, to think it over, to take neither the defense nor the offense but simply to reply politely with a few appropriate facts.

Bryce Harlow is justly famous for being a sort of universal Mr. Fixit for every Republican administration since Eisenhower. I can't imagine what an accurate job description would say about him. He was, technically, counselor to the president. He was, actually, a roving deputy chief of staff, a prime minister without portfolio. I suppose that Clark Clifford on the Democratic side would be the closest similar operator. Harlow has the edge, however, having never been involved in a scandal like the banking one that lately has caused people to take a harsher second look at Clifford.

The controlling interests for the platform, finally, were those of Richard Nixon and Nelson Rockefeller. Both had nuncios who checked every word of the platform as it was being drafted, to be sure that the political religion of their popes was not offended. Rockefeller's people were, in my view, far and away the most nit-picking.

I am pleased to think, at this remove, that nothing Nixon or Rockefeller demanded, or that I wrote, really had any particular effect on the future of the Republic. Nixon was organized to win the nomination. Rockefeller had already made it clear he would not accept the vice-presidential spot. Why should he? Since he must have felt that he and his family damn near owned the country, why should he settle for any lesser spot on the management chart?

That is another pleasant recollection. In spite of the substantial wealth of the Rockefeller family (vastly greater than that of the Kennedy family), Nelson Rockefeller's shallows were utterly engulfed by the sheer drive and organizational thoroughness of Nixon and, later, Goldwater. And although Nelson was known to be as enthusiastic a womanizer as JFK, he could scarcely match the Camelot charisma of the Democrat.

It is hard to say where the real centers of political power lie today. In some ways, the movers and shakers seem to be the middle millionaires, the hard-pushing, cash-gushing people like the savings and loan mini-moguls, or the defense industry top managers. But as the television age has deepened, influence has become more scattered. Network anchors, handicapped only by the intense dislike they attract when their prejudices show too openly, are enormously influential. Newspaper columnists, by contrast, appeal to the really rather small intellectual community of other newspaper people, corporate philosophizers, academics, upper-level bureaucrats and militarists. That's not a bad constituency, of course. But there are greater ones just waiting to be tapped.

The Reverend Jesse Jackson was said to have tapped one with his rainbow coalition. But the most impressive that I can think of at the moment is the AM radio constituency of the talk-show host Rush Limbaugh. At this moment, in mid-1993, he claims a listenership of more than twenty million on more than six hundred radio stations, overshadowing the rainbow coalition or any other constituency outside of the major parties. What he will do with this sort of influence he is building remains to be seen.

In 1960, however, it was the White House staff, and the Nixon and Rockefeller people, who controlled the writing of the Republican platform, and the writer.

This is not to say that a ghostwriter is simply a stenographer. Far from it. The person who first drafts any statement does not set it in concrete, but does set it in a sort of thick mucilage. There is a powerful form of inertia in the process. Given a written statement, the managers and overseers first approach it planning to make changes if needed. The ghostwriter already has scored a big point. The biggies are prone to edit, not discard and start over again, unless there has been a simply outrageous departure from what was expected. Ghostwriters with any sense at all will make sure that they do not overstep that boundary. They may slant a statement. In fact they always slant a statement. But they must not try, for reasons of ego or ideology, to make it a brand-new statement. The time for arguing about fundamentals is before the writing has begun.

My bosses' biggest flap was over a Rockefeller insistence that the platform distance itself from Eisenhower's military-industrial statement and his relatively tight defense budget; the Rockefeller people insisted on a plank that would say "there should be no price tag" on American defense. They got what they wanted, a fairly open-ended defense plank.

The Eisenhower people and the eventual candidate, Richard Nixon, were placated with a ringing defense of the general's presidency.

I did not believe that I was there to espouse anything or anyone. I was there to write clear phrases where appropriate and vague ones where controversy was to be avoided. This made the job pretty plain sailing for me. But it was inevitable that when faced with a battery of memos and notes, I would pick and choose for emphasis the things that struck me, personally, as most commendable. I had no official responsibility, yet the nature of my job gave me a fair amount of power. On the other hand, the same is true, in different ways, of many of the others who connive in the construction of a national political platform.

Writing for individual politicians is a different matter. There is a terrible amount of power—far, far too much—granted to anyone who drafts statements for public figures.

It is an impressive little exercise of power to write the snippet planks that form a party platform. When it comes to writing entire speeches or articles or even books for politicians, the inertia factor gives the writer the central, if unacknowledged, role. In those cases, the client is faced with a fairly substantial hunk of wordage. A wily ghost may even insert some obviously silly stuff so that the client can have the immediate pleasure of blue-penciling something and perhaps be distracted from any more significant substance in the body of the work. But the idea of changing an entire statement, particularly when it is even a fairly accurate reflection of pre-draft talking and memos, seems to be too much for most politicians.

The most chilling part of the ghostwriting business is that it even exists in public affairs. Letting someone else do a major part of the thinking and expression for a public figure has become the accepted, even the standard, practice. Yet if politicians are not elected for what they think, for what *are* they elected? The answer has come to be that they are selected mainly for their appearance, their style of presentation, all of the familiar cosmetic features of modern politicking as entertainment.

Most people I know accept this as a fact but add that there is more to it than that. Fine. Isn't it reasonable to expect that the "more" would include some form of cerebration and contemplation on the parts of the politicians? And might we not expect that it should result in the politicians telling us what they think, in their own words rather than in ghosted simulacrums?

By the time the convention for the 1964 nomination rolled around, I was director of special projects at the American Enterprise Institute in

Washington. This time I was not loaned to the Republican Party: I was, you might say, jettisoned to it.

Protocol insisted that I could not remain on the staff at the nonpartisan AEI while writing a Republican platform, a task to which I had been invited through the impressive, if invisible, political influence of William Baroody Sr., founder of AEI. AEI was in fact at that time an equal-opportunity supplier of political wisdom. While there, I had begun writing for Barry Goldwater, who had applied to AEI for help in research—which included help in how to present that research. I had also written for Hubert H. Humphrey.

The behind-the-scenes overseers of the 1964 Republican platform still included Ed McCabe and Bryce Harlow, and also now Malcolm Moos, author of President Eisenhower's startling "military-industrial complex" speech, who represented the ex-president. The persistent Nelson Rockefeller was represented by various people, including the former editor of *Life* and a former Eisenhower speechwriter, Emmet John Hughes, who had moved on to work for the Rockefeller family. He stayed off to the side, preferring to deal with more lofty types than I.

Then there was President Eisenhower's vice president, Richard Nixon, who had retained influence but who tended to act for himself rather than through an agent. Nixon, for whom I wrote a magazine article later on, was more his own man when it came to speeches than anyone else I can remember. He really did draft them, on legal pads. Most of the ghost help he got was in the research and then in the later, cleaning-up-the-draft stages.

The main tension in the platform writing, as it would be in the nominating convention, was between the interests of Barry Goldwater and Nelson Rockefeller. It could not have escaped the notice of the Rockefeller people that the deck was stacked, with AEI dominating platform research and with me at the typewriter.

Actually, in my view, the most impressive part of the entire 1964 platform process came in a hearing of the official platform committee of the national Republican Party. The platform committee mainly is a place for people to have brief moments of show-off, sound-off prominence. When Goldwater, an obvious strong runner for the nomination, appeared, the Rockefeller people on the committee were primed to ask him questions which, they must have hoped, would show him to be a heartless cost cutter and old-fashioned conservative, perhaps even a bigot.

They were particularly sharp in their questioning about Social Security and other assistance for the elderly. Someone attempted to skewer Goldwater with a question about just who should have primary responsibility for the care of elderly people; he probably expected a hard-sounding let-them-shift-for-themselves answer. But Goldwater received the question with a puzzled expression as though he really couldn't believe that anyone would ask. His answer: "Their children, of course."

Goldwater felt that way about his own family. In fact, as I quickly learned, he always formed his strongest, often most controversial opinions on the basis of personal experience rather than ideology. I don't think most people understood this or, if they did, appreciated its profound importance. Certainly, the response to that answer, as could have been predicted given the hostility of the press, was that Goldwater was unrealistic, that he was insensitive—all of the politically correct criticism with which we are now groaningly familiar.

Oh, Barry, oh, Barry. The candor of that answer, its uncontrived sincerity, was so revealing, as were the sly attempts of the Rockefeller crowd to trap and harass him, like a bunch of bullies ganging up on Billy Budd, or Darth Vader besetting Luke Skywalker.

I am pleased to note that although writing a national political platform, let alone two, sounds impressive, the work was simply done on sand. It was transitory. It was ritualistic. Prenomination platforms are exercises in political make-work, full of sound and fury and signifying virtually nothing. They are marvelous stages for people to have their five minutes of fame showing off and sounding pompous and all-important. In the end, though, they are slender reeds for public policy determination.

Can you think of anyone except hostile columnists ever reading them after the convention has selected a nominee? More telling yet, can you think of any politician actually running on a platform, much less keeping many of its pledges, promises, and promulgations? The platform is never elected president. A person is. And what that person will do as president has little or nothing to do with the party platform.

13

Goldwater

I must remind you, lords, senators, that extreme patriotism in the defense of freedom is no crime. And let me respectfully remind you that pusillanimity in the pursuit of justice is no virtue in a Roman.

—Cicero

Politics, to the conceivers of its ideal form, is mutually tolerant compromise among diverse peoples. American politics has strayed sadly far from that Jeffersonian ideal.

Politics has become sheer power. Power over people. Power to *be* over people. Politics, in the ringing phrase of the *Critical Studies* lawyers at Harvard, decides who gets what. There may be democracy aplenty in this new politics. There is little liberty. Small room for diversity. Less and less tolerance in a politics of correctness and cultural ghettoization.

Most people have at least begun to realize this after decades of wrongheaded schoolbooks teaching that politicians are public servants. A Nobel Prize has been awarded to an economist who has proposed that politicians by and large make their decisions on the basis of what will benefit *them,* not the public. Politicians are not servants. They are masters. Politicians make law and law is the way to say who gets what in a mixed economy.

In twenty years of working with many of the most important politi-

167

cians of our time, I found only one man who was an exception to that rule. So far as I know, after working with him as closely as anyone could, I can honestly say that Barry Goldwater is wholly unaffected by power. He has not lusted after it. He has never succumbed to its temptations.

The public seems to have come to understand that, among politicians, there really is something special about Barry Goldwater. I think that the explanation of what some call his honesty, others his naturalness, is that special relationship he has had to power. He has had some sort of real power his entire life but he has never let it become the focus or purpose of his life.

When he was young, going to work in his father's department store, he did not choose the glamour and power of administration. He flew goods out into the Indian areas. He traded the way his frontier ancestors must have. He liked to do things, not just have things.

In the Arizona National Guard, he ignored the don't-tread-on-any-toes treadmill of military success. He helped desegregate the guard, a toe-stepping adventure if ever there was one. In the Second World War, he didn't try for a deferment or a cushy job of the sort many sons of wealthy families received. He flew as an ordinary ferry pilot, taking planes across oceans and mountains, always under the risk of enemy attack.

I started working with Senator Goldwater about a year before his nomination as the 1964 presidential candidate of the Republican Party. I worked with him as a writer and researcher. I was with him when he was nominated. And, during the presidential attempt itself, I sat with him in the campaign plane every day of the entire unsuccessful trip toward the White House.

We became very close friends then. We remain friends, separated only by distance, today.

And here are some of the very vivid recollections I have of this fine man and good friend.

Prior to the beginning of the 1964 presidential campaign, Senator Goldwater was speaking to Sen. John Tower of Texas. Senator Goldwater suggested that he and I might rent a small jet and just fly from town to town, talking about the issues, meeting people, barnstorming, like a pair of old-time pilots. Senator Tower, of course, passed it off as a joke. But we talked about it and might well have done it. We did not because Senator Goldwater felt a strong responsibility to the Republican Party; he recognized that an important part of his campaign would be to strengthen the entire party organization. Thus, he submitted to a conventional campaign, with the party organization fully involved—hoopla, hurrahs, and four-ring campaign stops. Still, I know what the senator would have preferred: to fly his own plane, to fly his own campaign.

There were moments to remind me of this throughout the campaign. For example, the senator was always opposed to motorcycle escorts from the airport into town. He kept asking why we couldn't just go by cab or limousine like other people. He was never comfortable with the pomp of politics. And he had one other reason for hating motorcycle escorts: He was always afraid that someone might be hurt in one of the noisy, fast cavalcades. He never felt that his getting somewhere on time was worth risking someone else's life.

There was the matter of going to church. As the presidential campaign got underway, the public relations people began planning all of the conventional coverage of the candidate. One of the hoariest of campaign conventions is the coverage of the candidate attending church.

Senator Goldwater has a deeply held, personal religious faith. He doesn't talk about it. He doesn't argue about it. He doesn't use it to score political points. He just has it. And he does not attend church on any regular basis. So, when asked to go to church so that the photographers could snap him, he simply said no. He didn't go. If he had been as eager for the presidency as was, for instance, Lyndon Johnson, he would have gone everywhere, done anything. Not being willing to do so, he lost.

If there is a lesson in that, it is not a comforting one.

Then there was the matter of the Texas tax threat. Campaigning in Texas, the senator received a phone call from an until-then staunch supporter. The supporter was distraught. He was going to have to host a gala dinner for Johnson's running mate, Hubert Humphrey. Almost in tears, he explained that the president of the United States had just phoned him. He said he had several years' worth of the man's tax returns in front of him and that they made most interesting reading. Then he directed him to have the dinner for Humphrey. The supporter told the senator that he just couldn't afford the sort of extensive tax audit he had been threatened with.

Had Goldwater lusted after power, he could have turned that sorry story into a major campaign issue. He never considered it. He had listened to a friend in confidence and he would keep what he heard in confidence. The friendship was more important than the power.

It was his very personal view of politics that left the senator more baffled than angry when Nelson Rockefeller harshly denounced him after a long conference in the senator's Washington apartment. During the meeting, Rockefeller had said over and over that he understood what the senator stood for and was sympathetic to it. After the meeting, in the hallway of the apartment building, Rockefeller was set upon by a dozen newsmen. Without a twitch, he told them that he had listened to everything Goldwater had said, that he didn't understand most of it, and that he disagreed with the parts he *did* understand.

Rockefeller's reaction to the senator's speech accepting the nomination was as ill spirited. One phrase from that speech has echoed over time to define for many people the entire Republican presidential campaign of that year. At the time, the Rockefeller people worked hard to turn it against Goldwater. Yet, though the phrase is a bombshell of phrasing, it is not explosive in content: "Extremism in the defense of liberty is no vice. Moderation in the pursuit of justice is no virtue."

The wording itself was buried in a long letter written to me by Harry Jaffa, known then as a historian of the Lincoln period, now a professor at Claremont State College in California. He later said that he had gotten the phrase from a Lincoln speech. The novelist Taylor Caldwell said she had traced it to Roman antiquity. I had the opportunity to make it famous in the acceptance speech, which I wrote for the senator. There are parts of that speech that should have received the attention of the "Extremism" statement. Alas, they were not aphoristically memorable. A major part of the speech, for instance, was devoted to a vision in which young people currently inspired by movie stars and athletes would become inspired, instead, by engineers building bridges across uncrossable chasms, by researchers cracking the ancient mysteries of disease, by scientists looking to and past the frontiers of the solar system.

But "Extremism" caught the ears and grabbed the spotlight. Extremism in the pursuit of liberty is no vice. Moderation in the pursuit of justice is no virtue. People had been calling Goldwater an extremist from the beginning of his campaign for the nomination. He wanted to say clearly just what sort of an extremist he actually was.

A powerful expansion on the extremism theme came shortly after Goldwater's acceptance speech, during a debate at Oxford University, when Malcolm X said: "My reason for believing in extremism—intelligently directed extremism, extremism in defense of liberty, extremism in quest of justice—is because I firmly believe in my heart that the day that the black man takes an uncompromising step and realizes that he's within his rights, when his own freedom is being jeopardized, to use any means necessary to bring about his freedom or put a halt to that injustice, I don't think he'll be by himself." Goldwater himself had earnestly, if clumsily, tried to explain "extremism" by saying that the Allied invasion of Europe on D-Day was certainly extremism in the defense of liberty.

Extremism in the pursuit of liberty is no vice. Moderation in the pursuit of justice is no virtue. Think about it.

The mean-spirited nature of the Rockefeller campaign against the senator before, during, and after his nomination can be illustrated by two incidents. One involved Social Security. A headline in a New England newspaper said something to the effect that "Goldwater Would Abolish Social Security." Nowhere in the story, however, was there a single quotation, citation, or observation to back up the headline. The story was about the senator's familiar, proven charges about the actuarial flimsiness of the system. The headline writer simply gave it the headline which, I suppose, he thought would most harm the senator. Our staff did some digging afterwards and discovered that subsequently the headline writer had been hired to work on some Rockefeller enterprise or other.

The other incident was a brief one in New York City, where the senator was changing planes during the campaign for the nomination. His presence attracted a crowd and the usual TV cameras. There was one fellow whose enthusiasm for the senator was most unfortunate. He kept shouting appalling sentiments, such as his hope that Goldwater would put "them niggers" in their place. His shouted comments were so obnoxious that I shoved through the crowd to his side and asked him to shut up. Seemingly dismayed, he did. I was curious as to who he might be. Was he just a bigot on the loose? Not at all. As a sharp-eyed New Yorker working for Goldwater pointed out, he was a state legislator, a Democrat, and, as it turned out, a Rockefeller supporter.

There was only one time I can recall when the senator actually felt he'd taken a low blow at Rockefeller, and that was in private. Rockefeller had divorced his wife of many years and remarried a younger woman. They had a child. In 1964, this was not a pleasant family portrait for a candidate for the presidential nomination. Goldwater made nothing of it publicly but, once, when meeting with Rockefeller, he started the amenities by saying, "Well, how's the kid?" Goldwater felt that really was unfair, and he never repeated it. Talk about Billy Budd in politics!

Then there was the matter of race riots—this time nothing to do with Rockefeller, but instigated by some of our own supporters.

Early in the campaign, word came to the senator that some hotheads actually were planning to foment race riots in the hope that they would swing voters toward the hard law-and-order line of the Republicans.

Here's a tricky question: How can a candidate control such crazies? They are there in both parties, surely. (As pointed out above, one New York Democrat, from the state assembly, followed us around for a while shouting really vile racist slogans from the crowd, while seeming to support Goldwater, in order to make it appear that the senator had wild-eyed racist supporters. Could the Democrats control him?)

The fact the senator had to face was that the race-riot crazies were truly loose cannons, working on their own and subject to no one's control. The senator could have gone public with the story, getting off the hook should anything terrible happen. But he wasn't looking for an excuse and he wasn't looking for a headline. He was looking to stop violence. And he did.

The day after hearing about the loony race-riot scheme, he called in a reporter from a major daily newspaper and gave him an exclusive interview. Generally, it just concerned the senator's analysis of the campaign to that point. But at the end of it, as though it were an afterthought, he handed the reporter an irresistible and exclusive piece of information. If during the course of his campaign, the senator said, there should be any racial violence that could be attributed to it, he would resign his candidacy immediately. He had removed, with one skillful and heartfelt promise, every motive that the crazies could have had for their lunatic scheme. He didn't score any political points with that at all. He didn't advance or improve his power at all. He just did what he felt was right. That was totally typical of my friend, my dear friend from Arizona.

I recall also a campaign trip to Philadelphia, one on which my older son accompanied me, that revealed the profound decency of the man. In the afternoon before the senator's appearance, there was a briefing to review a television ad that supporters had put together to exploit the ever-present, always popular issue of moral decline in America. It was the sort of slimy, self-righteous imagery that has come to dominate American politics today. It showed topless (but appropriately censored) women at a public beach and had the stern voice-over, holier-than-thou condemnation of the country's slide into moral decay. Before a word could be said, the senator turned to my son—then sixteen years old—and asked his opinion. Young Karl said the ad was silly, had nothing to do with the ideas of the campaign, and was dirty politics to boot. Goldwater agreed. That was it; the ad was pulled, and the campaign stuck to the high ground of principles and substantive issues.

There are two incidents involving aircraft that should be mentioned in my account of the Goldwater campaign. In the first, the senator had casually suggested to the pilot of our luxurious chartered jet by way of a joke that he make a high-speed run back and down the runway after taking off. He didn't mention it to anyone else, including me. The way the plane was set up, the senator and I sat together in the front seats of what otherwise would be the first-class section. Other campaign people such as Denny Kitchel, the manager, had seats there too. Beyond the first-class partition, in rows of triple seats, were seated the traveling press.

After takeoff, from somewhere in Pennsylvania as I recall, the pilot did a very quick backward turn, and headed almost straight down toward the ground. The shrieks and blubberings from the press section were alarming. Some of the reporters actually seemed to be praying. Goldwater, looking through the window, absolutely unconcerned, made me want to follow suit. Suppose we did crash? It had been a good ride so far. As it was, of course, the pilot straightened out just above hangar height, roared down the runway path and then roared up again to his assigned flight pattern.

Afterward, it took all of the senator's best efforts to keep the pilot from losing his license. He probably should have warned the press in advance—but then they never warned him when they were about to make high-speed runs through his campaign.

The other incident was probably more frightening than the runway one, except that nobody but the senator and I and a hired pilot knew about it. We had chartered a modernized DC-3 to fly to Manhattan for a meeting. As we moved toward the runway at Washington National Airport, Senator Goldwater suggested that I sit up beside the pilot. I accepted the invitation eagerly. When we got to the runway itself, the pilot jumped out of his seat and, with Goldwater shouting encouragement, insisted, "Go ahead, take it off. It'll damn near fly itself if you let it." Having long admired the DC-3 and even written encomiums to its aeronautical virtues, I was delighted and off we went. It actually seemed easier than taking off in the many smaller aircraft that I had piloted.

Happy as a hog in wallow, I got the compass headings and assigned altitudes for New York and proceeded to fly us there—or almost. As we approached the traffic control area for New York, even I realized that it would be imprudent to go any farther. I left the controls, walked back to where the senator and the pilot were sitting, and said that if one of them didn't take over we would certainly have a chance to see how well and how long the lovely aircraft could shift for itself. The pilot's response was prudent and quick and the meeting in New York went fine, although its subject matter has long since been outshone in my memory by the wonder of piloting that great plane.

The election itself finally caught up with us. I had thought, seeing the huge and wildly enthusiastic crowds that showed up for every Goldwater rally, that there must be an enormous number of Americans just itching to vote for the senator. Looking back, it seems apparent now that the huge crowds, the chants, the adoration, were the entire picture. There simply was little depth of voting beyond the true believers, the already converted.

Polling after the election indicated that the issue that Johnson had most successfully pressed against Goldwater was Social Security. What Goldwater actually had said about Social Security was that it had become dangerously insecure in its financing, that too much of its money was in use as loans to various parts of the federal budget deficit. It was his recommendation that the entire system be made sound by permitting people to substitute private pension systems (yielding far higher returns), retaining the federal role in Social Security strictly as a safety net for those who could not obtain private insurance. All of his warnings about the Social Security system have been proven to be accurate and substantial. Reformers are still trying to figure out how to make the system sound. But back in the '60s, Goldwater, the messenger, was shot for bringing the message.

The matter of nuclear war was second to the Social Security issue in moving people to vote for Johnson, according to the polls. Goldwater had been cruelly maligned in a TV commercial showing a little girl plucking petals from a flower as a voice intoned "Ten, nine, eight . . ." until an atomic explosion obliterated everything. The voice-over made it clear that a vote for Goldwater was a vote for just such obliteration. The commercial was designed, we are told, by that now-lovable TV personality, Bill Moyers. Shame.

What Goldwater had said about nuclear weapons was (1) that they had never been tested under battlefield conditions, (2) that field commanders in Europe should have the discretionary power to use tactical nuclear weapons if being overrun by a Soviet invasion, and (3) that although the warheads had not been sufficiently tested, the inertial guidance systems of some of the missiles themselves were good enough to "lob one into the men's room at the Kremlin." Rather than dispute the technical point (which was admittedly shaky, given the other charge about no battlefield-condition testing), the press overwhelmingly chose to play the statement as saying that Goldwater *wanted* to lob one into the Kremlin men's room.

The minor flap about Goldwater wanting to sell the Tennessee Valley Authority was just another big media lie. What he had suggested was divestiture of the system from the *federal* government. It should be offered first, he said, to the states where it operated. After that, if the states didn't want it, it should be offered to the communities where it operated facilities and then, and only then, to private companies.

On election night there was the usual returns-watching party at the Goldwater home in Paradise Valley, just outside of Phoenix. Almost everyone there seemed reconciled to the fact that we weren't going to win. I still clung to the notion that voters would, at the last moment, in some resurgence of American thoughtfulness, recognize the quality in Goldwater and the con-man in Johnson and vote accordingly. Perhaps they did. Perhaps they wanted someone who would billow out the public money and not someone who would pull it back and protect it. It really is tough to run against Santa Claus.

As the evening ended there was a good deal of weeping and wailing, literally. The senator seemed absolutely unperturbed, perhaps relieved, epitomizing the power-and-personality problem. People driven to rule, people such as Lyndon Johnson, are the ones least to be trusted with power. Governed by ambition and pride, they are absolutely not to be counted on for prudence, thoughtfulness, or restraint. But it is the lust and the ambition that make them indomitable campaigners. And in any case, people do not seem to vote for ideas at all any more, but only for personalities.

What *were* the great ideas of the last several presidential campaigns? Dukakis, for instance, was not defeated because he offered no inspiring ideas, though he didn't. He was defeated because he is drab.

Bush called Reaganomics voodoo economics when contesting Reagan for the nomination. By the time Bush was seeking the nomination again, Reagan was a personality-cult hero, and his economic policies had led to an extended prosperity which Bush opportunistically embraced until, finally elected, he began tossing key elements overboard to reestablish federal hegemony over the economy and to prepare for a war which made Reagan's adventure in Grenada look like a high-school dance.

Isn't it odd that millions of people, probably including some of the most competent people on earth, will vote quadrennially for people who tell them, right to their faces, that they, the campaigners, are uniquely qualified to tell all 250 or so million of us how to run our lives, spend our money, organize our businesses, regulate our commerce, relate to other peoples in other lands, and even how and when to go off to kill some of those people? It is, as the king of Siam says in the musical, "a puzzlement."

The day after the election, Barry Goldwater started building a color television set which was still working when last I visited him in Paradise Valley. During the campaign, the senator had gone to special pains to dig out some old equipment and have it shipped to my older son, Karl Jr., who had gotten his amateur radio operator's license when he was twelve years old. It was another indication of what mattered to the senator—things like kindness and friendship.

The senator's own amateur radio activities revealed another facet of the man. In a long story on the closing, after forty-five years, of the Heathkit build-it-yourself line of electronic kits, the *New York Times* quoted the senator as saying: "It's just that people today are getting terribly lazy, and they don't like to do anything they can pay someone else to do. . . . I think the current generation is certainly missing out." The senator was eighty-three, and just remarried, when he said that. During the forty-five years before, he had flown his own plane about twice yearly to Heathkit headquarters in Benton Harbor, Michigan, to buy kits. By the time the company went out of business, the senator had built a hundred.

After the election, a defeat of some magnitude, you may recall, there was a brief time when the future of the Republican Party seemed balanced on whether Dean Burch, a longtime Goldwater associate, would remain as chairman of the Republican National Committee. I have never heard a convincing argument one way or the other as to whether Dean could have stayed. I've always felt he could, that despite the Goldwater defeat, there was sufficient internal party support for the senator and his people to keep them in place. But the fact was that Dean seemed to want to get out of the job and its pressures and to return to his law practice in Arizona. His new wife certainly supported the move.

And so Dean left (though he would return later, in the Nixon administration, as the assistant to the president in charge of liaison with the Congress). The party was turned over to people who were determined to compensate for the election defeat by distancing the party from it and from its perpetrator. It was not until Ronald Reagan's ascendence that a more Goldwaterite attitude and crew took the party over again—a shift that might not have been possible without the groundwork laid by the senator.

With Dean gone, the bars clanked down at the National Committee. Anyone retaining an open loyalty to Goldwater and unwilling virtually to denounce him was on the outside. Which is just where I found myself. Again.

I was not outside on the Goldwater camp, however. William Baroody, founder of the American Enterprise Institute and a major player in the Goldwater campaign, arranged for Tony Smith, Goldwater's press secretary, and me to have an office together where Tony could work for the senator-in-exile and I could write a book about the campaign (*In a Cause That Will Triumph*, Doubleday, 1967). We were supported by funds from a few other die-hard Goldwaterites such as Roger Milliken, who, as a great patron of the arts, I also approached later on for assistance when I began to do metal sculpture. He only supported the work of dead artists, however, and I had to make it on my own. It turned out to be a good experience which I will discuss later on.

Along with working on the book, I began to write a newspaper column whose proceeds the senator generously gave to me. I am sure that there are some close to him who regret that the support went largely to subsidize my association with the New Left, to pay alimony, and to become a hippie—things also covered separately later on.

By 1968, Goldwater had decided to run again for the Senate. That meant the end of the column but not the end of our association. Despite the fact that members of the Goldwater staff were convinced that I had become a longhaired, bearded, dope-smoking, acid-freak hippie and a New Leftist besides, Goldwater wanted me to write speeches for the Senate campaign.

He was certainly following my old dictum that ideology should never get in the way of a good friendship. The fact was, as much as the staff found it hard to believe, that my own ideology had not shifted much, if any. I had, indeed, gone from considering myself a conservative to thinking of myself as a libertarian, or anarchist; but then I had previously thought that there was a place for libertarians on the conservative side. Bill

Buckley listened attentively to and provided magazine space for one of the most hard-line libertarians of all, Frank Chodorov. Goldwater himself reflected many libertarian points of view—his stand against conscription, his tacit disapproval of laws against victimless crimes, such as pot smoking. Dean Burch, who once again was running the Goldwater campaign, has strongly, as an attorney, defended violators of antidrug laws.

I recall Goldwater saying that he never could understand the anti-marijuana law since cowboys in Arizona, before the Harrison Narcotics Act, smoked it regularly and were never more peaceable than when they were doing it. We never discussed the harsher narcotics such as heroin and cocaine since neither of us was interested in using them.

At any rate, when I got the call to come back to Arizona to write speeches, it was made clear that I was to do it in a clandestine manner, with no publicity and complete anonymity. In fact, I had been registered at a motel, away from the campaign offices, under an assumed name.

Daily, Dean Burch sent a topic or two over to the motel and by day's end would have someone pick up the copy. We spoke by phone if there were nuances to be noted. Otherwise, I remained completely detached from the campaign except for frequent secret trips up to the senator's house and except for a weekend quail-hunting trip with the senator's sons, Mike and Barry Junior.

One weekend, I was invited to stay at the senator's house, occupying the lovely guest house by the swimming pool. The same building also housed the senator's impressive amateur radio studio, one of the most complete and powerful ones in the nation. Thoughtful friends had provided me with a block of hashish that looked ever so much like a giant Hershey bar. So I was relaxed even if anonymous. The senator, coming into the pool house one day, smelled the fragrance of hashish smoke and, smiling, said "I recognize that." It was then that he explained the popularity of marijuana and its derivatives among old-time Arizona cowboys. He never mentioned having smoked any himself. Whiskey was his drug.

One of the speeches that I wrote during the campaign was delivered by the senator at Arizona State University, in Tempe. I wrote it following a long discussion with the senator about Students for a Democratic Society, the most publicized of New Left groups. During that discussion, I read aloud the part of SDS's founding Port Huron statement dealing with foreign policy. To the senator, and to me, it sounded brilliantly iso-lationist, in the Taft mold. The senator's reaction was that it could have been written for Young Americans for Freedom, the foremost right-wing youth group. I explained that it really couldn't have, because YAF was deeply committed to the expansion of the American empire through military power. Now Goldwater was as interested as anyone in the strength of his country and was delighted when its influence spread. He deeply felt, however, that this influence should and would be spread through the impact of American culture and commerce, not troops. The collapse of Communism under the pressure of exactly those things has certainly proved his point.

I had also described to the senator that there were very distinct factions developing in SDS, including the anarchistic or libertarian, Midwest or Prairie Power faction. We discussed the difference between the laissez-faire attitudes of libertarianism and the classically-liberal economic but culturally orthodox attitudes of conservatism.

The senator's Arizona State speech opened with the phrase: "I have much in common with the anarchist wing of Students for a Democratic Society." Surely there are ears still ringing with disbelief about that one. But it's a fact.

Incidentally, the first members of the Weatherman faction of SDS whom I met had been Youth for Goldwater leaders previously. Where else could they go? Many had been drawn to Goldwater because of his clearly radical opposition to pervasive government, even his potential to become a fervent anti-imperialist, given his strong belief that we could oppose Communism more effectively with culture and commerce than with guns. There was nothing so basic, so radical offered by Democrats or by other Republicans.

There was only one difficulty for me in writing speeches for the senator at that time. I made it a provision that I wouldn't write anything specifically supporting the Indo-Chinese war or "law and order" in any sense that included crackdowns on culture or art or on the free flow of information. It worked out.

Later, after the senator's shoo-in reelection to the Senate, my wife, Therese, and I were part of a demonstration that included a sit-down outside the Senate chambers. It was a star-studded event, with a few Hollywood celebrities; many authors, including Gary Wills; the producer Joseph Papp; and the author of a famed computer language, a fellow named Iverson.

While we sat on the floor outside the Senate chambers, waiting to be formally arrested and taken outside for curbside booking, several people with whom I had worked as a Republican came by. One, Strom Thurmond, simply growled at the seated crowd. Another, Jerry Ford, actually stopped to say hello and argue earnestly about the justifications for the war. Ford is such a decent fellow that it is no wonder people find only his clumsy golf strokes to ridicule. As a president he was gracious, humble, and very conscientious.

And then Senator Goldwater came by. He asked one of the protesters, the professorial Robert Jay Lifton, whether Karl Hess was among the huddled mass. Lifton pointed to Therese and me and Goldwater came over to chat. He observed that he would have been disappointed had I not been there. He didn't defend the war but, instead, mused on the possibility that this could be the last bloody adventure of its sort. George Bush proved him technically wrong on that one; but, in the truly long run, in the genera of Vietnam-type wars, he may be as correct in this prophecy as he has been in so many others.

A good example of Goldwater's commonsense insight has proven to be his redefinition of the idea of convergence. The orthodox view was that the Soviet Union and the United States would move slowly together and converge at some point of mutual reliance and security. Goldwater, in a paper prepared for the command and staff school of the air force, argued differently. In his view, the two superpower competitors would indeed move together. But rather than stopping at a point of convergence, they would continue to move past each other until Russia became a free society while America, inextricably yoked to the vast expansion of its apparatchiks in the federal and state bureaucracies, would move past freedom and toward a culturally hidebound, economically overregulated society.

Each day, as the socialist structures crumble in the former Soviet Union, new federal regulations covering everything from financial privacy to land use to racketeering statutes which can be used against any person offending a district attorney make Goldwater's prediction seem solidly prophetic.

Even in the administration of Ronald Reagan, a Goldwater manque, there was evidence of this inexorable crawl. Many new security and secrecy regulations were put into place, many economic privacy laws were done away with, and various anti-organized crime laws were enacted which soon came to be employed not against mobsters but against any economic targets the avid sin-seekers could spot.

It now is difficult to imagine a president of the United States actually turning back federal power. Goldwater, if elected, would have tried. He wrote to me some years back that "I am more of a Jeffersonian than a Republican or anything else. In fact, I think he was one of the greatest men who lived in America. If we could pay more attention to his preachments and his philosophy, I think the country would be a lot better off." I agree, and I know Goldwater would have tried, but I suspect little would have changed—a sad reflection that is even truer today. With about half of the entire population receiving some sort of economic transfer benefits from the federal establishment, the constituency for liberty is under serious siege, at the very least.

One of the great mistakes made by Senator Goldwater as well as many other conservatives, it seems to me, was to suppose that simply devolving power to the individual states would create a barrier against the creeping inflation of federal power. One of the few long-running arguments that I had with Senator Goldwater concerned his faith in that proposition and my skepticism about it.

The truth, still emerging, seems to be that the individual states do not want to get away from the federal teat. They want it to nourish them. The optimistic view says that experimentation and variety are possible in the fifty states in a way they are not in the unitary federal government. But that's a fading optimism. Most of the federal grants that the states so avidly seek come accompanied by federal guidelines.

If there is optimism, it is to be found, I believe, in contemplating the refusenik attitude of more and more Americans who withdraw as much as possible from involvement with large units of government and devote their energies to reenergizing local institutions, right down to the neighborhood level. Local democracy, town-meeting-style, may still be possible. And its practice would encourage the return of liberty, rather than command, as a national goal.

If that ever happens, Barry Goldwater will have contributed mightily to the triumph of the cause.

14

New Left

On such a basis do we offer this document of our convictions and analyses . . . rooted in the ancient, still unfulfilled conception of man attaining determining influence over his circumstances of life.
—Introduction, Port Huron Statement

When I left the Republican Party, after the Goldwater defeat, I was contacted by Marc Raskin and Richard Barnet, codirectors of the Institute for Policy Studies. The Institute was then characterized as the foremost New Left think tank. Raskin and Barnet invited me to hold a seminar on what they viewed as some radical aspects of the Goldwater campaign, thus proving themselves more perceptive than most of the journalists covering the campaign. Almost every journalist had condemned Goldwater for terminal conservatism with never a discussion of the radical aspects which Raskin and Barnet could so clearly see.

It was they, not the oddly incurious press, who understood that Goldwater had very little support from big business, that his insistence on competition as indispensable to a free market had scared the huge corporations. These giants of free enterprise had become addicted over the years to collusion with the government and to the sheltering protection of government regulations which hampered market entry and produced excessive restrictions against innovative products. Too many of them

183

were used to government's helping hand in what amounted to welfare programs disguised as redundant and unquestioned defense appropriations. Goldwater was suspicious of all that. He did not feel that a corporation should be subsidized with funds coerced from working people—any more than he believed that an artist or a scholar or a farmer should be. The support of big business flowed naturally to Lyndon Johnson, who knew how to wheel and deal with corporations that felt they had the right to be treated as virtually a fourth branch of government.

The people at IPS also knew how deeply skeptical Goldwater had been of the Kennedy-Johnson war in Indochina. These New Leftists, and not the press, understood the significance of his calling Kennedy on the great lie that there were no U.S. combat troops in Vietnam. (Goldwater once asked that I check on what decorations were being awarded soldiers in Vietnam. It was revealing: Hundreds of combat decorations had been handed out for a military maneuver that was supposed to be absolutely noncombative.)

It was the people at IPS, not the liberal press with their eyes screwed tightly into their prejudices, who could see the significance of Senator Goldwater's very first (very first!) campaign pledge: to end the draft, the draft that made the Vietnamese adventure possible.

And it was even the folk at IPS who listened carefully when Goldwater advocated selling TVA—to the states where its facilities were located, or to local communities, or, if none of them wanted it, to auction it publicly—anything to get it out of government and into the marketplace where its work could be effectively assessed.

Years later, it was a friend at IPS who enthusiastically called my attention to the fact that Ronald Reagan had devoted three of the syndicated radio broadcasts he made prior to the presidential campaign to a plan to end the federal welfare system by letting neighborhoods take over the task. The final payments of welfare fund money would go to those neighborhoods that were able to create local enterprises which would absorb the employable poor—a fair version of many New Left proposals.

The moderate IPS people such as Raskin and Barnet, not the Utopian Marxist sloganeers at the Institute, understood that there had been an Old Right in this country—a faction that was isolationist in foreign policy and supportive of competition rather than privilege in business. I was welcomed to the Institute by at least those two as a representative of that Old Right who could engage in fruitful dialogue with the New Left.

At the same time, I had run into several laissez-faire capitalist economists and historians, notably Murray Rothbard and Leonard Liggio. An article by Rothbard in the left-wing *Ramparts* magazine, in particular, was an ideological eye-opener. It described anarchism, a position well to the right of Right and well to the left of Left. I had never really thought about or known much about anarchism (or libertarianism), but reading about it made me think that I had been one all along. So, I wrote to Rothbard and he generously invited me to come to New York, stay in his apartment, and join the nightly get-togethers of what then seemed to be the entire libertarian anarchist movement.

My first night with the New York anarchists was an epiphany. It was classical salon, a roomful of a dozen or so extraordinarily bright and witty men and women united by enthusiasm for liberty. There was only one difficulty. They never slept, at least not at night. The usual schedule for this engaging bunch was to sit and talk, laugh, analyze, make outrageous proposals for the abolition of public policy, occasionally play a game of Risk, go out around 2 A.M. for a gnosh, then back to talk until dawn.

All-night movie-going was also a passion of the group, and the weirder the film the better. *Invasion of the Body Snatchers* was the runaway favorite thanks to Rothbard's straight-faced, brilliantly funny interpretations of the film in which the invading pea-pod people were loudly applauded as an oppressed minority finally squaring things up after all these years. Sometimes the films were unbearably boorish, and in one instance so bad that we rose in revolt, stopped the projector, delivered a few harangues on the stage, collected rain checks for the next film, and then went our merry way.

It was from this group and in this crazy, abandoned milieu that I learned, with great excitement, about a grand tradition in this country that seemed to fill in all the places where the Republican Party was looking so weak: deregulation, the withdrawal of subsidies to business and agriculture, and voluntarism to replace such coercions as conscription. That tradition, of course, was anarchism: not the anarchy of regicides in Europe, but the anarchism of, for instance, Dorothy Day's Christian communes, and of laissez-faire capitalism and human association based on voluntary agreement and absolute individual responsibility.

Anarcho-syndicalists and other left-wing anarchists, naturally, gag at the notion that any form of capitalism could fit into a free society. But most of them are decent enough to admit that people should be free to make choices other than those that the syndicalists prefer—so long as they do not use force in the process. Thus, or so it seems to me, they will have to accept the embarrassing but inevitable option of free markets, property rights, and capitalist, or private, ownership of the means of production. And as strange as it may sound to anyone steeped in images of anarchy as a lawless and violent force, the voluntaristic society envisioned by the American anarchists that I met seemed like a Jeffersonian or classical liberal dream come true.

It was with all these ideas roiling in my mind that I entered into debates at IPS with a real-life Communist, Alfred Henley. I have forgotten how we got started on the debate series, but once we had decided to do it, the institute's publicity drew a faithful and interested audience of several dozen people over two or three months of weekly sessions. The idea was to argue out the differences between the Communist ideal of revolution and the anarchist.

Anarchists have been arguing against Communists since the nineteenth century. The argument always has centered on a familiar question: Should we seek freedom, with all its risks, or a centrally planned society, with all of its assurances of efficiency? But the idea of an erstwhile prominent Republican taking the anarchist side was enough of a novelty to bring people to the meetings despite the expected familiarity of the positions.

It all went as could be expected. Henley inveighed against racism, colonialism, and capitalism, all of them to be dealt with by revolution right around the corner. To counter, I proposed liberty—my arguments perhaps initially not very exciting compared to the revolutionary rhetoric that an educated Communist could bring to bear. And Henley was not only well educated in ideology, he was a true believer and one with a good deal of personal appeal.

He was small, trim, white-haired, sharp as a tack, and quite polite in his eloquent attacks on my position. He made only one mistake—but that single one won the day for me. He misjudged his audience. He misjudged the New Left just as badly as did the FBI and the Republican right wing.

He made his mistake when he said, somberly, that I would "never understand revolution until you have had to order an execution." I'll never forget that moment of brilliant clarification. That's exactly what Communism was about. Killing people. I didn't even have to make the point. Most of the young people in the meeting were not only New Lefties, they were hippies. The idea of executions was probably the only thing that could have chilled them even more than my occasional references to property rights as a basis for freedom. (Another moment of clarification came in an IPS seminar where Saul Landau, the filmmaker, then an IPS fellow and devout Marxist, seriously explained how the world *should* behave. I asked him how in the world a person could acquire such wisdom as to tell three billion other people, with historically noteworthy differences and preferences, how to live their lives. Landau replied, still seriously, that it was nothing mysterious; it was a science, Marxism-Leninism.)

I don't expect that I gained many converts to free-market capitalism or anarcho-capitalism, as some call laissez-faire capitalism. But I know that Henley didn't make any converts either. Eschewing both his collectivist ideals and my libertarian ones, most of the people who attended the debates seemed to have settled on positions which were like but predated the Green Movement, based on a hazily pretty hope that people could live together voluntarily but purged of desires to compete, to own, to fiddle with nature, or to go to the stars.

Just a few more words about Henley and his gentle, lovely wife. Henley, who boasted that he once had been bawled out by Stalin personally, was an optical scientist. As the result of good work and the acquisition thereby of some patents, he was moderately well-to-do, certainly to the country club level— a bourgeois temptation that I'm sure never even crossed his mind. He did, however, live in a lovely home in an upper-middle-class bourgeois neighborhood in Washington. I attended several cocktail parties there with many ordinary-seeming middle-class people (surely they couldn't all be Communists!).

It was at one of these parties that Mrs. Henley made an extraordinary suggestion. Knowing that my wife, Therese, was a skilled editor, she wondered whether Therese might be interested in working on the magazine *Russia Today*, the official domestic house organ of the Soviet Embassy. Without betraying the real shock that the idea was to us, we tried to pass it off as just cocktail chitchat: Therese said, "How nice of you to ask. . . . I'm really quite busy," etc.

I've wondered ever since, however, whether the suggestion was altogether innocent or a planned temptation. If Therese had followed through on the offer, or even gone to visit at the magazine offices, it could have suggested the real possibility that we were involved with the Left for reasons other than my own indiscriminate political curiosity. Perhaps we were counterintelligence agents!

As I came to expect, the FBI got it all screwed up. In material I later obtained under the Freedom of Information Act, they noted that I had *collaborated* with a Communist in a series of seminars. That, of course, made me at least a Communist sympathizer. On the other hand, the FBI also got the color of my eyes wrong, suggesting that their snoops never looked at me straight in the eyes. And, as I mentioned earlier, they listed Therese, my Wisconsin wife from a Czech-German background, as a Spanish woman named Theresa.

One of the bruited-about explanations for my move to the New Left was that I was a government agent of some sort. The most terrible explanation was that I had simply become a modern liberal. I would have preferred being explained as having been landed from a Chinese submarine. Liberal. Ugh.

Actually, several government investigative agencies were interested in what I was doing. The CIA had an impressive number of pages with my name on them but mostly censored-out blank spaces below. Under the Freedom of Information Act you can, indeed, get a lot of material, but the agency from which the material is being sought has considerable latitude in deciding what can, for national security reasons, be blanked out. I was surprised to get any CIA material at all, having long heard that they didn't do domestic investigations. Another myth exploded. Oh, my.

The most ingenious part of the FBI's surveillance as I began working with people on the New Left was the assignment of a really likable truck driver, Joe Barrett, to make friends with me and to keep tabs on me. Joe turned up for the Hess-Henley debates and hung around after one of them to talk and to express strong agreement with my position. There didn't seem to be anything that he wasn't willing to do to help me. Drive me around, get carry-out meals, all manner of really friendly things.

One ride that he gave me was to a meeting in nearby Virginia, where I addressed a group of students preparing for various law-enforcement careers. Law enforcement? Yes, they were interested in my description of just exactly what the New Left represented. Was it open and honest? Was it part of the Great Red Plot? I gave them my best "open and honest answer," arguing that the New Left was as opposed to the authoritarianism of the Old Left as they were. That was my belief then; with some modifications, it remains my belief regarding the New Left in its early days.

When we returned to Joe's car after the meeting, he asked that I step around to the back and take a look in the trunk. There, like the most tempting of sirens, he showed me a Schmeiser submachine gun in shiny, good condition. Now, for someone who has grown up with guns and truly likes them, the sight of such a weapon is centerfold material. Joe wondered if I might like to have it. Oh, would I! But prudence, for one rare moment, inspired me to thank him and point out that such weapons are difficult to own legally. I would have to decline his kind offer.

Actually, a couple of years earlier, I had purchased a Thompson submachine gun from what seemed a dependable source. My younger son, Eric, who would later become a world-class rifle shooter, took a strong fancy to it and I let him have it only to discover, to my amazement, that he had passed it along—fortunately with its vital parts spot-welded shut—to a school classmate whose father was a senior official of the FBI. I would love to have had the thing back but I (1) couldn't afford the exorbitant tax levied against such weapons, (2) couldn't afford the ammo to use it, and (3) couldn't really imagine pressing a senior FBI guy's son on the issue.

It was not too long after the Schmeiser incident, which seemed to have impressed Joe, that he told me about his connection to the FBI. He said that the bureau had promised to help him obtain medical services at the National Institutes for Health for his young daughter, who was suffering from a lengthy illness, if Joe would, in return, report on my activities. But, he said, he finally concluded that his employers were probably more of a menace to the Republic than I was. He said he would continue the charade, but suggested that I might start writing memos detailing my activities directly to the bureau to save us all a lot of trouble. Not ever having been conscientious about keeping records or making regular reports on anything, I enjoyed the suggestion but never followed it.

A more flamboyant incident occurred through the action of my old friends at what had been the House Un-American Activities Committee and was, at the time of the incident, the politically cleansed House Internal Security Committee (HISC). They must have been honestly baffled and honestly suspicious of my political weaving and bobbing. I must admit that any investigative agency might have had cause to wonder what was going on.

To satisfy their curiosity, the staff at HISC enlisted the services of a young man just out of high school named Don Meinshausen. Don, a member of the conservative Young Americans for Freedom, joined SDS—a group he secretly loathed at the time of our first meeting—as a paid informant for HISC. His assignment was simply to hang out with me. After a few months of doing this, he was to testify at a public hearing;

they expected that he would expose the violent and threatening nature of the New Left, SDS, and its most odd new ally, me.

We came to be good friends. Actually, very good friends. And this led to his telling me one day about his work for HISC. Like the FBI informant, Don had concluded that I as well as SDS were no menace to the Republic, but that maybe the House Internal Security Committee was. Disingenuous as it might be at times, the New Left looked to him as American as apple pie. He had a rather heroic plan to put his new conviction into practice. He would show up for the scheduled public hearing but, instead of exposing the Red menace, he would candidly expose his own doubts about HISC's own activities.

Probably a teenager couldn't have been expected to bring off this audacious plan without a hitch. The hitch was a beauty. He had carefully written out his testimony and had been, literally, sitting on the several pages of it in the hearing room. Then for some reason he changed his seat—and forgot to take his testimony with him. An HISC staffer picked up the pages, glanced at them, and then, shocked, read them carefully.

Don was immediately withdrawn from the list of scheduled witnesses. Undaunted, teenage zeal aflame, he talked a few reporters into meeting him in the corridor outside the hearing room where he ad-libbed the testimony he had so carefully written out. A credit to his generation. The whole thing appeared here and there as a small story, but it made a large impression on me, as it did on Don.

In August 1969, YAF held its annual convention in St. Louis, Missouri, to "Sock It to the Left." Don was there, but as an ally rather than infiltrator of SDS. I was there too, but as master of ceremonies for the formal fracturing of the conservative movement. Rallying under the famous St. Louis arch, with such notables as Robert Vaughn and his traveling Marxist advisor looking on in fascination at the unfolding of political history, classical liberal dissidents (anarchic, libertarian, and individualistic) socked it to the Right by calling for an end to the war in Vietnam, the draft (a Selective Service card was later burned on the convention floor), and the modern liberal state. To an angry conservative chant of "lazy fairies," YAF's classical liberals split from the group and set in motion the rise of the libertarian movement and the birth of the Libertarian Party. Don and I have remained friends ever since.

In the basement office to which I was assigned as an associate fellow at IPS, I was host to many of the transient scholars or hotspurs who saw

IPS as a sanctuary of sorts. The most interesting of them was the poet Allen Ginsberg, who prepared for several seminars in my office (actually just half of the basement, made quite livable with plenty of lights and working surfaces supported by empty 55-gallon metal barrels). Allen was a delight and a surprise to me. For one thing, he got me over my reservations about hugging as a form of greeting. For another, he completely disabused me of any prejudices that I had about the Buddhist mysticism by which he ordered his life. It had been my crude assumption that no one could be taken seriously who chanted and rang tiny bells before a supposedly scholarly seminar—on worldwide drug trafficking, for instance. But after the tinkle and the chant, Allen would launch into detailed, carefully studied and documented discourses that were models of Western linear, scientific thinking. He remains a friend.

There was another transient in my office who remains a mystery and a confusion to this day. His project was to research the CIA and try to document misbehaviors. Just as a passing idea, I suggested to him that he might have fun trying to document who actually worked at an agency then so secret that it wouldn't permit its name to appear on the sign pointing to its headquarters in Langley, Virginia. (The sign in question read "Fairbanks Highway Research Station.") I recall that back in those days a certain congressman needed an estimate of the total number of people employed by the CIA—and the only source for such information was the Soviet Embassy, which readily obliged with a figure.

My suggestion to this young man was that he position himself on a hill overlooking the road into the supersecret headquarters and, through binoculars, check the license numbers of cars going into the agency and then recheck them at shift-change time. Those who stayed all day, for several days, probably were employees. The license numbers could then be checked through the various departments of motor vehicles, and the names and addresses made public if he liked. Apparently he did so, and one of the alternative newspapers in Washington printed just such a list of his observations.

Months later, another alternative paper printed an exposé of the young man himself. They had obtained convincing evidence that he had been an informer for the CIA. Wheels within wheels!

What was it about the New Left that attracted me without at all disturbing my Republican upbringing?

The New Left that unfolded itself for me was as isolationist as my old hero, the late Sen. Robert Taft of Ohio. But the New Left had the public relations sense to call it anti-imperialism. (Oddly enough, so did some publications of the John Birch Society, such as Garrett Garrett's *People's Pottage*.) Also, the New Left—again, that part that first attracted me—was oriented toward neighborhoods, toward localism, and away from central bureaucracies.

This thrust toward decentralism, community, and small-scale organization that so excited me would eventually be overturned by the growing domination of the New Left by Maoists, Marxists, Leninists, and West Coast Utopian socialists such as Jane Fonda's former husband, Tom Hayden, whose one great contribution to the New Left was his major role in drafting the Port Huron Statement. After Port Huron, as did so many on the New Left, he became a public scold and an advocate of a modernized but still vulgar Marxism. Even as formerly Marxist states were heading directly toward market economies and even capitalism, Hayden was determined to turn Santa Monica into a command-economy, social welfare state, somewhat on the model of Cuba.

But for a time, for me, the New Left looked good and it felt good, and the Port Huron Statement—the founding document of SDS—seemed a platform with principle, punch, and possibility.

Far wiser Old Righties than I felt the same. Murray Rothbard and Leonard Liggio, for instance, edited an admirable journal called *Left and Right* to show the positive relationships between the Old Right and the New Left.

The dippiest part of my association with the New Left was a brief attraction to the Marxian notion of the labor theory of value. (Ironically, it was an anti-Marxist who led me into my infatuation with the labor theory of value, Jeremy Brecher, an apostle of the work of a Dutch political philosopher who, Jeremy claimed, got to the best ideas of Marx long before the Master himself.) It is a tribute to the numbing power of peer pressure, friendships, and disillusionment with old values that I could have had even a brief interest in what soon struck me as the most fundamentally silly economic notion ever brought forth—a sort of economic Flat Earth Theory. Little wonder that people held thrall by this philosophy have never prospered. Fortunately, I recovered my senses before the labor-theory virus had become fatal.

Of all Marxist ideas the labor theory of value—also known as surplus labor value—is the one most often used to attack free-market capitalism. The theory says that the only value in any product is the human physical labor that went into its production. If there is other value added by intellectual effort then it must be counted as service to society and not carried on the books as payment. There are some things people should do simply because "society demands it."

Here's an example of the labor theory of value in action, just as described to me by a college student studying under a Marxist professor:

Suppose that you want to have a table painted. Someone comes along who says he will have the table painted for $100. Finding people who want things painted is his business. The price seems fine to you and the deal is made.

The person who agreed to have the table painted, according to Marx, is a capitalist, because he did not mean to paint the table himself. He was arranging for someone else to do the actual physical labor. He would put up the capital (money) to get the job done, but would not do the actual work.

He spends ten dollars to buy the paint and brushes that will be needed to paint the table. That money, used for starting-up costs, is called capital. It is money that people have saved out of work they did in the past.

The capitalist finds an unemployed person who will be happy to paint the table for $50. The deal is made. The table is painted. The painter receives $50. The capitalist has already spent ten dollars for material, so he pockets $40 in profit. Profit is the difference between all the costs of getting a job done and the selling price. Loss is when the cost of getting the work done turns out to be more than anyone is willing to pay for the work or the product.

Marxism claims that the capitalist should have no role in this affair, and that he doesn't deserve a penny. Yet the unemployed person who actually painted the table is now $50 richer. The man who wanted the table painted now has a painted table, for a price he was willing to pay. And the capitalist is paid $40 for having ensured that these satisfactory events should have taken place. It is hard to see how the professor thought this example would wean his students from capitalism.

But for many people in poor parts of the world, who may have watched local store owners, truck owners, or other small businesspeople make money while others remained poor, the idea of blaming capitalism and capitalists for their own poverty has been very attractive. Moreover, they may have seen people become very, very rich either by controlling the government, or by making deals with it. Obtaining huge amounts of land in this way is one of the chief sources of great wealth in poor or underdeveloped countries. And graft is confused with capitalism.

In socialist countries, the role of the hated "capitalist" is played by the government bureaucrat. The past decade has not been kind to his image. In country after country, socialist bureaucrats have stood revealed as incompetent, often felonious, and usually parasitic. I would not give odds that the senior remaining Communist dictator, Fidel Castro, does not have a cash stash somewhere beyond his three-mile limit.

Other things, of course, troubled me about the New Left. Too many in the movement expressed a visceral hatred for America, a sentiment I never shared and one I combated by always making a distinction between a nation I disliked politically and a country I loved immensely.

For example, a friend of mine named Andrew Kopkind, a fine writer, full-time radical, and coeditor of our short-lived *REpress* newsletter on late sixties political and police-force repression, visited North Vietnam in 1969. When he returned he brought with him some rings made of scrap metal of shot-down American airplanes and numbered to identify which airplane they had come from. He gave me one of the rings. I wore it for several months as a symbol of opposition to the Vietnam War, until it dawned on me that I was celebrating the death of a warrior. I was ashamed. The war was bad, but never could it have been so bad as to deserve the boasting of a countrymen's death—the death of a neighbor, a friend of a neighbor, a loved one. I returned the ring.

I was bothered also by the New Left's use of jargon—such as using praxis rather than practice, of replicate rather than duplicate, a special language invented seemingly to prove that when New Lefters spoke even of the ordinary things of life they were speaking as intellectually superior people. I was also puzzled with special New Left pronunciations, like Neeka-rawa instead of Nicaragua—though, of course, never Coobah for Cuba. I was bothered too by the New Left's conviction that there was a "working class" rather than the sprawling middle class that includes manual workers, production workers, professionals generally, and just about everybody except the actually rich and the politically powerful. I suppose that conviction was somehow linked to yet another: the New Left doctrine that poor people, simply by being poor, were virtuous and wise.

Violence was another trap into which some New Lefters tragically fell as the movement progressed from optimism to despair. I had no wish to go in that direction. I believed then, as I do now, that violence against people and property can never be a revolutionary act; at best it is criminal activity and at worst it kills people, alienates people, and destroys peoples' jobs. It is simply sheer terrorism; I was and I remain steadfastly opposed to it. The only violence in that period that I took part in was Alan Ginsberg's abortive attempt to levitate the Pentagon. I thought it was a great idea, one that would have put the New Left in tall clover if it had worked. Had Ginsberg succeeded, he (1) would have become the wealthiest person on earth and (2) would have had the resources to buy a thoroughly peaceful revolution. Other than that, my closest flirtation with violence was the occasional thought about how much fun it would have been to launch the Washington Monument like a rocket.

None of these aberrations, however, dim the fondness I feel toward those times and the great expectations I held in the early years of the New Left. SDS, for example, began as a student organizing effort to aid poor urban neighborhoods in the Northeast. There was less ideology in those days and more practical, local problem solving. I recall an SDS group in Newark, New Jersey, who tackled a traffic light problem with what seemed to me inspired, decentralist, even libertarian zeal.

The problem was an intersection which, people in the neighborhood thought, needed a traffic light to be safe. The city decided that the light wasn't needed. But the neighborhood people continued to insist it was. The SDS solution would have made the Founding Fathers proud. Just put up your own light! And they did—a jury-rigged affair that blinked on and off, a tiny little beacon of freedom of local choice.

My attraction to the Black Panthers, like SDS, was again my liking of direct, *nonfederal* community action. Members of the Black Panthers, including Huey Newton, would show up at IPS from time to time. In the late '60s, IPS was a New Left salon. Frequent pilgrimages to its seminars and offices were simply part of doing radical business in Washington, D.C.

One of the more unusual yet regular visitors to IPS was a group of poor white southern Appalachians closely allied with the Black Panthers and led by a remarkable individual known as Preacherman. The alliance between the two seemed odd to me until I thought about subterranean Appalachian coal mines, the layers of coal dust on workers' arms and faces, and just how irrelevant skin color must have been under those conditions. I liked Preacherman and his friends because they were southern and they didn't feel guilty; they felt the Stars and Bars were their symbols, not just the property of plantation owners and mine operators. I liked their attitudes; they seemed to be decent people. And they introduced me to the world of the Black Panthers.

My dealings with the Panthers were mostly on the organization's edge. I knew the white media, I knew the kind of things to which people would respond either with hostility or sympathy, and I knew that police weren't pigs and whites weren't honkies. I advised the Black Panthers to drop the hostile jargon and just talk about their programs, which I believed were constructive and splendid. Their school milk program was a fine example of local effort to feed poor neighborhood children. But the Panthers didn't stop there; they wanted their own schools. I don't know what those schools would have been like, but I am certain they would not have been any worse than state-run inner-city schools.

The Black Panthers also had a stern prohibition against any drug that had to be injected. In Cleveland, for example, the chief of police attributed a drop in the dope trade to Black Panther vigilance. And in Adams Morgan, my own neighborhood in D.C., the Panthers let it be known that heroin dealers were not welcome on neighborhood streets.

My tie to the Black Panthers was minor and short-lived, and any importance it had was mostly in my effort to reach old-friend conservatives with the message that the Panthers were not the demons they imagined. I asked them to forget the group's newspaper—which was edited so far as I could tell by Marxist-Leninists, stank, and was jargon ridden—and to think instead about the fact that the Black Panthers were doing what they, the conservatives, had dreamed of doing all of their lives. I know that when Huey Newton showed up at the state capitol in Sacramento with a bandolier of ammunition over his shoulder and a shotgun in one hand, he was fulfilling the fantasy of many conservatives in this country.

For me, however, the Black Panther's notion of neighborhood was most important. They didn't compete for or take the government grants that were seriously and possibly permanently corrupting black neighborhoods. Some members of the Black Panthers were probably bad, but most of them I trusted; they talked practical neighborhood business. They wanted to be free, not integrated. They spoke about individual choice and local community, stressing the libertarian value of self-determination. They were community builders.

Black Panthers and SDSers aside, what endeared me most to the New Left was its incisive criticism of modern American liberalism. Where Republicans were spiteful, the New Left's criticism was very thoughtful, rich in analysis and documentation. They saw liberalism, in short, as an incipient form of fascism. They saw through the liberal belief that the most powerful support of empire came by way of a tranquil domestic population, tranquilized by the exercise of central authority. The New Left simply took the Old Right's observations and analyzed them more deeply. Being a Taft Republican, I understood that; being a libertarian anarchist I embraced it.

15

True Believer

Humaneness consists of never sacrificing a human being to a purpose.
—Albert Schweitzer

There is one minor peril associated with minor celebrity. I think of it as the Old Gunfighter scenario. There you are, standing at the bar, minding your own business when in comes this stranger, wearing a brand new gunbelt, shiny Colt Navy models in the holsters, Stetson thrown back, and an evil leer on his face. "Say there, old man," he says, "I hear you're pretty fast on the drawn conclusion. Well, I reckon I'm a lot faster and a lot meaner. Go on, now. Draw your First Principles!"

As the libertarian humorist Dave Barry would say, "I'M NOT MAKING THIS UP!" Once, a young man came to visit. He was very complimentary. One of my books had helped introduce him to libertarianism. He surveyed my bookcases, saying that he thought he could get to know me better by knowing my library. I discouraged that hope by telling him that we had given away most of our books a year or so ago and that the remaining ones were mostly reference works with a only a few revealing favorites—Mark Twain, Ben Franklin, Mr. Jefferson, Charles Murray, and Nietzsche. He then got to the serious matter, the face-off at the Epistemological Salon. It went like this:

"I see that you have a copy of the Bible."

199

"Yes. I consider it a very important book. Although I am an atheist."

"Are you an atheist because you believe that the existence of God cannot be proved? Or, do you hold that it simply has not *yet* been proven?"

"I am an atheist because I do not believe in the existence of gods. I agree with Cardinal Newman that it's a matter of faith. Either you have it or you don't. I don't."

"But doesn't that mean that you simply do not know? Doesn't that make you an agnostic?"

"So far as I'm concerned, and since it is all a matter of opinion, I feel that I can say that I do know. I know that I do *not* believe. What more do you want?

"Don't you feel it would be better to be sure? Isn't some sort of ultimate sureness what we are all seeking?"

"Not me. Just about the time it seems that there is some sort of ultimate sureness, it gets to be Monday morning and somebody has come up with a new notion that opens new doubts in that ultimate sureness. I think that's exciting. To know that you know all that can be known would be dispiriting. It's the questions that keep us going as thinking creatures. Not just the answers."

"All right, then let's shift the subject a bit. Do you believe in the Copenhagen or the Realistic interpretation of the Heisenberg Indeterminacy Principle?"

"*Who cares?*" I asked. "Whether I *believe* in one or the other won't change the principle. I'm not working on any experiments in the area. I have friends who are, and they will certainly let me know what they think as they go along. In the meantime, I can comfortably afford to wait and see. It's the same with God. Whether I believe or not is not likely to cause a panic in his, her, its, or their neighborhood. And what you think of my opinions is certainly not the center of your life—at least, I hope not. Surely you don't think of such things when you are making love."

As the face-down died down, the visitor, an impressively studious and philosophically sophisticated young man, seemed to have no more reason to stay. He had, apparently, no interest in my character or real life. Had he had such interest, he could have asked if I honor contracts, if I pay my bills, if I lie, cheat, or steal; or if I covet my neighbor's ass, if I'm faithful to my wife, if I honor my father and mother, or if I like the Three Stooges, and do I betray my friends. Those strike me as important matters; far more important than my *opinion* about gods or quantum mechanics.

After my principle-slinging visitor had left, I recalled a brief lesson a physicist friend of mine had given me on quantum mechanics—and, as it turns out, on gods too. The Copenhagen interpretation is the generally accepted view of quantum mechanics. In fact, there really isn't a Copenhagen or Realistic version of the uncertainty principle; it is more correct to say that the uncertainty principle is a part of the Copenhagen interpretation.

The argument between the Copenhagen and Realistic schools is as ancient as philosophy itself and goes like this. Do objects exist in an independent, *realistic* manner, apart from any observer, and can this independent nature be known? Copenhagen quantum mechanics answers no. It argues that although objects may well have independent features, it's irrelevant to worry about them; they can never be known. All we can learn about a thing or a system is what we observe, and in the process of observing it we invariably disturb and change it. Because of that, we cannot learn anything absolute or realistic about an object; we can only observe its response to our stimuli. The Realistic folks don't like this: they prefer to believe that there is an absolute nature to the world out there, and if we are clever enough (quantum mechanics being not quite so clever) then we will be able to figure it out.

Quantum mechanics, Copenhagen-style, does not fret over gods and absolutes. It says only this: "When I observe the thing I call an electron, *this is what I see.*" The Realistic interpretation is not so easily satisfied; it goes the additional epistemological mile to make a claim that classical quantum mechanics would never dare. It says in bold and certain words: "When I observe an electron, *this is what the electron is like.*" It makes the quantum leap from observation of simple, verifiable fact to a statement of absolute, unchanging truth. The difference is profound; it is the gulf between believers in simple things, like the shadows left by excited electrons, and believers in true things, like the fixed and certain nature of an electron. It is the difference between accepting what lies before us, and which is observable, and what lies beyond us, and which is a matter of faith.

Faith has always, for me, been the prime matter of religion. I was born and raised Roman Catholic but when I ceased to attend mass it was not a question of rejecting the church. It was the far more fundamental question of lacking, or being unable to achieve, faith. Either you have got it, I have come to believe, or you haven't. I can't recall ever having it although I certainly went through all the motions of belief, First Communion, Confirmation, Sunday school, and being very impressed by and deferential to priests.

Two priests, both Paulists, who did their best to lead me to faith, were Father Eugene Burke and an associate of his, Father John Shearin. I recall a story told by Father Burke that, uncomfortably, seems to fit me to a tee. A man is approached by his parish priest who, in distress, says that, "I've heard that you have become a Protestant." "Oh, no," the man replies, "I've become an atheist. I've lost my faith, not my reason." Having been a Catholic taught me all that I had to know to become an atheist. None of it ever tempted me to become an undifferentiated Christian.

My most extravagant attempt to achieve faith came when I was working as director of special projects at the American Enterprise Institute. The proprietor, William Baroody, was a Lebanese Eastern Rite Catholic. He and his large family were the most overtly religious Christo-Catholics I've ever known. Their faith overwhelmed everything they did. You could not understand their politics without understanding their religious convictions.

So impressive was their intermingling of politics, neighborliness, everything with their religious faith, that I decided to give the faith business one more sincere shot. To that end I actually went to church and prayed for the gift of faith. I kept that up throughout the Goldwater presidential campaign, even attending mass regularly with the other Catholic members of the campaign staff, most notably Tom Dunlavey who was as comfortable with his own faith, and as modest about it, as anyone I've ever met. A truly good man.

My prayers were not answered. The gift of faith eluded me. I did not, however, become antireligious. I was like Senator Goldwater in that I did not go to church. Unlike the senator, however, I did not have any religious feeling at all. The senator did. It was private and personal which, I have been told by some strict constructionists, doesn't count. At any rate, the senator simply refused to believe me when I said that I did not believe in God. He said, "You believe in things as much as anyone I know." But, I tried to explain, one of the things that I so deeply believe is that there isn't any you-know-what. He would sigh and we would go on to other matters.

The closest I have ever come to experiencing a religious feeling was after reading Whittaker Chambers's moving, magisterial book *Witness*. He made Christianity seem central to civilization itself. I have, since then, had a different feeling about civilization. I believe that civilization grew

Top: Undated photo of Karl's father, Carl Hess Jr.

Left: Karl's mother, "Gaga," on September 12, 1915. Photo taken at Rock Creek Park, Washington, D.C.

Karl at fifteen—and looking almost exactly like his father.

Karl at thirty-four. In the spring of 1957, he was living and writing in New York, and doing a lot of fishing and shooting at the Rod and Gun Club.

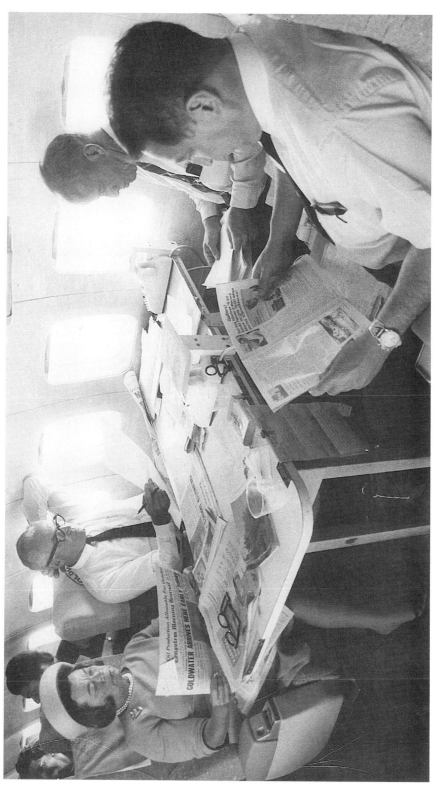

Karl (far right) with Barry and Peggy Goldwater on the presidential campaign jet in 1963.

Top: Karl and Therese at a seminar in the early 1970s, Washington, D.C.

Left: Karl is arrested at the "Redress of Grievances" antiwar demonstration in 1971 at the U.S. Capitol.

Right: Karl with trout tanks that were part of the experiments undertaken by the Community Technology Group in 1973-75, in the Adams-Morgan neighborhood of Washington, D.C.

This is the earth-bermed, passive solar home Karl and Therese built, with the help of sons and friends, in the mid-1970s, near Kearneysville, West Virginia.

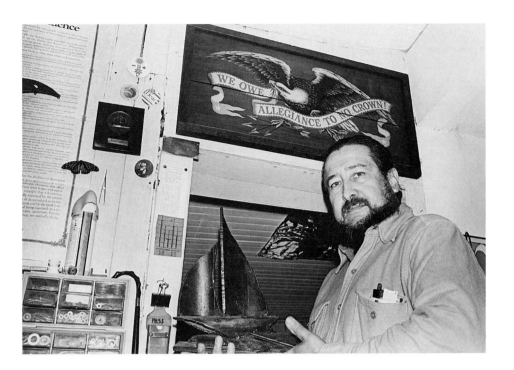

Top: Karl in his welding office in West Virginia, holding one of his metal sculptures and standing beneath his favorite art. (Photo by Stan Jennings, Jennings Publications.)

Left: Karl the welder, at home in West Virginia.

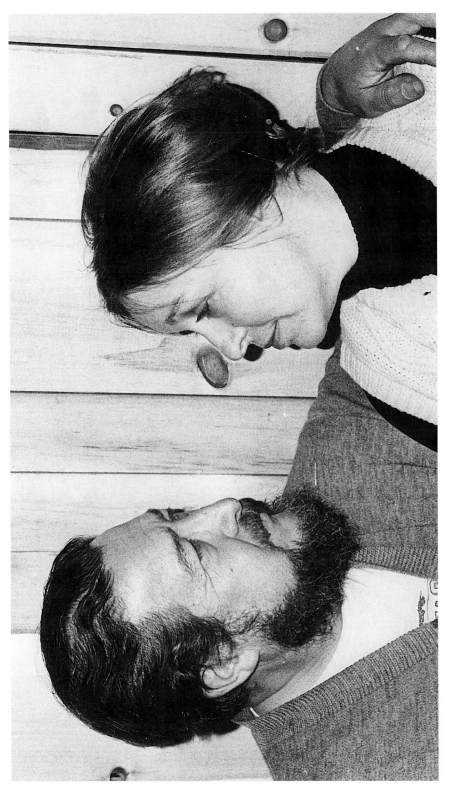

Karl and Therese in 1980, at home in West Virginia.

and spread because of the market and the freedom to travel to and from *market places* and to sell at them. Christianity, Islam, and Judaism may take missionary pride in taming the wild and the wild peoples but the fact of the matter, in my view, is that marketers and merchants have been the true carriers of civilization. It is the merchants who have most needed a peaceful and civilized world in which to do their business. The great religions have all been and largely remain warlike. The proposition needs to be repeated. When goods cross borders, soldiers don't need to.

Believer or not, religion remains an important aspect of the world in which I live and I do not find it an unattractive aspect, just an unavailable one. When I was accepted onto the list of people eligible for a heart transplant in 1991, some of my dearest friends, fundamentalist Christians, organized a prayer group to come to our house and pray for my health and for a new heart. They came every few months to restate their prayers and their friendship and I never got through one of the sessions without unashamedly weeping for the depth of their feeling and the warmth of their love. They were sweetly tolerant of my own lack of faith. They gave Christianity a good name.

I suppose that if I had to pick something with a religious tinge to it that I appreciate, it would be Buddhism. My own version of the Bible, the eleventh edition of the *Encyclopaedia Britannica*, points out that Buddhism is not so much a religion as an ethical philosophy. I have taken to telling religious solicitors, of which there is a substantial supply in West Virginia, that I am a Buddhist. This has easily and not acrimoniously ended many of the solicitations. And who knows? Maybe I am a Buddhist. I know that I heartily approve of the old Buddhist saying that if you meet with Buddha on the road, you must kill him. I gather that this means that if an actual person tries to submit you to their authority—as a road-met Buddha might—that you should cast that person aside, rejecting anything or anyone, or any symbol that would substitute for your human responsibility to make up your own mind.

That's my kind of religion, or whatever it is.

I am, nonetheless, curious and empirically minded about the religious experience. Not long ago, on a Saturday evening, Therese and I attended the dedication of the new Petra Worship Center in Martinsburg at the invitation of its minister, Earl Hairston, a onetime tutor in the local literacy program and a great admirer of Therese for the literacy work she does. The center, a partially redecorated nightclub once famed as a black hangout and a location of considerable sinning, from dope dealing to murder, had a congregation that evening which appeared to be about a third black, a third Latin, and a third white. Hairston, a former street dude now working days as a counselor at the local juvenile detention facility and, as he put it, full time for Jesus, blended nicely with the restored surroundings.

He, or rather his appearance, was the first surprise of that evening. He was tall and strikingly handsome, proportioned like a gymnast but with shoulder-length hair which, in the African mode, was very oil-shiny and curly. The second surprise was the dedication itself. It was not your typical Protestant thank-you-lord now let's have some refreshments event. It was a musical extravaganza, a participatory witnessing event in which, from the moment we arrived, until we had to leave several hours later (in deference to my physical tiredness), many of the hundred or so people there stood, swayed, danced in place, shouted joyfully to their God, and occasionally went to the base of the bandstand-altar to kneel and pray. One person fell supine upon the floor. Others were joined by people who helped them pray by holding them, always joyfully, lovingly, and without inhibition. There was no sense that they were doing it to impress anyone in the audience. It was very personal, even intimate, even though in the most publicly exposed setting imaginable.

And the music. Standing between rock-band amplifiers were a white keyboard player, a tall, balding man dressed in necktie, businessman's striped shirt but no jacket, and showing the first bulging sign of over-weightness; a swarthy player of electronic drums, mustached like a Mexican bandit; a lithe, movie-star handsome Latin playing acoustical Conga drums; and a white guitarist, very Irish-looking, playing one of those electronic wonders trimmed down to just strings and enough instrument body to support the strings. He, the guitarist, moved almost constantly in the familiar rock posture of one leg straight, the other bent and seeming to pull the whole person along in a series of spasmodic jerks. Their music, all unfamiliar to me, was rock rhythmic, but in a distinctly Jewish minor-key mode. It was wonderful to hear. The words were undistinguishable to me but apparently not to the audience which joined perfectly with shouted repetitions of key phrases. One I recall, and in which I happily joined, called for giving a shout of victory.

There were no breaks. As one song ended and another began there were many shouts of "praise God" by the musicians and the audience, but then it went on, at the same infectiously high-energy level. Meanwhile, many people just stood and clapped in time to the music. Others stood and swayed, their hands raised (in what seemed to me remarkably graceful fashion). A few fell to their knees for a moment. One woman, near us, stood, hands raised and swayed, her face glowing in adoration, while her infant child, in a sort of basket, looked on happily and with never an outburst of tears or anxiety. I thought at the time that even though the mother actually was swept along by the music and the worship, that she too seemed calm even though energetically moving. There was no protocol or ritual. Everyone there showed some form of exaltation in the way that, obviously, they felt most appropriate.

I had to sit but did not feel that anyone would venture to ask why I wasn't standing. I never felt that I could get away with that sort of nonconformity when, as a practicing Catholic, I attended mass and dutifully followed every detail of the rubric of the ceremony. Although we had to leave after just two hours, it is our understanding that this impressive participation would go on until midnight or later as the congregation worshiped ecstatically. Earl Hairston called the next day to make sure that we hadn't been frightened or offended by the vigor of the worshiping. We assured him we had not.

During the event at a particular moment, I had a feeling that I was looking at the goings-on through open doors. Ahead was the future in which I foresaw powerful replacements for mystical religious affiliation. Looking backwards through another door, was the scene of the worship center, a present that surely must be a comfort to those who properly are not concerned by the future I so eagerly await. Human, posthuman? I really don't know. I do not, however, feel that the people at the worship center are deprived of anything important by not sharing my visions. Their own seem to be sufficient for their days and needs.

My evening at the Petra Center exposed me to the living core of religion, the body-swaying, hand-clapping, heartfelt shoutings of people that is one of many aspects to neighborly life in West Virginia. I can't imagine West Virginia without it, even though I can't imagine myself as ever more than an accidental observer of its more personal enthusiasms. The main thing is that it is a deep, profound, and important way in which people affiliate with one another and engage themselves at the local level. It is manageable, mostly decent, rarely ideological when it comes to practical things such as welding cracks in a backhoe shovel or blading ruts in a common-use dirt road, and hardly offensive to believer or nonbeliever so long as the matter of faith is not allowed to interfere with the matter of being a good neighbor.

I recall, for example, a fundamentalist preacher who would visit me at home from time to time, yet never for the purpose of speaking about religion. He supported his ministry by striping parking lots—a fact that greatly impressed me. He was an ideologue who was *working* to support his ideology, making the propagation of his belief a noncoercive, nonpolitical matter of a friendly and fruitful market negotiation. It was a wonderful way of doing what he believed in, and doing it in a way that made his religion a creation of labor, and not merely a product of belief.

Apart from religion, he was simply a Berkeley County neighbor, a man with whom I could discuss local affairs and mutual friends. The only preaching he ever did, and it was quite harmless at that, was to bring an Amway representative to my house. But even the Amway man, a believer in his own right, was more neighborly than ideological. Both men were friendly and inoffensive, solidly anchored in local affairs. They, as well as the worshipers at the Petra Center, were the part of religion I could see and understand without faith. That is not to say that I found their faith objectionable. I have, personally, no objection to religious faith, which I simply regard as a comforting and powerful opinion. I do, however, object to any sort of "faith" as a basis for social organization (beyond, at least, the level of voluntary association) or as a foundation for public policy. I know that none of these people treated or viewed their faith in that manner. Yet, their world of hands-on religion and simple neighborliness was a world apart from the mysteries and mysticisms of life after death that make up the "system" of spirituality in most of the religions of which I am aware and which is the heart of the Catholic faith that I once embraced.

Life after death, it strikes me, is a powerful and attractive notion. It also is a horrific way to inspire crazed fervor among soldiers, terrorists, and others plying a violent craft. Perhaps it was because of the time I spent working at the morgue, but the notion of mortality and its end has never seemed frightening to me. It just seems natural. Even while awaiting a heart transplant and being so keenly aware of the limited possibilities of my survival, the idea that it all, someday, would just end, shut off, close down, go blank, was not frightening. It was and is mainly inconvenient. I wish it would not happen. But since I know it will, I am resentful only of the time it will take away from being with Therese.

Now, if you do not feel an intense need to believe in life after death, and you are not inclined toward raucous revivalism, what else is there about religious faith that could tempt you? As a young Roman Catholic the very panoply of the ritual of the mass was tempting. It was fine to hear the anthems, it was appealingly mysterious to hear the chanting of the priests, it was good to be an insider taking part in an ancient and mystical rite, to be separated from those vulgar religionists who just said prayers and listened to preachments of uncertain origin. Being a Catholic in those days was to know certainty, to know certainly that there was a world of religion sloppily parading by in the outside world but that in the dark and incense-filled precincts of The Church, you were participating in the original thing, the unbroken line of faith from the crucifixion to this day. You were different, special, set apart in the world, like being a marine. Heady stuff.

I don't really recall when the first doubts infiltrated my smug feeling of being an insider in this ancient matter. The kids I had spent time with in my early teens included a number of flamboyant atheists but I still went to mass with my mother. Later, as a full-time anti-Communist, there wasn't time to doubt. There was just time to fight the godless Communists. Going to mass seemed a powerful gesture against Communism, a powerful anchor for the reason I was anti-Communist.

Also, I had never heard any reasoned arguments against religious faith. Perhaps that was why I never questioned it, at least not until I attended a series of seminars discussing the Objectivist philosophy of Ayn Rand. The Rand attack on religion was quite powerful and her books such as *Fountainhead* and *Atlas Shrugged*, which greatly impressed me—and still do—made it necessary to at least consider religion as an undesirable doctrine of self-sacrifice.

In all, my previous armor of ritual and mystery were insufficient to the blows dealt it by an increasing interest in science and by the unshakable arguments of Ayn Rand. It slowly but surely became apparent to me that I had been a believer only, not a believer with true faith, but one who just embraced the comfort and certitude of the rituals and the good feelings of association with an ancient and powerful organization.

Catholicism, of course, was not my only encounter with religion and the temptings of true belief. I spent the '50s as an ideologue in the company of ideologues. I was part of the extreme Far Right, a dedicated, believing anti-Communist who put up with the fringes of that spectrum in the name of a cause. I am still an anti-Communist, but with this difference. Anti-Communism is no longer a purpose in my life, nor would it be again should the Communist empire miraculously reemerge. To seek "a" purpose of life, I now believe, is to ignore the individual's purposes. Ideologues, of course, are given to the former. I am more taken by the latter, the little things that I can see and touch and understand, such as making a fine weld, writing a good speech, calculating this or that angle, writing a poem to Therese, or watching *Smokey and the Bandit.*

My empirical bent does create problems for some of my friends who still dabble on the edges of ideology. I recently wrote to one of them about my growing discomfort with the idea of rights. I applauded her notion of self-ownership; it is the most obvious of positions and, in my opinion, the most materialistic. However, she saw it as a moral value, which if true becomes a splendid point of merger with my materialism. I enthusiastically endorsed her efforts, though I told her of my great uncertainty.

I remain unsure as to how rights can exist on their own and beyond agreement. Tell me about a right that exists in such a way that simply proclaiming it assures the existence of the thing or right being proclaimed and I will be a believer.

I recall how often, during the wild '60s, the police would bang people about while the bangees shouted, in obvious outrage, "You can't do that to me! I have my rights!" I do not mean to suggest that an attachment to material things such as one's unbeaten body or self-ownership is in any way weakened by a simultaneous attachment to morality. Certainly that is not the case. It's just that rights have no legs to stand on other than the material ones given to them by people.

I suppose we always have phantom audiences in mind when we flounder about in the realm of rights, morality, and ethics. (One of the two books I've written for kids lately tries earnestly to make a distinction between morality, with what seems to me to be its unavoidable reference to supernatural authority, and ethics which are, in my view, ways of behavior always modified by material situations.) At any rate, two of the phantom audiences that spring up when I think of rights and morality are the libertarians who hold that if your opinion is correct, you are correct, and the morally unshakable. I am sure that we all have known libertarian after libertarian who can quote the gospel and sing the anthems but whose personal behavior is obnoxious, undependable, and not at all neighborly.

I have come to prefer to wait and see how people act before I take too seriously how they talk.

As for the morally unshakable, there is, alas, a real downside to the situation. Immediately following the Korean War I was a member of a Defense Department panel charged with finding out why some soldiers, taken prisoner, held out against their captors' threats and even torture while others quickly gave in. The perhaps not surprising answer was that people with deeply held religious beliefs held out best.

We did not, unfortunately, have the latitude to see if similarly committed atheists or holders of nonreligious moral convictions did as well. Surely in such a situation of captivity, the presence of a power that cannot be imprisoned has obvious advantages. I certainly would not argue with the idea. The downside, of course, is the sort of religious fundamentalism that sweeps away all reason and demands total fealty.

My rights-inclined friend agreed with my concern for the excesses of fundamentalism. She reminded me, thinking it supported the point, of the Ayn Rand adage about people who won't accept the 2 + 2 = 4 argument unless it is to their advantage. I took exception to her point, for her dispersion described a community of people who are anything but psychologically dense. They are called mathematicians.

I ended my letter to her by telling her I was greatly relieved to hear that she would not let a loved one die rather than take state cash. This was, with my failing heart, an issue of some import to me. My own view of the most dipsy ideologue of all time was one of Hitler's cronies who reportedly bled to death in a Berlin gutter rather than accept help from a Jewish doctor. What a dummy!

Ideologues detached from real life are truly frightening. They live by a logic that is no longer familiar or desirable to me. But it is infectious, and for some people deceivingly noble to live and die for something that transcends the material things of life, that puts a grander purpose to living than creating a tool to make living easier, a piece of art to make it more pleasurable, or a person to love and be loved by.

Perhaps the best example of what I mean came in the form of a question asked during the intellectual whirlwind of one of IPS's ongoing seminars by Milton Kotler, who remains a hero of mine for asking that question and for being a decent, polite, civil person even when surrounded by snarling, unsmiling World Saviors.

Someone was giving a standard radical recitation on the one, the true, the only way to hammer the future into proper place. Milton asked: "What would be in it for you?" The person was offended, obviously. Absolutely nothing, he snapped back.

The changed world he wanted was needed not because of doing him any particular good but because it would serve the people, save the people, do something or another wonderful thing for the people.

Milton was unable to proceed much farther on what was obviously a sensible series of follow-up questions. By the time he got to "but aren't you one of the people?" the seminar was demanding that he shut up, sit down, and that we get serious again.

Ever since then, I have always made that Kotler question an early one in discussions of how the world should run (pardon me, *be* run). It seems to me that Emma Goldman was right when she beautifully stated that if she couldn't dance, she didn't want to be part of anyone's revolution. I expect, for the same reasons, that a person of ordinary sense should be able to tell you in clear terms why they *personally* would be better off in their future Utopia. If they actually would have nothing to gain, why bother? Even a rich person wanting to impoverish their country club colleagues should be able to explain why the egalitarian changes they usually espouse would be more enjoyable for them.

There is a wonderful book title that says something like *Never Trust a Naked Man Who Offers You the Shirt Off His Back.* I say never trust a fiery orator who offers you the shirt off someone else's back while never discussing his own future wardrobe.

16

Motorcyclist, Hippie,
Welder, and Sculptor

The order is
Rapidly fadin'.
And the first one now
Will later be last
For the times they are a-changin'
   —Bob Dylan, "The Times They Are A-Changin' "

I got my first motorcycle shortly after the '64 election while I still lived in the Virginia suburbs of Washington, D.C., and while I was still married to my first wife. It was not much of a bike, just a 50 cc toy poodle of a Honda which I rode from Annandale, Virginia, to various high-toned jobs in Washington, fully suited and neatly necktied. Yet it was enough of a bike to raise a few eyebrows. My wife thought it was the onset of some sort of senile dementia. Friends thought I had lost my mind. Well, maybe I had. At least I had lost my heart to the machine.

I was hooked on motorcycles thanks to the '64 campaign, or more exactly the Hollywood "celebrity crew" that traveled with Goldwater and campaigned for him. Actors like Fess Parker, a big-time cyclist in his own right, talked the glories of the sport and captured my fancy. By the end of the campaign I was ready to break social convention and make the move from four to two wheels. It was a big break too; it was not chic in the mid-

211

60s, as it is today, to have a motorcycle. Then, it was hideous—at least to my circle of neighbors and friends.

This first motorcycle, hardly large enough for my size and hardly powered enough to make it over steeper hills, was my act of separation from a lifestyle and a style of work that no longer made sense to me—no longer held my interest or affection. It was part of the disillusionment that had come on the heels of the '64 campaign loss, and the sense that I had crossed a divide from which there could be no turning back. It was like painting yourself blue. Once you paint yourself blue, you can't go to the country club anymore. I did, and I couldn't.

I have never regretted painting myself out of one life into another, nor have I lost my admiration for two-wheeled transport, even though my deteriorating health now precludes it. Many times when you are about to make a change, it is helped by some symbolic act that gives your neighbors and friends something they can really understand. Falling in love with motorcycles did just that for me. It removed the mystery of where my thinking was heading and the different world toward which I was moving. It was an overt act that invited them to make a decision about me. They could say I was crazy without any ambiguity. They could speak to me truthfully because they were convinced I was crazy, and because they knew I really didn't care. Later, after I and my motorcycle had made our quixotic exit, they might even start thinking about it themselves, wondering whether my craziness was truly as daft as they first imagined.

I did not stick with my first bike for long. As I quickly learned, you can't own just one motorcycle. What you do—and what I did for nearly a decade—is to invest in a long series of motorcycles. I quickly graduated to a 160 cc Honda, which lasted until it was demolished by my older son on a Friday night spin with a girlfriend. Compelled by circumstances, I moved on to a 500 cc model, and then finally made the leap to real bikes. All of this, of course, came at a time when I was getting a divorce, leaving politics, and heading hippieward in a hurry. Some people ascribe their elevation to higher consciousness to LSD; I ascribed mine to two-wheelers and the internal combustion engine.

A Triumph Bonneville 650 cc—a British motorcycle—was my first big, street bike. It had the most classic of classic motorcycle lines, and, for the sheer pleasure of it, it had tremendous acceleration and speed. I would often crank it up on the highway, sometimes above 100 mph. It was fun, a show-off thing, zipping past people in their fancy cars, hurtling oneself across open landscape, the fresh air, the immediacy of speed, the uninhibited sense of freedom. There was the downside too, the wild vibrations common to that temperamental breed of British bike that literally shook and tore three sets of license plates from their bolted moorings.

But motorcycle riding was never meant to make sense in a tidy, logical way, apart, that is, from maintaining the function and running of the machine. What we enjoy most in life rarely has a rational basis in either the wanting or the enjoyment of it. I don't believe it is possible, for example, to establish a rational basis for liberty. It's wholly aesthetic. I can't justify it beyond that. You can establish a rational basis for not stepping off a three-story building, but not for social activities such as the way you like to live. That's the nuts and bolts of motorcycling. When the parts are working logically as they should, something other than linear thinking takes over to make riding a motorcycle the great thrill that it is.

My bike phase peaked once I had left the Virginia suburbs and completed my divorce. I moved into a scruffy apartment near George Washington University on 21st and F streets. Among my new neighbors were a number of postgraduate students who were also hooked on bikes. We formed a motorcycle gang of sorts in which I was the only one without a Ph.D. One of the gang, I fondly recall, was stopped by a D.C. policeman while riding his ancient Harley. The policeman went through the standard questions, some of which my biker-friend couldn't answer (such as, "where is your license?"). The policeman then asked, sarcastically, "How far did you get in school?" "Ph.D.," replied my friend. That seemed to outrage the lawman who promptly took him off to jail.

Motorcycles—at least in the mid-60s—set you apart from polite society. They were a sign that you were somehow different, undesirable, and undeserving of even the most furtive and fleeting of glances. I remember, for example, the last time I saw Arleigh Burke, admiral and onetime Chief of Naval Operations. I had written some speeches for him and I had worked with him in setting up the Georgetown Center for Strategic Studies. We had been fairly close at the time, but when I left politics in 1965 we naturally lost contact—that is, until I motorcycled into the alley of one of D.C.'s more famous buildings to pick up a friend.

While I was waiting, Arleigh Burke stepped into the alley. I didn't have a helmet on, although I was wearing well-worn leathers. I'm there, I'm naked to the world, not hiding, and he walks directly toward me, looks at me, and then walks past me without a hint of recognition. He didn't know who I was *because* I had never been a person to him before. I had always been a certain set of clothes, a certain rhetoric, and none of that had anything to do with motorcycles, a person standing there in dungarees and a black leather jacket. You kid yourself if you think you're a person in these situations. You're just a performer, playing a role.

Street riding was only half of my passion for motorcycles. I also raced them. I road-raced a Yamaha, cross-countried a Ducati, and used a Bultaco Sherpa S for everything in between. I even won a few of the cycling events that I entered. But all of that came to a crashing—*and prudential*—end after I crushed my knee in a moto-cross race and had to spend the dog days of July through September in a full leg cast. I learned that summer how to bend a coat hanger wire into odd shapes to reach every itch. I also learned how to live without motorcycles. Nowadays, if I even look at one, Therese pulls in my leash. Just as well. But Lordy, how I miss my bikes!

Well before I raced bikes on road and dirt courses, however, I was racing headlong into hippiedom. By the late '60s I was there, motorcycle in hand, dope in pocket, and hard rock music pounding away. I moved from my apartment on 21st and F streets to what was then the rundown, disreputable, unfashionable Buzzard Point boatyard on the Anacostia River, just above Ft. McNair on the Potomac and some distance below the Washington Navy Yard. I lived on the *Tranquil*, a houseboat owned by my lady friend—a woman who had long shared my love of bikes and who had spent the past two years with me at 21st and F.

Our move to Buzzard Point was yet another break with the past, a further cutting of old ties and an immersion into a new and changing world. I would write political things in the boat cabin; weld and sculpt in Buzzard's only boat shed; and drink Tivola Red, grill a steak, and smoke dope on deck in the late summer evening with my boat neighbors. My girlfriend and I lived the life of the stereotypical hippie couple right up to the day she sold her boat and then left D.C. to be a lesbian in California.

"Hippie" meant many things in the late '60s. The idea of community was its great driving force. There were, of course, hippies who could see in the movement simply a way to be colorfully irresponsible—to be drugged out or drunk without being what their parents might have been in the same situations: addicts or drunks. Today, with marijuana having become about as middle class as the dry martini, I wonder how many hippies remember their past in terms of drugs? My sense is that they remember more important things—such as the community idea.

My favorite radio talk-show host, Rush Limbaugh, a social conservative who probably would detest a libertarian like me, has lately come to describe hippies as "longhaired, maggot-infested, dope-smoking" weirdos. Today, that description probably fits more construction workers than it does any persons who could be fairly called hippie in the '50s–'60s definition.

Nonetheless, his emphasis on appearance makes a point. I believe it is possible to assess the triviality of a movement by the moment when wearable fashion becomes its principle identification. Hippiedom died when long hair, rather than any particular way of living, became its icon. Hippies, of course, did not vanish, but the brief and joyous notion that they were part of a movement did. Long hair, colorful dress, and dope live on, but mostly as an empty shell of mimicking consumption. Hard-core hippies, I suspect, now hide in neatness and small business.

The same can be said for the triviality of the late '60s hate-America fad, the part that worshiped Yasser Arafat and the PLO. It never was a real movement, not in the sense that the anti–Vietnam War peace movement was. But it became a conspicuous nonmovement with nonvitality when wearing the checkered scarf of the PLO became so stylish that even rich movie stars could act like terrorists without risking anything more than a costume clash.

The Irish Republican Army has not yielded to fashion, nor to negotiation, and continues to be, if not much of a movement, at least a very lethal little wager of war.

The famed student revolt of the '60s wanted to wage war too, and was at least raising a little hell until it got a uniform, the army fatigue jacket and worn blue jeans. When revolting students started spending considerable time in abrading and sloshing the field jackets and jeans into fashionable shabbiness, the movement from movement to fashion was clear.

The civil rights movement still has an important movement component, but it also has a new fashion which could vitiate the entire thing. The fashion is the kente cloth, that brilliantly colored African, horizontal, linear patterning which now may be seen adorning pillbox hats and, most importantly, long scarves reaching around the neck and down each side of a person's body to arm's length.

A judge in Washington, D.C., recently forbade an attorney from wearing his kente scarf in the court because of its possible biasing effect on jurors. The aggrieved lawyer said that his religion demanded that he wear it. The religion was not identified but could be assumed: the religion of fashion which intrudes when real faith and real movements wane.

I became a hippie because it seemed the thing to do in the '60s. Everybody I met after leaving my first marriage was one. They all seemed wonderfully happy, so why not? To my older friends, I already was a hippie, having become one the moment I first rode a motorcycle—which was about the time I was director of special projects at the American Enterprise Institute. My first wife likely spotted the danger signals when she first sensed I was unfaithful to her—not long after I had first met Therese but well before I was divorced. An insufficient zeal for fashion was another tipoff, although the hold of fashion in hippiedom was as rigid and zealous as at Neiman-Marcus.

Blue jeans. Military fatigue jacket. T-shirts with outrageous political slogans. Work boots. At least the work boots were my choice, and were acceptable. Sandals seemed to be the most highly regarded footwear along with no-wear. Bare feet were considered a sign of inner purity, a return to the prized values of the noble savage. Sandals and bare feet always seemed to me an invitation to severe pedal damage from, for instance, having heavy things dropped on your toes. But then, not too many hippies in sandals, or barefeet, were toting around heavy objects or doing splinter-rich manual labor.

And then there was dope and sex.

I became a dope fiend for reasons that were far removed from a search for god, truth, or transformation. I became a dope fiend, to the extent that I did, because my girlfriend at that time was one, so were the people with whom I was then living, and because it was pleasurable in a perfectly middle-class way; i.e., it produced a more pleasant high than whiskey and didn't make me throw up.

I became a sex fiend first, as a reaction to falling in love, the first time, with Therese Machotka, and then, later, as a perfectly natural reaction to living with another young woman who (a) was preoccupied with the subject and (b) was half my age, very healthy, even athletic.

I became a nudist, of sorts, as a perfectly natural reaction, it seemed at the time, to the fact that hippies were supposed to have an open, bourgeoisie-shocking uninhibited joy about their bodies. Actually I have gone nude in mixed company more after returning to the regular middle class than when I was a hippie. The coed hot tub, for a time, perhaps still, was a familiar middle-class fixture.

It was my younger son, Eric, who had to go along with a lot of my exploratory foolishness. I recall that on one trip to a communal farm, he was really dumbfounded to observe that everybody working there was naked. The observation seemed to have no prurient implications at all—just shock. I don't think it hurt him in any way. He is a remarkably tolerant young man and, now, a loving father. His own father's hippieness was something he put up with, with grace and love. It is with those same qualities that he has approached our relationship all along.

In all of the fiendish pursuits, I now am convinced, one powerful driving force for many people was neither sensual nor ideological but simply sensational: the realization that the parents of the hippies would be more outraged by dope and sex and nudity than by more socially acceptable activities such as felony crime or drunkenness. Parents seem to rally around children accused of ordinary crimes or succumbing to familiar country-club vices. They did not rally as quickly, or even ever, around children who offended all middle-class values to become hippies.

Much of the business can be described as the *graffiti effect*. For much the same reason that people scribble outrageous graffiti on walls, many hippies were scribbling their deeply felt sensitivities and differences on their lives so that the bourgeoisie would see them and be properly offended. It was also done, of course, to say as loudly as possible that "I am different. I am more free. I am more sensitive. I am more, more, more. . . ." The fact that many of the hippies with whom I associated were supported by their parents, or by trust funds or allowances, was not counted as significant because, after all, hippies did not then care about money. As they opened shops or began peddling dope, or what-have-you, the great force of capitalism would sweep them away. Even so, hippy capitalists usually could be counted on to be the most vocal booers and hissers whenever even the word *capitalism* was brought up.

The *graffiti effect* can be seen in much more decorous surroundings than hippie communes. At operas, you probably have noted, there are people who shriek their approval when the time to applaud comes around. I suspect that those who resort to the loudest bravos are doing so in thrall to the *graffiti effect* desire to make sure that everybody understands that they are truly opera lovers and as lovers of such impressive sensibility, may be expected to do more than simply applaud when it becomes orgasm time. At any rate, I am convinced that what lies at the core of looking different, acting different, smelling different, or what-have-you, is this simple behavioral fact: to make sure that people understand that *we* are different and that *we* are better than the ordinary run of people.

Is, for instance, a gold Rolex usually worn because it keeps better time than a Timex? Of course not. It simply costs a lot and sets the wearer off from the crowd. I owned a Rolex for a while but the fact that getting it cleaned cost many times as much as the purchase of a Timex and the fact that it didn't keep better time than a Timex, finally convinced me that a Timex would be a better choice. I bought one, for about $14, and it keeps scrupulously accurate time; its face, with large numbers, is quite easy to read. I gave the Rolex to my older son. It cost him $200 to get it cleaned, a regular necessity—like tuning a Jaguar.

But he can now experience the little thrills sometimes provided by having such a watch. I recall that on an airplane trip, I was carrying an Air Rhodesia flight bag and wearing my Rolex. The couple next to me apparently observed all of this because I heard the man whisper to the woman "mercenary!" I did try to walk a little bit like the Duke when I had to go to the john.

Being a hippie in the '60s meant for me something more profound than being a poster child for rebellious fashion. Hippie was more than just looking different; it was being different. It suggested that those who called themselves hippies actually were different, living in a different and iconoclastic way, rejecting core values of Western civilization, having entirely too much fun in a world where fun was supposed to end with a person's twenty-first birthday.

I have often dreamed of a survey of parents that would ask if they would prefer to have their child killed in a war or become a hippie. There is something noble, many parents seem to feel, about a gold star in the window. There is nothing even admissible about having a kid who is a hippie. A current survey would have to ask if the parents would prefer to have their child killed in a war, such as the Gulf one, or be a spike-haired hard-metal freak or a devotee of rap.

Despite the most blatant racism, anti-Semitism, anti-Asian bigotry and even urges of violence in so much rap and hip-hop, its brutal messages still seem more acceptable than the flower-child messages of the hippies. Better to have a kid who hates than one who loves too much. One possibility is that parents simply were jealous. Here were the kids having all that fun. Why didn't the parents have all that fun? Because they had to take care of the kids, right? Sure, being a parent amongst the flower children was quite an awkward situation, sometimes leading to prudential kid-warning conservatism and sometimes leading to excesses in attempts to prove even more hippie than thou—or thou.

One enduring virtue of the hippie culture was a sense of self-reliant independence, of decentralism carried to any extreme, including the notion that just one individual could secede from society and make it, all alone; an idealized form of hermitism.

A minor manifestation of this was the proliferation of handcrafts, including a sentimental return to carding and weaving wool garments. I know one woman who, to this day, makes cloth and then clothing from the hair of dogs. But her husband is a college professor and, even though they live in an adobe house and have no electricity, they travel widely and send their kids to upper-class private schools. Why not?

A major manifestation was technological hubris, the notion that a right-minded person could do anything if they could only find the right tools. It was a noble idea. But foolish. I can sum it up, I hope, by reprinting a letter that I sent in July of 1990 to Jeffrey Hart, a magisterial conservative presence on the faculty of Dartmouth College:

> This letter, an apology, is long overdue even though possibly beyond your caring or memory. Nonetheless, I beg your patience and your attention to it.
>
> Some years ago, when I spoke at Dartmouth, you and I got into a crazy sort of shouting match over the division of labor. We exchanged rather acrid letters on the subject also.
>
> In that exchange, I shortly came to realize, you were absolutely correct and I was absolutely trendy, ideological, and wrong.
>
> It was during my headiest days working with and trying to understand the New Left. I do not for a moment regret the time spent doing that. I learned a lot from the experience. I have always sought close-on observation and "hands on" learning. That "get in and look around" process, although congenial for me, has proven terribly irritating for people whom I have respected and whom I have come to respect. You are included on both ends of that formulation.
>
> The center of our small storm in the lecture hall was your insistence that you would prefer not to go to the trouble of learning how to and then making your carbon-composite tennis racket.
>
> My position, being mind-tossed by visions of people, in their own communities, being able to do everything, was that you not only could but should make your own tennis racket.

As with many wholly ideological exercises, I did not care to grasp the essential fact of the matter which was that I couldn't make the tennis racket either. Moreover, being a welder at the time, I soon realized that I could not generate my own acetylene or oxygen in sufficient quantities to be significant for my work. Still, I must admit, as an ideologue, that I resisted the realization as much as possible.

Perhaps it was when my aorta burst, while lecturing in Connecticut, that I most gravely realized how essential is the division of labor to the world I actually love.

(Senator Goldwater, when I worked with him, often quipped that, if given a good mirror, and some sharp tools, he felt he could perform a good range of surgery on himself. I know the feeling of wishing that were so. The Senator never, however, proposed that he could personally, or even with the neighbors, build the sort of high performance aircraft which were the delight of his life. The Senator, of course, was joking about the surgery. I would not be joking had I made the same statement. Alas.)

When my aorta did burst, requiring an entire squad of surgeons and attendants to remove my heart and re-line and stitch up the offending artery, I had nearly terminal proof that the division of labor is one of the most sensible arrangements humans have contrived.

I now have a more Jeffersonian approach to the matter. I would like to be able to do everything. I try to do what I can but I more sensibly now reserve my strength and time for things I do better than growing vegetables or making your tennis racket. One of those things, I hope you will be interested in knowing, was the authorship of a book published two years ago. It is entitled *Capitalism for Kids*. Writing for children seems to be quite compatible with my abilities and my ambition although I am also working on an autobiography, in which reflections on the division of labor, and this apology to you, will be included.

Hippiedom, like motorcycles, was a brief interlude in my life, a handful of highly energized, transforming years that spanned the post-'64 election period up to my marriage to Therese in 1971. Yet during that interlude, and continuing beyond, something else happened that would change my life forever, and in more substantial ways. In the throes of motorcycling and a hippie lifestyle I became first a welder and then later a sculptor.

My career change started at a motorcycle race. I discovered that no matter how skillful a rider you are—and I was far from being skillful at the time—things break, and the only way to fix them is to weld them. So

I decided I had better learn how to weld metal and keep my bike running. In addition, I needed a way to make money; I needed a trade to live by. Having been essentially purged from the Republican Party after Goldwater's defeat, politics was out of the question. Except for a syndicated column that I was writing for the senator, my sources of income were slim. So I started welding classes at Bell Vocational School in 1967, and graduated the following year.

I learned two things at Bell. The first was how to weld and the second was a lesson in arts and aesthetics. Each student was given a work booth and a metal working table. Our first lesson was to weld a metal rod to that table. Then, for the rest of the year, we spent our time attaching metal pieces of various shapes and thickness to this pipe. The idea was to practice welding an assortment of metal sizes in as many combinations and from as many positions as possible. It's not hard to figure out the permutations. There were a hundred students, each with a hundred pieces of metal, and the possibilities before each of them for the placement of those pieces of metal on those pipes were infinite.

You might think, so what? After all, half of them appeared to have come on Harleys and the other half were likely fleeing one law-enforcement agency or another. They fitted the mold of dumb people—they weren't like you or me, they didn't speak good English, so they just had to be dumb. But they weren't. Not once did I see a student's booth adorned by pieces of metal that were ugly. They weren't always beautiful, but they weren't bad. There were no dreadful monster beaks jutting out from the rods. Everything appeared remarkably balanced; each student was making pleasant patterns and designs from randomly selected pieces of metal. It was good stuff, as good as the stuff you can see at the Guggenheim. I will wager to this day that if you had cut off any or all of those "sculpted" rods and mounted them on a good piece of wood, and then given them fancy names, you could have had them on exhibit in New York within a week. They would have sold like hotcakes.

Why? The answer is not mysterious. What happens, for example, when people put apples in a bowl? They don't just pour them in haphazardly; they put them in, one carefully here and another carefully there. They shift and rearrange them until they are pleased with what they see. Most people have this most extraordinary sense of pattern, placement, design—of aesthetics. It is innate; we strive for decoration because decoration is so important in our lives.

My lesson in arts and aesthetics at Bell Vocational convinced me to be both a commercial welder and a metal-welding sculptor. I knew the commercial side would earn me at least $10/hour and I guessed that the other would top that by at least a factor of ten. As it turned out, I was right on both counts.

My career in commercial welding took off immediately. I set up a business partnership with a biker-friend, Don Breid. We had attended Bell together and, as it turned out, we made a good team. Don was not an educated person; I doubt seriously if he had ever read a book in his life. But he was amusing and smart. We worked well together because he didn't make any demands on my obscure talents of intellectualism and I didn't make any claims on his unique skills. We just liked to weld, and we figured we could make money doing it by working together.

Our business, which we called K-D Welding, was based on a simple observation: heavy equipment at construction sites always breaks when it is being used, and it is almost always used during the daylight hours. Further, it is impossible to find someone on the spot, during the day, to fix it. Repairs by necessity have to wait for the next daylight day. But Don and I had a brilliant idea. We went to construction sites around the D.C. area and told the supervisory foremen we would work at night—that whenever anything breaks during the day to call us, give us access to the site, and by the next morning when the equipment is needed it would be ready.

K-D Welding was a good idea, one that people liked, one that could have been franchised—especially if we had been better welders. But we had just finished classes at Bell and there were a few imperfections in our technique. One imperfection was quite funny. We were working on the banks of the Potomac on what I believe was the stormiest night to ever hit Washington. We were repairing large dump trucks, or more accurately the protective guards that surround the body and cab of the trucks and that are frequently damaged. One of the guards, the one we were working on, was a projection that extended over the top of the cab to protect it from falling pieces of junk, debris, and dirt. There was a fracture in it and our job was to repair it.

One of the great perils in arc welding, particularly for new welders with unrestrained enthusiasm, is burning holes in the objects of repair. Don and I did just that, cutting a visible circle in the cab's protective shield. Holes, of course, are easy to repair, but the weather was deteriorating by the minute and Don did not want to spend any more time at the site. After staring at the hole for a few moments, Don very matter-of-factly said, "Let's leave it like that. If anybody asks about it, we'll say we left it there on purpose as a drain hole." I thought to myself, "This guy is smart." He had the conviction that he could pull it off, which to my mind shows strong character and a good deal of self-confidence.

All of our welding, of course, was done at night, and much of it was within blocks of the Capitol building. What I recall most from those nights were the lights of our arc welders. We would show up shortly after sunset and work into the early hours of the morning. Invariably, some poor old drunks would show up to watch our work. We would warn them about the danger of looking directly at the light from our arc welder—a light of such intensity that it could blind onlookers or, at the very least, give them the sensation of eyelids filled with coarse sand. They never listened, and after awhile we gave up trying to warn them of the danger. What we didn't give up on was marveling at the light show we created every night.

Except for a few street lights, our work sites were unusually dark. But the intense light of our arc welder changed all of that. An arc welder in action is like a sweeping spotlight at an airport. Lots and lots of light is generated. When we worked, the play of the light and the projection of every shape and size of shadow imaginable on the tall buildings that surrounded us created a light show of overwhelming proportions. We enjoyed and absorbed the art of the shadows with equal enthusiasm and amazement. It didn't matter that I had read about art and Don hadn't; we both had the same reaction and pleasure.

I am convinced that if most people, those with or without a reading education, were not systematically discouraged by phony experts into believing that one has to know something to appreciate art, the majority of them would be much more inclined to include—and appreciate—art in their lives. This was certainly true with Don; he loved our nighttime light shows. We would talk about them till three or four in the morning. We weren't hurried; we had lots of time to think and look. It was absorbing, colorful, and even inspiring. Welding was an extension of how we felt, an occupation and a commitment not of our intellect, but of our entire beings to the melding of light, metal, and shadow. It was the best job I have ever had, and because Don and I did it at such an unusual hour, we were able to command premium pay for it. If I could be a welder again, I would choose to do it just that way.

My partnership in K-D Welding did not last long—though not because of a lack of either work or enthusiasm. Shortly after I graduated from Bell, the Institute for Policy Studies started to put increasing demands on my time. In addition, I was still writing a column for Senator Goldwater and I had just started working with Thomas Reeves on a co-authored book, *The End of the Draft*. So, I shifted from commercial welding to art welding, a more specialized use of my new trade, but one that could be scheduled for any time of the day and one which, I quickly learned, is per pound the most lucrative use of welding. And in my case, I found that metal transformed into a vague shape was almost as valuable as platinum.

I had my first art showing at a Georgetown gallery not long after I left K-D Welding. *Time* magazine covered the show and called it "eye-riveting." It was a sellout. When asked to explain my work, I wrote this brief overview:

> Rather than trying to duplicate the fine arts, representational style of tra-
> ditional cast and carved sculpture, I have tried to make designs in steel
> which express the innate quality of the metal itself, its texture, weights,
> and strength. Steel is the heart of productive life as we know it today. It
> is to us what wood and stone were to other times. My work doesn't try
> to do anything more than simply turn this crucial metal into decorative
> patterns without ever losing sight of the inherent, commonplace utility
> that is the basic purpose of such metal.

My work was good. I thought doing the sculptures was immensely enjoyable and I thought it was better than almost anything comparable on the market. In fact, the only other similar uses of metal at the time were tricky things, like one artist's constructions of long, tapered beams on axles that swiveled in the wind. And then, of course, there was David Smith, a former production-line welder at Studebaker who happened to have an excellent eye for what metal should look like. But beyond these few people and myself, there were not many artists doing abstract metal sculpture.

If I had been more sensible and patient about living just one life, I would have liked to have been a full-time metal sculptor. People liked my work. The Corcoran Gallery gave space for it. It was abstract, but it was also pleasant to look at and it made a strong statement about the function and nature of steel. I would distinguish my work from other arenas of abstract art, however. Jackson Pollock is a good example of what I mean. He is an interesting old character, maybe, but his fame is due not to the quality of his works but to David Hunter of the Indianapolis Art Museum who wrote a book about what Jackson Pollock meant by his paintings. That's not hard to do. Without reading one page of Hunter's book, anyone can look at one of his paintings and say what it meant. It meant that he was smoking while he was painting, and that is why there are ashes all over it. It meant that it was painted on the ground, which explains much of its contour. But mainly it meant that the free market works. You can sell anything in the free market. It's all subjective—precisely as von Mises said; people attach value to things and, when they do, a price is set.

Most of my sculpting was done at a studio garage I rented on Capitol Hill. Besides welding steel into art, I learned a lot about children—in this case, black children. I learned they hated school, and I learned exactly why. School meant nothing to them, certainly no more than a Jackson Pollock painting. They resented reading about Charles Dickens's world of English poverty when they were as poor as the dickens in their own American world. Their rats were as big as Dickens's rats, and given a choice between the two they were more interested in their own. I found, however, there were things they would learn if those things had immediate application—such as measuring metal for cutting. They were intrigued by what I was doing, and I let them measure everything I could think of, thinking that measurement was one way to get them intellectually interested in the material world that so fascinated me.

The only exception to my regular use of the Capitol Hill studio for metal work was a trip I took in the winter of 1968–69 to Rhodesia (now Zimbabwe) to weld a sculpture for the Archives Building in the country's capital, Salisbury (now Harare). I was particularly fond of Rhodesia; I never believed it was the racist society that South Africa was, and I felt a great deal of sympathy for its declaration of independence from Great Britain.

My very close friend, Wainwright Dawson, set the trip up and arranged for a shop where I could do my work. It was a native African welding shop, one where the highest-paid welder was black. They provided the equipment and the steel I needed. The design for the sculpture came from my reigning interest in triangles—a fact explained by a recent discovery I had made of triangular pieces of metal left over from a commercial cutting job in D.C. So, I used a triangular model—I did a sculpture of floating triangles (all with open centers), one in an upright position to frame the piece and the other floating three-quarters above in a somewhat slanted orientation. It turned out well. It was unveiled in a public ceremony, and Ian Smith, then president of Rhodesia, gave a brief speech.

I still love welding, particularly gas welding—the mode I relied on most when doing my metal sculptures. Today, a faulty heart precludes the kind of heavy lifting that is the stock of the trade. Still, I dabble from time to time. The last welding I did was in the late '80s when I ran an 85-foot arc bead flat along a lowboy designed to carry a replica of James Rumsey's steamboat as part of a local celebration. All I had to do was lift the stinger and meld myself with the light, the metal, and the shadows. It wasn't the light show Don and I were accustomed to, but I am sure he would have understood.

17

Technologist

A human being should be able to change a diaper, plan an invasion, butcher a hog, conn a ship, design a building, write a sonnet, balance accounts, build a wall, set a bone, comfort the dying, take orders, give orders, cooperate, act alone, solve equations, analyze a new problem, pitch manure, program a computer, cook a tasty meal, fight efficiently, die gallantly. Specialization is for insects.
—Robert Heinlein, *Time Enough for Love*

It was August 18, 1992, and I knew that I was very sick, suffering another congestive heart failure whose frequency had increased from once every three months to once every other month. The time to die, I learned later on, was within a few days given what seemed to be the unalterable course of my failing heart.

Then, while lying on an examination table, with a notice felt-penned on my back by Therese (*Caution: Open Other Side*), the head of the cardiac transplant unit of the University of Virginia Hospital in Charlottesville came in and almost casually said, "Well, do you want to do it?" A heart had come in, he explained, and if further checking found it suitable it was all mine! Hard to believe after almost a year on the waiting list.

I had gone on the transplant list in October 1991, during one of my many bouts with congestive heart failure. Medically, there seemed

227

nothing to it. Stitching in a new heart, surgeons told me, is actually one of the simpler sorts of surgery. The more difficult part, as I quickly learned, is the waiting. You simply cannot schedule the availability of a heart. It makes waiting a fairly anxious affair. It also puts you in an interesting state of mind when you contemplate such things as the Christmas holidays. While others may think of rolling in the olde Yule log, I thought of the possibility of high traffic-accident rates and the rolling in of hearts.

The logistics of heart transplantation are interesting, too. When an appropriate heart is reported to what amounts to a regional clearinghouse, a doctor from the University of Virginia medical center zooms off to inspect and, if suitable, harvest it. As he heads back to the hospital, someone activates a long-range beeper which Therese carries with her at all times. Upon being beeped, she loads me into the car and off we go. The trip to Charlottesville takes two and a half hours if we aren't fussy about speed limits. There is a total window of four hours to get on the table.

None of this was necessary. I was already in the hospital when doctors learned of a locally-available heart. I accepted it graciously. Around midnight, a nurse gave me a shot which, I presumed, was just to calm me down. A few minutes later, I thought, I awakened feeling good but groggy. "When do we begin?" I asked. "It's all done," one of the surgeons replied. I had been out for more than twelve hours.

After a long stay in the medical center—complicated by a nasty little bug, Cytomegalovirus, which lies dormant in most people—I was wheeled over to a rehabilitation hospital. My initial reaction was sheer annoyance; I wanted to go home. "Do you know where you are?" asked Big Nurse. "I'm right here," replied Little Smart Ass. "Do you know who's president?" Who cares? Why don't they leave me alone? But no—and fortunately—they didn't.

My first full taste of the project came with physical therapy in a gymnasium-type room with large padded mats along the wall. Resident thereon were some badly banged-up people: amputees, head-trauma victims in plastic helmets, people in a variety of casts—and me.

Again, annoyance, when my first task was announced: get out of my wheelchair and take a few unassisted steps. Hah! Why didn't they ask me to do something challenging? By the time I had struggled out of the wheelchair and taken *two* steps, I was aware that the rehab people knew more about my condition than I did. I came to this conclusion as I slid slowly down onto a mat.

In two weeks, I learned to walk again, slowly and carefully, with a cane. I also learned that the physical therapy room was a stage on which important social lessons played themselves out. No matter how bad off a patient seemed, therapists pushed and pushed, urging them take one more step, to go another few feet on the exercycle, to keep going. With their help, people who might have just become wards of the state were, instead, struggling to regain control of, and responsibility for, their own lives. Some of them must have been hurting badly as they struggled to take the next step, to go the extra foot—but they persisted. My beau ideal was an elderly woman whose legs had been amputated but who was unstoppable in her determination to walk and walk well on the jointed metal sticks which now were her legs.

An old technology had given her a way to walk again, and a novel one was giving me a chance to just live. A new pump had been sewn into my chest. As simple as that—well, almost. The transplant people at the University of Virginia had been plagued by a TV show in which people reported changes in personality of friends and family members who had received replacement hearts. They talked of men having homosexual tendencies after receiving female hearts, and white people who walked and talked differently after supposedly receiving hearts from black donors. Aside from the fact that donor information is kept strictly confidential, the physiological impossibility of these things is rather firm. Nonetheless, so long as people *think* that something is happening, it might as well *be* happening. Alas.

What I believe is that what I *think* is crucial to defining me and to operating me. All of the other gooey stuff—colon, bowels, lungs, kidneys, etc.—may be replaced without any noticeable change in a person's thinking, capacities for love, loyalty, contemplation, creativity, good or ill nature. The dear old brain, however, remains the operator in chief. Snip a hunk of it and you go silly, clip another and you can't walk or talk. Meantime, the other stuff seems to know what to do without being told.

A poet-biologist has pointed out that if the various organs had to be told what to do, we would collapse with switchboard jam-up. I certainly, however, have no wish to impugn the organs lying below the cranium, nor do I want to reduce poetic imagery to a minor role by discounting the symbolism of guts, true grit, and a noble heart. I just want to make it clear that when people say they are following their heart and not their head, that they cannot mean, way down deep (in the bowels for instance), that they have been able to close down Mr. Brain, abolish language, and do something without reference to the symbols with which our mind is stuffed. One may feel that a message is coming up from the bowels. But without the thinking, I feel, it would remain a rumble, perhaps pretty and deceptive like a baby's smile with gas, but still *just* an act of digestion and not at all like the happiness of the loving parent who *thinks* that the kid is beautifully, beatifically, beamingly in ecstasy.

I see technology in this light—nothing metaphorical or mystical, simply a product of a thinking mind, a wondrous tool to change how we live. That is how I viewed the transplant—from the eyes of a onetime teenager who had delved into the simpler mysteries of chemistry and had spent a summer at the D.C. morgue learning about life; from the mind, not the heart, of a onetime aspirant to MIT who now, a half-century later, had not a single regret for straying from the straight and narrow path of science to the more convoluted and varied paths described in this book.

Strange as it may seem, it makes sense. I am by personality a poet and an engineer (or at least a tinkerer), by curiosity a scientist, and only by a long series of strange circumstances, a professional political scientist.

Properly speaking, I am an admirer of technology rather than a strict technologist, though I have done my share of using science to address everyday concerns. It—the dreaming and inventing of new technologies—is one of the many divisions of labor to which I have reconciled myself over the years and willingly left to others. In fact, most people are comfortable with the idea of not being able to do everything themselves. They call on a plumber when the drain clogs. They call on a surgeon when an appendix ruptures—or a heart needs replacement. They call upon an investment counselor when a stock seems to be going haywire. They call upon a lawyer when some other lawyer files a suit against them. They call the local library when there's a book they want but do not have. There are, of course, people who try to do as much of the needed work as they can possibly do—all by themselves. But no one can do everything; everyone relies on the division of labor sometimes. There are limits to what each of us can do, and a graceful acceptance of those limits could be called a sort of wisdom.

There is one area, however, where limits and a division of labor are not gracefully accepted by most people. That area is human intelligence. Some people who accept the division of labor do so with a tacit belief, apparently, that they are intelligent enough to do the needed work but that they are just too busy, or too occupied with more important matters.

Egalitarianism, that evergreen mirage, may be acceptably discarded in almost every walk of ordinary life—but not in the matter of intelligence. We are all born equal, people say, and after that it's up to you. Every human mind is endowed with certain inalienable rights, such as the right to do anything that it wants. It has become a modern mantra: I am a person of infinite worth. I can do anything I want. Listen to the talk shows on TV, for instance, with the newly empowered people telling you how, since they have come to love themselves, they can do anything. Self-esteem is the ticket to infinite wonders and limitless accomplishment.

What nonsense.

I have been loaded with self-esteem since I could walk and talk. Yet I have not mastered calculus. I've tried, but I am simply not smart enough. My intelligence is high on the verbal side of things, and low to stupid on the math side. I have mastered fractions enough to do simple cabinetry and I actually enjoy reading the *Elements of Euclid*. But I am as likely to come up with a geometric concept of my own as I am to sprout wings and fly across the ocean. Being a poet and a very practical engineer is one thing; being a genius in math and the physical sciences or a serious technologist is yet another.

This has never made me feel inferior. I do, after all, have a nifty little scientific calculator that does all sorts of arcane work for me without my ever having an idea of what it's up to most of the time. I'm smart enough to use the calculator—that's all.

Thomas Jefferson, in a letter to John Adams in 1813, spoke against the sort of intellectual egalitarianism that is so faddish today:

> There is a natural aristocracy among men. The grounds of this are virtue and talents. . . . There is also an artificial aristocracy founded on wealth and birth, without either virtue or talents, for with these it would belong to the first class. The natural aristocracy I consider as the most precious gift of nature, for the instruction, the trusts, and government of society. . . . May we not even say, that form of government is best, which provides the most effectually for a pure selection of these natural aristoi into the offices of government? The artificial aristocracy is a mischievous ingredient in government and provision should be made to prevent its ascendency.

Should that be equated with Plato's rule by philosopher princes? Not unless you can find a convincing similarity between the grim prospect of Platonism and the yeoman naturalism of Mr. Jefferson.

The point, for me, is that Jefferson spoke of people naturally endowed, the sort of people I think of when I think of someone like the late Richard Feynman, scientist, bongo drummist, plain-language expositor of problems and solutions. I have neighbors who are part of the natural aristocracy; I have other neighbors who are just plain dumb—all naturally—not by schooling but by native intelligence.

Why is it offensive to think that some people are smarter than other people? Isn't that just a reflection of the division of labor?

Again, watch the talk shows, those constant peerings into modern angst. The most troubled people, you can place bets on this, are the people who have poor language, thus poor analytical abilities of any sort, and who, because of that, feel buffeted by fate, helpless, angry, defended only by powerful opinions and distrust of anyone who does not share those opinions. They are not as intelligent as the people in the audience, but the people in the audience are not much different, just better dressed because they are going to be on TV and they are looking for a moment in the camera's eye. If notions of human intelligence can be applied to any of the hosts or hostesses of these shows it must be with careful reluctance.

Those hosts-hostesses must be aware and even appalled by the incredible soul-squalling and situation-baring that their guests are prepared to endure. Surely such people, seeking the public pillory like junkies after cocaine, cannot be considered very smart. They do not seem qualified for the natural aristocracy. So what? Would most of them actually be offended to discover that a poet or a rocket scientist had a higher IQ or a greater SAT score? They might not, but liberal defenders of the idea of intellectual egalitarianism probably would.

As a writer and a self-taught engineer, I am sensitive to the intellectual division of labor, yet I am not offended by it nor am I troubled by the natural shortcomings in my own affinity to the theoretical sciences. These are facts, ones that I can live with comfortably and without regret. A good friend, for example, earned his Ph.D. at the University of Wisconsin in high-energy physics studying what I believe, at this point in time, is the world's most uninteresting question: the origin of the universe. Some people are driven by that sort of curiosity, but I suspect many of them are really driven by the realization that (1) if they come up with answers, they still won't know for sure—it's an academic exercise that can go on for a billion years—and (2) even if they do find out, they can't do anything about it. The difference between these two essential attitudes—the engineering and the scientific—is telling.

I have an engineering attitude that is flawed sometimes by a scientific one. I occasionally get inordinately curious about weird things—which I guess is the scientific part of it. I sometimes like to know why something happens. But my general attitude is an engineering one which is simply, "Well, if it works, it is not absolutely necessary for me to understand why." I can tell you, for example, precisely where, in a speech I have written, audiences will laugh, cry, cheer, or do whatever. I sense it. I could spend some time trying to understand why I sense it, but I don't know what good that would do since I don't miss *not* knowing.

My engineering attitude was shaped in my youth. I nurtured it as a child when, in early years of sickness from pneumonia and rheumatic fever, I would spend hours building a mountain of gadgets—just as I love to do today. That early proclivity toward modest invention reinforced my engineering outlook. My mother was important, too. I think she was an engineer; she didn't care so much why things worked, but if something did work she was red hot on it.

Natural limits to my scientific prowess do not lessen my fondness for technology nor diminish my love of tools. If anything, they heighten and expand my regard for science, not because science is a truth or because technology is an absolute value—which is false in both instances—but because science as the way of exploration and technology as the process of building profoundly affect the way we live.

I am not brash about science and technology, though I do claim an engineer's pumpkin grin for pieces of machinery and electronics that do what we want them to do. There are, for example, thirty-six electrical outlets separately wired along my desktop. There is also a 36-inch slide rule in my drawer just in case the outlets fail and my scientific calculator stops working. These are tools that I truly love, *not* adore or worship, just love. Sure, I still read literature, even some classics. I enjoy them. Other people's learned opinions are the gossip of the upper middle class to which I belong. But good and effective tools are the Excalibur swords of the doing and the daring class, to which I also belong, and always will.

Making tools—whether dreaming up the theory behind them or forging them from molten steel or inert electronic parts—is admittedly not my strength in the great division of labor. But that is unimportant. What is important is that I understand how to use the tools before me and that I understand the reasons and consequences of what I do with them.

Even though an engineer in mind-set, I am firmly wedded to Western science and the scientific method. Some time ago I attended a Green conference where the "scientific wisdom" of ancient peoples was touted over the experimental scientific approach of Western culture. Someone argued that earlier cultures had mastered the proper use and conservation of natural resources—what they called wise and appropriate science. They bemoaned the apparent fact that this venerable body of "scientific" knowledge had been overlooked or simply ignored in the march of modern technology.

I spoke up, suggesting that this ancient wisdom was not science at all. It is, in fact, long-term observation confined to a very specific and usually small geographic area. And it is absolutely appropriate to its purpose which is to exploit available resources. If, for instance, it is observed, possibly over centuries, that some herb has a certain curative effect or that some crop grows best in some color soil, it would be folly not to do the things that work. And we admire those who do such sensible things. In my view, however, it does little good to equate such long-term, sensible observation with the altogether different processes of the Western scientific method.

In the first place, there is no concept of truth in Western science. Its project is to discard older explanations for newer and more encompassing or profound ones. Further, although it is observation-based, it seeks to unwind or understand more about material-world processes. This leads to a major practical difference between Western science and ancient wisdom. The Western process largely is portable. Its theorizing tends to be toward the understanding of general principles of operation. The other source of wisdom is rarely portable. When local conditions change, the long-term observations that have served so well, even for centuries, are thrown into disarray and, by and large, cannot react quickly. Western science at least provides the possibility of immediate response to sudden, even cataclysmic change.

The development of pollution-eating microorganisms (a major project today) is an example of this sort of quick response due to deeper process knowledge. People without such quick-response abilities have, over the centuries, been wiped out by plagues, famines, and other such sudden dislocations of the very environments which they had counted on to be stable and unchanging. I am not opposed to any local sorts of science. Far from it. My enthusiasm is for the culture of the West and not against the culture of anyone else. My fear, however, is that there is a gathering movement in this country eventually to ban forms of scientific curiosity, by force.

A good example of this is Jeremy Rifkin, the leading public critic of genetic engineering. Much of his objection to genetic engineering is based upon familiar themes: the science is terribly elitist, being practiced by only a few people; it is terribly dangerous because of the possibility of nightmarish new microorganisms being created in the laboratory and permitted to escape to ravage the planet; it is terribly anti-egalitarian because it might prolong the lives of those who could afford it, permit parents to select traits for their children, and so forth.

The facts weaken all of those points. Genetic engineering is becoming a respected and widespread technical discipline, immensely useful to farmers, to the ill, and to those who need new tools to help clean up the environment. Its basic equipment is dropping so in cost that even some backyard experimenters may be expected to take advantage of it. Fears of monster organisms have abated, safety procedures voluntarily have been adopted, and the "natural" scourges such as AIDS continue to make even science-fiction "monsters" look pale by comparison. Finally, those who can afford it already prolong their lives with good diet and nonabrasive lifestyles, and parents always have selected traits for their children, wittingly or not, in their own choices of mates. Genetic engineering doesn't change any of that, it just adds a more conscious dimension to it.

Still, Rifkin is committed to using government to kill the science and technology of genetic engineering. Similar protests are popping up in other arenas of scientific inquiry. There, as well as in the field of genetics, the ultimate objection is that such scientific probings into the unknown are unnatural, and against the will of God. Not surprisingly, some of Rifkin's most vocal supporters are religious fundamentalists who, apparently, couldn't agree more with his fears.

My adult dabbling in science and technology started in Washington, D.C., after my exit from Republican politics. It was modest at first, serving the practical needs of motorcycle maintenance and the emerging needs of arc welding and metal sculpting. It soon edged further into my life, first because of the need to keep the houseboat on which I lived afloat and second because I became, by default, the resident expert in appropriate, community-based technology at the Institute for Policy Studies. It did not reach its zenith, however, until after my marriage to Therese.

In 1973, Therese and I formed a group called Community Technology. Its purpose was simply to demystify technology so that instead of seeming a mysterious force it could become a part of everyday life, a catalyst to community self-reliance, a way to give people greater control over their individual destinies, and a servant in direct service to human needs in a local setting.

That local setting was the Adams-Morgan neighborhood. It spanned some seventy blocks in the center of Washington, D.C., and, at the time, had a population that was 58 percent black, 22 percent Latin American, 18 percent white, and the remainder mostly Middle Eastern. It was a neighborhood in transition, economically quite poor but culturally diverse and exciting. It was, we believed, the perfect place to try an experiment in participatory community that would make technology accessible and understandable to those who choose to use it. There was, we believed, a need for Community Technology. While neighbors, citizens, and community leaders worried about every other aspect of the neighborhood, there seemed to be no one very concerned about its material base—how it could produce things.

Our answer was inexpensive, available, and decentralized technology—giving local residents the tools, and the scientific understanding, to produce what they needed and where they needed it most: at home and in community. There was nothing extraordinary or presumptuous in our belief that average citizens could master the basic science and technology needed to be more self-reliant. After all, we live in a world where all normally intelligent people use a very scientific approach in dealing with material things—it's just that most of us don't realize it.

Most people *have* to be scientists of sorts to function effectively nowadays. The car you drive has roughly the explosive potential of a whole box of artillery shells. When you turn on a water tap, you're working with hydraulics—a science that was unknown until the twentieth century. And look at the average kitchen. It's an alchemist's laboratory. You've got to use scientific methods when you handle such equipment or you'll kill yourself.

So it occurred to Therese and me that if we could show the people in our rather downtrodden neighborhood that they were already thinking scientifically, then just maybe that fact would give them the confidence to think and do more for themselves, and to listen less to the politicians. This was the grand scheme for Community Technology, one that seemed right for the time, practical—not utopian—in its vision.

Socially it was a failure. We constantly worked against the "official magic" of city and federal government, the propensity of central authorities to offer citizens magical solutions to local problems. They would *give* something to everyone. They would give some a social worker, others a pass to the hospital, money, or food stamps. The only thing they would never give is the capacity to produce wealth locally. In short, they would never end poverty; they would just alleviate it. We suggested that *it* could be ended. But, given the choice between working hard to end poverty and not having to do anything and have *it* alleviated, most people made the choice to let somebody else give them the essentials of life. Why work when you can just shake the magic tree?

Community Technology (CT) did succeed in a more modest, and maybe more important, way. It demonstrated that an urban neighborhood could be self-sufficient in the production of its food and wealth. The heart of Community Technology was a warehouse in Adams-Morgan that we rented at a bargain price and outfitted with the tools of our chosen self-sufficiency. Financially, CT was a shoestring operation, supported in small part by the Institute for Policy Studies and in much larger part from Therese's salary and from the income of my lecture circuit. There was no formal structure, no officers or elected leaders to CT; there was just a small, informal core of active people who worked together cooperatively and mostly in a thoughtful manner.

We did many things at CT, but the one activity that stands out most was our experiment in rearing trout indoors to feed the neighborhood outside. The cast of characters in that experiment was remarkable. CT's resident advisor was a wonderful older fellow by the name of Fernwood Mitchell. He was not a political activist as some of us were or had been; he was just a scientist. Fernwood had designed a fish-rearing system of great repute in Canada. His skills were essential.

Besides Fernwood, there was Jeffrey Woodside, my hippie hero. I groaned inwardly when I first saw him at an early CT meeting. If you had sent to central casting for the perfect hippie, you would have gotten Jeff. He was bone thin and tall, had long reddish hair in a ponytail, wore tattered jeans, and was so absolutely calm that I presumed he had to be stoned on grass. I groaned because I was certain he would say "wow" at every opportunity and that he would be a groupie of the project rather than an active and creative member. What stuck in my mind as I looked at Jeff was the then-popular saying that the only problem with geodesic domes was that they were all built by hippies. Having been a hippie myself, I was touched by their sweetness and their great affection for affection, but God they were so careless of detail! I had come into CT with a Western, linear way of thinking, and Jeff seemed its antithesis.

I was wrong. Toward the end of the meeting as Therese and I were getting acquainted with the group, Jeff walked over to us and matter-of-factly said, "I'm a high-energy physicist, but I love this kind of work. I'm a fairly good carpenter and I am really enthusiastic about the project. I would like to work at it as close to full time as I can." As I mentioned to him later, and as I quickly confided to Therese, if there had been a preacher on the premises I would have demanded our marriage immediately. He was everything that was good about a hippie: considerate, sweet, contemplative, and playful. But he understood also the difference between a 90-degree and an 89-degree angle—and the devastating effects the difference could have. He would later become a full-time theoretical physicist at the University of Iowa, but for the time being he was the rock-solid core of our little enterprise.

And then there was C. J. Swet. He was an MIT graduate, a Quaker, and a former scientist at the Johns Hopkins University physics lab. When the lab began a weapons research program a few years earlier he had refused to work on it and the university had let him go. Unemployed and in his early forties, he and his wife, Emily, moved to a small Maryland farm where they subsisted on the harvest of staple crops. His presence at CT was a constant delight, even though his practical skills had long since been compromised by the sheer mass of what he had learned at MIT and Johns Hopkins. Emily also worked at CT and, like Jeff, was a figure from central casting, though in this instance the paragon of an iron-willed but confectionarily sweet, small Quaker lady.

All of us—including others like Fernwood, Jeff, and C. J. and a handful of old, tough radicals—embarked as mariners on an uncertain sea. In our case, of course, it was an indoor warehouse sea where we hoped to raise rainbow trout for commercial sale and local consumption. We knew the project would float, but the details of how to keep it afloat took a great deal of innovation.

My contribution, of which I am rather proud, was the fish tanks. I built them from wood, sealed with fiberglass resin. I reasoned that a tank designed to hold water inside is nothing but a boat in reverse. And having recently lived on a boat, I knew that boats could be made that floated; that they didn't have to leak. Within weeks I had built a series of four-foot cube tanks that didn't leak and that soon became home to thousands of rainbow trout.

More than tanks were needed, however. We also required a filtering system to remove the high—and lethal—concentrations of ammonia left from the rapid accumulation of fish wastes. There are many ways to handle this problem, but the one we chose was the simplest. A number of bacteria feed successfully on high-ammonia wastes. They can live almost anywhere, but they thrive particularly well on natural substrates such as old clamshells. So, we found the clamshells, dug up a few spoonfuls of dirt that were full of all kinds of bacteria, including the ones we sought, and dumped it all into the filtering chambers of our wooden fish tanks. The bacteria took hold immediately.

The other challenge to the trout-rearing project was to find a cheap source of motors and pumps to aerate the tanks and to propel a constant current of water against which the fish could swim. I knew that all the motors and pumps we needed were right in our own neighborhood of Adams-Morgan—in the form of discarded washing machines. Most washing machines get thrown out not because of a motor or pump failure —the pumps being simple centrifugal devices—but because of some failure in this or that insignificant part. I was right, and we soon had tanks filled with trout, bacterial filters cleansing the water of ammonia, and motors and pumps working diligently twenty-four hours a day.

Each tank was packed with trout. In fact, they were so closely packed that they would wear out their dorsal fins by the time of harvest. The pumps maintained a strong, steady current to ensure that food reached every fish—they ate constantly—and to make sure that the fish were working vigorously against the flow of water to keep them healthy and to build and tone their muscle. Although the trout seemed too busy to care, this rearing practice bothered some people. It did not phase Jeffrey Woodside. One time, I fondly recall, a volunteer asked, "Are those fish happy?" Jeff, who looked as though he had been hit by what we used to call a swivet—a bag full of human solid waste—answered, "How in the world would I know whether fish are happy or not? I've never seen one laugh. I've never talked to one. But ours are alive and gaining weight faster than rainbow trout do in mountain streams. They must be doing well. Plus, they taste good."

Jeff's answer further endeared him to me. I am not a great advocate of animal rights. In fact, I question the entire notion of rights even as applied to people. Nonetheless, I don't believe in cruelty to anything, including animals. I have, of course, killed thousands of fish in my life, but I have never for a moment felt that the fish I hook and fillet are surprised by that fact. I am just a bigger fish chopping its head off. Why should the fish care *who* does it?

I will admit deer bother me a bit. Their eyes are some evolutionary trick to elicit a phony reaction and a miss on an otherwise sure shot. They look sweet and pitiful. But they also look good in the frying pan. I don't have a problem with that—nor did the crew at CT when it came to growing, harvesting, and eating fish. We simply ignored the sweetly intended inquiries into the happiness of our trout.

What we didn't ignore was the fact that we could not have done the project with any commercial species other than trout. If we had tried to raise rabbits—which would have been easier to rear and would have had a very high-protein content—the dozens of kids that visited the warehouse daily would have invariably named each and every rabbit. Nobody to my knowledge has ever killed and eaten a rabbit named Charlie or Lenny. But with fish we felt safe. No one could tell them apart, and if they couldn't be separated, they couldn't be named. Raising fish was a good choice.

One other thing we did not ignore was the sensitivity of our trout to climatic environmental disaster. Rainbow trout cannot tolerate warm water, especially if heated to the temperatures common in summertime Washington, D.C. We had a choice, therefore: We could cool the water directly with a refrigerant system, which was the expensive way to do it, or we could cool the warehouse room—which turned out to be not only cheaper, but much more efficient. Cooling the room, however, created another problem. If the air conditioning went off for more than an hour or so due to a power outage, auxiliary generators would have to be brought on line to restart the cooling process. Quickly switching between the commercial power lines and our generators was the project's Achilles' heel. One time when the switching did fail, we lost several full tanks of rainbow trout to a small variation in temperature.

The fish project was a good experiment. We produced lots of fish and we learned new and critical technologies for community self-reliance. We anticipated, maybe foolishly, that the citizens of Adams-Morgan would flock to our warehouse to volunteer for work and to buy the fish we grew. They didn't. We did the work and we ate the fish ourselves. Adams-Morgan, as it turned out, was not the right place to do the experiment, and it was certainly not the right place to build the community participation we sought.

Perhaps the reason is exemplified by a sad encounter I had with a young boy, ten or eleven years of age, who came to the warehouse one day and asked me if I had a job for him. Other kids and adults had asked the same, and we had happily found things for them to do—including, if need be, running up and down the streets of Adams-Morgan shouting mantras of praise for our project. I told him "sure," and asked what kind of work he would like to do. He answered that he didn't want to work; he wanted a job. This was sophisticated thinking for a ten-year-old, so much so that I could hardly believe it. I said, "What do you mean you want a job but you don't want to work? What's the difference?" He answered, "A job is where you pay me and work is where I have to do something."

His words were discouraging, yet instructive. They spoke reams about a neighborhood more accustomed to welfare than self-help, more attuned to the rule of others than to the rule of self and neighbor. There was another child who hung around the warehouse. He was about five, and had been terribly abused by his mother. He came to visit almost every day. He would cling to my leg, wrap himself around it, and ride it for hours. I loved that little kid. He was so sweet. I thought, what a shame: in a few years he will learn like so many others in the neighborhood the difference between work and a job.

Community Technology died shortly after Therese and I left Washington for the hills of West Virginia in the summer of 1975. In fact, a lot died, including our faith in the community in which we had lived.

The catalyst for our leaving Washington and losing faith in Adams-Morgan was crime. We had been robbed before. Our apartment had been broken into on several occasions and our Ford pickup had been vandalized on an almost regular schedule. None of that had discouraged our fealty to our neighborhood. But it all changed quickly that summer.

Therese and I had gone to Goddard College in Vermont, where I was teaching in the social ecology program run by Murray Bookchin—an academic anarchist who always referred to me as the redneck anarchist. We were there only a few days when we got an anguished telephone call from the woman who was sitting our house. While she was out doing laundry, in the middle of the afternoon, someone had torn our apartment door completely off its hinges, entered, and stolen everything of value we owned except for Therese's typewriter. We returned home immediately.

We were both devastated. Nothing was left: My prize target pistols were gone, and even the simple flutes that gave Therese and I so much pleasure in the late summer evenings were missing. These were things we realized we would never have again.

Making matters worse, the apartment was an absolute mess. Everywhere we looked there were signs of the break-in. What bothered Therese the most were the orange remnants of dusted fingerprints left over from the police investigation. They were nagging reminders to both of us that someone we did not know, yet who bore us ill will, had been rummaging around in our things. We no longer felt safe in our home or in our neighborhood.

Fortunately, we had a choice. Well before the robbery we had looked at land along the Opequon Creek in the Eastern Panhandle of West Virginia, some seventy-five miles west of Washington. Rennie and Pam Parziale, close friends and kindred exiles from Washington, had already settled there and had found a parcel of land they thought would be ideal for us. It was twelve acres of riverfront and upland meadows nestled in a sharp bend in the Opequon with a steep hillside rising from the opposite shore. It had water, it had trees, it had wildlife, it had meadows, and, most of all, it had privacy. We fell in love with it immediately. Therese put a down payment on the land, with the idea that she and I would move there in ten or so years after our work in Washington was done.

The robbery changed our plans. With our apartment ransacked, our possessions mostly gone, and our sense of security fatally wounded, the allure of Washington faded fast—and fastest for Therese. Shortly after our return from Goddard she told me she had made her decision. She was going to West Virginia and I was welcome to go with her. People say that certain events lead to a flashing of one's life before their eyes. Well, when you get a mandate like that from someone whose absence for just a moment you can feel—say going in and out of a room—it does not take long to say, "What do you want to take?" And I said just that.

We packed up the essentials that we still owned. We had, of course, several thousand books, institute-type books mostly on political science which look terribly impressive on walls but which few people, including myself, ever read in their entirety. We decided to offer them in trade for books that might actually be of use to us in West Virginia. We didn't get a single nibble on our offer. So, we then offered to swap them for tools. We advertised on bulletin boards and in the local newspaper our desire to trade a set of politically correct books for a good set of socket wrenches. Nothing. The market had made its decision: The collective political wisdom of the ages was not worth a good set of forged-steel hand tools. It was sobering for me to realize how many of the books people own are simply amulets, ornaments bought to perform some magic work, as if just having them makes someone a better person. I know they don't, but the thought is hard to resist.

We left the books behind, packed only the few things we thought we would really need—which were few indeed—and headed to our new home on the Opequon, approximately midway between Martinsburg and Kearneysville, West Virginia.

For the first year-and-a-half we rented an old farmhouse on a parcel of land bordering the upper edge of our homesite. And with the savings Therese already had on hand and the insurance money from the D.C. break-in, we were able to begin construction of our new home, an earth-sheltered, solar-warmed 2,000-square-foot single-level house that was both elegant and efficient in its basic technology and surprisingly inexpensive in its construction.

Building our home was largely a family affair once the preliminaries were done. A good friend with a backhoe extended the dirt road onto our property, dug out and leveled the building site, and helped install our septic system. The local concrete company poured the slab. The electric company brought in the power line. And a local contractor drilled our water well. Beyond that, every block, pipe, wire, window, door, frame, board, bolt, and nail was placed, screwed, and hammered in by Therese, me, my two sons, and an occasional visitor.

The idea of the house was quite simple. Built into a hillside cut that sheltered the north facing back wall and then opened to the south with a phalanx of windows and glass sliding doors, the structure enjoyed the natural cooling effect of the earth in summer and the natural warming effect of the sun in winter. Therese drew the general plan for the house, a post-and-beam design built on ten-foot-square grids with two counterangling roofs.

Occasionally, as we labored away, we would consult the master plan to remind ourselves of the bigger picture. But usually we simply relied on hand-scratched measurements and scribbled sketches ironed out at early morning breakfast sessions to set the building agenda for the day. Looking back at the casual and largely unplanned way we pieced together our home (there were no county building codes apart from well and septic field requirements) my faith in the ordering influence of chaos and the ability of almost anyone to master the simple skills and tools of living is reaffirmed.

We made mistakes, of course. A write-up of our home in the book, *Thirty Energy-Efficient Houses. . . You Can Build,* correctly points out that "the lack of proper plans meant that there was uncertainty in the placement of underfloor drainage piping." It's true; we just put in a lot of drainage connections and figured we'd work out the fixture layout later. We also made a big mistake when we installed the submersible pump into our well. We didn't read the wiring directions as we should have, and the pump's motor fried itself almost two hundred feet below ground. Other than costing a sizeable amount of cash to replace it, it did give us hands-on experience pulling a forty-pound dead weight with plastic piping and rubber spacers several hundred feet against the forces of gravity and friction. Still, we mostly had fun.

To this day, we think of our south-facing gem as dearly as we would a poem that I had written or a picture that she had painted. We had built a house that we loved, that drew friends and visitors from around the world to our hearth, and that had cost to floor, wall, and roof only $10,000.

We were especially proud of the low cost. To save as much money as possible, we went to sales, salvaged building materials, bartered for supplies, and relied on the informal West Virginia used-parts network to locate and buy what we needed. A retired naval commander who lived not far away in an old brick schoolhouse and who collected bankrupt hardware stores as a hobby was most helpful. He provided at a sharp discount many of the tools, much of the hardware, and all of the glass sliding doors that lined the front of the house. We also bought Andersen basement windows that were of a discontinued size and on sale at a local auction for almost nothing, and then used them to create an open and lighted space between the overlap of the two opposing roofs. When we bought them, we didn't have any idea where we would use them, but figured we'd work them in somehow—and we did. We also saved money by buying dented corrugated aluminum roofing. It was cheap, easy to install, and the dents were barely noticeable. The paneling on the outside of the house came from discarded lumber at the site of an old barn. We bought used appliances at the local auction house, and our bathtub—a six-foot-long stainless-steel commercial dough-mixing tub—was a constant source of surprise and amusement to first-time visitors.

Tools and appropriate technology took on a new and more immediate meaning for me as the house went from vision to reality. I was no longer doing an experiment for *others,* to see if a warehouse full of trout-packed wooden tanks could feed a neighborhood of thousands of people. I was building the place where Therese and I would *live.* I was using tools and technology in a way that mattered profoundly to both of us—and, as it turned out, would also come to matter to our growing circle of friends and neighbors.

Renewed in our love for tools and our commitment to community-based technology, Therese and I started the Appropriate Technology Group in 1976 and continued with it until about 1980. It served the Eastern Panhandle of West Virginia, bringing members together on a monthly basis at different homes and at various project sites to share technological information and to help one another with tools, projects, and problems. Our show-and-tell project was our house, its efficient use of energy, and its innovative construction. An array of other projects, ranging from organic cattle farming to building a functioning duplicate of the locally famous James Rumsey steamboat, kept us engaged in a constant process of learning and creating. So successful was this effort that I enjoyed brief moments of technological notoriety. In 1978 I was elected to the West Virginia Academy of Sciences, named to the Appropriate Technology Task Force of the U.S. Congress's Office of Technology Assessment, and nominated to the Governor's (West Virginia) Advisory Committee on Appropriate Technology.

These years of immersion in small-scale technology changed forever my thinking about the utility of politics and politicians and the importance of tools. I had no lingering, sentimental sufferance for the pompous delusion of politicians that they somehow significantly improve the way we live. It was nonsense. Through taxation, rules, regulations, and war, politicians historically have destroyed people's lives and obstructed their economic progress. The real work of the world—the way we live our daily lives—has been changed by tools and by the people who create them.

I do not mean by this to disparage social or political theory but simply to put it in a prudent place. Inventors, scientists, artists, and merchants change the way we live. Social theorists and political philosophers usually just explain it. At best, they predict it. In either case, they only alter the rhetoric by which people describe how they live. There are, of course, thinkers of the caliber of Charles Murray who compile and analyze facts that can influence local, national, and global events. Still, I believe the rule holds: No political or social scientist in the history of the world has ever changed the way people live.

Even our Founding Fathers didn't change the way we live in any compelling or profound sense. The Bill of Rights was brilliant, of course, and you might make a small case for it as an agent of change. But after two hundred years we are still fighting for our civil liberties, still faced with righteous patriots who have decided in the name of country that burning the flag of the United States should be a violation—not a protected action—of the Bill of Rights. I am not impressed by that; I always have thought that changing the world meant *changing* the world. Sadly, I am not convinced that either the Founders or the Bill of Rights changed anything, fundamentally.

And neither did Christ, as far as I can see. The rhetoric of people who became Christians changed tremendously; it became virtuous to be your brother's keeper, and just maybe some additional charity flowed from it. But the injunctions put on murder and covetousness seem to have changed nothing. People still worship idols in the form of "official" authority, and they still rob, steal, and go to war in obedience to those icons. Christ may have been a kind and generous man, but he was not a world changer. A far better candidate for world changer is Euclid, who lived some three hundred years before Christ. He made it practical to measure things previously unmeasurable, and in so doing revolutionized every aspect of past and present life.

Karl Marx gave us *Das Capital* and scientific socialism; yet in the great reckoning of world-changing events the best that can be said of him and his social theories is that they helped modernize Russian czarism into twentieth-century Leninism and Stalinism. At the same time Marx was conspiring with Engels, Boole was busy inventing algebra and the Wright brothers were soaring to the heavens above Kitty Hawk. Which men and which ideas actually changed the world from the gritty industrialism of the late nineteenth century to the affluent age of information at the cusp of the twenty-first century?

Much the same can be said of Henry Ford. While nations waged war and politicians bickered over national boundaries, Ford changed the world with the automated production of affordable cars. No invention, short of the oxen yoke which first harnessed nonhuman power to human purpose, has so altered the way people live. Consider also the computer which was born in the crucible of World War II. Global warfare replaced old governments with new governments and redrew political boundaries to match the conquests of battle. The computer, in contrast, is now making government redundant by transferring the information and the power needed by people and neighborhoods to govern their own lives. And in Poland, the force that led freedom to triumph over Soviet tyranny was not Christianity or the solace of John Paul; it was the toolmakers and tool users of the Polish shipyards.

My point is simply this: What really changes our world and the way we live in it are devices and innovations. If you want to know what is happening in a society at any point, look at the tools—not the rhetoric, not the books, not the philosophy. If a tool is available you can bet somebody is going to use it, and if it works well you can be certain the world will never be the same again. The free market, for example, is such a tool. Wherever there is unfettered commerce, ordinary people thrive.

Governments, of course, are inclined to proscribe tools. Yet try as they might to constrain free markets, outlaw certain technologies, or proclaim others to be nefarious or uncivil, tools that work and the people who use them cannot easily be stopped. Such attempts have not succeeded to my knowledge—and if they have, they have been so successful that they remain a well-kept secret from all of us. Even then, it is only a matter of time before the secret leaks and the idea or tool opens up to one and all. Genetic engineering is like that. Even with Jeremy Rifkin's prophesies of doom, I don't believe it can be ultimately stopped—and I don't want it to be. In any case, gene-splicing equipment is not prohibitive; it can be bought for as little as $40,000.

There are, I am certain, thousands of people in this country who could afford the cost and who would be delighted to innovate with $40,000 gadgets. I just wish there were a million, and I wish every one of those million could put their energies to the job of innovation and invention. For if we have one assurance in life, it is that diversity breeds new tools, and that new tools open our minds to greater knowledge and our lives to greater possibilities. I say let a thousand genes blossom.

Putting political or social theories ahead of tools carries real societal costs. The sad decline of General Motors is a perfect example. Its early dominance in the automotive field came under the leadership of an engineer, Charles Kettering, not an MBA. Yet since the MBAs (the politicians of manufacturing) have taken over, GM has slid downhill. Only lately has GM begun to dimly recognize the role of advanced tools and technology as more important than short-term profits, golden umbrellas, and competition, not for customers, but for internal corporate advancement. One exciting evidence of change at GM comes, ironically, through the creation of a subsidiary company, Saturn, which is tool-driven, doesn't even have a personnel department, and is based on the sound engineering organizational principle of individual responsibility and autonomous work teams which are free to and encouraged to innovate rather than play office politics. The result is an American car that has the quality to compete bumper-to-bumper with the best from Japan and Germany.

There are, I believe, many reasons to care about tools and technology. They feed us, they shelter and clothe us, they entertain us, and they do the physical and mental work that might otherwise lie beyond our powers. For me the glorious feature of tools and technology is the power they have to free people and to give them the means to control their own lives and to participate in the governance of their own neighborhoods.

Regrettably, there are *uses* of technology which stand in the way of individual freedom and local self-reliance. Organization is the key. Some technologies, such as refining uranium for nuclear weapons or nuclear reactors, simply cannot exist without the centralized wealth and police power of the nation-state. Neighborhoods can't afford the process, and free markets will never sustain such costly ventures on the scale pursued so far by the federal government. Nuclear fission can be used in nondamaging ways, and it may still play an important role in future society. But nuclear power and nuclear bombs are not socially appropriate technologies; they are the outcomes of state socialism, not free markets and free people.

Government can also put tools and technologies to nefarious uses in the name of internal state security. Republican and Democratic administrations seem intent on passing laws to give government greater access to private communications, especially those by computer. Even in England, where Margaret Thatcher made progress in reversing the tide of government, internal security laws continue to mount. Invasive government, however, is no longer the threat it once was. The technology is now in place to batter it down. Poland's revolt was virtually operated via tape recorders and fax machines. American contact with Chinese fax machines continues apace. There just aren't convenient ways to keep secrets anymore except in the furthest backwaters and even those increasingly are being assaulted by information.

The joy of technology is that it does not seem susceptible to monopolization. The state must depend on it but cannot dominate it. As a programmer friend of mine (who uses a NATO satellite as his personal, informal bulletin board) says: "They can listen to everything we do, but now we can listen to everything *they* do." More importantly, the sort of clever folk who become programmers are far and away the least dependable personalities that I can imagine for ensuring state obedience and protecting state security. The really good programmers are sporting, playful, and poetic. Yet the state must depend on them for much of its new work. The state cannot, however, depend on them to put up with endless foolishness. The recent computer virus horror stories strike me as simply being some programmer's interesting reminder that the state can't hide anymore.

Here is where tools and technology seem so liberating; they are moving toward decentralized deployment. Cottage industry now includes gene splicers and cybernated milling machines, not to mention endless attics of retrievable data. More importantly, tools and technology are moving toward miniaturization, a key feature that makes it possible to decentralize their deployment and command. Decentralization and miniaturization, these are the undoing of central power, the features that must strike terror in the heart of any old-fashioned tyrant. They are the tools and technologies that empower people and that will change the world dramatically in spite of what rulers wish.

My observation is that tools and the producers who use them are looking more libertarian every day. Politicians and academicians, I fear, remain stuck in the pyramidal past. Politicians have the raw power, the gun power, and academics have the power of policy persuasion over elected leaders. Everyone else has production power and smart power— the power to create tools of beneficence. And there is, I believe, an increasingly painful wedge being driven between the gun power and smart power people. I don't think gun power will make it for much longer, although it surely won't vanish overnight. Gun power simply can't grow turnips or program machines. Prosperity, which is the inevitable result of advancing technology, is the greatest friend that peace could ever have. For it is merchant adventurers, not soldiers, who have carried cultures around the world, battering bigotry and weakening jingoism. People who are well fed, and who have good stereo systems and durable, fast cars are not likely candidates for slogging around in the mud while other people shoot at them.

"Ah-ha," the socially sensitive may say, "but what about the new tyrants, people such as Donald Trump?" Ridiculous. Donald Trump, whom I secretly admire for his flamboyance, simply does not hurt or oppress people. What difference does it make if he has billions of dollars? He doesn't just bury the stuff in his backyard. He invests it. Jobs come from it. Such an oppressor! Only the very meanest and shortsighted people, I believe, are still beguiled by the notion that the best society is one in which merit is not rewarded, nor incompetence reproved, and in which everybody has the same as everybody else. People of meritorious ingenuity have gifted us with technology that is magnificently liberating. Think of the next stage of tools when such lovely ideas as nanotechnology (manufacturing on the molecular level) fully develop and when we start mining the asteroid belt, or simply going *out there* into a new age of exploration.

[Editor's note. The text that follows was excerpted from the taped interviews of Karl Hess by Charles Murray. It is included because it casts important clarification on what Karl meant by alternative technology and the limits he ascribed to it.]

We all make errors of exaggeration or outlandish claim in the course of our lives. I admit to one crucial mistake in my thinking about alternative technology. It is not, however, a mistake about alternative technology; it is a mistake about attempting to see alternative technology as a full alternative.

In the film, *Karl Hess: Toward Liberty*—which won the 1981 Academy Award for best short documentary—I talk at length on appropriate technology. I say that people should be able to create and maintain their own technology. I believe that is essentially desirable. I think it is also essentially impossible. The maintenance of technology is an obligation. If you have stuff, you should know something about it and be able to keep it going. But creating it?—*no!*

Now, is it reasonable to think that alternative technology can always substitute for more intensive centralized technology? The answer lies in what we mean by alternative technology and how we envision it happening. First, alternative technology is just that—an alternative to centralized power and production. It is an alternative to mass agriculture; it is an alternative to mass production, to all massive, centrally controlled, bureaucratically defined operations.

Second, its spirit is admirable. I believe, for instance, that huge central power-generating plants will disappear over time, in part due to their inefficiency. Approximately 12 percent of the power they create is wasted in just sending it through long transmission lines—and the metal for those lines is becoming more expensive. But that does not mean that it is now effective or efficient for people to generate their own electric power. One exception are people who live five or more miles from a power line. Economically, they would be better off generating their own electricity by putting up solar cells and tying them into a bank of storage batteries. But who in America, apart from a handful of ranchers, hermits, and survivalists, lives that far from a power line? Still, self-sufficiency in power generation will happen eventually, and it *will happen* precisely because of advanced and high technology—because advanced and high technology will pave the way for alternative technology.

This is where I made my mistake. I thought the tools of alternative technology were not susceptible to improvement by high technology. In short, I failed to see that building a proper solar-powered generator or an appropriate wind-powered generator takes more than a felicitous gathering of enthused techies; it requires the genius to dream up the technology in the first place and, in the second place, the means to forge it into tools that are useable by nonscientists.

My attitude on food production would probably disqualify me altogether from the alternative technology movement. I don't like gardening. When I have done it, I found it boring. I would much rather be off somewhere else doing something I do better, such as writing a poem or contemplating my navel. Also, I don't care for the typical vegetables most people grow in their low-tech, high-organic gardens. I don't like much of what passes for healthy food, but that is my choice and my problem.

My mistake was posing as someone who believed in the dictum of grow your own. But it was an easy deception because we weren't doing much gardening in our experiment in Adams-Morgan. We had a high-technology fish farm going, and that suited me perfectly. We had motors to keep the fish alive; all we had to do was check every so often to make sure the electricity was still going. That's my kind of technology.

Much of the hubris of alternative technology stems from the *graffiti effect*. Some of what I said in *Toward Liberty* fits that category. Sometimes, to attract people's attention, you do or say things that are outrageous or shocking. Alternative technologists do that today. Many of them are good at what they do, but more often than not they are high-tech people posing as low-tech prophets. I suppose I was too, in a way.

For example, I made a comment about MIT in *Toward Liberty* that was totally inaccurate and which I regret to this day. A wind generator is truly an elegant device, but to imply, as I did, that the high-tech advances flowing from MIT were any less elegant is simply stupid. The people working there are producing elegant devices: tools that, once conceived and marketed, have the potential of transforming how all of us live.

My stepping back from the edge of unthinking allegiance to alternative technology, and my willingness to see that it does not have to replace its high sibling, but only emerge from it, is a reflection of how less an ideologue I am today. Alternative technology people have been mostly ideologues, certainly no less so than anti-Communists. They are both true believers.

A German politician once said, "Whenever I hear the word 'culture' I reach for my pistol." Well, whenever I hear the word "ideology" I reach for mine. I am not an ideologue now, but I once was. Sadly, so many of the people I associated with were also ideologues about alternative technology. None of us saw what was right before our eyes—that tools succeed by spanning the dark chasms of ideology, and that ideology is all that impedes the human mind in its search for liberating technologies.

18

West Virginian

In the days of Herod the king, behold there came wise men from the east to Jerusalem. Saying, where is he that is born King in Israel, for we have seen his star in the east, and we are come. . .

There's a star of mystery here too.

Herod, in these hills.

Magi in these woods.

Somewhere, a child.

And he arose and took the young child and his mother and came into the land . . .

They came into the land.

Along the Ohio, along the Greenbrier,

Wheeling Creek, Turkey Run, Ice's Ferry.

And two Fort Pitt deserters living in a sycamore tree.

Then was fulfilled that which was spoken by Jeremy the prophet, saying, In Rama there was a voice heard, lamentation, and weeping and great mourning, Rachel weeping for her children . . .

And they weep sometimes at Cabin Creek.

Always at Buffalo Creek.

And in places where only lamentations and never the light can touch.

At Monongah and at Farmington, Consolidated Number Nine.

Numbers that weep and tears without number.

And when they were come into the house, they saw the young child,
with Mary, his mother, and fell down and worshiped him.

At Potomoke Church and Old Rehoboth.

Old Stone Church.

The New Awakening, The Old Time Ways.

And when they had opened their treasures, they presented unto him
gifts, gold, and frankincense, and myrrh.

Gifts too at Shenandoah Bloomery, a burning spring in Kanawha.

Tarr's Furnace, Monongahela Oak, and almost everywhere—

that brooding dark rich river of ore,

sprung like a leak beneath the earth and on it.

And being warned of God in a dream that they should not return to
Herod, they departed into their own country another way.

Other ways, always other ways.

Mother Jones raising hell at Holly Grove,

Daniel Boone and the Point he called Pleasant.

Old man Brown and all his sons,

Rumsey and all his dreams.

Johnny Appleseed.

And a woman named Carol Jean Bain, but you may not remember her.

It's just that, here, it seems, they've been leaving Herod all the time!

Into their own country.

Another way.

Saying arise, and take the young child and his mother, and go into the
land of Israel, for they are dead which sought the young child's life.

Dead, too, The Mingos, Shawnees, and Delaware.

The Iroquois signed on the line at Stanwix Fort.

Chief Logan, mourning,

sown in the terrible time, the bloody ground.

It wasn't always nativity.

Notwithstanding, being warned again in a dream, he turned aside
into the parts of Galilee.

And still, from dreams still warned, a few turn aside.

Newcomers on the land, seekers, finders,

first timers, last chancers, root sinkers,

digging in and digging out. Looking.

And every one a neighbor.

When they saw the star, they rejoiced with exceeding great joy.

Stringed notes rising in the hollows.
Foot stomping, hand slapping, knee jigging,
eye laughing, voice shouting, sounds in our hills.
And he came and dwelt in a city called Nazareth, that it might be ful-
filled which was spoken by the prophets. He shall be called a Nazarene.
And the names still go calling here:
Boone, Clay, Hardy, and Logan.
Mineral, Mingo, Pleasants, and Roane.
Peapatch, Panther, Pie, and Sarah Ann.
Gauley Bridge, Paw Paw, and Hurricane.
Nitro, Munition, Petroleum, Sweetsprings, and War.
Montcoal, Mt. Hope, Mt. Storm, and Ellamore.
Big Chimney, Letter Gap, Smoke Hole, and Gassaway.
Athens, Cairo, and Galloway.
Gem, Power, and Tunnelton.
Boomer, Bragg—and Bethlehem.
And the angel said unto them, fear not, for, behold, I bring you good
tidings of great joy, which shall be to all people.
—Karl Hess, A West Virginia Epiphany

The first time that I ever was in West Virginia was when I was thirteen years old, hanging around with an older bunch of kids in Washington. One of them, whose name I forget, had just inherited $11,000. Remembering the money and not the person is not a comforting thing, but I cannot divine any greater significance to it than the fact that $11,000, back then, was inherently memorable.

The heir, being unmindful of the future and enthusiastically thinking of the moment, did what exactly every other one of the group would have done in his place. He bought a car, a used but quite glossy LaSalle sedan, and invited a carful of his friends, including me, to come with him on a trip of no particular purpose or destination. The purpose turned out to be to drink as much beer and eat as little food as possible. The destination, through a geographic alchemy beyond understanding, turned out to be Bluefield, West Virginia.

My impression of the trip is singular. I remember thinking that the most beautiful women in the world lived in Bluefield. Perhaps they do, although subsequent trips to the town have failed to verify it for me. What does live in Bluefield are West Virginians, an amazing mix of people who, as I discovered then and then rediscovered four decades later, are simply wonderful and eccentrically odd.

Coming back to West Virginia in 1975, this time to live and stay, was partly by accident and partly by planning. The accidental part was the force of circumstance—the need to get away as quickly as possible from the sight and remembrance of orange fingerprints. The planning part was a careful weighing of West Virginia against Arizona and Vermont, the two other states Therese and I found attractive. We had spent several summers in Vermont at Goddard College, and the thought of more summers there was comforting. The only problem was winter. Arizona solved that problem, of course, but it posed other obstacles such as summer and the sheer distance from family. West Virginia won out. It had low taxes, its body of laws was slim compared to our other choices, and it was nearest my mother.

Whatever practical matters guided our choice *to go* to the state of West Virginia, our decision *to stay* there came from a growing fondness for the people and the land. We simply fell in love with our neighbors, our community, and our plot of land in the small bend of the Opequon Creek. Good fortune also came from bad luck. We had enough money from the insurance claim on the Washington robbery to start building our earth-sheltered house. Therese found employment at the local hospital as head of volunteers and public relations, and I continued writing and welding for a living. We had come home to the place of our deepest affection by merely driving seventy miles west of the source of our greatest disappointment.

Friends have asked me over the years since moving to West Virginia if more money would have changed our lives. "No," I tell them. We have always had everything we need—grassy fields, a sturdy toolshed, a well that produces good water, a forest with walking trails, a creek to swim and fish in, deer, raccoons, and most of all, a wonderful house. All of those things have made for a very special place to live and work.

I recall harried friends from Adams-Morgan coming at unpredictable times to visit and then to meditate for hours in some corner of our house, at some hidden recess on our land, or in the crook of a towering sycamore on the banks of the Opequon. I am thankful that our move to Kearneysville kept our old friends near. I am also thankful for the new friends we found. Where we live—at exactly 39° 22' 50" North and 77° 55' 55" West in West Virginia's Eastern Panhandle—is small enough that we have come to know and care for our neighbors, and it is spread out enough that our neighbors have, by custom, respected our privacy while managing always, and always without being intrusive, to check on how we are doing. We built our house without a single lock, and not once has anyone entered without permission.

There are many remarkable things about West Virginia, its Eastern Panhandle, and the rural countryside of Kearneysville. Our immediate area was carved out of Virginia in the middle of the War for Southern Independence as a way of excising from that state a substantial rail center in Martinsburg. I am pleased that it happened, although I remain depressed by the tolls of the dead and the leviathan state that came as the outcome of civil war. But West Virginia has never depressed me. The people are of great character and are mostly great characters. The state, in turn, has one of the lowest crime rates in the nation, one of the lowest alcohol and drug abuse rates in the nation, and the nation's highest resistance to the use of seat belts—thus indicating that West Virginians are able to control base lusts but will not brook anyone telling them how to save—or destroy—themselves. West Virginians, by and large, are ingenious, generous, unpretentious, disrespectful of authority, and more intent on enjoying life than worrying over the statistical aberration that they are, per capita, the least wealthy in the Union.

We made new friends in the usual ways, from workplace and marketplace and simply visiting those who lived nearby. But what did the trick quickest was what we were doing on the land and the welding skills I had brought with me. When Therese and I moved to the bend in the Opequon, we were just another two outsiders who had escaped Washington and who had bought property and were building a house—a house which, not incidentally, was considered by many of our neighbors to be one of the more silly projects in the world.

One such skeptic and neighbor was Rodney Loy, a backhoe operator who lived just across the creek from us and who had agreed to dig out the building site for our home. I will never forget the puzzlement and the friendly sense of humor he brought to the job. As he finished digging the foundation into the hillside, he pointed to the results and observed that it was much like "one of them Polish swimming pools—a hole in the ground with only three sides to it."

"Rodney," I pleaded, "you've been in barns around here that have been built underground. What have you noticed about them?"

"Well, they're cool."

"That's right," I said. "If you dig a little bit below the surface of the earth the temperature of the dirt in that entire area will remain very close to 55 degrees all year long if you cover it over. It doesn't matter if its zero outside or 100, it's going to stay close to 55 degrees."

"Well," he admitted with new respect in his voice, "I guess that makes sense."

And as we lined the three-sided hole with cement, cinder block, and wood, it made more and more sense. Rodney understood function; he was uncommonly intelligent, not poetically so, but always sharp and acutely attuned to tools and their outcomes. What earned his respect was that something as unfamiliar to him as our earth-sheltered home was doing what was most familiar and desirable to him: making an economical dwelling. He accepted the house, and us too, once he saw that what we were doing was more than a faddish fantasy. It made common sense, and in West Virginia that is the sort of thing that matters most to people.

We had won Rodney's respect, and with it a willingness to trust us in other ways. As part of our agreement, I had offered to swap whatever I could, including my welding skills, to pay for his backhoe work. Rodney took me up on my offer. He told me that he needed a set of metal boxes to install on his backhoe and that he wanted me to weld them together. I went to work immediately, with the entire Loy family looking on, watching everything I did like a brood of eagles. When I had finished, and after each family member had had the chance to kick at, hammer, stand on, and thump the boxes, the older son spoke up: "Held together pretty good, didn't it?" Well, that was it. From that point on I could have been their father or brother. In fact, Therese and I went to almost every family reunion they had after that. And it was because the welds held.

Some years later when my neighbors learned of the film *Karl Hess: Toward Liberty*, and the fact that it had won the 1981 Academy Award for best short documentary, my standing in the community did not fall by much. They took it as just another West Virginia eccentricity that could be excused and that would be quickly forgotten. After all, their concern was that the welds held—that I could *do* something, not that I was somebody or some momentary celebrity as defined by newspapers and magazines that most of them never read or, if they did, took with little more than a grain of salt. They had faults, but being pretentious or putting up with pretentious people was not one of them.

Barter, in fact, turned out to be an excellent way to get to know our neighbors. It also turned out to be absolutely entertaining. My welding skills were always in demand, and there was always some service or new tool I needed, and the best way to get it was by trade. Therese, however, was always best at bartering. A neighbor up the road had decided to run for magistrate and needed campaign pamphlets. Therese needed manure for the garden, something the candidate had in abundance from his stables. Therese designed the pamphlets and he delivered the manure. It was the perfect, poetic swap. She got a bunch of it, he got a bunch of it, and she became the first member of our household to ever be involved in a successful election.

Earthy practicality and unpretentious nature were just two of the virtues that endeared me to West Virginians. A healthy disregard for government was another. For example, I was pleasantly surprised by the attitude of most people in the area toward taxation. I happened to be at the county courthouse when a women who worked there asked me if I was the guy who didn't pay taxes. My first thought was that I'd be in jail by tomorrow. So, I answered cautiously. I told her that I had refused to pay some taxes because I didn't think they were very just. I imagined bells and alarms going off throughout the courthouse. Instead, she said, "You bet they're not. I wish you'd show me how to do it." There was not a bit of resentment in her voice, just, "Yeah, I'd like to stop paying taxes too, but I just haven't figured out how."

Another example. Not long after our arrival, I went to the local laundromat to do the weekly wash. Mrs. Butts, the caretaker, asked if I had heard about "all that trouble they had at that Indian reservation up at Wounded Knee." I said—thinking this was an open invitation to disaster —that I understood there were problems and that the people there had some complaints. Again, I miscalculated. She took my cue and assailed the government for what it was doing to Native Americans. As I listened to her, it struck me that I was now living in the part of the country where the FBI, revenuers, and the U.S. Marine Corps wouldn't even make the bottom of the list of local heroes.

Generosity is yet another virtue that I find so attractive about West Virginians. The people here practice charity, and they practice it because their parents did, and before that their grandparents. They do not regard charity as an act of condescension; they regard it as an act of neighborliness. They understand charity, but they do not tolerate begging. They read in a newspaper, for example, that the Jenkins family was burned out of their trailer on such and such a day, that they need clothes of various sizes, and that it will be collected at the southside firehouse. And then if you drive up to the firehouse on the selected day there will be lines of cars winding around the block, and you will have to get in line and wait your turn to give. It's always this way, and I hope it always stays this way.

People in West Virginia genuinely care for one another, certainly more than they care for all the rules and regulations that government invents to make their lives safer. Being a good neighbor is high on the scale of social and economic priorities. I recall the visit of the county electrical inspector. As I mentioned before, there were virtually no building codes in Berkeley County to interfere with the construction of our home. There was, however, a requirement that all wiring be inspected and approved before the power company would deliver electricity. When the county inspector showed up and examined our improvised wiring scheme, he knew right away it wasn't according to code. Still, he reasoned that it *looked* safe enough and that he would approve it on a temporary basis. It's been almost two decades now and I feel confident that temporary means permanent.

Neighborliness sprinkled with a healthy dose of common sense also explains the great affection Therese and I felt for Mrs. Everhardt, the first postmistress we had in Kearneysville and the constant sentinel over our post office box and privacy. She knew—from local gossip and an article in the local newspaper—that I did not pay federal taxes. So she took extra precautions. Whenever someone would stop by the post office to ask directions to our house, she would make them wait while she called Therese or me to make sure they were the sort of people we wanted as visitors.

And then, there were the auctions. Back in Adams-Morgan on any typical Saturday night, we might spend $40 for a good dinner and an arty movie down at Dupont Circle. But in West Virginia it was different. The Loys introduced us to Casey's Auction, where for $40 we not only got a Saturday night's entertainment, we also got a whole truckload of old mirrors, discarded chairs, overpainted chests of drawers, and other used but salvageable things. The auctions—our "Saturday night special"—launched six of the most enjoyable and memorable working years of my life. From the summer of 1978 until my first heart surgery in 1985, Therese and I repaired and refinished old furniture and sold it on Saturdays at Eastern Market in Washington, D.C.

I continued my writing and lecturing as before, but for Therese it became full-time work. For both of us, it was the best time of our lives. Weekly, we would visit every antique shop, auction, and estate sale in the area, and at home we worked together constantly, sometimes past midnight, repairing (my job) and refinishing (her job) a litany of antique objects. I was able to spend spring, summer, and fall not only doing what Therese and I considered more fun than effort, but *working* in the place I enjoyed most—in the work shed we had built ourselves and equipped with every imaginable tool, experimenting with new materials and different ways to apply tools to them, making something of value to other people, and humming and whistling away the worst of heat and humidity in hours of absolute pleasure and enjoyment.

Therese specialized in refinishing mirrors. At the local auctions and at Eastern Market she was known as the mirror lady. My talent was figuring out alternative uses for all sorts of seemingly worthless things. One of those things was discarded sewing machines. In those days, Futons and floor mattresses were the rage in the city, and it seemed only sensible to use the wooden sewing-machine housings as low Futon side tables. Drawers from the housings could be stacked and framed to make spice racks. Wrought-iron legs became bases for various coffee tables and other side stands, and the metal foot treadles became pot racks and other hanging decorations. About the only thing we couldn't make use of were the sewing machines themselves. Today, there are still about thirty of them stowed away in our storage shed.

I also sold sculptures at Eastern Market, though not the arty ones I had shown at Georgetown galleries. Some were fashioned from preexisting metal parts—like the sewing-machine treadles or decorative gratings from turn-of-the-century homes. The most popular items, though, were garden decorations that Therese would outline in chalk on sheets of rusted metal and I would cut and weld to steel rods to be stuck in the ground as support. We made some impressive pigs and roosters—and some garden mice that to this day are mistaken for cats or possums.

No matter what we made for the weekend, the ceremony was always the same. The night before we'd pack the bed of the Ford pickup and cover it with a tarp—or, later, stuff the Ford Econoline van as full as possible—and at 4 A.M. Saturday morning we'd take off for the market. We'd arrive at six, along with the produce and flower vendors, and promptly grab a market breakfast and a coffee to sip on while setting up our display. All the vendors knew each other and were a close and friendly lot. We did a lot of bartering among us before starting the cash deals with shoppers. Buying would start immediately, though, often before we'd finished setting up. Capitol Hill townhouse owners were always eager to see, and have, what we brought in from the country.

Because of my tendency to agree to almost any offer from a buyer, I was early on banned from handling sales. So, while Therese made the deals with customers, I was left to sit in the sun on a bench and schmooze with various locals whom I knew from the old days. Whether a congressman or news reporter or war protester or hippie from Buzzards Point, they would look, do a double-take, and ask the inevitable, "What on earth are you doing *here*?" And I became the sidewalk philosopher I had always wanted to be.

At dusk, we would load up an unsold item or two and head, hot and sweaty, back to the Opequon, counting cash and checks on the way and making plans to reinvest it at some upcoming estate sale or auction. We didn't get rich from this activity, but we made enough to cover our costs and daily living expenses—and we had fun being crafters and small entrepreneurs. We probably would have continued the work for many years were it not for my health. Heart surgery in the spring of 1985 to replace a damaged aortic valve ruled out lifting heavy objects, and prudence ruled in finding another way to make a living.

In retrospect, those are the years that remain fondest in my memory and that had the greatest impact on my thinking. Living and working in a small town helped refocus my attention on the actual practices of neighborliness and away from the distractions of global problems created by, but not solvable by, authoritarian politics. The political fantasies that had excited me as a youth became inconsequential against the backdrop of Kearneysville, the Opequon, the toolshed, and most importantly, Therese. My lack of enthusiasm for saving the world was exactly counterbalanced by my enthusiasm for saving or, at least, enhancing, my neighborhood. I became convinced that where I was, in ideas and physical location, was where I had always been headed and where I will remain. Unless, of course, I have substantial reason to change my mind! But that hasn't happened. The landscape, the people, and the idiosyncratic culture are too compelling.

A weakened heart, a continuing need to make a living, and an affection for a political party that campaigns on a very nearly straight anarchist platform persuaded me to assume the editorship of the *Libertarian Party News* in the spring of 1986. A number of my closest friends were startled by my decision, wondering why the author of "The Death of Politics" would involve himself, beyond a statement of support, in any political activity at all. I tried to answer their concerns in the first issue I edited of the *LP News*. I explained that in "The Death of Politics" I had written about the obsolescence of coercive, traditional politics and about the understanding that all human social arrangements could be voluntary and that, indeed, only such arrangements can assure peace and prosperity and fully encourage the human imagination.

I emphasized that to the extent, and only to the extent, that the activities of the Libertarian Party hew to the engagement in politics as a way to diminish coercive authority—in short, to the extent that Libertarian political activity acts solely to serve liberty and never to reinforce coercion and the initiation of violence—to that extent I believed what I was doing to be compatible with the views I expressed in "The Death of Politics."

I also tried to clarify an ongoing libertarian debate over whether I was or was not a capitalist. I wrote that I am by occupation a free marketer (crafts and ideas, woodworking, welding, and writing). As a frequent barterer, I am a capitalist of the laissez-faire persuasion. I am not a defender of state-corporate capitalism, the capitalism of the two larger political parties. Nor do I hold that capitalism is the only way in which a free market may be maintained. There are other sorts of agreements about property and ownership and money which, if made and maintained voluntarily, seemed to me to be libertarian. I am, to give a shorthand summary of it all, a free-market pluralist. And I joined the Libertarian Party and became the editor of its newspaper to engage in and affiliate with a party of defensive politics; *self-defensive* politics, as I saw it, aimed at rolling back the coercive apparatus of the state.

I suppose I was mostly on the edge of the Libertarian Party most of the time. As editor of the *LP News,* I believed it was crucially important to keep hammering at the idea of a world beyond politics. Libertarians, if they wanted to, could do this in every candidacy, pledging to abolish, not pass, laws and, if daring enough, even pledging to abolish the offices to which they were elected—as some, I am pleased to note, actually have. Or, if they really wanted to affect the way people think about things, they could become teachers, software designers, skillful geneticists and nanotechnologists, active and visible capitalists, good neighbors, and constant commentators in the media.

I wanted to remind party members that the Libertarian Party is not the center of the libertarian movement, as if that movement had a center at all. A party and a movement must be seen as very distinctly separate. Movements involve shifts in the way people view important issues. Parties, at best, involve the hope to influence legislation. At worst, and now more characteristically, they just involve the election of public officials and the distribution of the spoils of office. The Libertarian Party, despite all of the pious talk about being "the party of principle," is still a political party. It has chosen the legislative course and, if it can elect more people to office, it certainly can begin in small increments the repeal of government. Noble ambition.

But to get elected it is quite clear that the purity-principle approach of many libertarians is of strictly limited appeal. To insist that the passerby in politics has to sign up for total agreement with a long menu of libertarian principles is a splendid way to stay in the church preaching to the choir. I know that there is substantial gratification in feeling absolutely pure and uncompromised and I believe that choosing such a course is ethically fine. I also feel that a person can choose a form of guerrilla warfare, in which you snipe at targets of opportunity to present liberty's view on any target of current convenience. I am inclined to guerrilla warfare myself, and I believe I brought a taste of it to the party.

As editor of the *LP News*, I worked to bridge the gap between party and movement. I feared that the internal politics of the party, if constantly brought forward to dominate every page of the *LP News*, would simply feed the ingrown and even incestuous notion that "getting ahead" in the party is crucial to the success of the libertarian movement. There were, I argued, two distinct versions of what a Libertarian Party paper could be: one reaching out to people, or one aimed inward. I was convinced that most of the members of the party wanted to reach out, to build constituencies, suggest and take actions, even build or join coalitions. I was also convinced that a considerable number of people who had taken the pains to seek and win internal party offices were more interested in keeping the party tightly disciplined and internally correct.

This I feared most: I saw a growing tendency for the Libertarian Party to be organizationally dominated by ideologues. They wanted to peddle principles, just as the Republican and Democratic Parties peddle emotional ideologies: love it or leave it, help the poor, etc. And they wanted to do it nationally, which is just where they don't stand a chance. Libertarian principles are not likely to be even heard in the din except by people already in agreement. Locally, however, things are different. There, the party has a real chance to be heard if it concentrates on issues rather than principle-purity.

Hobbling local, issue-oriented politics in the Libertarian Party is the presidential campaign. It brings out the absolute worst in libertarians who behave at nominating conventions just the way they would at a Democratic or Republican one. It projects an image that is not as convincing intellectually or as influential generally as are the independent works of libertarian artists, inventors, writers, and other activists.

To combat these tendencies I devoted my editorship to an open, tolerant, and intellectually diverse *LP News*. I reached out to people who shared libertarian values but who, for whatever reason, preferred to work with one of the major national parties. More power to them. I also reached out to libertarians who, sensibly, just wanted to be free and not engaged in any high-profile hooting and hollering. More power to them. If it hadn't been for my injudicious past and a sort of automatic attention-getting, that would have been my own preferred path. While doing all of this, I reached out most strongly to libertarians who were already party members, knowing that their choice to be political messengers would never hamper the libertarian movement—except to make some libertarians mad—but would, as I imagined, enhance and make it stronger. I looked at my editorship as a means to keep the anarchist vision alive in the party and as a tool to build a bridge between party members and the libertarian movement. I owed allegiance to no party faction, preferring instead to believe and write that there is no such thing as a bad or second-class libertarian.

My interest in the Libertarian Party was always in its membership and never in its organization. It represented a significant network of people with interest in liberty, just as the *LP News* represented an effective tool to make the network more effective and more ecumenical. I made my personal prejudice clear from the start: information is the heartbeat of liberty and the sturdiest safeguard against tyranny. It is *networks* of information that are spreading freedom today, even under the guns of tyrants everywhere. It is networks of information that can extend and protect liberty here at home. To the extent that the Libertarian Party and my editorship of the

LP News could serve to weave networks of information among the friends of liberty, I remained loyal to the spirit of "The Death of Politics." I hung on to a slim reed of politics, against the better judgments of many of my closest friends, because I saw so many good people in the Libertarian Party working to make it a truly libertarian group, decentralized and communicative, an information network rather than an organizational hierarchy.

My ideas got me in trouble. I was criticized for not editing a purely political paper, but editing, instead, a movement newspaper. I happily plead guilty. I was reprimanded for running an ad in the *LP News* that urged libertarians to join the Republican Party. I happened to disagree with the ad, and I later wrote a commentary against it. But I also disagreed just as strongly with the idea of rejecting paid advertising because of what amounts to a difference of opinion. I believed that if libertarians could be harmed by such an ad, the party was in more serious trouble than simply having an injudicious editor. At times, I felt as though I was being nibbled to death by insatiable mice. Always, however, there was strong, heartwarming support among party members for what I did with the *LP News*. That support kept me going; it made all of the criticisms and all of the usual clashes of personalities sufferable distractions in an otherwise exciting five years.

Dwindling strength and declining endurance dictated my departure from the *LP News* in the summer of 1990 and a stunning question from a stunning lady hastened it. Therese asked me why I was, in editing the paper, doing something that others could do while neglecting to do what only I could do: such as completing my autobiography. I couldn't argue with her reasoning; it made, as usual, iron-clad sense. So I submitted my resignation; turned over the editorship to my longtime friend and partner, Randy Langhenry; and got back into the business of being a West Virginian with one last tale to tell.

Except for a brief but health-aborted run in 1992 for governor of West Virginia (I received a new heart on August 19 of that year), my active role in the Libertarian Party ended. What did not end, however, were the local affiliations and engagements that both preceded and coincided with the lecturing, writing, furniture fixing, and editorship of the *LP News*.

My earliest local involvement, along with the Appropriate Technology Group, was with the Berkeley County Big Brothers/Big Sisters program. Shortly after we moved to West Virginia, Therese took a job as director of volunteers at Kings Daughters Hospital in Martinsburg. Larry Lawson, only twelve years old at the time, came to her and asked to be part of the hospital's volunteer program. Because he was so good with elderly patients, Therese bent the minimum-age rule and enrolled him in the volunteer program. Therese was also in charge of the hospital's Christmas party and persuaded Larry to dress up as an elf, in a green jumpsuit that extended from head to pointed toes with bells on them, and help give out awards and entertain the crowd. That was where I first met him. I was deeply impressed by his willingness to saunter about in such a costume and by his enthusiasm and enjoyment for what he did. He was inventive, outgoing, funny, and courageous.

I had been thoroughly won over to his wonder-kid personality by the time Therese went on the board of Big Brothers/Big Sisters and learned that Larry's name was on the little brother's waiting list. She asked if I might be interested in becoming his big brother. I said an unconditional yes.

Our big brother–little brother relationship was probably atypical. We didn't go to zoos, visit museums, go to bowling alleys, go camping, or sit on the banks of the Opequon and fish. Mostly, Larry visited me at the house and worked and talked with me in the toolshed. He told me he was the only male member of his family who hadn't spent time in jail. After a time, he invited me to visit his extended family in "the holler" not far from Winchester, Virginia. I was struck by the invitation, mainly because Larry had always made a distinction between "your people" and "my people." Once we were there, however, I was treated like one of his people. Although obviously without money and probably undereducated, they impressed me in the same ways Larry did. They were funny, they knew how to enjoy life without the mantles of wealth, and they were strikingly ingenious in the ways they built and decorated their homes.

I tried to help Larry in his studies at the local high school, though I made it clear to him that I had never gone that far in school myself. I remember one assignment in particular: Larry was to interview someone for a class project, and since I was the most convenient and available someone, he interviewed me. Therese and I looked over the paper before he turned it in and complimented him on how well it was written and presented. The teacher didn't agree; she ignored the mechanical correctness of Larry's report and was outraged by the content of the interview (which had to do with my opinions about public education). She gave him a D. Larry and I had a serious talk about what had gone wrong and I suggested that he tell his teacher that it was wrong to judge him by what I had said rather than how he had fulfilled his assignment. He did just that and got his grade changed to a B. He has since graduated, married, and become a successful trucker. We still keep in close contact, and I consider our friendship to be one of my greater achievements.

[Editor's note. Karl wrote a poem to big and little brothers and sisters and read it at the Berkeley County Big Brothers/Big Sisters annual meeting in 1979. It was later published in the organization's monthly newsletter, The Informer. It does not expound upon global issues or ideologies. Rather, it shows as well as anything he has written his commitment to volunteerism, his concern for children, and his personal ethic of neighborliness. The text follows.]

What It's All About

There's a saying around here . . .
No-one is ever so tall as when they bend to help a child.
There's another saying . . .
Only people who are very strong will take the risk of being
    gentle.
And hands that help, I've always heard, are holier by far
than hands that only pray.

Big Brothers and Big Sisters are tall like that. They're strong
    like that.
Their hands and their hearts help and help, and then help some
    more.
It's what it's all about. It's the only reward there is.

I heard someone talking to a Big Sister once. They were criti-
    cizing her
Little Sister. "Gosh," I heard them say, "I wouldn't spend time
    with that kid
for a hundred dollars." "Neither would I," the Big Sister said.
    No.
Dollars couldn't buy her time. But love could. And it did.

What are these people like beyond all that?

Well, a Little Brother is a package of energy wrapped in equal
  parts of

incredible noise and mysterious silence. Little Brothers can talk
  faster

than an auctioneer when they're telling you about something
  special they saw.

Five minutes later they can contract a severe case of lockjaw
  and leave you

talking to yourself while they drift off into that special, secret
  world

that hides way back in their heads.

Little Brothers can climb trees like squirrels. Then they can
  stumble flat

on their faces going up two steps. Little Brothers have another
  special talent.

On any given afternoon they can make you swear that they
  should be locked up

in a pickle-barrel and fed through the lid until they are 16. Five
  minutes

later, they can have you bragging about "you never did see a
  kid as good as

that" and "wait until I tell the people at work what that rascal
  did."

Most of all, Little Brothers are part of the sunshine that makes
  the skies

just a little bluer for Big Brothers.

Little Sisters are something else again. There are times when
  you swear

they could walk on air and that every single one of them was
  destined to

be a dancer in a ballet. Just about then, that same Little Sister
  will turn

around with all the grace of a truck making a U-turn on a turn-
  pike, knock

down three rows of cans in the supermarket, send an innocent
    bystander
sprawling to the floor, and then look you straight in the eye and
    ask
who in the world ever caused all that commotion!

Big Sisters are people who understand questions like that.

Little Sisters see special things everyplace they go. Where you
    see
houses, they may see castles. Where you see some skinny kid
    with three
teeth missing, they see Robert Redford. Big Sisters are people
    who
understand that when you see things like that you don't need
    glasses.

Little Sisters can't stand crawly, squirmy things and they all say
they'd faint if just about anything goes wrong. But Little Sisters
    can
hold a bird with a broken wing so softly that it probably thinks
    it landed
up in a cloud. There is a rumor that, on the other hand, they
    cannot hold
anything with grease on it, particularly things like socket
    wrenches.
Big Sisters are people who know that that is only a rumor—but
    that it
sure helps to keep your hands clean.

Little Sisters are bundles of deep mystery wrapped up in the
incomprehensible lyrics to the current Top Forty.

Little Sisters are the songs in the music that Big Sisters make
    out of life.

Big Brothers are understanding on the other end of a phone line.
    Big Sisters

are hugs on the other end of a walk.
Big Brothers are magicians who always know where the fish
   are biting, and
even more important can tell you why they weren't biting at just
   that
particular time.

Big Sisters are magicians who can turn a long silence into
   sudden
understanding—just by being there.

Big Brothers are the reason bears never get you on camping
   trips.
Big Sisters are the reason the blues never get you on any trip.

Big Brothers and Big Sisters are patience wrapped up in visions
   of what
the future can be like when that future is matched up with their
   own
Little Brothers and Little Sisters.

And all of them, Bigs and Littles, are just people, after all,
People wrapped up in the loving care that is the only real, little
   hope
We have for this very big universe in which we live.

Big Bothers/Big Sisters drew my attention to literacy, to what, I believe, is one of the most powerful tools in the workshop of the entire world. It is a basic tool.

Consider this for a moment. There is nothing in the world that you cannot teach yourself by using a book—except one thing. You cannot teach yourself *to read* by using a book. But, once you have been taught to read, you can learn everything else by reading. It is as though you were in an apprentice program. Once you have been taught the use of a basic tool, you can move on toward journeyman. But until you have mastered that basic tool you are stuck, dead in the water.

Everyone can understand the advantage of being able to read a No Smoking sign in an area of volatile chemicals. Sadly, some people—adult people—can't read that sign. Now, solving that particular problem isn't too hard; practically anyone can be taught to recognize a few key words. Learning *to read* is a different matter. Reading is more than just memorizing or decoding a few words or even a lot of words. Reading means to get meaning out of written words *and* to put meaning into written words. Written language skills, like oral language skills, are very complex and must be acquired early in life to be mastered.

In West Virginia, as in the nation, adult illiteracy statistics are very depressing. As many as one in every five adults cannot read well enough to cope with everyday reading requirements. But the figures have never depressed me as much as actually knowing someone who is cut off from the words in the world around him. The doors that slam in the face of a person who has trouble reading make sounds much more impressive than all the governmental statements on illiteracy.

The personal tragedy of someone left alone by the death of a spouse and unable to handle all the written material that the other person used to handle; that's more impressive than all the charts.

The parents who can't help children with schoolwork because they can't read may feel a sort of heartbreak that no official facts or figures could ever tell us about.

The fact is that not being able to read is a deeply personal tragedy for many people, a problem that they feel is beyond solution, a problem they don't even dare to tackle because they might feel ashamed or they might believe it just isn't right for a grown man or woman not to be able to read. The point, of course, is not whether it is right or wrong, shameful or not, to be able to read or not. At stake is simply the ability to survive.

Literacy is the basic tool in the workshop of the entire world. It is the lever that moves thoughts into action and designs into machines. Whether we read or not we all think in words. Just try to think without having a word form in your mind. It probably won't happen. Words are the tools that make humans so different from everything else on earth. There are ants that use simple mechanical tools. There are larger animals that do the same. But human beings have and use the tools of words—in thoughts, in spoken language, and in printed language. And that makes us very different—for better or for worse.

What I see as essential at the tool level of literacy is critical thinking. For people who have been disenfranchised from the reading world, there is the possibility of appealing to the native intelligence which has enabled them to survive into adulthood without being able to read or write. They are, many of them, very clever. And that's something that can be built upon by encouraging critical thinking as the pathway to literacy.

For others, there is a greater stumbling block to literacy. They cannot read or write well because they are mentally handicapped, despite the forced, romantic, wishful thinking that every ignorant person is a noble savage just waiting to be launched into salon appreciation of the finer things in life. These people demand patience and understanding and not forced deference and demands which often are cruel and patronizing, even though well intentioned.

To them, critical thinking could well be the difference between victimization and some sort of independence—although many of them, stuck on welfare, for instance, cannot be expected to be or, indeed, want to be fully independent. To simply think critically about the claims of consumer-product advertising might be the extent of liberation that could be hoped for. It is a small victory, but one that we should attempt and celebrate.

Whatever the individual nuances and circumstances of illiteracy may be, it is, I feel, one of the great human tragedies. It is a tragedy that children are able to grow to adulthood without mastering the most essential of human tools. It is a tragedy that children today are caught in an education system where the official measure of literacy is the possession of a high school diploma, not the honed skill to read and think critically irrespective of formal schooling. I am biased of course; the best I can formally boast of is a junior high school diploma and a mother who put reading and critical thinking ahead of the statutory requirements of school attendance.

I am not surprised there is something called a literacy crisis in West Virginia and in the nation. The crisis is that nobody seems to have even a foggy notion of what they're talking about. It's a veritable Tower of Babel, with every shade of expert speaking in a different tongue, and every illiterate child and adult stumbling for words because no one seems to grasp the vital core of education, the absolute need to master the one tool that opens the doors to all other tools—the basic human skill to read words and critically think about them. Instead, our schools, both private and public, have become so detached from the enterprise of critical thinking—preferring the content-soaked conventions of liberal and conservative social and political theorists—that people by and large have come to prefer to take sides rather than to take time to think.

Today, adult literacy and childhood education claim what remains of my time to write and to be part of my community. My interest in both stems from a lifelong occupation with human freedom and the dawning realization that individual and neighborhood liberty have little to do with what constitutions say and even less to do with the ideology of human rights. They have, to the contrary, everything to do with the words—*the tools*—people master and apply to the processes of critical thought and creative living.

My work with adult literacy, like the Big Brothers/Big Sisters Program before it, started, as so many things have, with Therese. She was working at the Martinsburg library when an opportunity arose for the two of us to attend a two-day training session hosted by Literacy Volunteers of America. The program was inspiring; it convinced us that we could do something about illiteracy in our own community, and that the way to do it was to start a local volunteer tutoring program.

Therese developed the program through the local library and, as she often was inclined to do, found a role for me: I became a tutor, a promoter, and a member of the board of directors. For much of the '80s, for me, and for Therese up to this very day, literacy work became a labor of love. We both became involved at the state and national levels eventually, with Therese doing training and program development while I served on boards and delivered keynote addresses. My speech at a national LVA Conference was said to be the most well received in years because, oddly enough, I was the first keynoter for that organization who was also an active literacy tutor.

It was the tutoring, not building or administering a literacy program, that most interested me. I enjoyed the challenge of working one-on-one with people I thoroughly respected and enjoyed, hoping at the very least to share my love and enthusiasm for the tools of words and the absolute joy of thinking about them—and, as I strongly urged, doing something with them. I had several literacy students during this time, the early and mid-'80s, but one in particular affected my life, certainly as much as I influenced his.

Melvin Peck had been a cable splicer for Western Union when a job-related back injury sent him home for a long convalescence. The injury never completely healed, ruling out any chance of his returning to his old job. The company did offer Melvin an inside office job that didn't require backbreaking labor, but did require reading and writing skills. The only problem was that Melvin didn't read or write very well. That brought him to the Martinsburg library's literacy program and, more specifically, to me, his new tutor.

Melvin and I worked on the basics, such as sight word and phonics, but also on practical things such as writing letters to his former employer and working on his outstanding liability claim against Western Union for disability benefits. Our efforts paid off after about three years of tutoring: Melvin substantially improved his reading and writing skills, Western Union gave him a fair settlement, and we became the best of friends.

Melvin's friendship taught me new lessons on neighborliness and volunteerism. We were comrades in bodily afflictions, I with my heart and he with his back, and that conspired to make us a most unusual yet cooperative pair. And we remain that way today. Except for Therese, of course, and Charles Murray, who in recent months has become a regular visitor and a newfound friend, Melvin is probably my closest friend and most constant companion.

Melvin seems to know everyone within a thirty-mile radius of Martinsburg. This has proven immensely useful to me in my neighborly probe beyond the Opequon to the surrounding hills and hollows. Because of Melvin, my circle of friends has expanded. We have spent afternoons at local shopping malls—America's newest and most democratic town forums and public gathering places—meeting and talking with anyone and everyone. It is obvious that a growing number of people actually want to spend more time there. I can understand why; it's socially infectious. It can even drive you to do outlandish acts of graffiti, like having your ear pierced, which is exactly what I did one day when Melvin left me alone on a bench with no one to talk to. I now wear a rather striking, small lightning bolt in my left ear.

Melvin is more than just a companion, though. He is a man of ceaseless charity, giving his time and labor to many needy families in the area—and particularly to those who are elderly and alone. In our case, Melvin has taken over most of the mowing of our three-acre lawn, and every bit of the repairing of our aging tractor-mower. When Therese traveled extensively before my heart transplant, it was Melvin who shuttled me to the grocery store and accompanied me to the Ponderosa Restaurant for the best salad bar in the Eastern Panhandle. Now that I have a new heart, it is still Melvin who fills in for the many tasks I cannot do. He has even shared with me his veteran secrets of fighting back pain, now that my own back is in painful revolt against the antirejection medicines that preserve my heart, and my life.

There is, of course, a modest price. I must listen to the wildest and most exaggerated tales likely ever told on this side of the Opequon, and told in a syntax that is uniquely Melvin, and that absolutely cannot be parsed. I don't mind though. He delights in astonishing me; he loves to make me laugh with his stories. I suspect the reason that the tractor-mower breaks down so often is that Melvin continuously thinks of yet another yarn to spin. It's called being a West Virginian, a good neighbor, and a caring friend.

[Editor's note. Karl's involvement in issues of adult literacy tied directly into his concerns for the state of childhood education and his writings on the subject. "Illiterate adults," *he wrote,* "once were illiterate children. It is the *illiteracy* of children which is the root of the problem which today often is described as a crisis of functional literacy in the adult population."

The source of that illiteracy, he believed, lay in a schism between education that seeks merely to teach facts—what he called content teaching—and process education that seeks "to develop the mind as a supple, creative organ of human action." *Only process education, he argued, was conducive to the critical thinking necessary to combat illiteracy and to prepare children to be free, responsible, and creative adults. He felt that liberty hung in the wavering balance between a populace educated to think and a populace drilled for rote memorization.*

He wrote Capitalism for Kids, *in part, to make the case that liberty and critical thought were handmaidens to one another, and that children's minds were the crucible where the two commingled in productive harmony. He wrote that,* "Education is more than a feel-good exercise. It is the most exciting exercise because it involves the mind. Young people should be taken seriously and much more, rather than less, should be asked of them at this crucial time in their development."

Karl left no autobiographical text to complete his thoughts on childhood education, but what emerges from the bits and pieces he did leave behind is a vision and a passion for the potential of the youthful mind. He spoke of its nobility and he argued for the crucial need to exercise it from the earliest age. Cutting across the landscape of gimmick-ridden teaching theories, he stuck to his basic premise: teach a child to read and reason and you will have given the child the only tools he or she will need to complete the task of their own education.

That is why he spoke and wrote so adamantly against the prevailing mind-set of more and more money as the only solution to plummeting student knowledge and test scores. The fault, as he saw it, was not in cash-poor schools; it was the failure of schools—and parents—to nurture and develop the basic tools of the child's mind.

It is important to keep Karl's interest in education in the perspective he intended. He was never a scholar who sought information for its own sake. Information was just one of many sets of tools to be used by people in their pursuit of happiness. So too was the critical, thinking, reasoning mind. Nurturing that mind so that it could transform the data of the outside world into the nuts and bolts of everyday living was, he thought, the surest path to individual freedom and to stable, vibrant communities.

Below are two statements that speak to his concerns for children and community of place. The first is a brief note he wrote to his grandson, Patrick Hess, on the occasion of Patrick's second birthday, on July 29, 1992. The second is a much longer essay, "Gossip vs. the Five Hundred Mile Stare," that was published several years ago in a local quarterly publication called The Good News Paper. *They need no further explanation.]*

Letter to Patrick

Dear Grandson:

Please pardon the tardiness of this gift to celebrate your birthday. Your old Grampaw has been pretty puny lately and moving even more slowly than usual. But he and Therese think of you always and with deep affection and love.

Our gift to you is a book about one of the most powerful tools of human intelligence: the concept of concepts. If you will just remember that they are just tools, and not binding laws or moral edicts, you should be able to avoid the major errors of ignorance, bias, and the lack of curiosity.

Always question authority, Patrick. Don't be a boor about it, just questioning things to be a smart-ass. Be a scientist. Ask questions to advance your knowledge of how the world works. And do not settle for answers that are mere jargon or official or conventional wisdom. Do not stop asking questions until you actually feel that you understand what is being said or, alternatively, understand that what is being said is just nonsense. What human beings do at the top of their talent is to speak clearly, write clearly, and demand that others do as much.

There also is a smaller book along with the big one. It is for your Dad but he will probably share it with you. Live long and prosper.

Gossip vs. The Five Hundred Mile Stare

Gossip has got a very bad name these days. Talking about your neighbors or your town, or yourself, is in many quarters considered to be small-time, low-life, petty, unworthy stuff. The sort of thing that the better people do not do.

Instead of gossip we are urged, for the good of society and the enlightenment and elevation of our consciousness, to have concerns for and opinions about The World. It is said that we live in The World.

Now, I understand the theory of living in The World. I know that The World does exist. I have, in fact, circumnavigated it and can attest from the witness of my own senses, that The World exists, with its teeming races of people, its great stew of mountains, plains, oceans; its cackle, creep, and gaggle of odd beasts and birds.

And, in a sense, we *do* all live in The World.

Some of us also live in the Eastern Panhandle of West Virginia. Some of us even live on the Opequon Creek, a place so tiny in the scheme of things that no map of The World even bothers with it.

Which is just what bothers me.

A map that does not include the Opequon seems as deficient, to me, as a history that does not include my Mother. I concede utility to such a map or history but I cannot concede it great importance.

What's this? A map of The World not being important!? A history with kings and queens, and even presidents, not being important if Thelma Snyder Hess is not included!? Looney tune time, eh?

Yet . . .

The utility of a map of The World is that it will show you that it is so many statute or nautical miles from Here to There. Should you wish to go There, however, the important thing is either to be able to walk it, ride a beast, or have at your disposal some imposing substitute such as a Pontiac Grand Prix or a Boeing 747. It would also be important if you, or someone in your party, knew how to drive, pilot, and navigate. Those are important matters. The map of The World is rather a frilly thing designed to permit you to have a fancy opinion about your trip and whether or not it will take you through Paris or Beckley, West Virginia, or over them. The important maps for the real work of getting from Here to There can, I assure you, be counted on to occupy themselves with what could be called cartographic gossip: a lot of information about creeks and hills, buttes and mesas, reefs and rocks and, of course, radio beacons rooted in some local soil lest your grand trip become a brainless meander through The World.

Same with history. Knowing the succession of the Tudor kings of England is fancy trivia. Knowing why people permit themselves to be ruled is just as fancy but not nearly so trivial and becomes actually important if it permits you, personally, to sensibly position yourself in relationship to some authority or another. We can, of course, learn much from history but, as a very wise adage tells us, what we learn mostly is how not to repeat it. History, as with those maps, is most important when it tells us not just about the past but gives us hints about the future and most especially our own. Just as the maps that are important tell us about where we, you and I, are located at any given moment, so must important history tell us where we, you and I, are located at any given epoch. Maps without travelers are empty. So is history without you, without us.

Which brings us to my Mother.

She was, in my case, just as yours was in your case, an important source not only of genetic inheritance but of environmental conditioning. Parents are our history to a very significant degree. They are important history. It is *useful* to know about other people's history. But *your* history, that is IMPORTANT.

And parents, it may be noted, are the gossip of genetics, the small talk of environment. We may look to Darwin or Scriptures to understand The World and how the abstract "We" came to pass in it, but when we are very curious about *our* not-at-all abstract, very concrete selves we must at least glance at our parents. We must descend from the Grand Discussion to, of all things, gossip.

Which brings us to this newspaper.

This Good News Paper is, essentially and importantly, a gossip sheet. Gasp. A what? Alas, it is true. A gossip sheet, a journal full of small talk about the minute matter of our neighborhood, a place that, like our creeks, does not even show on maps of The World, a place and a people who are never cited as the concern of Great Men, or Women, involved in the big time stuff.

We must live with this.

Matter of fact, we have no choice. No matter the exalted state or range of our opinions, even if we happen to be The President, the place where we live and the place where we do things is not so much The World as it is our neighborhood. But surely this doesn't apply to the truly great, to The President, does it? It does.

The President has opinions, of course, about the entire universe. But to storm the moon, Saturn, or the Kremlin, even the President must act right where he is, at home. He then must depend upon a very complex chain of responses from other people—*all acting at home*—to get anything done. If any significant one or number òf them do not act, right where they are, at home, so to speak, then nothing gets done beyond The President having had a very big idea that got exactly nowhere.

It is not likely, however, that Presidents can be taught simple truths since they live at a fair remove from simple events and can be excused for thinking that the world actually behaves according to the physics of high school books of instruction on how your government operates. The rest of us have no such excuse. We have the lessons of our lives, every day, to tell us that if we do not do things where we live then we may end up doing very little at all.

Not that there are not serious temptations to think otherwise. The most serious of these temptations is a highly agitated mental state that I have come to think of as The Five Hundred Mile Stare. It develops in the following, almost invariable, sequence.

Something wretched happens somewhere in The World, usually at a great distance from the person involved, thus the name The Five Hundred Mile Stare. Actually, five thousand miles is even better, as will be demonstrated.

Now, this may seem a mean-spirited cavil, akin to thinking that a person should know the tilth of their own soil before declaiming on world erosion, but it seems to me that the first concern of anyone interested in saving children would be to save a child. 1 also believe that there are children in our neighborhood, our community, our counties, who urgently need help. While applauding the rescue of a child in the tropics, might we not also think of a priority for a child down the street?

You can see where this is all leading. Back to gossip.

Helping the child near you is a sort of gossip, a discourse upon your relationship to your neighbors, far different from the mightier discourse upon your relationship to the world, pardon me, The World.

Lest we not demand greatness from our every action, however, let's see what demand we can put on this little idea of helping the child nearest to us rather than the one farthest from us. Let us say that the distant child needs the help more desperately. Overlooking the difficulty of even making the determination, think for a moment of what we are left with after the determination. We now have launched the distant assistance. But the child nearby is still in pain. Are we to call upon some distant person to help that child because we are helping a distant child? We could be getting ourselves into a mess. Then how about a compromise? Help the local child and then, help the distant one.

Such compromises seem to make good sense, to me. They are the stuff of which the fascinating adage, "Think Globally, Act Locally," is made.

And what that means, I believe, is that to save the world we must gossip a lot right here at home, gossip about whether we are kind to one another before we leap to battle a Cruel World; gossip about the dignity of ourselves and our friends before being outraged by affronts to the Dignity of Man, the Dignity of Woman. Gossip about the price of progress and the meaning of progress along our creeks and not just across our rivers and oceans.

People who cannot gossip but who can only talk in great concepts are forever, as in the case of the once-ruling Russian Communists, grinding along their famous highways of history on paving made of the bodies of people who once were their neighbors but now are just their subjects.

They are not alone. The best and the brightest even here are said to be concerned always with great concepts rather than small potatoes. They feed on great concepts. I eat small potatoes. No wonder that great concepts often must explain that the general good (i.e., the good of the great concept) must roll majestically over the individual person or place. Thus does history triumph over gossip and silence the petty tongues of men and women talking about themselves when they should be serenading the leader.

Having observed the distant, wretched happening, the person becomes outraged and determines to do something. Nothing, of course, can be done way out there where IT is wretchedly happening. Something must be done where you are, a tribute to the inflexibility of the rule of local action but no deterrent to the person with the Five Hundred Mile Stare. What they contrive to do, first of all, is to have an opinion. Should this opinion be one that would not have occurred to any of the neighbors, so much the better for it will mark you off as a person of special sensitivity and even special knowledge. It may be seen as being to the social graces what owning a Ferrari is to automotion. Very big stuff.

The person with the Five Hundred Mile Stare may now be set off at cocktail parties and other neighborhood gatherings by a particularly pained expression. The better people will all know, and respect the fact that this angst is caused by the person's advanced anguish over the distant situation. This is all that need happen although it is true that, sometimes, people with a Five Hundred Mile Stare will be found circulating petitions or even collecting money on behalf of their anguish. Of the fate of petition, I have little knowledge. Of the fate of money collected for distant distress I have some knowledge and considerable trepidation inasmuch as substantial fractions of this well-meant money inevitably must go to sustain a professional staff which can obtain free TV commercials so that ever more people can donate money to enable the staff to get ever more free time on TV.

Does this mean that it is silly to care about distant distress? Not at all. It suggests to me only that there might be more direct ways to get things done in this respect than in having correct opinions about it. There was a time, for instance, when church people concerned by distant distress would simply bundle up food and clothing, medical supplies, and what-have-you, put it in a local truck which would haul it to a harbor where a ship, chartered by many church groups, would unload it, then proceed to deliver it to missionaries in the distant place who would then distribute it.

Local action, in effect, all the way. In these more sophisticated times, however, such chores are given over, more and more, to professionals who are said to know what they are doing and who, indeed, do keep impressive forms, in quadruplicate, to prove it. They also command excellent salaries, which may prove that they are smarter than missionary Christians at that.

A closer look at the most highly developed Five Hundred Mile Stare can make a path on which we may return to gossip.

One pronounced form of the Five Hundred Mile Stare is to save children. This seems reasonable since anyone lacking an urge to help children is approximately as unnatural, it seems to me, as a person who wanted to help none else.

In the grip of the Five Hundred Mile Stare, however, it is not sufficient to save just any child. It is mandatory to save all children. Save the children, it is demanded. It may remind you of serving the people. It is a very elevated ambition. No small time stuff there.

Does this mean that there is no general good, no great speaking to be done above the buzz and hum of homely gossip? The general good, I believe, can only be defined by the particular person. That, after all, is how it always *is* defined, by particular people. It is similarly true of the landscape. What is good at the top of a mountain may be simply terrible in the fold of a valley. Good is too ancient a problem for us human beings to be conveniently relegated to the sure and the compartmentalized. It is our great, ongoing human debate. Great speaking? Socrates, Christ, the Buddha talk of little things, of mustard seeds and a single person. So does quantum mechanics. The eye of the observer, not the universe, is the first concern for all of them. The universe, they might be saying, is itself just gossip so far as we can be concerned.

The universe, which may not care a fig for us, can only be cared for by us in our gossip, which is our talk of where we live, because it is only there that we intersect the universe.

But is anything I have written sensible? Who knows? We must gossip about it. That, too, is what good neighbors do.

19

Therese

There is no way to own the sky
And yet we fly, and yet we fly.
Fish and the whale all roam the ocean,
Yet there's a shore on the edge of the motion.
Moving 'round, moving 'round, moving up, moving down,
Put your feet down on the ground and, if you've a mind to,
Let's walk together.
Let's walk there together.

There is no way to own the day,
Yet for every flower there's a sunny ray.
Grain and vines all over the land,
Yet there's a place for a forest stand.
Moving 'round, moving 'round, moving up, moving down,
Put your feet down on the ground and, if you've a mind to,
Let's walk together.
Let's walk there together.

There is no way to own the gale,
Yet we sail, yet we sail.
Lands and islands, voyages and quest,

Yet there are harbors, yet there is rest.
Moving 'round, moving 'round, moving up, moving down.
Put your feet down on the ground and, if you've a mind to,
Let's walk together.
Let's walk there together.

There is no one who owns another,
Sister, brother, kin or lover.
Yet there's sharing, yet there's caring,
Yet there's calling and yet there is hearing.
Moving 'round, moving 'round, moving up, moving down.
Put your feet down on the ground and, if you've a mind to,
Let's walk together.
Let's walk there together.

We'll go and we'll see, together.
Together, we'll go and we'll see.

—Karl Hess, "Wedding Song," January 1971

Edward the Eighth, during his brief run as king of England, said that he had learned only two things of value during his reign: To never miss a chance to sit down or to relieve himself.

Well, he was British. Two things were probably enough.

For an unruly American like me, there is one I would add: Be in love. The form of the love may be varied, and even change from time to time, but the principle holds: Be in love.

I can remember the time when I was in love with trap and skeet shooting. My over-and-under Browning was my personal gauge of beauty. Its rich, blued barrel, its superb balance and pointing seemed more lovely to me than any maid or mistress. Tracking a target and breaking it was orgasmic. I was in love.

Then there was the Macintosh computer that my friend Bob Kephart gave me. If I could have been wired directly into it, I would have readily surrendered my autonomy.

But arching over all those loves there were greater ones. First, the love of my two sons. Just watching them is a lover's vision. Talking with them is a constant excitement, pleasure, and mind-opening.

And then and always there is Therese. Being in love with her has made all other loves not less, but less commanding. I would not trade a minute alone with her for an eternity in someone else's paradise.

> *Her Bath*
> *copper green earrings*
> *brush comb a shining hair*
> *scent of fair flowers*
> *warmed air traces of mist*
> *And her footprint on slate*
>
> *Her Bed*
> *high hill of pillows*
> *glasses book and papers*
> *love laid beside her*
> *day poured into night*
> *hands touch silently*
>
> *Her Landscape*
> *cat curled purring*
> *birds whirl high singing*
> *wild yarrow yellow*
> *hawks gliding easily*
> *with her sun at the center*

—Karl Hess, "Haiku (sort of) for Therese"

There are other loves of course. I love my country—which is West Virginia. I still have trouble putting up with that other one that surrounds us. And I love my friends.

You can be in love with many things, with many people, but, in my view, the essential action is to be in love with something, with someone, at every moment of your life.

Perhaps it is an obsession with an accomplishment—climbing a mountain, discovering a new particle in physics or a new arrangement in genetics, tracking down the intransitive form of some verb in an Icelandic saga, getting rich, getting even—whatever, so long as it has the passion and the focus that we associate with romantic love.

The love of *occupation* is most likely to occupy us in our earlier years. It often is said to be equal to love for a person, for a lover, or for our children and, indeed, it seems difficult to sort it all out. But this I am certain of; there are few people on earth who are not in love with something. Einstein was in love with concepts that kept eluding him. Surgeons are in love with the fight with death; they persist to win. Love in this sense is relative, each person sorting it out as best he can.

My own sorting through the matter has led me to my own final solution.

The love of a friend, lover, wife, child, or husband, is the singular, most compelling form of love. This is the love that can endure all of the other loves and passions and obsessions of an active life and remain steady and sure as the great constant of one's life—at least it has for me. I have learned that when all is said and done our most momentous statements finally shake down to what amounts to opinion. Thus it is my opinion, one which guides my life and has guided it for many years, that the old-fashioned, hand-holding sort of love is the love that lasts and which, finally, overshadows all of the other loves.

There is a perfidious form of love also: the love of power, the urge to tell other people what to do and how to live their lives. This is the passion of some preachers and most politicians, people who are not in love with *other people* or with *curiosity*, but only in love with themselves, their position, their power. They are not very trustworthy people; they often are dangerous people.

From my perch on the edge, I have concluded that despite all of our ideological pretensions and zeal to save the world, that it is the person we are in love with that is the central purpose and parameter of most of our lives. Nothing in my entire life has made me as happy as being with Therese, nothing as unhappy as not being with her, or displeasing her. Love is such an obvious central core of human happiness that I am appalled that people are so quiet about it—so hushed, so ashamed to be open and forthright about the most important aspect of human life. Most of the words that people have put down on paper in the history of the human race, I believe, have had to do with love. Still, there are signs.

Therese and I attended a bluegrass concert recently, in an open field on the sort of warm, wonderful day that seems like a dream in an afternoon's nap. I noted with actual and sudden astonishment the couples coiled and twined in so many different ways. Hair fallen over arms, thick, skinny, tattooed, clean, yuppie arms. All sorts. I was mesmerized by the sight of love—that strongest affiliation—and how it brings people together as powerful sculptures, individuals pressed against other individuals, volunteers in union. I came once again to my most optimistic thoughts. Humans really are, by and large, amazing and wonderful. Some are unhappy in any combination of coupling. But most aren't. They make a go of it. Of love, of another person, of the grand sum of all things.

Next is winter.
Why.
Because summer died.
Of joy.

Next the ferret plans.
Why.
Because lions starve.
After overeating.

Next the sheltered fires.
Why.
Because pyres flicker out.
In the rain.

Next is planting.
Why.
Because reapers dream.
Never awakening.

Next is choosing.
Why.
Because all-ness emptied.
Into nothingness.

Next is now.
Why.
Because sometime vanished.
Into yesterday.

Next is here.
Why.
Because someplace sank.
Into nowhere.

Next is someone.
Why.
Because everyone vanished.
In the day.

Next is knowing.
Why.
Because feeling failed.
Staring blankly.

Next is feeling.
Why.
Because knowing failed.
Squinting narrowly.

Next is person.
Why.
Because there is.
Nothing else.

—Karl Hess, "Anthem-song of the Persistent Rationalist"

In a recent letter, after returning from his honeymoon, Senator Goldwater wrote at length and lovingly about how falling in love had transformed his life, even in his eighties, and made him a better man than he ever thought he could be.

I have, in fact, been in love with three women, four if my mother may properly be included. My first wife, a lovely, intelligent woman, a reporter for the *Washington Star* when we met, put up with me through a period when I was so self-absorbed that I am afraid I treated everyone as just the furniture in the grand salon of my life. It was immensely unfair and even hurtful to a fine woman.

I was in love with the young woman who lived with me on a boat at

Buzzard's Point, at the confluence of the Potomac and the Anacostia Rivers in Washington, and at the juncture of my past and present. She was the princess of my hippie period.

And then there was and is and always will be Therese.

Therese Ann Mary Machotka. Even her name sings in my mind like an anthem.

Morning is a soft sound made of goose down
Still, water thick and waiting
To pour across gray smooth rocks
Living with the lady across the creek
The lovely, loving amazing lady 'cross the creek.
The making wonder world making lady 'cross the creek
The lady who makes the earth roll, the day rise
Living across the creek that crosses the world.
Lady, lady across the creek
Make it morning, make it glow, make it go
Start it up, sun it up, run it up.
Lady, lady living 'cross the creek.

Noon is fireworks made of wheat pinging bronze
Buzzing, lightheaded air exploding
To flood across the deep, ragged grass
Living with the lady across the creek
The lovely, loving amazing lady 'cross the creek.
The warm, wonder day making lady 'cross the creek
The lady who makes the air dance, the sun melt and flow
Living across the creek that crosses the world.
Lady, lady across the creek
Make it noontime, make it ripple, sparkle, spin
Bring it on, sing it on, take it on.
Lady, lady living 'cross the creek

Twilight is a cloud of rain clinging mist
Silent, curtain closing, whispering
To shut windowed lights one-by-one
Living with the lady across the creek
The lovely, loving, amazing lady 'cross the creek.

The quiet, time defining lady 'cross the creek
The lady who makes eternity stand still, sigh, softly glow
Living across the creek that crosses the world.
Lady, lady across the creek
Make it evening, make it glisten, smooth, still
Lead it in, close it in, gather it in.
Lady, lady living 'cross the creek.

Night is a silver whistle in blue-black woods
Boundless, edged by moonlit endlessness
To tunnel endlessly into tomorrow
Living with the lady across the creek
The lovely, loving amazing lady 'cross the creek.
The forever lady, star-arched across the creek
The lady who makes, keeps and lights galaxies
Living across the creek that crosses the world.
Lady, lady across the creek
Make it night, make it enfold, cover, shimmer
Deepen it, delight it, hush it away.
Living with the lady across the creek
Living, living loving with the lady 'cross the creek.
Lady, lady living 'cross the creek.

—Karl Hess, "Lady Across the Creek"

Therese. Of all my life's enterprises, being in love with her is and will always be the most important. Not the world and not the galaxy means more to me than just being with her. Just as the universe seems to expand and contract in some ageless breathing, my universe once expanded boundlessly and now contracts to a point of light, without ever, I feel, changing its composite matter. Being alone with Therese is my own idea of perfect happiness.

I give her not only my love but also I owe her my life. When, following the successful transplant of a heart, I fractured my spine and was for several months just about totally incapacitated, Therese tended me day and night, putting up with everything from fairly constant complaining to occasional incontinence. Without her there could be no me.

[Editor's note. On Earth Day, 1991, Karl spoke to students at Hedgesville Middle School as part of the Earth Day celebration. A few days later, a letter arrived from the students he had spoken to, thanking him for coming. They wrote:

You were most interesting and not at all boring as we had thought. You appear to be quite intelligent and have done so many interesting things throughout your life. We learned a lot, too, about your many jobs and this has helped some of us in planning our lives. We thank you not only for facts but for inspiring us to be what we want to be. We learned also that we want to be members of the smart group and not the dumb group.

Karl valued the thank-you; he framed it and hung it next to a letter sent to him by Pres. Dwight D. Eisenhower. Shortly afterwards, he wrote a letter on love to Laura Legensky, one of the Hedgesville students. That letter appears below, as well as an aside on love written by Karl to his lifelong friend, Ralph de Toledano, just thirty days earlier.]

Letter to Laura Legensky

I want to thank you for asking the most serious and important question of any asked during the morning that I spent at Hedgesville Middle School.

After I described the importance of love in our lives, you asked, "Is being in love fun?" It is. But it is so much more. In fact, to think of love as basically fun is to miss its deeper power. Yet, it *should* be fun, along with being comforting, exciting, challenging.

If it isn't fun then there may be serious reason to examine it. Perhaps it isn't love, but some lesser emotion such as physical passion, admiration, or, in the worst of all situations, attraction not to a person but to a person's possessions or minor accomplishments such as dressing well or throwing a ball accurately.

Love, if true and important, should be the center of your life and not simply an adornment to your life.

Imagine spending a lifetime with a person on a deserted island. Love can make such an exile a small paradise on earth.

People who love each other have the most valuable and significant asset available to most human beings. I say "most" simply because it is apparent that to someone like Mozart or to great scientists such as Watson and Crick, love of humans can be supplanted by love of craft. But that sort of love is rare. It actually is a definition of genius, in my view.

You said that your parents love each other. That is wonderful. There are entirely too few marriages, these days, founded on love. You are fortunate to have such parents. They are blessed to have love. They are fortunate, also, to have a daughter who is unafraid to talk about important things and who so obviously has a lively intellect and a good character.

I can best talk to you about love by talking about Therese.

Literally, from the day I met her more than thirty years ago, she has been the center of my life. There is nothing that I ever have done or can imagine doing that can compare to what she means to me.

From the first moment I see her face in the morning, to the conversations we have during the day, or just sitting with her watching the hundreds of birds who congregate near our house, or listening to music, or even just being with her silently reading, there is nothing that I feel we cannot share, nothing that we cannot honestly say to each other.

I have never in all of our years together wanted to be anywhere else more than I have wanted to be near to her. Traveling around the world is fascinating. But being with Therese is the most fascinating thing I have ever done.

We share everything. She edits my books, and argues with me when I write silly things. I take great pleasure in being part of her own work which mainly involves adult literacy.

We each have our separate talents, of course. She is a fine artist. I am a good writer. But more and more we find that we even seem to share our brains, saying exactly the same things in unison as we react to something.

I hope, Laura, that you will not settle for anything less when you find yourself loving someone. It can't be a one-way street. Love must be nourished by love. It is an enterprise of mutual interest. If it isn't it may be something but it certainly isn't love.

That is why, in answering your wonderful question I urged the class to be most careful about love, more careful about it than fashion, or cars, or sports, or money or anything else.

Some young people fall madly in love. Madly is a good modifier in the sentence. Falling madly in love has always meant, when I practiced it or observed it, falling in love with love and not with an actual person.

It is so exciting to feel swept away by a grand passion or unyielding lust. But it is a madness, and one which should be avoided if possible, or ended quickly if not. There then follows, the period of anguish when a person may feel that they will die. Most don't.

Getting over falling-madly-in-love is cured by a little time. And it is so different from actually loving someone. You'll know when that happens. It is such a serious thing that you will think about it and not just react to it. You will ask all of the sensible questions—about being alone with the person and not being bored, about comforting the person during bad times or illness, about having the most fun when with the person.

I am sure you are smart enough to have begun thinking along those lines already. You will love and love wisely. There is nothing more important. I wish you well and feel honored to have met you.

—Karl Hess, April 1991

An Aside on Love to Ralph de Toledano

Got to thinking about love songs the other day and my two favorites came quickly to mind. "You Have Cast Your Shadow on the Sea," from *The Boys from Syracuse*, and "My Love Is a Wanderer," as sung by Portia Nelson. Frank Norris steered me to the former, you introduced me to the latter. Now here is where I yearn for a minor miracle. Do you happen to have the Portia Nelson album? If so, could you tape it for me? I'll buy you a decent dinner when you visit us out here if you can do it! They really are great songs aren't they? Come to think of it, there just haven't been many love songs lately, have there? Happily, I observe that this does not mean that love is going out of style. It persists as the most important part of the lives of everyone I know. What has gone out of fashion, alas, is the unashamed discussion of it. I've suggested that love impact statements would be more important than environmental impact statements.

—Karl Hess, March 1991

T

When the day seems safer, brighter, aglow with hope
I know that you have entered the room or house.
When the evening seems softer, gentler, and sweet,

I know that you are in the room or about the house.
When sadness ends and joy, peace, and happiness abound
I know that you are in the room or about the house.
When every breath is taken in my life
I know that you are the completeness of my love.

20

Mostly on the Edge

Karl Hess, the gentlest anarchist of them all, came down from the West Virginia mountains the other day. He was dressed as usual, as if he were hunting for bear, but he joined some old friends in a posh K Street restaurant with the serenity of a man who has his values and his humor intact. He had been struck with a Great Idea.

Hess is well up in the running for the title of Most Unforgettable Character I have encountered on the campaign trail. We first met in 1964, when he was chief speechwriter for Barry Goldwater. He was then a conservative's conservative, somewhere to the right of old Bill McKinley, a gray-flanneled, clean-shaven, fire-eating apostle of free enterprise, balanced budgets and a 25 per cent annual return on investment.

Then, as you may recall he went through a convulsive repudiation of his suburban life-style. He separated from his wife, went to live on a houseboat, grew a fine black beard, made his living as a welder, tried the communal life in a rundown section of Washington, and finally moved to a cave house near Kearneysville, W.Va. He built the house with his own hands.

On this particular Wednesday morning, he had caught a 6:50 train to Washington, walked a mile to the Jean-Pierre, and was early for a board meeting of the Fund for Investigative Journalism. He ordered a no-vodka Bloody Mary and exuded good cheer. During the two-hour train ride to Washington he had perceived how the Iranian crisis might have been prevented; he saw how similar crises might be averted in the future. His Great Idea: Diplomacy by 800 numbers.

The details would have to be worked out, but the impressive cost savings are at once apparent. Instead of embassies, in the Hess proposal, we would have telephone booths. In every capital city, the State Department would arrange a bank of attractive sidewalk kiosks. The aggrieved Iranian, or Libyan, or Panamanian would insert a refundable coin, dial 800-632-9606, or whatever, and behold!

"State Department here."

"I am an aggrieved Iranian."

"Yes, of course, and what aggrieves you today?"

"Send us the shah, or I'll pull out this telephone by its roots!"

"By all means, sir, feel free to do so, and the best of the season to you."

Such colloquies, said my friend, waxing eloquent as the possibilities expanded, would save us all the expense of ambassadors, striped pants, tea parties and smashed windows. Hostages could not be seized, only phone booths. Deprived of embassies to arrange their nightclub visits, congressmen would tend to stay home instead of junketing abroad.

As for the gathering of intelligence, at modest expense we could subscribe to the Tehran Daily Bugle and the Tripoli Times. A corps of sweet-talking Kelly Girls could man a special State Department switchboard. Diplomacy would never be the same again.

If Hess runs for president, a prospect he is seriously non-considering, this would be but one plank in a platform devoted not to expansion, but to contraction. His whole purpose would be to disband the federal government, but to disband it "gracefully." One by one, beginning with the regulatory agencies, executive departments would simply vanish. After six months, he believes, "no one would miss them but the bureaucrats who used to work there."

The Constitution, alas, would continue to require a Congress, but with the Kelly Girls in charge of foreign affairs and no executive agencies to bother about, the Congress would have little to do. The liberties of the people, in sum, might be secure.

In his second month in the White House, Hess would wipe out federal aid to the states, the cities and the public schools. This would effectively wipe out public education, a prospect he finds enchanting.

He would end highway maintenance which in time would end driving, which in time would solve the gasoline problem and also revitalize the legs of the American people. This would help the horse industry also.

Down with government and up with anarchy! The platform, I am bound to say, has a certain splendid appeal.
  —James J. Kilpatrick, *Thoughts from a Gentle Anarchist*

Speech making is the craft I do best and the one in which I find the greatest joy. Why this should be I have no clear idea, though I suppose my mother's self-confidence played more than an incidental role. I also suspect that the accelerated pace of my early years made a verbal vocation a reasonable choice and, as it turned out, a truer reflection of my natural leaning to be a performer. Mind you, not a figure to be admired, *not* an ego to be inflated, *not* a leader in search of converts; just a stand-up commentator with a playful sense of humor and a fondness for ideas by which to tickle the imagination and to spur the mind to critical thought.

As a rule, I have never written my speeches down on paper, unless, of course, I have written them for others to read. My practice is to speak simply and straightforwardly off-the-cuff. I learn what people are most interested in, I talk toward that, I encourage interruption and argument, and I hope for a healthy questioning of *my* authority. I don't think I have ever made a public lecture without somewhere along the line making this last point. I believe the most important thing I can tell anyone about anything I have said is that if you *believe* it all you haven't been listening.

What I say *may* be true, it *may* have importance, but you have got to go to the trouble of finding out for yourself. It is not enough just to listen to me and to believe me. I don't want followers, I don't want to start a new church, or anything of the sort. I want to go to places where people take the time to think; I want to say things I have long thought about and see if anyone agrees, if anyone is excited. That, I confess, is my sole motive in writing this book—to entertain and to question. If there is a lesson to it, and quite possibly there isn't, I leave that to others much smarter than I to discern and make the case.

My world is here and now, along the Opequon. My life, of course, continues to be dominated by health concerns and the sense of mortality that it forces upon me like a tombstone waiting to plop on my head. Yet my spirits are high and I cling to the hope which is always up there, cheering from the top of the magic computer in my mind. I have my neighbors, my friends, Therese, and twelve acres of shale outcroppings, meadows, and path-laced forest that I would not trade for The World. I am limited to doing the only thing I am physically capable of doing: writing. Alas for sculpture, woodworking, and canoe trips. But maybe it is all for the best. I have an idea I'm better at writing than all the other stuff anyway.

So what does one write about at the closing of a life's story? Some great reflection, an eternal truth, an enticing vision to inspire and motivate? I have never been good at profound reflections, seeing very little need to dwell on what was. I confess a disinterest in truth, preferring instead to concentrate on what is and what I can do about it. And I'm not terribly clever at visions, especially since practical matters always seem to get in the way.

Not long ago, a close friend asked if I had any regrets about the course, and the details, of my life. "None," I said, echoing what I had already written at the outset of this book. There were, I noted, some things I would like to have changed sooner to have made my life—and the lives of the people around me—smoother. But what those changes amounted to was not so much a grieving for not having learned certain lessons, but rather an admission to having taken so long to learn them.

My attitude on war has changed over the years. As late as the beginning of the Vietnamese War, I was still infatuated with the romance and utility of armed conflict. I agreed with Gen. Curtis LeMay that we should bomb the North Vietnamese back to the Stone Age. If we had the weapons to do it, as I was certain we did, why not? War was big on my mind.

Things began to change about the time I associated with the Institute for Policy Studies and read—and reviewed for the *Washington Post*—the brilliant analysis of the Vietnamese War by IPS director and fellow, Richard Barnet. Earlier, I had argued the necessity of bombing the dikes in North Vietnam to flood the country and destroy its crop potential. But Barnett's book—as well as the writings of Bertrand Russell and the international war tribunal he assembled—gave substantial evidence that the United States had been bombing those dikes for years and it just wasn't working. That planted suspicion in my mind that maybe there was something wrong about war, that possibly we had been on the wrong side from the start, and that in all likelihood winning a war against a bunch of peasants was too much of a task even for a superpower. Nobody, as far as I could tell, had ever won such a war; Great Britain, to our great advantage, hadn't in the years following 1776, so why should we two centuries later?

My attitude on war is much different today, but not on humanitarian grounds or for pacifistic reasons. I am not against violence in principle or against people having fights in practice; I am merely against the prodigious waste of substituting war for commerce. Commerce has worked from the beginning of time. When people have traded together they have found ways to live together peacefully and productively. If winning in a global arena matters, then we should buy the world, not fight it or conquer it. Most people would love the idea. There are, after all, far more merchants and marketers in the world than warriors and marines.

I will admit that if somebody wants to start a trade war, I will be the first one out there waving the banners and saying hurray for Ford and down with Toyota. But if the Japanese happen to win, so what? Of what consequence is it other than the trifling detail that a bunch of us will start working for Toyota instead of Ford?

War, in contrast, has real consequences. It is, as the splendid but cranky libertarian Randolph Bourne has said, the health of the state. Wars, whether against other nations or between a nation and its citizens, are among the greatest killers in human history. But wars on such a scale don't happen by accident; they are prosecuted with design and intent. Governments, not just the wars they spawn, kill people with efficiency and dispatch. The counterargument, that without those governments people would run amuck, plunder, and kill one another, is less convincing to me than the long-observed and mortal facts of state warfare.

So, I have decided to sit out the next national or global war. But I will not sit out little wars. If, for example, war breaks out between Berkeley and Jefferson counties over *our* creek and the shooting starts—*though I doubt it will since my neighbors are marketers, not warriors*—I will shoot back. I have no Quaker inhibition to this sort of violence. I am not against shooting at people, I am just against being *forced* to do it and doing it for frivolous reasons. I believe that if you are going to shoot at someone it ought to be because your life is in danger, because something more serious than the welfare of government is involved. I would not, for example, hesitate for a moment to pick up a gun and defend any of my neighbors if they were threatened.

I have learned that there is a difference between the organized insanity called war and the smaller, defensive maneuvers of protecting our neighborhoods. A willingness to protect where we live—the communities and small platoons of our affections and affiliations as Charles Murray puts it—is natural and sometimes absolutely necessary. I think some neighborhoods in Washington, D.C., realize this; they know that if they were more heavily armed they might be safer. They could defend themselves better, and they *should* defend themselves. The defense of the *place* where you have your good life is a reasonable responsibility, one that you should at least be prepared to carry out. I also think that Robert Heinlein was right: an armed society is a polite society.

Having said this, I will also say that in the Second World War, if I could have successfully enlisted, I would have fought courageously. But that was true of everyone I knew. To object to that war you had to be so smart and so even-keeled in your emotions as to be almost unbelievable. The music was overpowering, Roosevelt was overpowering, and the fact that the Japanese—who didn't even invent the airplane—destroyed Pearl Harbor from the air was a maddening affront.

One attitude that has never changed is my immense love for America. I cannot imagine anyplace else in the world that would put up with me except here. Comparatively, it is the most free country on the face of the earth. I don't think there's any doubt about it. It is true for blacks living in the ghetto, it is true for people living in Beverly Hills, and it is true for people living in Hamtramck, Michigan.

I feel this way now, and I felt that way on April 15, 1969, when I wrote to the Internal Revenue Service that "I can not in conscience sanction [the United States] government by the payment of taxes." I love America dearly, and I know that it was in that spirit that I said no. But I now know that my refusal to pay taxes burdened others. It was not courteous to my wife, Therese. It cost her considerable money and years of worry. Nothing that I can imagine—and certainly not a stand on principle—will ever justify that cost.

I am pleased, though, for whatever inspiration my tax resistance has given to others in their personal resistance to an illiberal and oppressive IRS. I believe my example has caused more people to question the authority of that agency, though I suspect some people who have taken my lead have also spent time in jail. Those who have openly fought the IRS and gone to prison have generally argued their cases on ideological grounds, as if the only error made by the IRS was some technical infraction of law. My approach was simpler. I didn't contest their authority because it was unconstitutional or because I envisioned some abstract right to protect me. Who cares? They make the rules, not me. I simply said no.

Over time I have also learned to say no to the various ghosts and goblins of ideology that have strayed across my path. I have learned to stick to what I can see, touch, and love—my neighbors, my place on the Opequon, and Therese. Compared to friendship, ideology seems such a shallow, pompous thing. Opinions, I believe, are trivial, and institutional loyalty—which is part of opinion—is a travesty. I have been criticized rather sharply for saying that "given the choice between being disloyal to a friend or my country, I hope that I would have the good sense to remain loyal to my friend."

It's a strange criticism when you think about it. How in the world can a person be disloyal to a country? It's only possible if you think in terms of being loyal to a particular political administration or to some grandiose idea. Yet, I am convinced that such loyalty is unworthy of a human, especially when compared to loyalty to inquiry, to friends, to love, or to a dog or a cat. These I understand and accept; the other is just someone else's opinion about what I *should* think, believe, and do.

I am inclined toward the wisdom in Buddhism and Sufism that declares there is no truth and everything is permissible. I have found this to be a comforting guide to what we must challenge ourselves to do: to live constantly with self-asserted certainty in a world of absolute uncertainty. It is said in a similar vein that humans have visualized the universe but the universe doesn't care. That too, I feel, is an essential part of being wholly, consciously human; knowing that we are simply individuals in an uncaring universe.

All of this constrains us to know that what we do, we must do on our own simply because we will it. It also frees us to know that we can try to do whatever we wish. There is no truth, everything is permissible. Our kindness to neighbors, which I so treasure, is not dictated out of divine instruction; it is simply a choice. The churl, even the killer, is not evil or wrong, but simply a pest or a threat. The universe, no matter how hard we work to make it appear benign, will no more protect us from either pests or threats than will our incantations against such people. Action will. And included in that action is the possibility of a shared culture in which being a pest or threat is mutually agreed upon as being impermissible. But at all times, it is agreement, never right or wrong, sinner or saint, that makes human action compelling and effective.

People can, of course, dress up agreements with fancy concepts such as natural law, Christianity, or whatever ideology is closest at hand. Yet I feel strongly that the lever moving anything that is social always is agreement or lack of it. Indeed, civilization is a constant negotiating process. Those who see civilization as something steady are always depressed or alarmed that, despite their fondest hopes for stability, it keeps changing.

We should not be surprised that the only social areas that are slow to change, or unchanged over long periods, are very small and isolated by terrain (the reclusive tribe in the Philippines) or by policy (the Aborigines in Australia) or by choice (the Amish in Pennsylvania). In contrast, technological and market-based societies are fast to change and have shifting borders, or no borders, because they feed on ideas and often take pains to be open to them, which means opening their areas and culture generally.

Some people, on both the Right and Left of American politics, argue vociferously over the importance of ideology to the spirit and evolution of America. I disagree. I am convinced that the truly distinguishing mark of America is the hard-core practicality of its people, a practical nature that has made shambles of most attempts to overlay it with ideology. It is the very same practical nature that makes political lines hard to draw and that is continually surprising pundits. That explains, I suppose, the failure of the Left to make substantial inroads in American society. So many leftists are besotted with morals; they are mystics of their own revealed wisdoms, unconcerned with the ethics of neighborly behavior—the very ethics that might otherwise give them credence in the eyes of practical-minded Americans.

Much the same can be said for the conservative and, sometimes, the libertarian Right. Individual liberty, the very order of society itself, is said to rest on rights of some natural, immutable, or universal origin. As far as I can observe, such rights are illusions that do more mischief than good by persuading people to rely on what doesn't exist, to assume behaviors that are most curious, in order to preserve what is most essential to human happiness.

Consider the hallowed right to life, a right that is certainly attractive to most people. If I stood on the banks of the Opequon and proclaimed that right, twenty-four hours a day, in the face of marauding pests and threats, I would be dead within hours or days unless someone happened to agree with my exhortations. In short, the right would not save me, even as I proclaimed it to my death. Only the help of a neighbor could, and only then if I had the state of mind to shake loose from my beliefs and rely, instead, on the good will of human hands.

There is no right to life. There is no right to respect. There is no right to absence of pain. All of these so-called rights are just opportunities. This is neither good nor bad, right or wrong; it is just an observation, a statement of material reality. In this regard, chaos theory helps to remind us that no matter how arrogantly we may think of our ability to measure, to predict, and to plan things, we invariably fall short of our expectations. The earth just doesn't work that way. The smallest causes make the grandest events unpredictable, whether in weather, biology, or human affairs. Material reality simply trumps human hubris, stripping away the ethereal dressing of our ideologies and leaving in their stead the thin skeletons of our opinions, whether on rights, gods, or the Three Stooges.

In short, I am not in the rights business, believing, as I do, that there are no rights except through agreement. We have only those rights to which there is actual assent among some discrete group of involved people. Rights which are not based upon agreement are not rights at all but, instead, are dictates which imply the power of someone exterior to the situation to apply force, including lethal force, to enforce the dictate.

Set apart from and opposed to the power of guns are negotiations and agreements. They are the essence of both community and liberty in my view. That view, of course, is constantly changing. So are my neighbors. So is the world. To walk among the changes, self-assured and unburdened by ghosts and goblins, strikes me as the most wonderful of human attributes.

This is the freedom I have sought along the meandering path of my life.

This is the choice that defines who I am.

Charles Murray, in his wonderful book, *In Pursuit of Happiness and Good Government*, presents the notion that most people, in order to be happy, need two things: to be engaged in something they love, and to be affiliated with others in common pursuits. I find that notion profound in its simplicity. I have used those terms—*affiliation* and *engagement*—repeatedly in this book. They seem to summarize much of what I have sought and tried to incorporate in my life.

They are, I believe, the building blocks for who we are as individuals. Each person spends a lifetime engaged in a single overarching project: designing his or her own life. To be this thing, this person, to do it just the way you want, and to be satisfied with it, that is the major artistic endeavor and creation of our individual lives.

This thought came early in my own life. I gleaned it from my mother, from her insistence that I listen and learn from others, but when it came down to choosing and acting, I would be totally responsible for whatever I did. I was, she assured me, master of the one universe that counted most, the one inside my mind. The world, she promised, would not make me; I would make the world.

My life is so indelibly touched by my mother that I simply cannot come to any conclusion about whether I was born loving freedom or whether I was simply born to and then raised by a woman who took liberty as her main nourishment. I suspect there are people whose passion for liberty is altogether their own and even a conscious choice. I don't think I am one. The genes must have been terrific but the early childhood with that amazing woman was so emphatic that I cannot help but believe it was crucial.

Liberty for me boils down to a passion, somehow instilled, but a passion nonetheless. I have never been able to see my own passion for liberty as coldly rational; it just burns there, like the sort of love that causes you to suddenly cry, as I sometimes do, when I look at Therese in a certain light of day or a glow of night. I have done the same thing thinking about the sheer good feeling of doing work freely, without coercion, of doing it well, of building something, of thinking something. Love, passion, liberty.

I suspect all three are the same; at the same time, I suspect there are those who will challenge the equivalence, arguing that love and passion are emotions, while liberty is an ideology. If that is true, liberty is simply an opinion that carries no more weight than any other opinion. Its market is rarified and special, loyal and bookish, wonderfully worthwhile, but small nonetheless.

I prefer to see liberty in a different light. I see it as the freedom to move beyond the pompous preaching of an opinion to the simple practice of affiliation and engagement. I see in it the creative spark and the productive energy of doing, thinking people who make the tools that change the world. I see its meaning and significance to lie in what the individual gives to it in the sculpting of his life. And I see liberty's allure and market to be bright and broad, for I have learned the more free people are to pursue the artistry of their lives, to combine together to build their neighborhoods, and to make and market things, the better are their material lives and the more able are they to pursue their individual happiness.

Some years ago I was asked what great ambition drove me. I answered only that I wanted to be the perfect anarchist. Queried further on what I meant by the perfect anarchist, I added good friend, good lover, and good neighbor. That puzzled the interviewer. He had anticipated I would list "resistance to authority" as the defining character. Not satisfied, he pressed me further, asking if such simple things were really all that were needed to be the perfect anarchist. "Yes," I said, "what did you expect, a lot of rules?"

Since then I have not altered my ambition or my response. I don't think it's because I've stopped learning or because I've become resistant to change. I am still living mostly on the edge, though now it's mostly on the edge of the Opequon where being a good friend, a good lover, and a good neighbor come naturally. It's what I do the best and it's what I enjoy the most. Yet there are moments when my mind soars beyond the Opequon, when the realization dawns on me that nothing is fixed or constant.

Standing now at the hospital window, looking beyond to the hill where Monticello stands, I feel as though I am at the helm of a tall ship sailing toward a wonderful future—a future which always exists despite age or condition. Puccini's *Gloria* is playing. Who could fail to be moved?

Epilogue

The Measure of a Man

[*When I discovered the handwritten note that ends the final chapter of this book, and that came in the last days of my father's life, I recalled the epitaph I wrote for the* Libertarian Party News. *I wrote it right after his death on April 22, 1994, a year before I agreed to edit his autobiography, and almost eighteen months before discovering the eerie similarity between our shared glimpses of Mr. Jefferson's house on the hill from the hospital window. I offer these thoughts now because I believe they summarize as well as anything the measure of Karl Hess.*]

In the evenings of my childhood, before I could read a word on my own, my father would sit beside me and recite the barrack-room ballads of Rudyard Kipling. I remember still the Fuzzy-Wuzzy who broke the British square, the jinglety-jink of the screwguns above the pine and oak-scrub, the hanging of Danny Deever on a bitter cold morning, and the good old grinnin', gruntin', Lazarushian-leather Gunga Din. These were the images and heroes of my childhood, my earliest and most vivid memories. And that was my father, then and now.

But of course, there was much more. There were the people and places from a political world that I would never know except through his eyes—people and places like Whittaker Chambers and an incriminating pumpkin patch, and a Cuban revolution and a garage full of Browning semiautomatic rifles (my friends and I would stare at them in awe from a crack in the door). There were also the wilderness treks my father would take with his sidekick Bill Lewis into the great Adirondacks and the evening rides I would share with him on his sleek and beautiful Triumph Bonneville 650. Most of all, I recall our shared journeys in the paddy wagon to the D.C. police station to be booked and jailed for protesting the Vietnam War. It was a most unusual childhood, but then again he was a most unusual father.

The measure of the man I call my father is hard to capture for he was so much and meant so much to me. But on the wall before me in his office in West Virginia is the best measure I can find. To the far right is the Deal Junior High School diploma awarded to Josef Karl Hess on January 31, 1938. It is a modest diploma, one that Ph.D.-pedigreed scholars might scoff at, but one which my father displayed with pride. It is the only certificate of the state (other than a driver's license) that he would ever receive, and he kept it because it was all the formal education he would ever need. By the time he was fifteen he was reading and writing things that most scholars would take a lifetime to do.

To the left of the diploma is a photograph of Emiliano Zapata. Of the many heroes and heroines of the twentieth century, my father admired Zapata most of all. Emma Goldman and Petr Kroptkin were close seconds, but Zapata was a true democrat, a man of the people, a leader who was not a leader, a common man who rose to uncommon heights, a complex man of simple needs, a loving husband, and a caring neighbor.

Further to the left is a drawing of Barry Goldwater with this inscription: "To the best Tequila man, the best writing man, a good man, Karl, from his friend, Barry." For all the differences that the years brought between my father and Goldwater, the two of them remained steadfast friends. He was the only politician my father admired, and the only potential president he could possibly have served and still have remained true to his principles and beliefs.

Wedged between framed letters from Goldwater, Dwight Eisenhower, and Gerald Ford is a small portrait of Thomas Jefferson. Jefferson was my father's guiding star. He was a Renaissance man, a philosopher, a tinkerer, an inventor, and a spokesman for liberty and tolerance. (Hours before my father's death I looked from the hospital window in my father's room at the University of Virginia. I looked toward the small hill that lies to the left of Carters Mountain. The trees were not fully leaved yet, and I could make out the outlines of Jefferson's Monticello. It struck me as odd and prophetic that two men with so much in common would meet in death on this remote spot in the rolling hills of the Shenandoah.)

Farthest to the left on the office wall is a framed letter to my father from several elementary school students. Of all the letters he received in his lifetime, he liked this one the most:

Mr. Hess:

Thank you for being part of the Earth Day Celebration at Hedgesville Middle School. You were most interesting and not at all boring as we had thought. You appear to be quite intelligent and have done so many interesting things throughout your life. We learned a lot, too, about your many jobs and this has helped some of us in planning our lives. We thank you not only for facts but for inspiring us to be what we want to be.

We learned also that we want to be members of the smart group and not the dumb group.

None of these letters, pictures, or diplomas, however, measure the man as well as an oddity strapped by double-sided tape to the top of one of the picture frames hanging on the wall. A piece of paper is folded and attached and reads, matter-of-factly, "Parts Dept." Nestled in its fold is the artificial heart valve that my father retrieved from his discarded natural heart and a gold-capped tooth that was just recently removed. As piercing as the pain was in his last months, the humor that is quintessential Karl was devilishly alive.

In the last hours of my father's life, when the pain was even greater and immune to the massive doses of morphine, Therese, my brother, and I held his hands and spoke to him of our love and our life together. For a moment his forehead smoothed, his eyes glowed, and a twinkle of a smile spread from his lips. He looked at us, squeezed our hands, and spoke with firmness and finality, "Let's go home."

That is the measure of a man. Not the halcyon years of politics or the stacks of books, articles, and speeches he wrote. In the end, as in the beginning and the middle, all my father ever wanted and ever needed were family, friends, and good neighbors to love and laugh with and a place called wild and wonderful West Virginia to set his roots in and build a house that he could call home.

—Karl Hess Jr.

Selected Bibliography of the
Works of Karl Hess

[Editor's Note. The bibliography that follows is selected and provides only a narrow glimpse of the range of the writings of Karl Hess. It is drawn exclusively from his personal files. For that reason, it excludes many writings, most particularly those of his earlier years as a journalist, businessman, and political speech writer. The writings that are listed are those he chose to save and, presumably, the writings that meant the most to him. In addition, several entries lack dates or detailed publication data. Because the bibliography is intended to be suggestive rather than exhaustive, no attempt was made to track those publications down.]

Dated Entries

1957. "Should You Own a Gun?" *American Mercury* (April).

1958. *The Bookshelf for Boys and Girls.* Vol. 7, *Nature and Science.* New York: The University Society.

1967. *In a Cause That Will Triumph.* New York: Doubleday & Company.

1968. "Libertarian Outlook." *Politics* 4, nos. 1, 3, 5, 7, 9, 11, 15, 17, 19, 21.

1968. "Protest." *Political Success* (June).

1968. "Involvement or Resistance." *Political Success* (June).

1968 "An Agenda for Libertarian Activists." *Political Success* (July 5).

1968. "Target: Taxation." *Political Success* (July 19).

1968. "A Union for Forgotten Men." *Political Success* (August 2).

1969. "Notes on an Interview—and Anarchy." *Politics* (January 29).

1969. "The Death of Politics." *Playboy* (March).

1969. "The Lawless State." Lansing, Mich.: Constitutional Alliance.

1969. "My Taxes." *Libertarian* 1, no. 3 (May 31). Karl Hess wrote frequently for the *Libertarian* (later renamed the *Libertarian Forum*) and was the Washington editor.

1969. "Libertarian Outlook." *Politics* (May 21).

1969. "Conservatism and Libertarianism." *Politics* (June 4).

1969. "An Open Letter to Barry Goldwater." *Ramparts* (August).

1970. With Thomas Reeves. *The End of the Draft*. New York: Random House.

1972. "Letter from an Enemy of the State." *Outlook* (March).

1972. "The Rise of Radical Realism." *Business and Society Review* 1 (Spring): 102–105.

1973. "Beyond Decentralization." *Harvard Crimson* 24 (October).

1974. "When Push Comes to Shove." *Washington Post,* February 3.

1974. "The Material Base for Local Liberty." Caucus for a New Political Science Panel, *Dimensions of Community*, Annual Meeting of the American Political Science Association, Chicago, Ill., August 31.

1974. "The System Has Failed." *Penthouse* (August).

1974. "Washington Utopia: An Election Eve Dream." *Washington Post Potomac Magazine* (November 3).

1974. "Whiffs of Change." *Progressive* 38, no. 11 (November): 55–57.

1974. "Community Technology." *Sparks* 4, no. 2 (Fall): 10–14.

1974–1975. "Science in the Neighborhood." "Monthly Notes" in *The Neighborhood* (November 1974–April 1975).

1975. With Roy Klein. "Science and Technology." Institute for Policy Studies, *The Problem of the Federal Budget*. Washington, D.C.

1975. *Dear America*. New York: William Morrow & Company.

1975. With David Morris. *Neighborhood Power: The New Localism*. Boston: Beacon Press.

1975. "Technology with a Human Face." *Science* (January 31).

1975. "Americans Hate Politicians." *Penthouse* (February).

1975. "America Has a Crisis of Scale—Not Leadership." *Los Angeles Times,* May 20.

1975. "The Politics of Advice: The Baroody Connection." *Washington Post Potomac Magazine* (August 17).

1975. "Living Right (and Left)." *Washington Post,* October 19.

1975. "Bartering." *New York Times Magazine* (November 9).

1976. "Introduction." In Charles M. Wilson, *Let's Try Barter.* Old Greenwich, Conn.: Devin-Adair Co.

1976. "White Elephant Blues." *Rolling Stone* (March 25): 30–31.

1976. "What Happened to Conservativism?" *Libertarian Review* (May/June).

1976. "The Myth of College Education." *Playgirl* (October).

1976. "Getting Unhooked." *Skeptic* (November/December).

1977. "Gilmore: A Flick of the Mighty Beast's Tail." *Seven Days* 1, no. 2 (February 28).

1977. "From the Old Right to the New Left." *Washington Watch* 5, no. 19 (May 13).

1977. "Adams-Morgan: A Democracy That Dried Up." *Washington Star,* August 21.

1977. "Flight from Freedom." *Quest* (September/October).

1977. "Exposing the Great American Myths." *Gallery* (November): 53–55, 114–20.

1977. "Not Going by the Book." *Inquiry* (December 5): 6–8.

1977. "A Season, a State, a Poet's Tribute." *Shenandoah Poets.* Charles Town, W.Va.: Jefferson County Arts Council, 1977. Also published in the *Martinsburg Journal,* December 24.

1978. "Why Voluntary Simplicity Won't Destroy Us." *Alternative Celebrations Catalogue.* 4th ed.

1978. "Abolish the Corporation!" *Business and Society Review* 25 (Spring): 12

1978. "Living in Freedom." *Reason* (May).

1978. "Goodbye Barbara (Walters)! Hello Dolly (Parton)!" *Playgirl* (May).

1978. "The Future Is on the Edge." Testimony to Congressional Clearinghouse on the Future, July 19.

1978. "No Inalienable Rights." *Anvil* 28 (Fall): 9–11.

1978. "Don't Mess with Me!" *Penthouse* (August).

1978. "On Shelling It Out." *Rain* (November).

1978. "Your Money or Your Life." *Inquiry* (November 27).

1978. "Proposition 13: Saying No to a Government That Doesn't Deliver." *Gallery* (November).

1978. "The Water Crisis: Will There Be a Drop to Drink?" *Gallery* (December).

1979. *Community Technology*. New York: Harper & Row.

1979. "What It's All About." *Informer* (August).

1979. "The Day the United States Invaded Mexico." *Gallery* (October).

1979. "Land War in Lewis County." *Inquiry* (November 26): 15–19.

1979. "Contradictions of a Conservative." *Inquiry* (December 10).

1980. With Therese Hess. "Community Technology." *Potomac Guardian*. Bimonthly column from April 1980 through December 1980.

1980. "The Good Machines." *Quest* (February/March).

1980. "The Conspirators Behind the Third Wave of the New Age." *Next* (March/April).

1980. "Anarchism without Hyphens." *dandelion* (Spring).

1980. "My Life in Barter." *Comstock Quarterly* 1, no. 4 (Summer): 23–28.

1980. "Thriving without Money." *Quest* (July/August).

1980. "On Personalist Politics." *Rain* 7, no. 2 (November): 10–11.

1980. "Fascism by Any Other Name. . . ." *Reason* (December).

1981. *A Common Sense Strategy for Survivalists*. Alexandria, Va.: Kephart Communications, Inc.

1981. *Three Interviews*. Alexandria, Va.: Kephart Communications, Inc.

1981. "If I Were President . . . I'd Resign within 24 Hours." *Inquiry* (January 12).

1981. "In Pursuit of Wealth, Not Welfare." *Public Welfare* (Winter).

1981. "Getting Started in Barter: A Free Market Alternative." *Personal Finance* 8, no. 7 (April 1): 100–101.

1981. "The Politics of Place." *CoEvolution Quarterly* 30 (Summer): 4–16.

1982. "Organizing for Survival." *Survival Tomorrow* 2, no. 10 (October): 105–106.

1983. With David Morris. "Neighborhoods: The Space to Be." In John S. Friedman, *First Harvest: The Institute for Policy Studies, 1963–83*. New York: Grove Press.

1983. "Another Function of State Power." In *What Will It Take to Prevent Nuclear War?* ed. Pat Farren, 166–67. Cambridge, Mass.: Schenkman Publishing Co.

1984. "Foreword." In Morris and Linda Tannehill, *The Market for Liberty*. New York: Laissez Faire Books.

1984. "One Country—Two Cultures." *Reason* (June–July).

1984. "My Fellow Democrats. . . ." *Harper's* 269, no. 1610 (July): 32–33.

1985. "The Mediasphere 1985 or Programming Yourself." West Virginia Library Commission, *Film Services Newsletter* 8, no. 2 (Summer): 1–2.

1985. "A Review of Handcarved." West Virginia Library Commission, *Film Services Newsletter West Virginia Library Commission.*

1985. "America's Permanent Underclass." *Houston Post,* November 3.

1985. "The Opiate of the Masses." *Orange County Register,* November 6. Versions published in the *Plain Dealer,* November 3, and *St. Louis Post-Dispatch,* November 3.

1986. "At the Movies." West Virginia Library Commission, *Film Services Newsletter West Virginia Library Commission.*

1986. "A Response to Cities and the Wealth of Ideas." West Virginia Library Commission, *Film Services Newsletter West Virginia Library Commission* 9, no. 1 (Summer): 11.

1986. "What Do Kids Think about Government?" *Reason* (November).

1986. "Book Section." *Reason* (December).

1986. "The Drumbeat of Revolutionary Power." *Reason* (January).

1987. *Capitalism for Kids.* Wilmington, Del.: Enterprise Publishing.

1987. "The Most Unforgettable Libertarian I Ever Knew." *Liberty* (December).

1987. "Schooling: What's Education Got to Do with It?" *Mountain Pathways* (Fall).

1987. "Idiosyncratic Individualist." *Reason* (October).

1988. "Foreword." In Carl Watner and Robert LeFevre, *Truth Is Not a Half-way Place.* Gramling, S.C.: The Voluntaryists.

1988. "Your Money: Curse or Blessing?" *Liberty* 2, no. 1 (September): 42–44.

1988. "Rights and Reality." *Our Generation* 20, no. 1: 71–77. Also appeared in *The Anarchist Papers 2,* ed. Dimitrios I. Roussopoulos (New York: Black Rose Books, 1989), and *Renewing the Earth,* ed. John Clark (London: Green Print, 1990).

1989. "Draft Is Pinnacle of Liberalism's Outlook." *Plain Dealer,* January 30.

1990. "Elitism in Defense of Virtue Is No Vice." *Liberty* 3, no. 3 (January): 46–48.

1990. "The Official Truth and the Death of Thought." *Liberty* (May).

1991. "The Hope in the Schools." *Liberty* (January).
1991. "Godzilla Among the Greens." *Graffiti* 2, no. 9: 8.
1991. "Berkeley in the Sixties." West Virginia Library Commission, *Film Services Newsletter* 13, no. 3 (Winter 1990–91): 2.
1991. "Tools vs Philosophy." *Liberty* (July).
1991. "50 Really Stupid Ways to Save the Earth." *Liberty* (September).
1991. "Gospel in the Hills." *Charleston Gazette,* December 13.
1992. "The Cost of Kids." *Liberty* (May).
1992. "Cyberpunk." West Virginia Library Commission, *Film Services Newsletter* 15, no. 1 (Summer): 1.
1992. "America in Black and White." *Reason* (October).
1992. "What Should the President Read?" *Reason* (December).

Undated Entries

"A Practical Anarchy for Today's America." *Gallery.*
"An Objection to the Space Program." *A Week with Isaac Asimov,* The Institute on Man and Science, Rensselaerville, N.Y.
"Ex-Republican Bitten by a Panther."
"Nuclear Power Will Bankrupt America." *Penthouse.*
"Ronald Reagan's Winners—and Some Losers." *Gallery.*
"The Five Hundred Mile Stare." *Good News Paper,* Sheperdstown, W.Va.
"When Will They Ever Learn?" *Good News Paper,* Sheperdstown, W.Va.

Partial List of Ghostwritten Books

Norris, Frank. 1953. *Crime Without Punishment.*
Peterson, Elmer. 1954. *Big Dam Foolishness.*
Laird, Melvin. 1962. *A House Divided: America's Strategy Gap.*
Curtis, Tom. 1962. *87 Million Jobs.*
Goldwater, Barry. 1964. *Where I Stand.*
Siciliano, Vincent. 1970. *Unless They Kill Me First.*

Selected Writings

The Death of Politics

This is not a time of radical, revolutionary politics. Not yet. Unrest, riot, dissent and chaos notwithstanding, today's politics is reactionary. Both right and left are reactionary and authoritarian. That is to say: Both are political. They seek only to revise current methods of acquiring and wielding political power. Radical and revolutionary movements seek not to revise but to revoke. The target of revocation should be obvious. The target is politics itself.

Radicals and revolutionaries have had their sights trained on politics for some time. As governments fail around the world, as more millions become aware that government never has and never can humanely and effectively manage men's affairs, government's own inadequacy will emerge, at last, as the basis for a truly radical and revolutionary movement. In the meantime, the radical-revolutionary position is a lonely one. It is feared or hated, by both the right and left—although both right and left must borrow from it to survive. The radical-revolutionary position is libertarianism and its socioeconomic form is laissez-faire capitalism.

Libertarianism is the view that each man is the absolute owner of his life, to use and dispose of as he sees fit; that all man's social actions should be voluntary; and that respect for every other man's similar and equal ownership of life and, by extension, the property and fruits of that life, is the ethical basis of a humane and open society. In this view, the

321

only—repeat, only—function of law or government is to provide the sort of self-defense against violence that an individual, if he were powerful enough, would provide for himself.

If it were not for the fact that libertarianism freely concedes the right of men voluntarily to form communities or governments on the same ethical basis, libertarianism could be called anarchy.

Laissez-faire capitalism, or anarchocapitalism, is simply the economic form of the libertarian ethic. Laissez-faire capitalism encompasses the notion that men should exchange goods and services, without regulation, solely on the basis of value for value. It recognizes charity and communal enterprises as voluntary versions of this same ethic. Such a system would be straight barter, except for the widely felt need for a division of labor in which men, voluntarily, accept value tokens such as cash and credit. Economically, this system is anarchy, and proudly so.

Libertarianism is rejected by the modern left—which preaches individualism but practices collectivism. Capitalism is rejected by the modern right—which preaches enterprise but practices protectionism. The libertarian faith in the mind of man is rejected by religionists who have faith only in the sins of man. The libertarian insistence that men be free to spin cables of steel as well as dreams of smoke is rejected by hippies who adore nature but spurn creation. The libertarian insistence that each man is a sovereign land of liberty, with his primary allegiance to himself, is rejected by patriots who sing of freedom but also shout of banners and boundaries. There is no operating political movement in the world today that is based upon a libertarian philosophy. If there were, it would be in the anomalous position of using political power to abolish political power.

Perhaps a regular political movement, overcoming this anomaly, will actually develop. Believe it or not, there were strong possibilities of such a development in the 1964 campaign of Barry Goldwater. Underneath the scary headlines, Goldwater hammered away at such purely political structures as the draft, general taxation, censorship, nationalism, legislated conformity, political establishment of social norms, and war as an instrument of international policy.

It is true that, in a common political paradox, Goldwater (a major general in the Air Force Reserve) has spoken of reducing state power while at the same time advocating the increase of state power to fight the Cold War. He is not a pacifist. He believes that war remains an acceptable state action. He does not see the Cold War as involving U.S. imperialism.

He sees it as a result only of Soviet imperialism. Time after time, however, he has said that economic pressure, diplomatic negotiation and the persuasions of propaganda (or "cultural warfare") are absolutely preferable to violence. He has also said that antagonistic ideologies can "never be beaten by bullets, but only by better ideas."

A defense of Goldwater cannot be carried too far, however. His domestic libertarian tendencies simply do not carry over into his view of foreign policy. Libertarianism, unalloyed, is absolutely isolationist, in that it is absolutely opposed to the institutions of national government that are the only agencies on earth now able to wage war or intervene in foreign affairs.

In other campaign issues, however, the libertarian coloration in the Goldwater complexion was more distinct. The fact that he roundly rapped the fiscal irresponsibility of Social Security before an elderly audience, and the fact that he criticized TVA while speaking in Tennessee, were not examples of political naivete. They simply showed Goldwater's high disdain for politics itself, summed up in his campaign statement that people should be told "what they need to hear and not what they want to hear."

There was also some suggestion of libertarianism in the campaign of Eugene McCarthy, in his splendid attacks on Presidential power. However, these were canceled out by his vague but nevertheless perceptible defense of government power in general. There was virtually no suggestion of libertarianism in the statements of any other politicians during last year's campaign.

I was a speechwriter for Barry Goldwater in the 1964 campaign. During the campaign, I recall very clearly, there was a moment, at a conference to determine the campaign's "farm strategy," when a respected and very conservative Senator arose to say: "Barry, you've got to make it clear that you believe that the American farmer has a right to a decent living."

Senator Goldwater replied, with the tact for which he is renowned: "But he doesn't have a right to it. Neither do I. We just have a right to try for it." And that was the end of that.

Now, in contrast, take Tom Hayden of the Students for a Democratic Society. Writing in *The Radical Papers*, he said that his "revolution" sought "institutions outside the established order." One of those institutions, he amplified, would be "people's own antipoverty organizations fighting for Federal money."

Of the two men, which is radical or revolutionary? Hayden says, in effect, that he simply wants to bulldoze his way into the establishment. Goldwater says he wants, in effect, to topple it, to forever end its power to advantage or disadvantage anyone.

This is not to defend the Goldwater Presidential campaign as libertarian. It is only to say that his campaign contained a healthy element of this sort of radicalism but otherwise, the Goldwater campaign was very deeply in hock to regular partisan interests, images, myths and manners.

In foreign policy, particularly, there arises a great impediment to the emergence of a libertarian wing in either of the major political parties. Men who call upon the end of state authority in every other area insist upon its being maintained to build a war machine with which to hold the Communists at bay. It is only lately that the imperatives of logic—and the emergence of antistatist forces in eastern Europe—have begun to make it more acceptable to ask whether the garrison state needed to maintain the Cold War might not be as bad as or worse than the putative threat being guarded against. Goldwater has not taken and may never take such a revisionist line—but, among Cold Warriors, his disposition to libertarian principles makes him more susceptible than most.

This is not merely a digression on behalf of a political figure (almost an *anti*political figure) whom I profoundly respect. It is, rather, to emphasize the inadequacy of traditional, popular guidelines in assessing the reactionary nature of contemporary politics and in divining the true nature of radical and revolutionary antipolitics. Political parties and politicians today—all parties and all politicians—question only the forms through which they will express their common belief in controlling the lives of others. Power, particularly majoritarian or collective power (i.e., the power of an elite exercised in the name of the masses), is the god of the modern liberal. Its only recent innovative change is to suggest that the elite be leavened by the compulsory membership of authentic representatives of the masses. The current phrase is "participatory democracy."

Just as power is the god of the modern liberal, God remains the authority of the modern conservative. Liberalism practices regimentation by, simply, regimentation. Conservatism practices regimentation by, not quite so simply, revelation. But regimented or revealed, the name of the game is still politics.

The great flaw in conservatism is a deep fissure down which talk of freedom falls, to be dashed to death on the rocks of authoritarianism.

Conservatives worry that the state has too much power over people. But it was conservatives who gave the state that power. It was conservatives, very similar to today's conservatives, who ceded to the state the power to produce not simply order in the community but *a certain kind of order*.

It was European conservatives who, apparently fearful of the openness of the Industrial Revolution (why, *anyone* could get rich!), struck the first blows at capitalism by encouraging and accepting laws that made the disruptions of innovation and competition less frequent and eased the way for the comforts and collusions of cartelization.

Big business in America today and for some years past has been openly at war with competition and, thus, at war with laissez-faire capitalism. Big business supports a form of state capitalism in which government and big business act as partners. Criticism of this statist bent of big business comes more often from the left than from the right these days, and this is another factor making it difficult to tell the players apart. John Kenneth Galbraith, for instance, has most recently taken big business to task for its anticompetitive mentality. The right, meantime, blissfully defends big business as though it had not, in fact, become just the sort of bureaucratic, authoritarian force that rightists reflexively attack when it is governmental.

The left's attack on corporate capitalism is, when examined, an attack on economic forms possible only in a collusion between authoritarian government and bureaucratized, nonentrepreneurial business. It is unfortunate that many New Leftists are so uncritical as to accept this premise as indicating that all forms of capitalism are bad, so that full state ownership is the only alternative. This thinking has its mirror image on the right.

It was American conservatives, for instance, who very early in the game gave up the fight against state franchising and regulation and, instead, embraced state regulation for their own special advantage. Conservatives today continue to revere the state as an instrument of chastisement even as they reject it as an instrument of beneficence, The conservative who wants a Federally authorized prayer in the classroom is the same conservative who objects to Federally authorized textbooks in the same room.

Murray Rothbard, writing in *Ramparts*, has summed up this flawed conservatism in describing a "new, younger generation of rightists, of 'conservatives' . . . who thought that the real problem of the modern world was nothing so ideological as the state vs. individual liberty or government intervention vs. the free market; the real problem, they declared, was the preservation of tradition, order, Christianity and good manners against the modern sins of reason, license, atheism and boorishness."

The reactionary tendencies of both liberals and conservatives today show clearly in their willingness to cede, to the state or the community, power far beyond the protection of liberty against violence. For differing purposes, both see the state as an instrument not protecting man's freedom but either instructing or restricting how that freedom is to be used.

Once the power of the community becomes in any sense normative, rather than merely protective, it is difficult to see where any lines may be drawn to limit further transgressions against individual freedom. In fact, the lines have not been drawn. They will never be drawn by political parties that argue merely the cost of programs or institutions founded on state power. Actually, the lines can be drawn only by a radical questioning of power itself, and by the libertarian vision that sees man as capable of moving on without the encumbering luggage of laws and politics that do not merely preserve man's right to his life but attempt, in addition, to tell him how to live it.

For many conservatives, the bad dream that haunts their lives and their political position (which many sum up as "law and order" these days) is one of riot. To my knowledge, there is no limit that conservatives would place upon the power of the state to suppress riots.

Even in a laissez-faire society, of course, the right to self-defense would have to be assumed, and a place for self-defense on a community basis could be easily imagined. But community self-defense would always be exclusively defensive. Conservatives betray an easy willingness to believe that the state should also initiate certain *offensive* actions, in order to preclude trouble later on. "Getting tough" is the phrase most often used. It does not mean just getting tough on rioters, It means getting tough on entire ranges of attitudes: clipping long hair, rousting people from parks for carrying concealed guitars, stopping and questioning anyone who doesn't look like a member of the Jaycees, drafting all the ne'er-do-wells to straighten them up, ridding our theaters and bookstores of "filth" and, always and above all, putting "those" people in their place. To the conservative, all too often, the alternatives are social conformity or unthinkable chaos.

Even if these were the only alternatives—which they obviously aren't—there are many reasons for preferring chaos to conformity. Personally, I believe I would have a better chance of surviving—and certainly my values would have a better chance of surviving—with a Watts, Chicago, Detroit or Washington in flames than with an entire nation snug in a garrison.

Riots in modern America must be broken down into component parts. They are not all simple looting and violence against life and property. They are also directed against the prevailing violence of the state—the sort of on-going civic violence that permits regular police supervision of everyday life in some neighborhoods, the rules and regulations that inhibit absolutely free trading, the public schools that serve the visions of bureaucracy rather than the varieties of individual people. There is violence also by those who simply want to shoot their way into political power otherwise denied them. Conservatives seem to think that greater state police power is the answer. Liberals seem to think that more preferential state welfare power is the answer. Power, power, power.

Except for ordinary looters—for whom the answer must be to stop them as you would any other thief—the real answer to rioting must lie elsewhere. It must lie in the abandonment, not the extension, of state power—state power that oppresses people, state power that tempts people. To cite one strong example: The white stores in many black neighborhoods, which are said to cause such dissatisfaction and envy, have a special, unrealized advantage thanks to state power. In a very poor neighborhood there may be many with the natural ability to open a retail store, but it is much less likely that these people would also have the ability to meet all the state and city regulations, governing everything from cleanliness to bookkeeping, which very often comprise the marginal difference between going into business or staying out. In a real laissez-faire society, the local entrepreneur, with whom the neighbors might prefer to deal, could go openly into business—selling marijuana, whiskey, numbers slips, books, food or medical advice from the trunk of his car. He could forget about ledgers, forms and reports and simply get on with the business of business, rather than the business of bureaucracy. Allowing ghetto dwellers to compete on their own terms, rather than on someone else's, should prove a more satisfying and practical solution to ghetto problems than either rampages or restrictions.

The libertarian thrusts away from power and authority that marked the Goldwater campaign were castigated from the left as being "nostalgic yearnings for a simpler world." (Perhaps akin to the simplistic yearnings of the hippies whom the left so easily tolerates even while it excoriates

Goldwater.) Goldwater's libertarianism was castigated from the right—he received virtually *no* support from big business—as representing policies that could lead to unregulated competition, international free trade and, even worse, a weakening of the very special partnership that big business now enjoys with Big Government.

The most incredible convolution in the thinking that attacked Goldwater as reactionary, which he isn't, rather than radical, which he is, came in regard to nuclear weapons. In that area he was specifically damned for daring to propose that the control of these weapons be shared, and even fully placed, in the multinational command of the North Atlantic Treaty Organization, rather than left to the personal, one-man discretion of the President of the United States.

Again, who is reactionary and who is radical? The men who want an atomic king enthroned in Washington, or the man who dares ask that that divine right of destruction become less divine and more divided? Until recently, it was a popular cocktail pastime to speculate on the difference between the war in Vietnam under "Save-the-world-from-Goldwater" Johnson, or as it might have been under wild Barry, who, by his every campaign utterance, would have been bound to share the Vietnam decision (and the fighting) with NATO, rather than simply and unilaterally going it alone.

To return to the point: The most vital question today about politics— not *in* politics—is the same sort of question that is plaguing Christianity. Superficially, the Christian question seems simply what kind of religion should be chosen. But basically, the question is whether any irrational or mystical forces are supportable, as a way to order society, in a world increasingly able and ready to be rational. The political version of the question may be stated this way: Will men continue to submit to rule by politics, which has always meant the power of some men over other men, or are we ready to go it alone socially, in communities of voluntarism, in a world more economic and cultural than political, just as so many now are prepared to go it alone metaphysically in a world more of reason than religion?

The radical and revolutionary answer that a libertarian, laissez-faire position makes to that question is not quite anarchy. The libertarian, laissez-faire movement is, actually, if embarrassingly for some, a civil rights movement. But it is antipolitical, in that it builds diversified power to be protected against government, even to dispense with government to a major degree, rather than seeking power to protect government or to perform any special social purpose.

It is a civil-liberties movement in that it seeks civil liberties, for everyone, as defined in the 19th Century by one of Yale's first professors of political and social science, William Graham Sumner. Sumner said: "Civil liberty is the status of the man who is guaranteed by law and civil institutions the exclusive employment of all his own powers for his own welfare."

Modern liberals, of course, would call this selfishness, and they would be correct, with intense emphasis on self. Many modern conservatives would say that they agree with Sumner, but they would not be correct. Men who call themselves conservatives, but who operate in the larger industries, spend considerable time, and not a small amount of money, fighting government subsidies to labor unions (in the form of preferential tax and legal considerations) or to people (in the form of welfare programs). They do not fight *direct* subsidies to industries—such as transportation, farming or universities. They do not, in short, believe that men are entitled to the exclusive employment of their own powers for their own welfare, because they accept the practice of taxing a good part of that power to use for the welfare of other people.

As noted, for all the theoretical screaming that sometimes may be heard from the industrial right, it is safe to say that the major powers of government to regulate industry were derived not only from the support of businessmen but actually at the insistence of businessmen. Uneconomical mail rates are cherished by businessmen who can profit from them and who, significantly, seem uninterested in the obvious possibility of transforming the postal service from a bureau into a business. As a business, of course, it would charge what it costs to mail things, not what is simply convenient for users to pay.

The big businessmen who operate the major broadcast networks are not known for suggesting, as a laissez-faire concept would insist, that competition for channels and audiences be wide open and unregulated. As a consequence, of course, the networks get all the government control that they deserve, accepting it in good cheer because, even if censored, they are also protected from competition. It is notable, also, that one of the most fierce denunciations of pay TV (which, under capitalism, should be a conceptual commonplace) came not from the *Daily Worker* but from the *Reader's Digest*, that supposed bastion of conservatism. Actually, I think the *Digest* is such a bastion. It seems to believe that the state is an institution divinely ordained to make men moral—in a "Judaeo-Christian" sense, of course. It abhors, as does no publication short of William

Buckley's *National Review*, the insolence of those untidy persons who today so regularly challenge the authority of the state.

In short, there is no evidence whatever that modern conservatives subscribe to the "your life is your own" philosophy upon which libertarianism is founded. An interesting illustration that conservatism not only disagrees with libertarianism but is downright hostile to it is that the most widely known libertarian author of the day, Miss Ayn Rand, ranks only a bit below, or slightly to the side of, Leonid Brezhnev as an object of diatribe in *National Review*. Specifically, it seems, she is reviled on the right because she is an atheist, daring to take exception to the *National Review* notion that man's basically evil nature (stemming from original sin) means he must be held in check by a strong and authoritarian social order.

Barry Goldwater, during his 1964 campaign, repeatedly said that "the government strong enough to give you what you want is strong enough to take it all away." Conservatives, as a group, have forgotten, or prefer to ignore, that this applies also to government's strength to impose social order. If government can enforce social norms, or even Christian behavior, it can also take away or twist them.

To repeat: Conservatives yearn for a state, or "leadership," with the power to restore order and to put things—and people—back in their places. They yearn for political power. Liberals yearn for a state that will bomb the rich and balm the poor. They too yearn for political power. Libertarians yearn for a state that cannot, beyond any possibility of amendment, confer any advantage on anyone; a state that cannot compel anything, but simply prevents the use of violence, in place of other exchanges, in relations between individuals or groups.

Such a state would have as its sole purpose (probably supported exclusively by use taxes or fees) the maintenance of a system to adjudicate disputes (courts), to protect citizens against violence (police), to maintain some form of currency for ease of commerce, and, as long as it might be needed because of the existence of national borders and differences, to maintain a defense force. Meanwhile, libertarians should also work to end the whole concept of the nation-state itself. The major point here is that libertarians would start with no outstanding predispositions about public functions, being disposed always to think that there is in the personal and private world of individuals someone who can or will come along with a solution that gets the job done without conferring upon anyone power that has not been earned through voluntary exchange.

In fact, it is in the matters most appropriate to collective interest—such as courts and protection against violence—that government today often defaults. This follows the bureaucratic tendency to perform least needed services—where the risk of accountability is minimal—and to avoid performing essential but highly accountable services. Courts are clogged beyond belief. Police, rather than simply protecting citizens against violence, are deeply involved in overseeing private morals. In black neighborhoods particularly, the police serve as unloved and unwanted arbiters of everyday life.

If, in the past few paragraphs, the reader can detect any hint of a position that would be compatible with either the Communist Party of the Soviet Union or the National Association of Manufacturers, he is strongly advised to look again. No such common ground exists. Nor can any common ground be adduced in terms of "new politics" versus "old politics." New or old, the positions that parade today under these titles are still politics and, like roses, they smell alike. Radical and revolutionary politicians—antipoliticians, if you will—should be able to sniff them out easily.

Specific matters that illustrate the differences would include the draft, marijuana, monopoly, censorship, isolationism-internationalism, race relations and urban affairs, to name a few.

As part of his aborted campaign for the Presidency, Nelson Rockefeller took a position on the draft. In it, he specifically took exception to Richard Nixon's draft stand, calling it the "old politics" as contrasted with his own "new politics." The Rockefeller position involved a certain streamlining of the draft, but nothing that would change it from what it patently is—forced, involuntary servitude. Rockefeller criticized Nixon for having asserted that, someday, the draft could be replaced by a voluntary system, an old Republican promise.

The new politician contended that the Nixon system wouldn't work because it never *had* worked. The fact that this nation has never offered to pay its soldiers at a rate realistic enough to attract them was not covered in Rockefeller's statement. Nor did the new politician address himself to the fact that, given a nation that not enough citizens can be attracted to defend voluntarily, you probably also have a nation that, by definition, isn't really worth defending.

The old politician, on the other hand, did not present quite as crisp a position on the draft as the new politician tried to pin him with. Nixon, although theoretically in favor of a voluntary military, was—along with the presumably even *more* conservative Ronald Reagan—opposed to trying voluntarism until *after* the Vietnam war. Throughout the conservative stance one sees a repetition of this position. Freedom is fine—but it must be deferred as long as a hot war or the Cold War has to be fought.

All should be struck by the implications of that baleful notion. It implies that free men simply cannot be ingenious enough to defend themselves against violence without themselves becoming violent—not toward the enemy alone, but to their own persons and liberty as well. If our freedom is so fragile that it must be continuously protected by giving it up, then we are in deep trouble. And, in fact, by following a somewhat similar course, we got ourselves in very deep trouble in Southeast Asia. The Johnson war there was escalated precisely on the belief that southern Vietnamese freedom may best be obtained by dictating what form of government the south should have—day by day, even—and by defending it against the North Vietnamese by devastating the southern countryside.

In foreign relations, as in domestic pronouncements, new and old politicians preach the same dusty doctrines of compulsion and contradiction. The radical preachment of libertarianism, the antipolitical preachment, would be that as long as the inanity of war between nation-states remains a possibility, free nation-states will at least protect themselves from wars by hiring volunteers, not by murdering voluntarism.

One of the most medievally fascinating minds of the 20th Century, that of Lewis Hershey, sole owner and proprietor of the Selective Service System, has put this unpretty picture into perfect perspective with his memorable statement, delivered at a National Press Club luncheon, that he "hate[s] to think of the day that [his] grandchildren would be defended by volunteers." There, in as ugly an example as is on public record, is precisely where politics and power, authority and the arthritis of traditionalism, are bound to bring you. Director Hershey is prevented from being a great comic figure by the rather obvious fact that, being involved with the deaths of so many unwilling men, and the imprisonment of so many others, he becomes a tragic figure or, at least, a figure in a tragedy. There is no new or old politics about the draft. A draft is political, plain and simple. A volunteer military is essentially commercial. And it is between politics and commerce that the entrant into radical or revolutionary politics must continually choose.

Marijuana is an example of such a choice. In a laissez-faire society, there could exist no public institution with the power to forcefully protect people from themselves. From other people (criminals), yes. From one's own self, no. Marijuana is a plant, a crop. People who smoke it do not do so under the compulsion either of physiological addiction or of institutionalized power. They do so voluntarily. They find a person who has volunteered to grow it. They agree on a price. One sells; the other buys. One acquires new capital; the other acquires a euphoric experience that, he decides, was worth allocating some of his own resources to obtain.

Nowhere in that equation is there a single point at which the neighbors, or any multitude of neighbors, posing as priesthood or public, have the slightest rational reason to intervene. The action has not, in any way, deprived anyone else of "the exclusive employment of all his own powers for his own welfare."

The current laws against marijuana, in contravention even of all available medical evidence regarding its nature, are a prime example of the use of political power. The very power that makes it possible for the state to ban marijuana, and to arrest Lenny Bruce, is the same power that makes it possible for the state to exact taxes from one man to pay into the pockets of another. The purposes may seem different, but upon examination they are not. Marijuana must be banned to prevent people from succumbing to the madness of its fumes and doing some mischief upon the community. Poverty, too, must be banned for a similar reason. Poor people, unless *made* unpoor, will angrily rise and do mischief upon the community. As in all politics, purposes and power blend and reinforce each other.

"Hard" narcotics must be subjected to the same tests as marijuana in terms of politics versus antipolitics. These narcotics, too, are merely salable materials except that, if used beyond prudence, they can be quite disabling to the person using them. (I inject that note simply because, in my understanding, there remains at all levels of addiction the chance of breaking or controlling the habit. This suggests that a person *can* exercise a choice in the matter; that he can, indeed, be prudent or not.)

The person who uses drugs imprudently, just as the person who imprudently uses the politically sanctioned and franchised drugs of alcohol or tobacco, ends up in an unenviable position, perhaps dead. That, rationally, is his own business as long as he does not, by his actions, deprive you of the right to make your own decision not to use drugs, to assist addicts or, if you wish, to ignore them. But it is said, by right and left today, that the real problem is social and public—that the high price of the drugs leads the addict to rob and kill (rightist position), and that making drugs a public matter, for clinical dispensation, would eliminate the causes of his crime (leftist position).

These both are essentially political positions and clearly inept in a society where the line between mind-expanders such as coffee or LSD is highly technical. By choosing the economic and cultural approach rather than a political one, the antipolitical libertarian would say, sell away. Competition will keep the price down. Cultural acceptance of the root ethic, that a man's life and its appurtenances are inviolate, would justify defense against any violence that might accompany addiction in others. And what is there left for the "public" to do? Absolutely nothing—except, individually, to decide whether to risk drugs or to avoid them. Parents, of course, holding the purse strings of their children, can exercise a certain amount of control, but only individually, never collectively.

Incidentally, it is easy to imagine that, if drugs were left to economics and culture instead of politics, medical researchers would shortly discover a way to provide the salable and wanted effects of drugs without the incapacitation of addiction. In this as in similar matters—such as the unregulated competition from which it is felt people need protection—technology rather than politics might offer far better answers.

Monopoly is a case in point. To suppose that anyone needs government protection from the creation of monopolies is to accept two suppositions: that monopoly is the natural direction of unregulated enterprise, and that technology is static. Neither, of course, is true. The great concentrations of economic power, which are called monopolies today, did not grow *despite* government's antimonopolistic zeal. They grew, largely, *because* of government policies, such as those making it more profitable for small businesses to sell out to big companies rather than fight the tax code alone. Additionally, Federal fiscal and credit policies and Federal subsidies and contracts have all provided substantially more assistance to big and established companies than to smaller, potentially competitive ones. The auto industry receives the biggest subsidy of all through the highway program on which it prospers, but for which it surely does not pay a fair share. Airlines are subsidized and so protected that newcomers can't even try to compete. Television networks are fantastically advantaged by FCC licensing, which prevents upstarts from entering a field where big old-timers have been established. Even in agriculture, it is large and established farmers who get the big subsidies—not small ones who might want to compete. Government laws specifically exempting unions from antitrust activities have also furthered a monopoly mentality. And, of course, the "public utility" and "public transportation" concepts have specifically created government-licensed monopolies in the fields of power, communications and transit. This is not to say that economic bigness is bad. It isn't, if it results from economic efficiency. But it is bad if it results from collusion with political, rather than with economic, power. There is no monopoly situation in the world today, of which I can think, that might not be seriously challenged by competition, were it not for some form of protective government license, tariff, subsidy or regulation. Also, there isn't the tiniest shred of evidence to suggest that the trend of unregulated business and industry is toward monopoly. In fact, the trend seems in the opposite direction, toward diversification and decentralization.

The technological aspect is equally important. Monopoly cannot develop as long as technology is dynamic, which it most abundantly is today. No corporation is so large that it can command every available brain—except, of course, a corporate state. As long as one brain remains unavailable, there is the chance of innovation and competition. There can be no real monopoly, just momentary advantage. Nor does technological breakthrough always depend upon vast resources or, even where it does, would it have to depend upon a single source of financing—unless, again, only the state has the money. Short of total state control, and presuming creative brains in the community, and presuming the existence of capital with which to build even modest research facilities, few would flatly say that technological innovation could be prevented simply because of some single source enjoying a temporary "monopoly" of a given product or service. The exceptions, to repeat, are always governments. Governments can be—and usually are—monopolistic. For instance, it is not uneconomical to operate a private post-office department today. It is only illegal. The Feds enjoy a legal monopoly—to the extent that they are currently prosecuting at least one entrepreneur who operated a mail service better and cheaper than they do.

Politics is not needed to prevent monopoly. Unregulated, unrestricted laissez-faire capitalism is all that is needed. It would also provide jobs, raise living standards, improve products, and so forth. If commercial activity were unregulated and absolutely unsubsidized, it could depend upon only one factor for success—pleasing customers.

Censorship is another notable example in which politics, and politicians, interpose between customer and satisfaction. The gauge becomes not whether the customer is happy, but whether the politician (either singly or as a surrogate for "the public") is happy. This applies equally to "public" protection from unpopular political ideas as well as protection from pornography. Conservatives are at least consistent in this matter. They feel that the state (which they sometimes call "the community") can and must protect people from unsavory thoughts. It goes without saying who defines unsavory: the political—or community—leaders, of course.

Perhaps the most ironic of all manifestations of this conservative urge to cleanthink concerns the late Lenny Bruce. He talked dirty. He was, therefore, a particularly favorite target of conservatives. He was also an explicit and, I think, incisive defender of capitalism. In commenting that communism is a drag ("like one big phone company"), Bruce specifically opted for capitalism ("it gives you a choice, baby, and that's what it's about"). There is no traditional conservative who is fit to even walk on the same level with Lenny Bruce in his fierce devotion to individualism. Lenny Bruce frequently used what is for many conservatives the dirtiest word of all: He said capitalism. When was the last time that the N.A.M. did as much?

Lenny Bruce wasn't the only man to alienate conservatives by opening his mouth. In 1964, Barry Goldwater alienated Southern conservatives in droves when, in answer to a regionally hot question about whether Communists should be permitted to speak on state-university campuses, Goldwater said, flatly and simply: "Of course they should."

Even anti-Communist libertarians have no choice but to deny the state the right to suppress Communists. Similarly, libertarians who are aesthetically repelled by what they deem pornography have no other course than not to buy it, leaving its absolutely unregulated sale to producer, purchaser and no one else. Once again, a parent could intrude—but only by stopping an individual, dependent purchaser, never by stopping the purveyor, whose right to sell pornography for profit, and for absolutely no other socially redeeming virtue whatever, would be inviolate. An irate parent who attempted to hustle a smut peddler off the street, as a matter of fact, should be sued, not saluted.

The liberal attitude toward censorship is not so clear. At this point, it needn't be. Liberals practice it, rather than preach it. The FCC's egregious power to insist that broadcasting serve a social purpose is both a liberal tenet and an act of censorship. In the FCC canons, social purposes are defined so that a station can get good points for permitting a preacher free time but no points—or even bad points—for extending the same gift of free air to an atheist.

It is partly in the realm of air, also, that differences regarding nationalism between the old left/right politicians and the libertarian antipolitician show up. If today's conservative has his fervent jingoism for old nations, the liberal has just as fanatic a devotion to the jingoism of new nations. The willingness of modern liberals to suggest armed intervention against South Africa, while ignoring, even in terms of major journalistic coverage, slaughters in Nigeria and the Sudan, is a demonstration of interest only in politics—and in particular persons—rather than in human life per se.

Of course, conservatives have a similar double standard in regard to anti-Communist slaughter and anti-Communist dictatorship. Although it is not as whimsically selective as the liberal decision to be revolted or cheered by each particular blood bath, the conservative double standard can have equally tragic results. The distinct undercurrents of anti-Semitism that so obviously muddle many conservative movements probably can be traced to the horrid assumption that Adolf Hitler's anticommunism excused his other, but comparatively minor, faults. Somehow, anticommunism seems to permit anti-Semitism.

I have met in my time many anti-Communists who view communism as simply a creature of Jewish plotting for world dominion. The John Birch Society's separate chapter for Jewish members is a seriocomic reflection, I think, of such good old WASP anti-Semitism. The widely reported admiration of Hitler by the head man of the right-wing Liberty Lobby is a reflection, presumably, of the "you need a strong man to fight atheistic communism" school of thought. There are, of course, notable Jewish anti-Communists. And there are many anti-Communists who condemn anti-Semitism. But the operating question for most of the full-time anti-Communists that I have met is simply: Are you anti-Communist? Being also anti-Semitic is not automatically a disqualification on the right, though it usually is on the left.

Conservatives and liberals alike hold in common the mystical notion that nations really mean something, probably something permanent. Both ascribe to lines drawn on maps—or in the dirt or in the air—the magical creation of communities of men that require sovereignty and sanction. The conservative feels this with exaltation when he beholds the Stars and Stripes. The liberal feels this with academic certitude when he concludes that Soviet boundaries must be "guaranteed" to prevent Soviet nervousness. Today, in the ultimate confusion, there are people who feel that the lines drawn by the Soviet Union, in blood, are better than the lines drawn, also in blood, by American foreign policy. Politicians just think this way.

The radical and revolutionary view of the future of nationhood is, logically, that it has no future, only a past—often an exciting one, and usually a historically useful one at some stage. But lines drawn on paper, on the ground or in the stratosphere are clearly insufficient to the future of mankind.

Again, it is technology that makes it feasible to contemplate a day in which the politics of nationhood will be as dead as the politics of power-wielding partisanship. First, there is enough information and wealth available to ensure the feeding of all people, without the slaughtering of some to get at the possessions of others. Second, there is no longer any way to protect anything or anybody behind a national boundary anyway.

Not even the Soviet Union, with what conservatives continue to fear as an "absolute" control over its people, has been able to stop, by drawing lines or executing thousands, the infusion of subversive ideas, manners, music, poems, dances, products, desires. If the world's pre-eminent police state (either us or them, depending upon your *political* point of view) has been unable to protect itself fully behind its boundaries, what faith can or should we, the people, retain in boundaries?

It is to be expected that both liberals and conservatives respond to the notion of the end of nationhood with very similar shouts of outrage or jerks of reaction The conservative says *it shall not be*. There will always be a U.S. Customs Inspector and long may he wave. The liberal says that far from ending nationhood, he wants to expand it, make it world-wide, to create a proliferation of mini- and micronations in the name of ethnic and cultural preservation, and then to erect a great superbureaucracy to supervise all the petty bureaucracies.

Like Linus, neither liberal nor conservative can bear the thought of giving up the blanket—of giving up government and going it alone as residents of a planet, rather than of a country. Advocates of isolationism (although some, admittedly, defend it only as a tactic) seem to fall into a paradox here. Isolationism not only depends upon nationhood, it rigidifies it. There is a subcategory of isolationism, however, that might avoid this by specifying that it favors only military isolationism, or the use of force only for *self*-defense. Even this, however, requires political definitions of national self-defense in these days of missiles, bases, bombers and subversion.

As long as there are governments powerful enough to maintain national boundaries and national political postures, then there will be the absolute risk, if not the certainty, of war between them. Even the possibility of war seems far too cataclysmic to contemplate in a world so ripe with technology and prosperous potential, ripe even with the seeds of extraterrestrial exploration. Violence and the institutions that alone can support it should be rendered obsolete.

Governments wage war. The power of life that they may claim in running hospitals or feeding the poor is just the mirror image of the power of death that they also claim—in filling those hospitals with wounded and in devastating lands on which food could be grown. "But man is aggressive," right and left chant from the depths of their pessimism. And, to be sure, he is. But if he were left alone, if he were not regulated into states or services, wouldn't that aggression be directed toward conquering his environment, and not other men?

At another warlike level, it is the choice of aggression, against politically perpetuated environment more than against men, that marks the racial strife in America today. Conservatives, in one of their favorite lapses of logic—States' rights—nourished modern America racism by supporting laws, particularly in Southern states, that gave the state the power to force businessmen to build segregated facilities. (Many businessmen, to be sure, wanted to be "forced," thus giving their racism the seal of state approval.) The States' rights lapse is simply that conservatives who would deny to the Federal Government certain controls over people, eagerly cede exactly the same controls to smaller administrative units. They say that the smaller units are more effective. This means that conservatives support the coercion of individuals at the most effective level. It certainly doesn't mean that they oppose coercion. In failing to resist state segregation and miscegenation laws, in failing to resist laws maintaining racially inequitable spending of tax money, simply because these laws were passed by states, conservatives have failed to fight the very bureaucracy that they supposedly hate—at the very level where they might have stopped it first.

Racism has been supported in this country not despite of, but thanks to, governmental power and politics. Reverse racism, thinking that government is competent to force people to integrate, just as it once forced them to segregate, is just as political and just as disastrous. It has not worked. Its product has been hatred rather than brotherhood. Brotherhood could never be a political product. It is purely personal. In racial matters, as in all other matters concerning individuals, the lack of government would be nothing but beneficial. What, actually, can government do for black people in America that black people could not do better for themselves, if they were permitted the freedom to do so? I can think of nothing.

Jobs? Politically and governmentally franchised unions do more to keep black men from good jobs than do all the Bull Connors of the South. Homes, schools and protection? I recall very vividly a comment on this subject by Roy Innis, the national director of the Congress of Racial Equality. He spoke of Mayor John Lindsay's typically liberal zeal in giving money to black people, smothering them with it—or silencing them. Innis then said that the one thing Mayor Lindsay would not give the blacks was what they really wanted: political power. He meant that the black community in Harlem, for instance, rather than being gifted with tax money by the bushel, would prefer to be gifted with Harlem itself. It is a community. Why shouldn't it govern itself, or at least live by itself, without having to be a barony of New York City ward politics? However, I take exception to the notion of merely building in Harlem a political structure similar to but only separate from New York City's. And I may be doing Mr. Innis, who is an exceptional man, an injustice by even suggesting that that is what he had in mind.

But beyond this one instance, there is implicit in the very exciting undercurrents of black power in this country an equally exciting possibility that it will develop into a rebellion against politics itself. It might insist upon a far less structured community, containing far more voluntary institutions within it. There is no question in my mind that, in the long run, this movement and similar ones will discover that *laissez faire* is the way to create genuine communities of voluntarism. *Laissez faire* is the only form of social/economic organization that could tolerate and even bless a *kibbutz* operating in the middle of Harlem, a hippie selling hashish down the street and, a few blocks farther on, a firm of engineers out to do in Detroit with a low-cost nuclear vehicle.

The *kibbutz* would represent, in effect, a voluntary socialism—what other form could free men tolerate? The hash seller would represent institutionalized—but voluntary—daydreaming, and the engineers would represent unregulated creativity. All would represent laissez-faire capitalism in action and none would need a political officeholder or a single bureaucrat to help, hinder, civilize or stimulate. And, in the process simply of variegated existence, the residents of this voluntary community, as long as others voluntarily entered into commerce with them, would solve the "urban" problem in the only way it ever can be solved; i.e., via the vanishment of politics that created the problem in the first place.

If cities cannot exist on the basis of the skills, energy and creativity of the people who live, work or invest in them, then they should not be sustained by people who do *not* live in them. In short, every community should be one of voluntarism, to the extent that it lives for and through its own people and does not force others to pay its bills. Communities should not be exempted from the civil liberty prescribed for people—the exclusive employment of all their own powers for their own welfare. This means that no one should serve you involuntarily and that you should not involuntarily serve anyone else. This means, for communities, existing without involuntary aid from other communities or to other communities.

Student dissenters today seem to feel that somehow they have crashed through to new truths and new politics in their demands that universities and communities be made responsive to their students or inhabitants. But most of them are only playing with old politics. When the dissenters recognize this, and when their assault becomes one against political power and authority rather than a fight to gain such power, then this movement may release the bright potential latent in the intelligence of so many of its participants. Incidentally, to the extent that student activists the world over are actually fighting the existence of political power, rather than trying to grab some of it for themselves, they should not be criticized for failing to offer alternative programs; i.e., for not spelling out just what sort of political system will follow their revolution. What ought to follow their revolution is just what they've implicitly proposed: no political system at all.

The style of SDS so far seems most promising in this respect. It is itself loosely knit and internally anti-authoritarian as well as externally revolutionary. Liberty also looks for students who rather than caterwauling the establishment will abandon it, establish their own schools, make them effective and wage a concerned and concerted revolt against the political regulations and power that, today, give a franchise to schools—public and private—that badly need competition from new schools with new ideas.

Looking back, this same sort of thinking was true during the period of the sit-ins in the South. Since the enemy also was state laws requiring separate facilities, why wasn't it also a proper tactic to defy such laws by building a desegregated eating place and holding it against hell and high water? This is a cause to which any libertarian could respond.

Similarly with the school situation. Find someone who will rebel against public-education laws and you will have a worthy rebel indeed. Find someone who just rants in favor of getting more liberals, or more conservatives, onto the school board, and you will have found a politically oriented, passé man—a plastic rebel. Or, in the blackest neighborhood, find the plumber who will thumb his nose at city hall's restrictive licenses and certificates and you will have found a freedom fighter of far greater consequence than the window breaker.

* * *

Power and authority, as substitutes for performance and rational thought, are the specters that haunt the world today. They are the ghosts of awed and superstitious yesterdays. And politics is their familiar. Politics, throughout time, has been an institutionalized denial of man's ability to survive through the exclusive employment of all his own powers for his own welfare. And politics, throughout time, has existed solely through the resources that it has been able to plunder from the creative and productive people whom it has, in the name of many causes and moralities, denied the exclusive employment of all their own powers for their own welfare.

Ultimately, this must mean that politics denies the rational nature of man. Ultimately, it means that politics is just another form of residual magic in our culture—a belief that somehow things come from nothing; that things may be given to some without first taking them from others; that all the tools of man's survival are his by accident or divine right and not by pure and simple inventiveness and work.

Politics has always been the institutionalized and established way in which some men have exercised the power to live off the output of other men. But even in a world made docile to these demands, men do not need to live by devouring other men.

Politics does devour men. A laissez-faire world would liberate men. And it is in that sort of liberation that the most profound revolution of all may be just beginning to stir. It will not happen overnight, just as the lamps of rationalism were not quickly lighted and have not yet burned brightly. But it will happen—because it must happen. Man can survive in an inclement universe only through the use of his mind. His thumbs, his nails, his muscles and his mysticism will not be enough to keep him alive without it.

Playboy, March 1969

The Lawless State

The Nature of Government

Government has gone wild.

Today, in the land we like to think of as the most free on earth, government at all levels reaches into every level of our lives. It controls and it coerces, it bullies and it brags, it browbeats and it blusters. It grows and it grows, feeding without restraint on the energy, the talents, the hopes, the fears, and the futures of the people.

Endless arguing about, or even rigorous voting for "better" government has not and can not alter the fact that it is the nature of government, the state itself that has shown itself in such a dark light. For it is in the nature of the state and of government as it has developed to do all of the things that it now is doing—regardless of which partisans, which technicians operate it at any given point.

After each American election there are the weeks and months of elation in which partisans euphorically tell one another that "problems are going to be solved" by the "good" and "strong" and "wise" men about to take office. The losers, meantime, say just as flatly that the world is going to hell in a breadbasket.

And very little changes.

In terms of actual change, as a matter of fact, there hasn't been an election in the United States since its inception that has driven the country solidly onto a course toward less government and more liberty. Each, rather, has driven the country toward more government and less liberty.

Parties and promises notwithstanding, this is the way it is. To not recognize that one overpowering fact is to let the meaning of the entire political history of our time utterly escape you.

The nature of the state, the growth of government has been unchanged by politicians.* Only the politicians themselves have changed.

Too many Americans for too long have been diverted by the changes of faces and factions. They have permitted their attention to be diverted from the unchanging problem of government itself.

To the extent that they continue to be so diverted, government has a free course to continue its development toward despotism.

Particularly now, with one more election and with one more chorus of paeans and pliants, one more magic-lantern display of changing images in an unchanging show, those who profess an interest in liberty need to turn away from illusions and shadows and look at the actual and concrete facts of government here and around the world.

They need to ask not whether it is possible simply to tame government or make it more economical, or to make it more favorable to this or that ideology, class, or interest; they need to ask the most fundamental questions about government. What is its purpose? What is its limit? What is its legitimacy? What is its relation to liberty? To the individual?

Those who weigh the cost of government only in dollars will vote for the most economical government, the most efficient—perhaps not bothering to ask if that efficiency is in the service of or to the detriment of liberty.

Those who assess the value of government only in terms of its output of "good" programs will vote for the most active government—perhaps

---

*The references to government, except where otherwise specified, are to government as developed in a nation-state and as representing that state. Government is defined as the social instrumentality through which, by force, of which it claims a monopoly, the interests of the state are served. Specifically different from that formal concept of government as used here are the purely voluntary forms of social organization which, even in the absence of a state, most people probably would volitionally construct. Here, as will be obvious throughout, government and the state represent those social forms which rest not at all upon voluntarism but, in the final analysis, upon sheer force. The 'government' that did not and could not sustain itself by force would clearly have to be voluntaristic in nature and, as a result, would not be subject to the body of criticism presented in this statement.

not bothering to ask if the action serves the need or greed of some men or the liberty of all.

Others may measure government only by its arms and martial spirit, praising the way in which it guards the borders or the outposts but remaining curiously uninterested in the garrisons it may be building at home.

Some will ask only that government benefit them, protect them, comfort them, preserve their status quo and suppress any who would disturb it. And they too will have forgotten to ask any question at all about liberty.

Questions about liberty have, of course, long been most notably neglected by those who have called themselves liberals in America. One result has been that the entire liberal position now stands discredited and, even more humiliating to its leadership, hopelessly outdated and irrelevant.

But the same is more and more true of those who call themselves conservative. They too, more and more, ask simply who controls the government ("our" guys or "their" guys) rather than what should we do about government itself.

It has become, as a result, a political truism of our time that the differences between the two major political parties are marginal at best. One editor recently pointed out that in terms of sheer differences of political approach there now is more difference between factions behind the Iron Curtain than between the major political factions in the United States. It is not altogether fanciful to say that the United States has, finally, become a one-party state.

And it is merely common sense to observe that, beyond it all, government rolls along—widely accepted, widely supported, largely unquestioned as the father of us all, the focus of life, lever of all power.

Riots in the streets may concern some. Riots on the campus may concern others. But it is the riotous, growing power of *government* gone wild that should preoccupy the serious and concerned friend of liberty in this land once so hopefully dedicated to liberty.

It is in that dedication, as a matter of fact, that may be found the inspiration to return to concern about government itself and not simply to its current cost or management. For in that dedication we can clearly see a time when men, serious men, were concerned very candidly not with who should run the government but with how to restrain, repress and even eliminate government. They were concerned with purpose, not merely with program.

The deepest concern then, as it should be now, was not the sort of law to impose upon citizens, not the sort of order to impose upon citizens, not the sort of privileges and prerogatives to bestow upon government, not the tasks to assign it or the titles to enhance it. No. The concern was to impose law *upon* government.

It was to curb government; to cut it back and cut it down.

The concern was liberty.

The Declaration of Independence

The Declaration of Independence says it all and says it well.

". . . that all men are created equal, that they are endowed by their Creator with certain inalienable rights, that among these are life, liberty, and the pursuit of happiness. That to secure these rights, governments are instituted among men, deriving their just powers from the consent of the governed, that whenever any form of government becomes destructive of these ends, it is the right of the people to alter or to abolish it . . ."

To the men who founded the United States, that Declaration was the essence of the law insofar as the state was concerned. There were among those men, some, perhaps many, who had little sympathy for the state at all. They accepted it only as a necessary evil. Others conceived it only as an evil and not actually necessary at all.

All finally agreed, however, that they could live under or at least co-exist with an agreement of government, an agreement of lawful government that established the sole function of government as in "securing" the "rights" of the people: life, liberty, and the pursuit of happiness. Government would, in effect, be merely an instrument, voluntarily subscribed to, that would prevent *anyone* (including governments) from taking or abridging life, liberty, or the pursuit of happiness. That is all.

It has been the constant breach of that law that has marked the development of the state ever since then.

It is the gathering momentum of more and more breakage of that law that marks the only crucially important political question facing Americans, or, indeed, people anywhere. This is no longer a problem of any one state. It is a threatening reality in all states, around the world.

The Omnipotent State

Government, gone wild in growth and its powers, has gone also above and beyond the law. Today it is widely accepted, as a matter of fact, that *Government Is The Law.* Just as a "divine" king once could say, "I am the state," governments today everywhere say they are the law, even that they are the people.

Each citizen can ask himself the most grave questions in this regard. Frank self-answers should be revealing.

Do you feel that the state is more important than you are?

Do you feel that the state should enjoy freedoms that you do not?

Do you feel that the state should be able to rise above the law?

Do you feel that you could not live unless the state protected you?

Do you feel that you could not thrive unless the state nourished or subsidized you?

Do you feel that service to the state is more desirable or more noble than service to your self, your family, your neighbors, or your own ideals?

Do you feel that it actually *is* a privilege to pay taxes?

Do you feel that since the government, the state is more important than any one man, that every single man should be prepared to give his all, even his life, to or for his government?

Do you feel that the state is something with a life and identity of its own, beyond the men who might hold office in it?

Do you feel that "the government" and "the country" are the same?

Do you feel that, when all is said and done, your life belongs to your government?

Do you feel that your "rights" are given to you by government?

Do you feel that, when all is said and done, that if big problems are to be solved in this world that government will have to do it?

The crucial separation between men today is not anything more, or anything less than the separation between those who answer "yes" to those questions and those who answer "no." The only important gradations in the thinking that separates men today will be found along a scale of how *many* "yes" and how many "no" answers are given.

My own position is a resounding NO to every single one of the questions.

The demonstrated response of both major political parties, and including the new, conservative Administration is "yes" to at least a majority of the questions.

And it probably would be fair to say that the response of most Americans, sincerely and in heartfelt patriotism, also would be "yes."

That the so-called liberal response has been "yes" all along does not require exposition at this point. Readers of average care know this is true from a generation of reform-liberal, New Deal–type programs in which every action of government has been condoned and expanded. Liberal programs have, without exception, strengthened government and have rejected by their very actions one particular approach to problem-solving. That approach is liberation; the liberation of people *from* political control rather than simply trying to advantage them by political favoritism.

Conservative Contradictions

Conservatives, it now turns out, have little to crow about either. They have howled at the expenditure of tax-taken money for welfare programs but have jumped to support vast outpourings of the same sort of money for the entire panoply of the military-industrial complex and the garrison state; many supported racial laws at the state level but wept when reverse racial laws became Federal; many gleefully seek government subsidy of and protection of business even while they rail against government protection of unions; many ask tariffs to protect their particular interest; few object to farm boondoggling when it gives millions to a man with vast acreage, but many decry the support of another man with a small and unproductive plot.

The examples abound; examples of inconsistency, of outrage at government when it benefits someone else and red-white-and-blue support of government when it's "on our side."

Particularly today, the conservative contradiction is glaring. Of a sudden, as though smitten by righteous lightning, conservatives are discovering that government is good and big government is even gooder. Where is the conservative voice being raised to ask, of the new Administration, that it use its every power not to "improve" government but to, quite literally, get it off the backs of the people altogether.

Instead, the talk most popularly is of such things as "tax incentives," as though letting a man keep some of the money he has earned is an act of supreme wisdom and charity on the part of the government. Only those who, down deep, believe that the government actually does have first claim on everything legitimately, can find inspiration in a system that merely uses taxes to "pay off" this or that class or faction.

Where, instead, is the conservative voice that says do not simply reform the tax system; replace it!

There are few such voices to be heard. Ironically, only on the libertarian right and in some portions of the New Left or among true anarchists are there voices crying against not programs and not against personalities but against government itself.

It is in this very context and against this very background, of the widespread acceptance of government as good, that liberty must beg, must implore all with some concern for her to pause, to reflect—ultimately, to resist.

The Nature of Man

Philosophically, the resistance to government has roots running to the very nature of man himself. There are questions to be asked, in care and conscience, on that score just as on the political score.

Do you feel that your life is unimportant when compared to the lives of others?

Do you feel that the noblest thing you could do would be to give your life for someone else?

Do you feel that the value of each man is simply what "society" says it is?

Do you feel that man actually is incapable, as an individual, of "knowing what is right or wrong" and that only the wisdom of "society" can establish such values?

Do you feel that the life of each individual person belongs in large part to society?

Do you feel that individual men are nothing but that "mankind" is everything?

Do you feel that man's reasoning mind is just a veneer and that under it he is only another animal, very much like all others?

Do you feel that man is basically bad?

Do you feel that if man didn't have restraints he always would run amuck?

Do you feel that man's mind is so limited, in the long run, that it just isn't safe to think you know anything for sure?

Do you feel that your life is swept along, determined by invisible forces over which you have no control?

The person who answered "no" to the liberty-degrading questions listed earlier should answer "no" also to these life-degrading questions. But the sad truth is that to a greater or lesser degree the most acceptable answer has become yes, yes, yes.

Just as liberty has become a low order of priority for concern politically, so has the individual become a low order of priority for concern philosophically. And, of course, it follows. The collectivist view of society which dominates politics of both parties and most people today also dominates the view of man himself. In both instances the word of the day is that men must be ruled, that they are unworthy of liberty, and that progress is only possible through the programs of a special elite, the politicians.

To the abiding discredit of most of us, the fundamental question of liberty and man, of man versus the state, has been neglected, rarely even asked as right and left, liberal and conservative, Democrat and Republican have preoccupied themselves with the lesser questions of political spoils.

The challenge to liberals today is whether they will mutter in their tents about the amounts of welfare programs or the progress of some particular war or whether they will become concerned by the principles of liberty that underlie the programs and the conflict. Liberals cannot have it both ways.

The problems of poverty and prejudice are not solvable by piling official restrictions, more control, and more coercion on top of old, informal repressions. It is to the liberation of people, not their regimentation that liberals should have addressed themselves had they not been swept up in the current concern for political control as an end in itself.

Nor can liberals have it both ways about war. Wars are waged, solely, by governments. The bigger and stronger the government, the bigger and more likely the wars it will wage. Liberals who worship in the state, and forsake liberty, who oppose one war but whoop it up for others (against "bad" guys) are no friends of liberty or of peace.

Conservatives are similarly challenged and they have similarly failed.

After decades of platform ranting about the perils of big government they have been in the forefront of those who advocate all-encompassing government to protect industry, wage war (against *their* enemies, of course) and, above all, to establish and enforce norms of conduct and morality as they have conceived those norms.

Both liberals and conservatives, to sum it up, become preoccupied with the ways in which to *use* government, each for their own ideological or class benefit.

Neither have offered a body of libertarian doctrine. Neither have, so far, returned to the concern over liberty which marked the founding of the nation.

The Concern for Liberty

Actually, for liberals the question is largely academic. They have slipped so far from the mainstream of concern over liberty—a concern that is stirring the cauldrons of discontent everywhere in the world today—that few take them seriously in regard to anything today. This is particularly true of many activist young people, who abhor the bureaucratic pomposity of the liberals every bit as much as they detest the establishmentarian conformity of conservatives. For conservatives, or those who have generally been lumped in that category, the question is more tragic than academic. In the face of liberal collapse, when the time was ripe for a message of liberty, conservatives by and large have preferred to talk of status quo and of political platitudes, of problem solving, of "good government" and, woefully, of more government, always more.

The chief and perhaps only difference is that where liberals used to speak of greater government power to enact welfare programs, conservatives speak of greater government power to establish "order," by which is meant status quo.

In both cases power has corrupted, and always will corrupt whatever good motives may have been present at the outset.

In neither case has liberty become or remained the standard to which good men could repair. In both cases, power has become the goal, the means, and the end.

Where politicians flourish, long history harshly has taught us, people and their liberty wither. Where the state is god and the "public interest" worshipped, individual man will be found bleeding upon the altar.

To what extent has that happened in this land?

When Independence was declared in the land, those whose quest for liberty had made them revolutionaries listed the grievances that set them on their violent, illegal, disorderly course.

The detailed nature of those grievances has changed but the same attitude of grievance rightfully may be levelled against the government today; the government which, by displacing the sovereignty of individuals, has enthroned itself as a political monarchy, giving its subjects the chance only to change the wearer of the crown every so many years.

The monarch "erected a multitude of new offices, and sent hither swarms of Officers to harass our people, and eat out their substance" at the time of the Declaration of Independence.

The Federal and state governments do the same today.

The monarch, then, "kept among us, in times of peace, standing armies." The Federal government conscripts people in times of peace today.

The monarch then suspended "our own legislatures, declaring themselves invested with power to legislate for us in all cases whatsoever."

The Federal and state governments today regularly bypass the legislatures to rule by executive orders and regulation.

The monarch then "endeavored to prevent the population of these states" by land and travel restrictions.

The Federal and state governments today hold vast land areas away from the use of individuals and also closely regulate travel abroad and the conditions of building homes or settling in new places here at home.

The monarch then cut "off our trade with all parts of the world."

State and Federal regulations today straitjacket trade even between cities, much less nations.

The monarch then was opposed "for imposing taxes upon us without our consent."

State and Federal governments today, to be sure, obtain legislative consent for tax rates but then, in administering the rules of taxation with absolute power, actually determine who shall pay what and when just as effectively as though they passed the laws in the first place—without consent.

Last Great Bastion?

There are still some (sadly enough most are conservatives) who argue that despite it all, the United States remains the last great bastion of free enterprise and capitalism. The proposition needs to be examined.

Capitalism, first of all, implies ownership of property and the freedom to use it in non-injurious ways. Where is that freedom today? It is hedged in with so many bureaucratic regulations and restrictions—including the right of the government to expropriate property or, alternatively, destructively tax it—that capitalism in America can only accurately be described as a version of state capitalism, surely not free market capitalism.

As to free enterprise, that is part of the very crux of the discussion. How free is it? To what extent are conservatives defending, rhetorically, something which has ceased to exist anywhere except in their own publications? To what extent does the conservative defense of what is a far-from-free enterprise system actually retard, far from advance, any possibility of moving toward an actually free system?

It is to such problems that those interested in liberty should be seriously addressing themselves and not to merely whether this or that administration, or state government, is more or less "favorable" to business and industry. The fact that supposed free-marketers have so totally accepted the idea of state capitalism that they accept also, without a blink, the fact that government *can* favor or disfavor a particular enterprise is just a measure of how removed from concepts of liberty are most so-called conservative arguments about the economy.

Of singular significance along these lines is the prevailing attitude toward what is called "black capitalism." As stated by the conservative politicians who have proposed it, this is state capitalism of the most arrant sort. It begins with government guarantees and assistance, on a racial allocation, and it ends with the obvious strings of government red-tape laced entirely through it. Liberals, of course, aren't even that subtle. They attempt to buy off, or co-opt black Americans with unvarnished programs of control, rather like putting them on reservations to the accompaniment of promises of dignity and prosperity—perhaps of the sort enjoyed by that other Federally-favored minority, the American Indian.

To view this matter through the lens of liberty is to see an entirely different sort of picture; it is to see the challenge of actually liberating black Americans *from* state control, letting them, if anything, have special assistance in cutting *through* red-tape, in blasting apart the restrictions of labor unions, business and zoning codes and, above all, constant police surveillance over their daily lives. It would mean, for instance, giving more than lip-service to the idea of local control of local schools—a supposedly

conservative idea which went up in smoke the moment it was desired not
by white Americans, but by black Americans.

The same instinct which led some conservatives to defend the right
of some schools to teach and practice bias, in accordance with community control of the school, should certainly have led them to support black
control of schools in black neighborhoods even if the community wanted
to teach Swahili, black supremacy or whatever.

The issue involved is not the convenience or the customs of "society,"
the issue is the liberty of individuals and their *volitional communities.*

The issue is whether, when complacency may be so tempting to so
many, there still will be men willing to make enemies of the world if they
can remain friends of liberty.

There is nothing in the long history of men yearning to be free that
indicates the quest or even the goal is comfortable. There is everything
to indicate that it is exciting and creative and, depending upon your view
of man, rewarding in the only values that are meaningful, self-respect for
instance.

Government or Freedom

What then is the legitimate "political" concern of the person interested in
a free, volitional, community-based, individually respectful society?

Ideally that interest is reflected in seeking the end of the state itself.
Such an interest was, of course, deeply reflected in the debates that followed the Declaration of Independence and preceded the adoption of the
Constitution. Men who might today be regarded as rather anarchistic
strongly argued against the Constitution, feeling that it rather established
a state than guaranteed liberty. The Declaration itself seemed enough to
some and, indeed, upon reflection it might seem so to some today.

But, surely, the legitimate concern of a friend of liberty, even if it is
not directed frontally toward the ideal of no state at all, cannot be directed
in conscience toward *any* actions that would enhance rather than diminish
the power of the state, that would free from power, rather than limit it.

Thus, for the friend of liberty, today, yesterday, and tomorrow, the
crucial questions and answers always must be—wherever on the ladder of
state development he may find himself—"does this action increase the
power of the state? If it does, I shall oppose it. Does this action increase

the liberty of, or even the opportunity for individuals and their volitional communities? If it does, I shall support it."

How frivolous, or vicious seem the arguments of cost, of mere partisan advantage, or of vested interest and special favor, in analyzing legislation, when stacked up against the measurement of liberty itself.

How much sadder, therefore, that liberty is not the constant measure of action—particularly in legislation—rather than only a rhetorical decoration. And, lest it seem a paradox that legislation and liberty can even be discussed in the same breath (most, if not all, legislation being a restriction of rather than extension of liberty) it should be carefully considered that given any freedom of legislative choice at all, it still is conceivably possible to legislate *against* government as well as in favor of it.

Examples could be found in legislation to require the government to obey the law. The recent Freedom of Information Act was such an attempt, although one that has not proven wildly successful. It did attempt, however, to make the government behave as though its public property, which includes mountains of data, were *actually* public and not, instead, the private preserve and property of bureaucracy.

Several court suits are now outstanding to test this law. That government holds all the aces goes without saying.

A greater example, naturally, would be found in the passage of laws to make the tax collectors obey any law at all—such as equal treatment, candor of information as to their internal memoranda and operations (today a body of secrets more closely guarded than the atom bomb) so that citizens would know just what the rules might be on any given day; and so forth and so on down a long line of abuses which now mark this profession as the governmental counterpart of the Black Hand Society.

Laws designed to respect, rather than deny the right of every man to his own life, also could be passed—as for example in forbidding government the right to conscript people for any purpose whatsoever.

Laws designed to respect, rather than degrade, the minds of men, also could be passed, as in laws forbidding anyone, particularly any level of government, the right forcefully to practice censorship or enforce conformity. (It goes without saying, of course, that this would scarcely prevent a parent from "censoring" inputs to a dependent child, if the parent felt so unsure of the child as to think he or she needed it, nor would it prevent any other consensual relationships. If some people *want* to let someone else think for them, it probably would be impossible to stop them. But what eagerly should be opposed is their right to extend the action force-fully to cover anyone else!)

It is true that a libertarian concept of a legislature is largely negative. It envisions the only function of government, and voluntary government at that, as lying in the realm of providing, by community agreement, the sort of protection for individuals which, otherwise, individuals could and would provide for themselves. Sound arguments, of course, can be deliv-ered for the achievement of precisely this same sort of protection by non-governmental means, as through fee-services, voluntary arbitration agree-ments, commercial protective services, and so forth—or for the existence, side-by-side, of competing community and commercial services in all those fields.

The sheerly constructive side of libertarian views of society is in the liberation of men to try voluntarily any and all sorts of daring, innovative social forms, or stick with old ones if they wish.

The real point lies beyond the details. The point is that there is vast and legitimate room to discuss the forms of liberty without forever being bogged down in discussions of the form of the nation-state. The point, fur-ther, is that a serious interest in liberty, as opposed to a parlor-protest, rhetorical interest only in how to play the power game, will impel men to exert themselves in what is essentially the revolutionary direction of our own Declaration of Independence rather than in any more polite directions.

Liberty—The Unsettled Issue

Liberty is not by any means an even slightly settled issue in the United States. It is, rather, a deeply *un*settled issue. When liberals think they serve liberty by confiscatory taxation and when conservatives think they serve the same cause by opposing the ascendency of individual rights in courts we can see just how unsettled and disturbed the whole question of liberty has become.

Only one matter does seem settled. The state, liberty's arch foe throughout history, has increased its powers, scope, and—most signifi-cantly—acceptance every single year of the American republic. Each year has brought more and not less state power.

Today, characteristically, the legislature, which is supposed to repre-sent the people, is judged by the majority of citizens on the basis of how many enlargements of state power it passed rather than how many it resisted! The legislature has become, thus, not representative of the people at all. It is just as surely representative, in the main, of the state, of the bureaucracy, as is the executive branch itself.

Or, to put it another way, the issue of liberty can scarcely be thought of as settled when the Great Debate about it becomes the difference between 60 and 70 percent in taxation, the control of many or just some media, or any other such matter which even in its specification shows that liberty is not at issue anyway—but only some degree or another of state control.

At its most grim level, also, it must be recognized that there now exists in this land of liberty, virtually every institution of state power necessary to totalitarianism with the possible exception of a national police force. Even there, the growing surge to nationalize the police through anti-crime legislation that would, in effect, begin the Federalization of all police forces, leaves little room for a comfortable complacency in any area.

This is not to say, of course, that totalitarianism is right around the corner or that we have already passed the corner. That particular corner is one of the most difficult of all political landmarks to recognize. History strongly suggests, as a matter of fact, that the time when most persons recognize it is precisely the time when it is too late to do anything about avoiding it.

For that reason, among others, it strikes some that it would be better to stand up and appear even ridiculous and alarmist right here and now than to be calm, cool, and collected, properly docile and politically acceptable—while it became too late to do anything else!

The Tax Rebellion

Direct resistance may be the course others will select. Taking every available legal course to harass or even halt government programs is one avenue. Forcing the government to take, in its turn, legal action to compel the individual to comply with a government rule, rather than just voluntarily going along, is another course. Along such lines, of course, for those able to afford it, may lie many useful tests of the legality of government actions, particularly in the high-handed area of executive orders and regulatory law.

Ultimately, of course, every American holds in his hands the most explosive weapon that possibly could be turned against such a government as that of the United States as it has developed. That weapon is the sword of tax refusal.

It is clearly illegal, of course, to defy the government in regard to the payment of taxes. But prior to the clearly illegal areas of tax refusal there are many steps close to the borderline.

In this area, the unbounded imagination of Americans already has given the revenuers a massive migraine headache. Tax resistance is a fact. It is a growing reality. It worries the government. Their concern shows most evidently as they take harsher and hastier action to dampen the flames of this honest, grass-roots revolt.

Many will be frightened off by the toughness and the ruthlessness of the revenuers. Understandably. Yet, there is ample evidence to show that the spirit of resistance overall is rising, despite the repressive and retaliatory lashings of the revenuers.

Part of that spirit may feed on the earthy American feeling that "they can't put everybody in jail!" Or, in short, there *is* safety in numbers when it comes to fighting City Hall, or the White House itself.

Individual men and women, particularly those who have for so long been cruelly exploited by government—and this includes both the poorest and the most productive of our people—stand today at a point of decision that is made even more crucial because it is so honestly difficult for many to see it *as* crucial.

Life is, certainly in relation to other lands, good, sweet, and comfortable for many, if not most Americans.

Your Revolutionary Heritage

Many Americans are anxious, somehow fearful, somehow deeply disturbed that the quality of life in the land has lost many of its values, many of its virtues.

Creative and productive Americans of every race, of every degree of energy or education, from the mechanic at a cross-roads garage, to the stock-clerk in a department store, to the physicist, to the poet, to the musician, to the conscientious parent struggling to speak to a child suffering from the tongue-tied, mind-bent confusions of schools designed not to teach kids to think but to teach them simply to conform—all of these

Americans, and their counterparts across the globe, in hut, hacienda, or factory, are chafing under the load of government that has been pressed down upon their shoulders in the name of many causes.

Americans are faced with two vistas.

Across one they see the comforts of life in this lovely land—the barbecues, the patios, the second car, the color TV. Seeing this many will reject out-of-hand any idea that the times now call for the sort of spirit that swept the land in 1776. How foolish to rock the boat, they can rightfully say.

Across the other vista are the clouds, no larger than a man's hand, or fist; the resentments of regimentation, the realization of rising repressiveness in the society, the stark, staring vision of those millions around the world to whom liberty is not just a copy-book exercise but precisely the sort of exercise in which men put their lives on the line.

No man, surely, can see the entire future clearly now. But all who put their hand upon the ground can feel the tremors in the earth. And all who turn their heads from the familiar tasks before them can hear the wind that is rising.

There is nothing so certain as, or seemingly more painful than change. And changes there will be.

Each man now has only to answer whether he will stand pat and be changed, willy-nilly in a world he can wistfully say he did not want and did not make—or whether he will stand up, be counted, be confronted and be committed to the change to which his conscience and his reason dedicate him. There are just those two courses.

My course is clear. It is to stand for, and fight for liberty. For the liberation of man from a lawless state.

For, "when a long train of abuses and usurpations, pursuing inevitably the same object evinces a design to reduce them under absolute despotism, it is their right, it is their duty, to throw off such government, and to provide new guards for their future security."

That, Americans, is your revolutionary heritage from your Declaration of Independence. It is a proud one. It is right.

National Issues Series of Politics, Constitutional Alliance,
February 5, 1969

Anarchism without Hyphens

There is only one kind of anarchist. Not two. Just one. An anarchist, the only kind, as defined by the long tradition and literature of the position itself, is a person in opposition to authority imposed through the hierarchical power of the state. The only expansion of this that seems to me reasonable is to say that an anarchist stands in opposition to any imposed authority. An anarchist is a voluntarist.

Now, beyond that, anarchists also are people and, as such, contain the billion-faceted varieties of human reference. Some are anarchists who march, voluntarily, to the Cross of Christ. Some are anarchists who flock, voluntarily, to the communes of beloved, inspirational father figures. Some are anarchists who seek to establish the syndics of voluntary industrial production. Some are anarchists who voluntarily seek to establish the rural production of the kibbutzim. Some are anarchists who, voluntarily, seek to disestablish everything including their own association with other people; the hermits. Some are anarchists who will deal, voluntarily, only in gold, will never co-operate, and swirl their capes. Some are anarchists who, voluntarily, worship the sun and its energy, build domes, eat only vegetables, and play the dulcimer. Some are anarchists who worship the power of algorithms, play strange games, and infiltrate strange temples. Some are anarchists who see only the stars. Some are anarchists who see only the mud.

They spring from a single seed, no matter the flowering of their ideas. The seed is liberty. And that is all it is. It is not a socialist seed. It is not a capitalist seed. It is not a mystical seed. It is not a determinist seed. It is simply a statement. *We can* be free. After that it's all choice and chance.

Anarchism, liberty, does not tell you a thing about how free people will behave or what arrangements they will make. It simply says that people have the capacity *to* make the arrangements.

Anarchism is not normative. It does not say how to be free. It says only that freedom, liberty, can exist.

Recently, in a libertarian journal, I read the statement that libertarianism is an ideological movement. It may well be. In a concept of freedom it, they, you, or we, anyone, has the liberty to engage in ideology or anything else that does not coerce others, denying their liberty. But anarchism is not an ideological movement. It is an ideological statement. It says that all people have a capacity for liberty. It says that all anarchists want liberty. And then it is silent. After the pause of that silence, anarchists then mount the stages of their own communities and history and proclaim *their*, not anarchism's, ideologies—they say how they, how they as anarchists, will make arrangements, describe events, celebrate life, work.

Anarchism is the hammer-idea, smashing the chains. Liberty is what results and, in liberty, everything else is up to people and *their* ideologies. It is not up to THE ideology. Anarchism says, in effect, there is no such upper case, dominating ideology. It says that people who live in liberty make their own histories and their own deals with and within it.

A person who describes a world in which everyone must or should behave in a single way, marching to a single drummer, is simply not an anarchist. A person who says that they prefer this way, even wishing that all would prefer that way, but who then says that all must decide, may certainly be an anarchist. Probably is.

Liberty is liberty. Anarchism is anarchism. Neither is Swiss cheese or anything else. They are not property. They are not copyrighted. They are old, available ideas, part of human culture. They may *be* hyphenated but they are not in fact hyphenated. They exist on their own. People add hyphens, and supplemental ideologies.

I am an anarchist. I need to know that, and you should know it. After that, I am a writer and a welder who lives in a certain place, by certain lights, and with certain people. And that you may know also. But there is no hyphen after the anarchist.

Liberty, finally, is not a box into which people are to be forced. Liberty is a space in which people may live. It does not tell you how they will live. It says, eternally, only that we *can*.

the dandelion, Spring 1980

The Importance of Tools

Social and political philosophers analyze the world and try to clarify aberrations in the way we behave. They collect and interpret raw data on group human behavior. Economists, notably of the Austrian school, who actually are interested in economics and not in ward politics, help us understand why we cannot get rich by taking in each other's laundry or by building a solid customer base by cheating and overcharging so long as there is market entry for competition.

The eminent Austrian economist, Murray Rothbard, memorably points out that economists want *markets*. Politicians want *power*. Politics involve the forced *allocation* of what otherwise could be *traded*. The various sorts of philosophers and social scientists argue back and forth on politics—on the different ways of controlling or liberating tools, property, and wealth. They tell us why we should live differently. But not one of them, so far as I can see, has ever by a theoretical statement, or opinion, fundamentally changed the way we live together.

They formalize the rhetoric of history's vocabulary. They are the most highly lauded of intellectuals and even seem to define the term itself.

But consider: What was the first great transforming *idea* that turned humans from draught animals to creatures with enough time on their hands to contemplate rhymed speech, develop civil manners, the common law, music, and embark on space travel?

367

It was not Plato's notion of a philosopher prince. It was not Aristotle's common stonemason's notion that A is A.

It was not an idea from social, political, or economic philosophy although it is the sort of thing that has seemed to have been appreciated most, through the years, by the latter.

The great idea, the one that made human ascent to the stars *inevitable*, was the horsecollar or ox yoke. It was the agency of the first transfer of human need for energy to a non-human source. Once the ox was yoked, the nuclear turbine could not be far behind! The principle had been established. Humans could derive energy to do work from non-human, even inanimate sources. Even the discovery of fire seems pallid beside this. Fire did not become a source for energetic work, as a replacement for the ox, until years and years later, when technologies of smelting and the steam engine were developed. One brought the Iron Age. The other brought the Industrial Revolution. Now *those* were changes.

Tools *change* the way we live.

Philosophers try to explain how come.

Philosophies are powerfully held opinions. They can organize systems to command the use of the tools in this way or that way; to how they are to be used by this bunch of people or some other one.

Yet no tool, once conceived, has ever been known to have been successfully banned or monopolized except locally and temporarily, by any philosophy, law, or any other sort of opinion—no matter how powerful or popular the opinion.

Look to the tools and you see how humans will, over time, work and live together. Look to philosophies and you find out who detests or adores the vision. It seems, however, that the tools eventually prevail whether you or your political theory likes it or not.

The Chinese nobility was said to have rejected the use of gunpowder for war (perhaps to keep the warring field safe from gun-toting peasants). The Europeans did not. *They* were worried about the English long bow. And neither ban nor bother stood a chance against the roaring whirlwind of human ingenuity whence came the boom of the powder and the swoosh of the shaft.

Do not make the mistake that if all nuclear weapons finally are banned that this will contradict the point. The energy source surely will persist—safer, cleaner. The missile delivery systems will endure—perhaps to carry the mail, tourists, and ores back from the asteroids. Only a particular mechanism of nuclear detonation will be banned—and even that could be quickly revived in some political windshift or fairly easily stored away in some high-tech survivalist's cabin in the woods. Tools are immortal.

And here we stand, thousands of years along in developing every sort of religious, moral, and philosophical idea you can imagine and what actually has changed our contemporary world the most? Christian charity? Protestant individualism? Oriental mysticism? Marxism? Some sort of formally defined capitalism? Socialism? Communism? Pantheism? Mayan sacrificial ceremonies? Shrine shinto? Monarchism? Pacificism? Bellicosity?

You know the answer. Every peasant farmer trying to get a load of coffee to port knows the answer. It is said that Australian aborigines are fairly clear on the subject as well; surely after talking to a neighbor who has been to Brisbane.

So what is it?

The automobile, of course.

None of the great philosophers have had the impact on *this* living world as has the mass production of the automobile—the inevitable development of merging the first non-human motor, the non-human animal, with the altogether human device, the cart—whether the cart was intended to roll on wheels, skids, oiled logs or the bones of dead slaves.

There may be 73,000 Ph.D.s granted to prove that unless we had kings, queens, the Magna Carta, or the U.S. Constitution, we never would even have *had* the automobile.

I disagree. I believe that once a tool is demonstrated, and once someone finds that it makes their work easier or more effective, that the tool will, like it or not, *be used*.

Engineers, of course, devise the tools that work for us. They can do this without understanding exactly how all of the parts work or why.

If it works, it works.

Scientists, in contrast, are obsessed with knowing exactly why something happens, how it can be measured or located and whether it can be predicted. Engineers are artisans. Scientists are obsessed by curiosities.

In some cases, these days, the attitudes of the two are separating more widely than ever. In others they are coming closer together. The origin of the universe absorbs some of us. (Oy vey, what a big thing to worry about!) The manipulation of genetic material—like looking at the world through the *other* end of the telescope—absorbs others. Fusion energy and superconductivity, on the other hand, put scientists and engineers closer and closer together in their work.

More distant yet from the engineering mind-set is philosophy, the grand practice of the human mind. It can be an intellectual shorthand to let people know who we are. "I work at the five-and-dime but I am a Flat Earther, a Debsian socialist, and a Platonist." It is, most importantly, the way we discuss across generations, decent behavior toward each other. We should all be philosophers. I favor the physical sciences but I would never want a physical scientist to be unaware of the philosophies that have formed so many of the rules about how we use our tools and relate to our tool users.

Yet for all the philosophies, we live in a world dominated by one great tool, the auto, and shaped around the edges by a million others related to it.

Do I think that social and political scientists should be banned from even *having* opinions about tools? Absolutely not. Do I resent that they, more than any other intellectuals, easily promulgate those opinions and cajole or force others to follow them? Damn right I do.

Do I want my buddies in the tool room to make all of the decisions about tools? Don't be a ninny. Tool *users* should form their own opinions and then have to negotiate with other users as to what to do about it—in roughly the way the rules of the road at sea were worked out by merchant seamen who had far too much more important work to do than to be harassed by pet behavioral theories, conflicting signals, and collisions.

The arena in which such negotiations are carried out could be called a marketplace. It is there we find the people who truly *change* the world.

I am moved by them, just as I am deeply moved by the sheer beauty and effectiveness of a Viking longboat. I am also moved by good arguments about how and where to navigate them, whether plunder is an ethical use for them, and how to foster cooperation between members of the crew—and the boatwrights, chandlers, and others. I have not forgotten coordination, information-sharing and planning ahead as human graces. I am not against good conversation of any sort, from theological angel-splitting to libertarian cat and dog fights.

But I always come back to tools and their creators; they are what change the world and shape how we live our daily lives.

Three hundred years before the birth of Christ, Euclid set forth his elegant *Elements*. This singular act makes it more practical to measure land for ownership, design better sails, make navigation more dependable. Euclid could be said to have opened the door to the modern world. Christ has influenced millions, of course. But the behavior of those millions has not changed much. They still lie, cheat, steal, and kill with abandon—ironically, often in Christ's own name.

In about 1000 A.D., Venice consolidated its empire in the Adriatic. Ho hum—just more empire building made lofty with some new political rhetoric. At the same time, the mathematician Sridhara, and perhaps dozens more, proposed the concept of zero in number theory. Zero is one important reason you can count to twenty without taking off your shoes.

Cardinal Richelieu became the famed power behind the throne of France in 1619. At the same time, William Harvey discovered the way that blood circulates in the human body. Which event resulted in greater benefits to humanity?

In the 1660s, there were at least 50 major treaties and wars. Politics was sweeping the earth. At the same time, Isaac Newton described differential calculus. When war becomes just a dim memory, some part of some mission into deep space probably will be enhanced by calculus. If war persists, the calculus will help us hit targets better. Of ideas developed at the time it has clearly more clout than the socio-political ones.

In 1760, the British imposed the Stamp Act on the British colonists. About the same time, James Watt perfected the condenser that made the steam engine possible, the Industrial Revolution inevitable, and America a powerhouse of production.

And score a big one for the power of ideas in 1776: *The American Revolution—and its concept of individual liberty—brought forth a social-political idea that matched the world-changing ideas of science and technology.* For it created the environment for free people to develop the scientific and technological breakthroughs that ultimately benefitted mankind in such enormous ways.

The French Revolution? As a world-changing force, it cannot stand against, for example, Eli Whitney's cotton gin or his development of the manufacturing technique of interchangeable parts for mass-produced machinery.

The United States government announced the Monroe Doctrine in 1823. In terms of human improvement, it cannot stand against Charles Babbage and his calculating machine. The government gave us the seeds for foreign intervention. Babbage gave us the beginnings of the computer.

In 1903, Lenin and Trotsky formed the Bolshevik faction of the

Russian Social Democratic Party. In America, the Wright brothers' plane successfully flew. The Bolsheviks gave us a another form of despotism. The Wright brothers gave us the ability to fly.

In the 1930s, the Nazis won their 230-seat plurality in the Reichstag. Contemporaneously, Werner Karl Heisenberg was awarded a Nobel Prize for the matrix theory of quantum mechanics.

In 1962, the United States government committed itself to intervening in Vietnam. That was also the year that Crick, Wilkins, and Watson received their Nobel Prize for describing the molecular structure of DNA. Thanks to those three peaceful men, not to raging armies, the world will never be the same again.

And the breakup of the Soviet Union and the end of its tyranny did not happen by the persuasion of ideas, but by the power of appetites and practicalities. People wanted material things. Free markets provide such things; they are proven practices more than ideologies.

The market and owned property are more ancient than any currently popular ideology, even Christianity.

A substantial black market in cars and car repairs surely helped pave the way for *perestroika* which, in turn, yielded to the truly radical pressures of material appetites fanned by faxed, photocopied, video-taped and personally computed information. The Eastern European peoples yearning for freedom are yearning for, admittedly, an abstract idea; but they are yearning for it in hope of using today's marvelous tools and earning the material rewards associated with the tools.

Today, as in the past, ordinary people in the ordinary communities of their lives change the way they behave on the basis of the tools available to them or that they develop for their special purposes.

The tidal change in the status of women, at least in the Western world, had been an idea for centuries. But only when computers unsexed symbol manipulation, when machine shops became cybernated, when muscle was replaced by mind in more and more of the work we do, did the change actually happen.

Listen to the ideas. But *follow* the tools to see if and how the way we work and live is going to change.

An abbreviated version of this essay appeared in *Liberty*, July 1991.

The Good Machines

Fifty years ago Mr. and Mrs. Lyman Pierce of Idaho Falls, Idaho purchased a secondhand refrigerator from the Utah Power and Light Company. It was a General Electric Monitor Top. You've probably seen one in an old-time film or on a TV show about the '20s or '30s. It's the box with the cylindrical "head" on top. Looks a lot like a chunky white robot. For the half century that the Pierces' refrigerator has been around, it has run—steadily and efficiently—every single day. Now that's a good machine.

Unfortunately, the Pierces' Monitor Top is not typical of appliances. But, in a special way, the Pierces are typical of Americans. For Americans love machines. They also hate them. Griping about appliances falling apart has become a favorite national pastime. Much of it seems perfectly justified—the complaints of people whose common sense tells them that the throwaway society is not so much an engineering triumph as a bookkeeping bonanza, pushing fast bucks and suppressing good craft. TV ads foist gadgets that promise to make us better, smarter, sexier people. But we suspect that the reverse is true, that as we love machines more, we love ourselves less. That machines too often run us, rather than serve us. Beyond all that lies our longstanding romance with *some* machines—the ones that *have* lasted, that *have* done what they were supposed to do, and with little fuss. The good machines.

Perhaps the best example is the Model T Ford. Most of us seem to be born with an almost gene-deep regard for this first mass-produced automobile. Children who have never seen one sense that it was the best—the old-time, straight-goods paragon of fine machines. At antique shows, fancy touring cars bring cries of admiration, but reverence and quiet respect are reserved for the Model T Ford.

The first was produced in 1908. At the time there were more than 200 separate automakers, but the Model T knocked them all out of the ring in terms of sheer public appeal. For one thing, it cost only $850—less than half the price of any competitor's cheapest model. For another, it was simple to operate and, extremely important, simple to repair. The tool kit supplied with the car contained a pair of pliers, a wrench, and a screwdriver. Over 19 years, 15 million Model Ts ran off the Ford line and into the hearts of the nation's drivers.

Transportation is a natural area in which to look for good machines. In today's market, with many drivers afraid that their costly chrome-and-color chariots may last only until the last payment, the longevity of cars like the Model T is a maddening reminder of the pre-style engineering of the good old days. So is the mighty Jeep of World War II fame. The last one I owned, back in the '50s, had been through the war and was still going strong enough to pull a stalled car sideways out of an Ohio snowdrift. Twenty- and 30-year-old Jeeps are still in use and in great demand. Today a 30-year-old model is likely to sell close to its original price of $875.99. About half a million were produced during the war and many times that number since then, here and in 30 other nations where Kaiser Jeep and American Motors, as well as the original maker, Willys-Overland, operate plants.

For the city dweller, the Checker cab is one of the most cherished of good machines. The style has remained basically the same since it jelled in 1959—36 years after the company turned out its first cab. Since it takes an expert to date a Checker, it's hard to say how many 20-year veterans are still cruising. But it's possible to find cabs with half a million miles under their fan belts. Their reputation for endless operation is so good that not even the maker keeps track of mileage records anymore.

Of the great machines for air travel, the Douglas DC-3 is arguably the most impressive ever built. It was the plane that made a reality of modern commercial aviation, taking over from the Ford Tri-Motor to become the most successful passenger plane in history. With a 95-foot wingspan, a cruising speed of 180 miles per hour, and room for 28 passengers, the DC-3 went into production just before World War II. During the war it became the standard military transport plane, carrying everything everywhere. Hundreds of DC-3s, some with new wings tilted rakishly upward for better performance, still drone away in barely flyable places like the Andes.

But good machines don't have to be big or change the world. Take the Zippo cigarette lighter. No matter how many billion disposable butane lighters are sold in our fast-paced throwaway society, the Zippo, like the Model T, lurks in our national memory as a reminder of a time when things worked and lasted. The basic design for the Zippo was an early-20th-century import from Austria that caught the eye of George Grant Blaisdell, a bright, ambitious machinist in Bradford, Pennsylvania. Blaisdell didn't even smoke, but he did want to make a buck, and that's exactly what he charged for the first handmade models of his lighter. He called it Zippo simply because the name reminded him of another red-hot invention, the zipper.

Even though the Zippo worked every time you thumbed the wheel against the flint, even though its metal chimney made it nearly windproof, and even though you could run a truck over one and still use it—despite all that—the business didn't really take off until World War II. Then the entire output of Blaisdell's plant went straight to war. By the time it was over, the whole world had seen Zippos. Millions were made for the armed forces, and a scrapbook of fantastic Zippo stories made its way firmly into American folklore. The Zippo that stopped a bullet, then lighted a butt to calm the saved soldier. The Zippo that turned up 10 years later on an invasion beach and still worked when it was mailed to its owner, his name scratched on it with a bayonet. And so on.

The Zippo and the Model T are so commanding in their sustained impact on millions of people that they would likely turn up on anyone's list of good machines. Other choices are more personal, the result of individual experiences. One of my own candidates is the Royal typewriter Model KMM or KMG. (One is black, the other gray.) I've been using a Royal since they first came out, more than a quarter century ago. The machine is virtually indestructible. For a couple of years I had one aboard a boat, and there were times when it was used to hold open hatches, to weight down planks, and, of course, to type a thing or two. It even occurred to me that it could have been used for an anchor without too much damage. Solid, heavy, great. Since my own love affair with the model began, I have noticed more of them in publishing offices than any other nonelectric machine.

My personal choice for the best machine with the fewest moving parts would be the GI can opener of World War II. It's an inch-and-a-half-long, rectangular piece of metal with a notch that fits over the rim of a can. Hinged to it is a small, curved can-opener blade. Just open the blade at right angles to the little handle, punch the blade into the can, and with short chopping strokes open the thing. The next stop down the line would be *no* moving parts, and here the standard beer can opener might well win first prize. Which, considering the place where you store some of the cans it opens, brings us back to Mr. and Mrs. Pierce's Monitor Top refrigerator.

General Electric introduced the Monitor Top in 1927, the same year that Lucky Lindy flew the Atlantic and Babe Ruth hit 60 homers. It was the first tightly sealed electric refrigerator that wasn't pretty much just an old-fashioned icebox with an external compressor and heat exchanger added on. The Monitor Top was designed from scratch to take advantage of the modern miracle of electrical refrigeration. The compressor and heat exchanger—the coils and tubes that throw off the heat leached from within—were mounted up on top. Hot air travels up and, thus, away from the box—a simple principle ignored by today's manufacturers who persist in lodging the cooling motor underneath the refrigerator.

Like many good machines, the Monitor Top emphasized function and not fashion. Nearly a million were sold. The cost was $299 and the capacity seven cubic feet. That works out to about $43 a cubic foot, while many of today's models have come down to $25 or $30 a cubic foot. But then, how many of the new models will still be working in the year 2030?

Since the pen is said to be mightier than the sword, there is a good-machine entry in the handwriting field also—the Parker 51 fountain pen. Although the rolling-ball pen is today's best-seller, the 51 remains the most famous writing instrument in history, except for the quill pen. Introduced in 1941, the pen was meant to take advantage of a new fast-drying ink that the Parker company had developed. The design was streamlined and classy. The price was outrageous: $12.50, at a time when most pens were still just a couple of bucks. But it took off anyway. It worked well. It looked good. Almost immediately it became a status symbol. During World War II a Parker 51 went for as high as $200 on the black market. Dwight Eisenhower used one to sign the German surrender. All 324 signatures on Brazil's modern constitution were written with the famous pens. Queen Elizabeth used one to sign official documents and so did Marshal Tito. Harry Truman ended World War II with one. To date, more than 30 million have been made.

There is one good machine that is just an engine—the one-cylinder Briggs and Stratton engine used on everything from lawn mowers to go-carts. They come in a wide range of small-horsepower sizes, so it's hard to single out just one model for praise. With care they go on indefinitely. Without care—the way most people treat them—they go on far past the point where most other mechanical devices so roughly treated would have sputtered to a stop.

Agriculture, generally, has an impressive number of good machines. Tractors seem to go on and on, from farmer to farmer and auction to auction. Of all the long-lived, good-machine tractors, the McCormick-Deering (International Harvester) Original Farmall strikes me as the most sturdy. From 1928 to 1932 over a quarter million of the F series were produced. A casual tour of country fairs or local farms will still turn up a few, not to mention the dozens of 20- to 30-year-old representatives of the successor series, the A, B, H, and M.

Another good machine that may well make it to 100 years is the Maytag wringer washer. The classic model is the 32, built between 1937 and 1942. One measure of its longevity is that the company still provides spare parts and servicing for machines that are almost 50 years old. About one million of these familiar square-tub washers were built. My wife and I have a more recent model—only about 30 years old. But in our shed, there are pieces of perhaps a half-dozen year-or-so-old washers that quickly conked out. Meantime, our old, funny-looking Maytag cheerfully glugs and churns away as it has perhaps a thousand times before.

There's a good machine for cleaning houses too, the Electrolux Model XXX [vacuum cleaner]. The familiar gray leatherette canister with polished aluminum ends was a hot item right up to World War II. The number still in use must be enormous. You can hardly pass a used-appliance store that doesn't have some available, touted quite accurately as the equal of anything new on the market.

Unfortunately, the list of good machines is not endless. Fortunately, it's longer than the list in this article. Personal experience keeps tipping people off to good machines that the rest of us may miss—or have forgotten about.

Fire engines, for instance. American LaFrance, a major engine maker, has a famous pumper called the Century. The company says that with proper maintenance they're good for about 25 years, a respectable life span for a hard-driven machine. But many have gone well beyond the quarter-century mark—the property of small, out-of-the-way fire departments.

Toys are another unlikely contender for a good-machine list until we consider the hardy, ingenious Erector set, with its little girders, engines, and bolts, which may have started more people into engineering than MIT. And Erector sets, if you keep track of the pieces, can be handed down to your grandchildren.

Some serious points can be made about good machines. First of all, that there are so many fine, long-lasting machines is a pointed comment on today's run-of-the-store junk that lasts such a short time. Machines that last and work *can* be made. They *have* been made. They are *still* being made. But most machines, it seems, are not like that. Why? What would our economy be like if quality and not quantity dominated it? What would our lives be like if the quality of life, and not just the quantity of things in it, became most important? How much are we paying for fashion alone in what we buy these days? How much more would we have to pay for things that lasted beyond fashion? And what would the final cost be of a few good machines as compared to so many shoddy, cheap things?

Quest, February/March 1980

The Politics of Place

In the beginning there was the world—and everyone wanted to save it, savage it, change it, conserve it, Do Something To It. And then there was the self—and everyone wanted to soothe it, swaddle it, swallow it, save it, solve it, suck it, succor it.

Then a sort of synthesis and practicality. If you want to make the world a certain kind of place in which to live, you have to make the self a certain kind of life. To change the world you must first change yourself. Imbedded in that was a revolution against the mechanistic determinisms that had cranked us all up since Newton and Marx, Calvin and Falwell. Changing selves make changing times. If there are invisible hands they are nonetheless hands, human hands.

Good enough but not nearly enough. In between the world and the self there is a crucial terrain of action, human action. Once seen, the sight is ineradicable. It is the terrain of local place, the local place where you live. And just as ineluctably as the lesson of changing the self to change the world, its lesson is that in changing anything in the material world, and regardless of the lever you use, the fulcrum will be the *place* where you are. The march of a thousand miles begins with a single step, the view of the infinite universe is a sight from a single village, all tomorrow is perceived from a single today, every self on Earth is somewhere. We, all of us, even if intermittently, live in a place.

379

It is the processes and politics of place that will occupy many of us for a long time to come. What happens in those places, all poured together into the gulf where our world empties into and joins the universe will be very important work indeed, perhaps the most practical work we have ever done. These are gardens, these places where we live, and it is there that we set the seeds of our future not knowing, just hoping, that the harvest will be good. But, at least, we know that in such a place we do not just scatter seeds into the middle of air, pumping the air full of high talk and high times, only to have it all flop back to renounced ground sooner or later.

About the politics of place certain points may be made:

- **The politics of place does not discourage thinking intergalactically**, but it does discourage *simply* thinking intergalactically, or globally, without due consideration for what concretely and currently, you can DO about it. René Dubos once said "think globally, act locally." That's the politics of place. (Obvious option: you can *just* think and act locally, if you wish. That may be no better than anything we already experience but it is also unlikely to be any worse.)
- **The politics of place is damage-limiting**. Mistakes made locally may be more easily corrected, have fewer externalities than mistakes made by, for instance, national or international planning bodies. To the argument that D. K. Ludwig's despoliation of the Amazon basin is politics of place but also regionally and perhaps globally devastating, it must be pointed out that Brazilian central planning organizations, and not local politics, made the adventure possible. Without Brazilian police power, courts, land condemnations, and so forth, a localist revolt or resistance against the immense invasion would at least be possible and would represent the politics of place as different from the politics of international finance. Actually, no project of such scale is even likely without state support.
- **The politics of place can be knowledgeable**. Even with a Cray I or II computer it is difficult to keep up with the conjoined weather of the world. You can, however, stick your head out the window of the place where you live and see what's happening. Remote bureaucracies inevitably see your creek in terms of its average

streamflow and depth. You can drown trying to cross a creek that averages four feet in depth. And you cannot constantly pump a million gallons from a stream that averages that flow. Sometimes it is dry. You know that and see that—locally.

- **The politics of place can be experimental**. Who knows, you and I and all our friends may be dead wrong about everything we say. Still, we will try to make our vision of the world more and more concrete. Doing it locally, on a laboratory scale, seems more decent than lunging to commissar commands for the entire globe or universe. Our neighbors in the universe might be pleased also; as we might be if they show the same patience.
- **The politics of place can be flexible**. A goof in a local garage means you change a cutting tool, reset the milling machine, heighten the chain hoist, close the windows on the corner experiment on oil-enhancing bacteria, or whatever. A goof at General Motors or perhaps Genentech, means goofing along to protect your investment. Mistakes, in large organizations, are too costly to correct. They must be covered and continued.
- **The politics of place involves people**. The conventional politics of party and presidiums also involves people, of course, but in a different way. The principal people display and deploy symbols or guns, the constituent people display voter registration or identity cards. In conventional politics, at its very best, which is right here, voters elect people to be citizens, to make arguments in and about shared spaces. But the voters are not citizens, just voters. In the politics of place, if only because of proximity and neighborliness, arguments about shared matters go on constantly and are not just part of a formal, occasional process even if such processes are present also.

  In the politics of place people are constantly tempted to be involved, again by sheer proximity, while the politics of conventional representation or, worse, dictatorship is always far enough removed from everyday life to teeter on the brink of alienation, renunciation, or repression. Usually it falls over that brink.
- **The politics of place is gently federative**. The interests of people where they live inevitably flow toward immediately surrounding places, then to the universe or, at least, the region. But the impulses are generated from the interests of the people where they live and

not by strangers with distant (not necessarily broader) views. High blown, universalizing fiats that descend like hammer blows on people all over are what we're used to and what many politicians and most ideologues aspire to. No one not seized by a brain fever, I feel, can any more truly believe that they or anyone else is wise enough to assume the ruler role of delivering those hammer blows from the fist of their own fervor. If we have learned anything over these years, if there is anything that binds us together in some shared attitude, all of us who read and write in places like this, it is that the king and the queen are dead—and should stay that way!

The gentle possibilities of federation for the politics of place could take off some of the abrasive edges of ideology which have made it very difficult for long-term concerted action, by individuals and small communities of people, on great national or global issues.

Such action has meant that disparate interests have joined in very narrow causes (antinukes, for instance) that have in no way been able to mute ideological differences about many other issues. Meetings on federated issues have always been battlegrounds to fight out many causes other than the one immediately involved. One reason is that the cooperating groups, by and large, have been groups which are based upon debatable ideological points. Thus, people who oppose nuclear energy but also espouse state socialism may be offended, and become offensive, when antinuke folk who are, say, libertarian refuse to applaud tactics calling for state intervention in the nuclear industry. The point is that both the opposition to nuclear energy and the espousal of any particular *larger* system change are both wholly ideological and not practical issues for the people involved. They have no power to begin with and no practical way of offering alternatives. They must unite in negativity and even though that unity may produce vastly valuable results of public attention, little practical action can result. "Occupying" a reactor is an action, to be sure, but not a practical one. It is a media event, not a political and practical one.

On the other hand, when people are rooted in the politics of place, when they have an enduring place in a community, and a constituency of neighbors who will at least listen to them, they can enter into the largest sorts of federated activity without any hidden agendas or ideological reservations. They can, if they choose, go into the federated activity as representatives not of any ideology but simply as people from a real place. The interests of that community, in turn, are not likely to be the sort that anyone would even want to foist on anyone else. People with their feet solidly in a place, in a community, easily and commonly realize, it has been my observation, that their own situation is unique and that other situations are as unique as theirs. They recognize that rather than imposing ideologies upon each other, we urgently need to leave each other alone enough to get work done at home—so that if we wish, we can bring it full circle and enter into federated actions with others in other communities as prudence, practical prudence suggests.

To carry out the nuclear example one step farther: the only county in Maine which recently voted against the installation of a nuclear plant in that state was the very county in which the reactor would be located. For those people, nuclear energy is more than an ideological matter, it is part of their politics of place. The stronger their internal community, the more people have their neighbors' ears on such matters, the stronger long-term practical case they can make for excluding the nuke and for deploying alternative forms of energy. Their only hope now, I suppose, is in stiffening the spine of the localities and the county to produce new resistance—legal, social, and economic—against the reactor. Had antinuclear people in the past been more attentive to their work in their communities, their general positions in their communities, and not just antinuclear organizing, they might at least now be in a position to rally countywide support for nuclear alternatives as part of their active life in the community. To carry the message of a cause in a community when you are a generally respected neighbor is far better than when you do it as virtually your sole activity in public.

- **The politics of place is no more ineffectual than any other kind of aspirant politics.** Our friends who have ranted and raved for years about this and that being unacceptable still accept it all, as most mere mortals must from time to time. Some now bore us from within the various thises and thatses they once found so unacceptable but now find interestingly reformable. The politics of the 500-mile stare, the glazed-over insistence that having the correct line is living the correct life is still what it always was, merely correct, like rooting for the correct football team, and about as meaningful.

Maybe the politics of place won't work either. Maybe nothing works. That is one way to make up reality. Another is to go ahead and work a certain way as though it will work, or, put it this way, we have little to lose by concentrating now in an area that has been long neglected, overlooked, even despised. What else are you doing this week?

The politics of place has one thing very much in common with any other kind of politics or, indeed, any other kind of social endeavor. It involves constituency. Put it another way. It involves making friends and envisioning neighborly relations. Conventional politics does it rhetorically, as in merchandising, using the lingo of pulling together, common causes, and enlightened self-interest. The politics of place has to do it concretely, getting neighbors interested in something, working together to do it, letting other neighbors see the work, make judgements, and perhaps join the next step, the next work.

But can anything so meager, so parochial, so local have any levering effect on the world? Who knows? But here's a possibility.

There are 3,099 counties, or similar subdivisions, in the United States of America. If most of the people in all the counties started doing something differently, then the country would have changed (no matter what the government, the nation, did). If people in all the counties started going into business for themselves, then productive life would change. If people in all the counties started working together in different ways then commerce would change.

Or suppose half of the counties did something. Wouldn't that make a change? Experience suggests that social change always has been (in advance of the revolutionary leaders who ride the crest of the wave, parasites on the work of other people out in the boonies) accomplished by far less a movement of people—in the places where they live.

Now imagine a quarter of the counties changing, or some lesser number, whatever strikes you as an interesting critical mass. I think of ten percent as most interesting, 300 counties.

Spread out, that's only six counties per state.

You may already have a constituency for change, or conservation, in your own county. I'm trying in mine. Okay. That's two. We have 298 to go. I know many counties where there is a substantial or at least significant constituency for the politics of place as different from the conventional politics of party. You must know a few. Our number gets more and more interesting.

Everywhere I've traveled in this country over the past ten years, I have found healthy signs of alternative or preserving communities. I know that there are such communities in at least, in at the very least, six of the 55 counties of West Virginia, where I live.

These are places where people of alternative imaginations have access to their neighbors, where they can be heard. Some work on media, in radio and newspapers. Most are associated with food co-ops and such things. Most are respected in their communities as hard working, productive, skilled people. They are good neighbors, not hippie intruders, liberal weekenders, or conservative speculators. Some hold local offices. More could. All can influence such issues as:

- preservation of farmland.
- development of local business and economy as opposed to giving away local resources to lure absentee owners.
- development of cooperative or other non-absentee, non-state forms of land, production, and resource ownership.
- development of still more experimental communities, luring like minded people.
- local development of technologies appropriate to the temper, times, and desires of neighbors and communities.
- local arrangements to adjudicate the externalities which so far have slipped almost completely into the cracks of the vast corporate state—costs of toxic waste generation and disposal, costs of subsidizing political factions and favored businesses from general funds, costs of such nation-state resource allocations as cheap water for irrigation, cheap shipping for world traders, highways, and so forth.
- definitions of progress. (So long as there is a singular definition, expressed as the national interest, by national leaders, progress will be totally manipulative managerial technique and not a process in which diversity, individual differences and, very important, individual landscapes can play any part at all. The national interest, as it has worked out in history may be seen as the narrowest interest of all, reflecting the least and not the most of the aspirations of people generally who become simply a population. Populations are hopeless masses. Settlements are human places of accomplishment.)
- or name your own.

And, of course, that is the great point. The politics of place is the politics of *your* place, not mine. After you have understood and raised your own issues, after your neighbors have done the same, then and only then can we come to some sort of decent time in which our two places, and as many other places as are interested, can share, compare, cooperate.

The tactics of the politics of place may be as varied as the people and the places.

I have friends in Champaign-Urbana, Illinois, who have based their politics of place in a garage. Five or six years ago, people who had been constantly active in the politics of protest decided to settle instead into a politics of place. They organized a worker-managed auto repair shop.

When one of the mechanics ran for local office, city council, he did so as a familiar working man in the community. It was a far more solid base than a mere reputation as a political hothead would have been. He won, and has won since. His wife, meantime, has become a local tax official.

Even if they lose their offices in one of the constant reversals of tides in American party politics, they will never be less than influential members of their community and, of course, the mechanic can never be less than a respected workman in the community.

They have a base. They have friends and neighbors, they have an ongoing constituency of neighborliness. And they can have some association also with students of the University of Illinois which sprawls like a parasite growth across the communities. Rather than politically highly charged students having only the dim memories of the Sixties to guide their energies, they can see a working example of a politics of place.

Incidentally, one of the most important ongoing political and social activities in the area is a small bookstore, started and operated by one man who decided, also, to stay put in the community rather than roam the land crying doom or making dire threats. The store is a communications center, a dependable and broad interest source of books and magazines, and exactly the sort of commercial operation that fits perfectly into a politics of place.

In the Nashville area, people who used to be neighbors in Washington have also settled down, convinced of the value of a politics of place, and have organized a network of local farmer's markets which may do more to reintroduce local, small scale, nonchemical farming than any number of cult rallies or even publications.

This doesn't at all mean that the cult rallies and the publications in this or any other area, are lesser activities. They are simply different activities. They produce a sonorous background. The politics of place can produce the actual melodies which people can whistle right where they are, here and now.

The *CoEvolution Quarterly* has been filled, over the years, with other examples. The Institute for Local Self-Reliance in Washington publishes an entire newsletter about such things, about the politics of place. The National Association of Neighborhoods, also in Washington, is an organizational evidence of the fact that in literally hundreds of American communities people have, with either actual municipal status or without it, banded together in substantial numbers to make purely local solutions to problems which, otherwise, would be called national and, probably, insoluble.

And, of course, everywhere the technology of place, the developments of small scale, locally feasible technologies soars along. No politics of place need be without a material base thanks to the incredibly miniaturizing characteristics of every advancing technology from amorphous semiconductors to molecular biology. These characteristics are as strikingly different from the technologies of conventional wisdom—the production lines, static development, huge tools, vast capital demands, political regulation and privilege—as the communities of a libertarian society are from the communities of a regimented society.

The politics of place does not demand but certainly does not deny the possibilities of running for local political offices. In what I believe to be the best recent philosophical statement made on local politics, Murray Bookchin has written:

> If a decentralist opposition to the state, indeed, to the regimentation and militarization of American society, is to be meaningful, the term "decentralization" itself must acquire form, structure, substance, and coherence. Words like "human scale" and "holism" become a deadening cliché when they are not grasped in terms of their full logic.
>
> What is the authentic locus of this project? Certainly, it is not the present day workplace—the factory and office—which itself has become a hierarchical, technologically obsolete arena for mobilizing labor. Nor can the locus for this project be the isolated commune and cooperative, despite their invaluable features as the gymnasia for learning the arts and resolving the problems of direct action, self-management, and social interaction.
>
> The authentic locus is in a conflict between society and the state. And just as the centralized state today means the *national* state, so

society today increasingly comes to mean the *local* community—the township, the neighborhood, and the municipality. The demand for "local control" has ceased to mean parochialism and insularity. In the force field generated by an increasingly centralized and corporatized economy, the cry for a recovery of community, autonomy, relative self-sufficiency, self-reliance, and direct democracy has become the last residue of social resistance to increasing state authority. The overwhelming emphasis the media has given to local autonomy, to a militant municipalism, as refuges for middle-class parochialism—often with racist and economically exclusionary restrictions—conceals the latent *radical* thrust that can give a new vitality to the towns, neighborhoods, cities and counties against the national state.

By the same token, the municipality may easily become the point of departure for a broad-based, directly democratic, truly popular, and humanly scaled constellation of *social* institutions that, by their very logic, stand in sharp opposition to increasingly all-pervasive political institutions. This much is clear: the potential for a libertarian radicalism is *inherent* in the municipality. It forms the bedrock for direct social relations, face-to-face democracy, and the personal intervention of the individual, the neighborhood or commune and cooperative in the formation of a new public sphere. Rescued from its own political institutions such as the mayoralty structure, the civic bureaucracy, and its own organized monopoly of violence, it still preserves the historic materials for a reconstruction (and ultimately, a transcendence) of the polis, the free medieval commune, the New England town meeting system, the Parisian sections, the decentralized structure.

Historically, the municipality itself has been a battleground between society and the state; indeed, it historically antedates the state and has been in perpetual conflict with it. It has been a battleground because the state, until comparatively recently, has never fully claimed the municipality owing to its rich social life—the family, guilds, the Ecclesia, neighborhoods, local societies, the sections, and town meetings. These richly nucleated structures, despite their own internal divisions, have been strikingly impervious to political institutionalization. Ironically, the tension between society and state on the municipal level never became the serious issue it is today because the internal forces of the town and neighborhood still possessed the material, cultural, and spiritual means to resist the invasive tendencies of political forces. Municipal life—richly textured by family networks, local loyalties, professional organizations, popular societies, and even cafes—provided a human refuge from the homogenizing, bureaucratic forces of the state apparatus. Today, the state threatens to destroy this refuge, and municipalism has become the most significant terrain for the struggle against the state on nonpolitical grounds. The very concept of citizenship, not merely of civic autonomy, is at stake in this conflict.

It is crucial at this time for any movement that seeks to be socially relevant to the unique nature of the American crisis to recognize the meaning and significance of the civic terrain—to explore, develop, and help reconstitute its social bedrock. Local politics is not foredoomed to become state politics. To help organize a neighborhood assembly, to advance its consciousness along libertarian lines, to raise demands for the recall and rotation of deputies chosen by assembly, to draw clear distinctions between policy formulation and administrative coordination, challenge civic bureaucratism in every form, to educate the community in mutual aid, finally, to foster confederal relations between assemblies within a municipality and between municipalities in open defiance of the national state—this program constitutes "politics" that, by its very logic, yields the negation of conventional politics.

I feel that there is another dimension to the politics of place that is important. The politics of party and privilege is always the politics of rights. These rights are proclaimed and enforced by agencies of brute force, the police. They may be pleasant agencies or they may be harsh, and thus mark off the cosmetic difference between autocracy and representative democracy, for instance. There remains at the heart of the thing, though, a legitimized monopoly on violence.

Conservatives, who now command our own political heights, see this use of force to maintain and enforce rights (the rights of corporate law, a public infrastructure, and police protection of titles and contracts) as virtually the whole of the civilized order. Some have even taken Ronald Reagan to mild task recently for having used excessive anti-government rhetoric that weakens the hold government has on the loyalties of people. The columnist George Will has done this at some length.

Liberals also base their politics upon the use of force to create rights (the right to make GM recall cars, the right to take money from one group and transfer it to another and so forth).

It is the proclamation and enforcement of rights that is the very business of the politics of the nation and of national parties.

And, as may clearly be seen, the enforcement of one party's rights is always viewed as an assault on the other party's rights. This is correct. It is.

Now look at rights in the natural order. There are none.

You may proclaim, until you die of starvation, the right of all human beings to food but, if you do it alone in an unplanted field you will do it to no avail. What you may observe, with your last gasp, is that you were faced with a situation in which a responsibility, not a right, had appeared: the responsibility to grow food.

Any proclamation of rights is a proclamation of the need for somebody to *do* something or abstain from doing something. Party politics, or autocracy, is the conventional way in which it is decided exactly who will do the work or the abstaining. There is not known on the face of the Earth any right that is not so divided. No right ever proclaimed has applied to everyone in a society. (Killing is the most obvious example. The right not to be killed is one of the most ancient. Virtually every state says that its main order of business is to defend the lives of citizens. But then, alas, time after time, the state itself must kill them, in wars, in the execution of laws, in so many ways.)

The politics of place, because it is essentially neighborly, can attend to something that I consider to be considerably more satisfying as a human proposition: responsibility.

To the extent that social discussions focus on our responsibilities in the community and, inevitably, therefore, on whether we even want to be in it or not, then we can be discussing volitional commitments. To the extent that they focus on rights, we are discussing legalistic commitments which experience has shown, acquire a life of their own, and, sadly, a life that becomes superior to the lives of the people bound under them.

Conservatives regard this as the settled purpose of human settlement and they also feel that the longer such arrangements can bind people the better. They believe in single strokes of wisdom lighting the way for people forever. Many, because of this, have strong institutionally religious convictions and they are fierce constitutionalists.

Liberals regard constitutions as a way to make sure that people perpetually do what is regarded as good—regarded as good today, that is. Thus they have reduced generations of welfare clients to indolence and incompetence because, once, some people needed charity and some other people decided they should have it as a right forever. They also decided who would foot the bill.

In the politics of place, with people discussing their shared interests more face to face, and certainly more in the light of day to day observations, a strong case can be made for responsibilities and agreement rather than rights and constitutions which are as subject to interpretation as the Bible and as subject to privilege as the curia.

At any rate, you can make a local case for responsibilities, shared and volitional responsibilities, while you can never make such cases in national politics. There is no volition in the nation. The nation says you must. The neighborhood says you should, and the good neighbor says either okay or here's why I won't—and the discussion can proceed from there.

It must remain impossible to write normatively about what the politics of place would look like close up. It would look, in fact, like any damn thing that local folks could contrive. In one county or community it could mean a drive toward a virtual free port live-and-let-live arrangement with only tiny agreements to, say, not shit on the street, aggressively kill, or steal. In others it could mean a prim approach to religious observances, tidy dress, and quiet manners. It could mean anything. It could mean keeping some town, county, or community exactly the way it is.

Whatever it meant it would have little pernicious impact on other communities so long as the focus was inward, toward local affairs. As the focus shifts outward there are other possibilities.

A community can choose to be aggressive, trying to annex a neighboring community, for instance. Nothing new there. It is done everyday. But, in the politics of party, the target community has little leverage because the annexing community, characteristically has, because of its size, more clout with the politics of party in the area. In the politics of place, people could encourage themselves to be more stubborn about resisting such aggression, and aggressive communities, to the extent that the politics of place weakens the politics of power and party, would have less and less force to throw against the target community.

In some sweet by and by when local liberty has been achieved, of course, you might still worry that one community would go berserk and raid a neighboring one. It certainly could happen. It also would certainly be more desirable than having a nation-state do it either to the same community or to another nation-state—the difference between a brawl and a battlefield.

In most times the first response of an outward look from one community to another has been reasonably prudent: commerce.

But, actually, most such concerns for what if this and what if that are fairly silly. We live in a place already. That place is in a region. The region is in a nation and it, in turn, is on this planet.

By turning away from national politics toward local politics we are not risking the sorts of spasm changes which have made such travesties of the hopes of modern revolutionary idealists who begin the morning as sweet liberators and end in the evening as common butchers.

Such a turning is to do what the Industrial Workers of the World once urged its members to do: to make the new world in the shell of the old. A better place, I believe, than to try to make it either on the scaffold or in the dreamy midair of theoretical proclamation.

You do live in a place today. You do have neighbors. You do have ways formal and informal to talk to people about change or preservation.

Local office holding is just one way. The myriad boards, clubs, and associations of town and country, of city and county, are another way. Civic associations and their constant communicative activity, offer another path. Churches are ways. Bull sessions. Food and other co-ops. Programs at the local library. Letters to the local paper. Programs on the local radio. Membership in the volunteer fire department, the police reserve. Visiting, visiting, and more visiting. Gaining respect in the community. Being serious about what you do. Speaking plainly and simply. Understanding that you have neighbors, not subjects. Staying put. Forming little groups to do little things. Teaching courses in the adult education program. Starting a women's shelter. Working with kids. Being pleasant. Being stubborn when your neighbors can understand why. Not following leaders and watching the parking meters.

And, always, offering sensible alternatives and not just criticism. If you feel that the trash can be collected better by a private company, or a co-op, than by city workers, go into business and not just into a rage. If you don't believe in public schools, start a private one. If you *don't* anything, do something else. If you resent land speculation, join with your neighbors in land ownership. If you pity the hungry, feed them.

Where else but at the local level, where you are protected by the volitional agreements of your neighbors, could you expect to do anything opposed to conventional power. (The small California towns whose citizens protect their dope-growing neighbors are an example of a free market springing up where the state says it shouldn't and although I am, personally, without any enthusiasm for marijuana, I am enormously enthusiastic about the liberty and neighborliness which can shelter its growing locally rather than handing it over totally to the managerial chieftains of hierarchically organized crime. Nonetheless, that homely example shows just how far the politics of place can go even these days and against great state power. I hope more ordinarily productive examples will come to mind and to pass.)

The urge to save the world, in a piece and at once, will endure in many hearts no matter what. Suggestions regarding the politics of place can scarcely diminish that fervor. The urge to seize power will endure. The urge to be President, or Senator, or something, will endure. I don't suggest it won't and I won't even say it shouldn't. I can't, as a matter of fact, imagine what the loftily ambitious would do if they didn't have their high offices to seek and their parades to plan. So they will.

There are many, many times more of us who aren't in that league. We march to a different drummer, as one of our neighbors once put it. Where we live is such an obvious place to get on with our parade.

What have we got to lose? We are on the scene anyway. We never live in the entire world, although we may bother about it a lot. We live at home. Charity begins there, remember? So does everything else including the next batch of human beings. Even if our inclinations keep us turned to the world, shouldn't we do at least a little work at home? Being an extremist I argue that we should do most of it there. But, being an anarchist, I would argue that you have to figure out some ratio for yourself. If you would simply grant me the same responsibility without imposing a right to make me do otherwise, I would be pleased—and we can get on with our separate politics of place, mine being Berkeley County, West Virginia, and someone else's being the universe or some other place.

While some folks are trying to save THE children, it does little harm and, I think, a great deal of good for some of us to save A child. Some people may feel the same way about whales.

And so it can go for the entire range of human action and interest. Things *can* be done locally. Not everything. Some things. Can any more inspiring claim be made for parliaments? And do you now care to wait for parliaments to do whatever it is they do?

The politics of place, as it has turned out, is the place for me. I have tried to save the world by being at the peak of its political power, or very near it. I wasn't very good at it, but, as I see it now, neither were the others who were working at it. I have tried to save the world by crying wolf and by crying love and by crying stranger things. I think I changed much more than the world but, then, I must keep reminding myself that I am part of the world and if I never changed then the world couldn't either, not altogether.

I have advanced and I have retreated, mumbled, shouted, even prayed. I've watched people shooting and looting. I've been high and I've been low, dirty and clean, wild-eyed and wonderful, neat, natty, big and little, global and local. I like local best. I've had fans, followers, suitors, pleaders, bosses and neighbors. I like neighbors best.

It comes to that, doesn't it?

I really don't have THE ANSWER. I've never met anyone who did. Maybe it's there. I never stop listening. In the meantime, though, I hate to do nothing. So I do something. I do it at home, with my neighbors. I've worked with them in an alternative technology group that has been meeting once a month for four years. Local officials now ask our advice. I've done work with our local library. Therese does more. We've held film festivals that got across ideas it would have been hard to put in a letter to the editor (which I also write at the drop of an issue). I've spoken to and made friends in just about every civic club. A couple of us are joining the Moose which, one layer under the drinking, is a mutual aid society. Friends in the next county have a movie theater. That's interesting. Friends do a lot of farming, a lot of building. We've got a fairly steady stream of courses going at the local vo-tech center, in other schools. We helped put together a medical self-care course at a local clinic. We're part of this community. We respect it. We're getting its respect. We're all likely to change some in the process.

And what else can I do? Whenever I think of an answer, I do that too. But I'm mostly at home and I like it best there and it's where I see the world from. And so I have volunteered to work at the politics of place. There may not be any more than that to it. We'll just have to wait and see.

CoEvolution Quarterly, Summer 1981

Elitism in Defense
of Virtue Is No Vice

"**E**litism" is one of the strongest words people use to discredit activities they dislike. Its undoubted power to provoke antagonism derives from an earlier evoker of hostility, the concept of "meritocracy." In a meritocracy the major rewards of life are awarded to (or greedily gobbled up by) people who have performed something with merit—made a good deal, written a brilliant piece of music, discovered a new way to explain an aspect of the physical world, or something along these lines.

This arrangement is bad, it is argued, because it leaves high and dry all of the non-meritorious people who, through no fault of their own, do not acquire enough of those things or privileges necessary for a good life. The evolution from meritocracy to welfare state in this country was deemed necessary in the belief that the non-meritorious—previously attended to by charity—should have the requisites of a good life *as a right*.

As meritocracy vanished as a worthy social and political concept, a new assault word was needed; one that could be targeted not only against whole systems, but with surgical precision could be used against even the most minute part of any activity. Elitism is just such a word. In any social, political or cultural activity, any portion that is not demonstrably and *purposefully* egalitarian may be attacked as elitist.

Why being elitist is now or ever was "bad" has not been widely debated. In the heaves of the mid-century, equality and egalitarianism took on a broad and undifferentiated air of virtue. The civil rights movement seems to be mostly responsible for this development. From its undeniable moral power, the idea of equality became unassailable and then undefinable. To suggest that in some areas of human action equality is not only impossible but also undesirable—in art and science, for instance— is sometimes attacked as racist as well as elitist. It is difficult, apparently, for anti-racists to attack elitism without making it appear that racial minority populations are not themselves capable of achieving the high standards usually associated with an elite.

Although the arguments are usually quite vague, the charge is felt as sharp and stinging largely because, I am convinced, the media generally have accepted without any question the notion that elitism is inherently bad, so bad that everyone is expected to know that it's bad. The old definition of an elite as an especially privileged, probably undeserving group —an aristocracy—is not generally involved or evoked. The new elitism has to do with the supposedly rejected idea of meritocracy.

Ironically, many who launch attacks on elitism are themselves members of an observable elite of social workers and educationists specially trained to be social propagandists and organizers. Saul Alinsky's justly famed school for New Left organizers nurtured just such an elite corps. Harvard's law school today, at least in its "critical legal studies" enclave, also seeks to create an elite. Nader's Raiders are another obviously elite group that nevertheless can be counted on to use elitism as a pejorative term.

Social-activist elites deny their own elitism on grounds that their special training and obviously superior grasp of things is meant to serve the helpless and the dispossessed. And, to be fair, many of them actually make it their purpose to help people help themselves—actually to create a new elite of self-helping people in settings of squalor. It seems to me that the best intentioned of these activists are missing a useful tool. To achieve by merit, to do good work, to improve one's life, to be an elitist of accomplishment and energy has a worthy sound if disencumbered of the vague and voguish *charge* of elitism.

The arguments supporting the charges of elitism, as I have observed them, are usually contained in the headlines of the stories: with the word elitism being sufficient for the charge *and* for the explanation. In the text of stories there may be casual clauses referring to elitism as being separatist or favoring a bright minority, but little else.

When I worked closely with many on the New Left, the charge was as powerful and as vague as it is today. New Left *elites* were able to carry the charge successfully into the media without being bothered for a discussion of why elitism suddenly had become such a bad idea.

In those days I always argued in favor of elitism, thus reinforcing the idea of many associates on the left that, down deep underneath my army field jacket and jeans, I was a right-wing flake.

It was, of course, always unsatisfying to discuss elitism with Marxist-Leninists. It was their view, as succinctly stated in one seminar I attended, that the wisdom to tell other people how to live their lives was a science in which Marxist-Leninists had become superbly skilled. When I mentioned that that sounded like an elitism of which they obviously should be proud, I was asked to leave, having become an "obstructionist." The leader of that seminar has gone on to be an energetic supporter of perhaps the most elitist group in all the Americas, the Sandinistas. They are elitist, of course, in the old sense of people who are thought of or think of themselves as socially superior and thus entitled to power and privilege. They are not elitist in the modern sense of having achieved elitism through merit.

Elitism has become a totem word. It has great strength and may be defined by the user. My reference to a modern definition of elitism through merit is an example.

Unlike the Biblical doctrines, with which interpretations can at least be argued because of the availability of text, the *charge* of elitism has no standard text, or definition, and has become more of a meaningful sound rather than a meaningful concept. In movies there are certain musical themes that denote moods or dangers as vividly as if they were accompanied by written signs. Elitism as a charge has become like that. You *know* it's bad and nobody need bother to tell you *why* just as they do not need to give you a musicological explanation of Alfred Hitchcock suspense themes.

One of the most recent targets of the charge of elitism are the high schools of science and technology that lately have become fashionable in many educational jurisdictions. Since they are limited in number and thus not available to everyone who might want to attend, ways of apportioning space in them have become necessary. One way is to accept only students who have evidenced particular aptitudes or accomplishments.

Such procedures are, obviously, meritocratic, thereby elitist.

Even, however, if the schools admit students on a first-come, first-served basis, the *programs* in the schools may be attacked as elitist. They seek to create, it is argued, an elite class of scientists and technologists.

In this view—which goes back as far as the pioneer public schooler, Horace Mann—public (government) education has as its purpose the inculcation of officially determined social values and the fundamentals of citizenship such as loyalty to the national state rather than to localities or devotion to professions or crafts.

Private schools are, of course, considered pure poison by this view. They weaken support for government schools by siphoning off desirable students and thoughtful parents, and because they create students who may actually think of themselves *as* an elite simply because they got a good education.

Perhaps we should wish these charges to *stick*—for a very elitist reason. Even if government schools of science and technology are successfully opposed by anti-elitists, there is no reason to believe that this will stop the proliferation of special schools in the *private* sector. Successful attacks against government schools of excellence simply opens the market for more and more private schools of excellence.

Elite private schools attacked by Luddites might even gain from the attacks; the attacks could focus the attention of parents not on the plight of the government schools but on the potential advantages to their children of the elite schools. Hurrah!

The attacks against elitism in the governmental system of education might also inspire businesses and industries to start nurturing their own engineers, scientists, and technologists in their own schools which, unlike most of the government schools, presumably would emphasize the processes and practice of thinking rather than genuflections to Federal guidelines.

The need for elites, in the meritocratic and not aristocratic sense, is more clear now than ever.

It is by the business elite, the entrepreneurs, that markets are created which, in turn, create new jobs. It is by the technical elites that new products are made possible. And these products are not confined, as leftists would have you believe, to the ticky-tacky. They include, for example, the materials of medical treatment and the technologies of information.

Non-elite—that is, heavily subsidized, coddled, technically careless—farmers have been going out of business steadily during the past decade. These were defended in a series of Hollywood and TV films, in ways that included an interesting and subtle—and very propagandistic—version of the anti-elitist argument. The ability of the farmers to grow crops effectively and profitably was never the issue. The issue was refined down to the fact that they had been farming in one way and on one place for a long time and thus should be able to continue no matter what. The villains, usually, were the bankers—who make money from interest on debts in order to pay interest to depositors. The way that the careless farmers got into debt, foolishly expanding acreage and buying incredibly expensive motorized equipment to harvest dirt-cheap crops, was not the issue. The issue was simply their *desire* to continue to be farmers—no matter the cost to their neighbors.

In the meantime, an elite of farmers has been appearing, many in truck farming areas where careful consideration of the soil, substitution of low-cost organic fertilizers for high-cost chemical ones, and judicious use of efficient, small machines is paying off handsomely. The farmers who have been going out of business to the accompaniment of so much Hollywood angst have mainly been those who concentrated on the crops, such as corn, for which price supports have been available and which they have been growing by brute force rather than by technologically sophisticated methods.

Good farmers will not have to go out of business, *ever*, so long as any semblance of a market is available for their absolutely indispensable product. Poor, non-elitist farmers *should* go out of business lest millions someday starve because of an agricultural Gresham's Law disaster.

Now that the task of cleaning the environment is taken seriously by so many people—seriously enough to create a *market* for clean air and water—the need for an elite of superb technologists is urgent as is the need for inspired scientists to keep probing the conditions which we now describe rather primitively as pollution. The air will not be cleaned or the water purified by Everyman thinking clean and pure thoughts. Things are far too far gone for that. Everyman may have an essential role in *keeping* things clean later on, but the job here and now is going to call for some very smart people, an elite.

Such elites, in a meritocratic sense, seem strikingly non-threatening and wholly beneficial to me. What "mad scientist" has ever been mad enough to achieve political power, to become a mad overlord? And who on earth has not benefitted from the work of scientists generally, by the applications of technologists generally, and by the promulgations of technology through commerce of science, technology, and even culture?

Unfortunately, in one area where an elite is crucially necessary it is difficult even to begin the discussion. That area is the neighborhoods of very poor people, the neighborhoods of the underclass. These neighborhoods need parents who encourage their children to study hard and work hard despite the current fashion according to which schoolmates psychologically and even physically attack achieving students as being unbearable nerds or even as being class or race traitors, trying to be like "them," the enemy outside the projects.

And there *are* such elite parents in even the poorest, toughest neighborhoods. When discussing them, however, the media alludes correctly to their heroism and energy but rarely makes an invidious comparison with the non-elite parents. To do so would be, of course, *elitist*.

In the cultural area, The National Endowment for the Arts takes a subtly anti-elitist view, particularly pertaining to painting, music, and poetry. The elitist view, stemming from a meritocracy, would be that people who produce something popular and profitable are commendable and have, without force or favor, been able to convince people of the value of their work.

The richest musicians in the history of the world are the Beatles. They are a pinnacle elite all by themselves, just as Mozart and Beethoven were in their own times. They all became elite in the same meritocratic manner. They produced something that people wanted. Even when rich patrons tried to bolster some flaccid competitor, the elite composers won the audiences then and now. (Imagine Pia Zadora having to compete with Ringo Starr's latest tour.)

The National Endowment has a quite different view. It appears committed to supporting the least elite artists in the realm. Let someone appear with a well-written grant to display scribbles or scrabbles that would stand no chance in a free market setting, and the National Endowment rushes to oblige. Let someone discover that a monotone, repeated for minutes on end, is hot, high musical art and the Endowment orgasmically unquivers its golden bolts and lets them fly.

The great anti-elitist attitude of the Endowment over the years has seemed to be that anything that the public likes (say Andrew Wyeth) is essentially unworthy. Their mission is to find stuff that nobody wants and to thrust it forward. If the Endowment didn't support the stuff, who would? If nobody did, wouldn't that be censorship of a sort? Wouldn't we risk depriving future generations of good stuff if everything had to be seen as having merit *today*. Groan. Little thought seems given to *why* it wouldn't be supported in the first place. The off chance that the work is unworthy and that not even the passage of time could redeem it is, thus, struck from discussion by an essentially elitist decision (in the old, authoritarian, aristocratic sense).

Think of poor old Van Gogh. Lord knows he wasn't supported much by anyone other than his brother. He just painted and painted. Would it have been nice for him to have had an Endowment grant? Who knows? The point is that it wasn't necessary. His great, elitist work got done anyway.

There has been no other time on the planet that more urgently needs elitism in the meritocratic sense.

There is no time that has more needed courage in facing up to charges of meritocracy and elitism. Those who sense grandeur and goodness in merit often have kept their feelings concealed. I am sure that discussions can be stopped cold today when someone asks "are you defending the idea of a meritocracy" and no one has the courage to say "sure!"

It is rather like the discussion stopper "but, surely, you don't mean that you believe in survival of the fittest."

Well, I do.

And whether I did or not, it's the way things are.

The fittest are not the slyest or the cruelest or even the strongest. In the long run it seems that the fittest are the smartest, the most thoughtful. And, among other things they have, as individuals, practiced the sort of charity that has helped the less fit to survive. Or, as artists, they have inspired people to *be* fit. Or as scientists and technologists they have made it easier for everyone to survive, to be more fit.

Way back, when the financier Bernard Baruch was famous for holding "court" on a park bench across from the White House, I sat with him and asked for sage advice. He said "young man, you will hear trusts criticized by all of the politicians. Do not listen to the criticism of trusts. Join one."

Same way about elites and elitism. Be part of the former. Be exalted by the latter.

Liberty, January 1990

Rights and Reality

Social ecology has performed the distinct service of demanding that human action be considered a factor in the study of natural systems. Legislative acts are seen as transforming the landscape as much as volcanic eruption. Of human actions, none seems a more powerful tool for affecting the natural world than the attribution of rights. Rights are declared to conserve and rights are declared to despoil—the concept is a double-edged sword.

The biblically-stated right of human beings to dominate nature is impatient with scientific method's slow, experimental efforts to understand nature. The environmentalist idea of the social right to clean air contradicts the economist's view that we have the right to use raw materials as efficiently as possible. Everyone's right to have whatever one wants, finally, collides with the politician's mission to define those rights and allocate force to eliminate some and reinforce others. Any concept of rights is an invitation to trouble, and perhaps disaster.

Every single declaration of a right is nothing more than a statement of opinion or preference. Consider what would happen if a right were pronounced by people in the middle of a field. Let us say they pronounce the currently popular "right of every human being to have enough food to sustain life," and having pronounced it sit and wait for the right to be

403

translated into action. They would simply starve. The mere proclamation of the right would not produce the food.

What about their right to strike out on their own and seek food rather than wait for it? That could certainly be called a right—unless, of course, other people surrounded the field and would not let them out. But *they* have no right to keep others from seeking food! Sure. Tell that to violent brutes—or to educated members of an elite police force assigned to contain a certain population to an infertile area.

As long as any discussion of the natural world seeks to state or discern rights, the discussion should be labeled for what it is—a search for power. Rights are power, the power of one person or group over another. Even if one considers rights as descended directly from Heaven, with God's signature hot upon them, the very next consideration will be to find the temporal power to bop on the head anyone who will not respect (i.e., obey) the right.

The belief that there are rights that can be enforced without head-bopping is an illusion. Neither Christ upon his cross nor Mohammed upon his rock made any provision for a Sacred Defense Initiative by which some supernatural force would zap anyone not respecting a religiously-proclaimed right. After religiously-proclaimed rights, of course, it is obvious that all other rights are human contrivances.

There are those who, while admitting that rights are never real, nonetheless see them as a powerful rhetorical tool to discuss conduct more transcendental than merely the crude question of power. There is at least a natural right, they would argue, whereby one's personal boundaries should not be violated. Most people probably would agree to this—if not as a part of a developed theory, at least as a personal belief.

While I admit that this is a benign and generally demonstrable statement, I cannot say it is a wise one. Allow the mere mention of rights, even restricting that mention to the single most fundamental right, and the door is flung open for an ever-escalating war of rights against rights. Introduce the subject of rights into any discussion and the chances are overwhelming that you will get confrontation, bared fangs, bared interests. Rather than a reciprocal discussion of mutual interests those who introduce the matter of rights into the conversation actually introduce combative lines, one person's right facing off, armed to the teeth, against another person's right.

Take the right to life, a popular right currently, as an example. As one bitter commentary puts it, the anti-abortionists believe that life begins with conception and ends with birth. The right of the foetus, in other words, is simply selected as a particular cause for concern.

Right-to-life is not stated as an absolute and all-inclusive right, although the very wording certainly suggests such a universal concern. The right-to-life movement does not, to pursue this point, include a cor-related statement that all humans have a right to life. To do so would obvi-ously undercut the power of the very State upon which the anti-abortion-ists now depend for the eradication of what they see as a particular evil. What they seek, explicitly, is power—the power to punish any who would take the life of a foetus; not a right to life for the foetus, which may under certain circumstances be killed illicitly. It is a right of punishment for the victors in a legislative putsch.

If the State did not have the right to kill, then it could not exist. Without the ability, in the long run, to kill, how would a State impose itself upon other States, or protect itself against them, or even remain sov-ereign over citizens? The absolute essence of State power, from its ability to collect taxes to its ability to fend off invasion, depends without equiv-ocation on its ability (its "right") to assign its agents to kill someone. The greatest "good" that it does (say, solace the sick with services paid by taxes) is based on the State's power to punish, and, if need be, kill anyone who resists. But how can this be true in instances of the State merely arresting someone who does not "have the right" to violate State law? Surely this does not constitute lethal intent. Nonsense! Unless the right to arrest is coupled with the right to kill, then it is a game like rugby, full of bruises and contusions but with precious few appearances in court.

People have always been and always will be killed for trifling rea-sons, so long as any institution claims the right to protect itself and codify that right into either the legislative act of a democracy or the ukase of a tyranny. But whether the reason is trifling or grave, the fact remains: nowhere on this planet does the right to life surpass, in any agreed or widespread way, the might of political power. There simply is not, in short, any right to life. Those who say that there is are saying only that they feel strongly that people, or some people, should live. No matter how grandly they clothe their statement of rights, it boils down to their own opinion (or their own ideology); to render them effective would require raw, brute power—the power to kill. When people voluntarily agree to behave in a certain way or to abide by a certain rule, we are no longer speaking of rights but of an agreement.

Given as I am to Utopian dreaming, even I cannot imagine a group of people living together on the basis of rights alone. They may agree to certain things, and, as a libertarian, I acclaim all voluntary agreements, but they must acknowledge the fact that the agreement is just that. It can be broken by the will of a human being, just as it was formed by the will of human beings. Powerful and often binding cultures can grow around such agreements, to be sure, but it will be continuity of agreement and not rights that keeps them going. And when there is a breach of the agreement, the decision must be made whether the others will punish or expel the person in disagreement, or simply ignore the offense. Whatever the decision, the lie will be put to the idea that the group was living together on the basis of rights. They were living together on the basis of agreement, the best thing that human beings can come up with as a guarantor of peace and fair dealing.

Why humans should be ashamed to call their extraordinary capacity to agree with one another just that and only that is beyond me. To agree seems wonderfully human. To talk of rights floating above our heads must invoke the superhuman, the supernatural, the theological. Only by proclaiming rights to be divine, it seems to me, can they be elevated beyond the status of agreements.

In every instance in which the capacity to agree has been codified into some right or another, I have seen or sensed mischief. The glorious Bill of Rights of the U.S. Constitution would be altogether glorious if it was simply a guideline for agreement, a statement of what is reasonable so that people might assure each other when settling down to live together.

Alas, it is nothing of the sort. It is a mere detail in a writ which, at its most powerful, grants absolute powers to the State and even provides that no one may withdraw from that power no matter how grievously offended one might be. The Constitution doesn't actually come right out and say this, but it does give a certain group the "right" to interpret its every word. And, quite sensibly from an institutional point of view, one of those interpretations makes it criminal to secede from the thrall of the Constitution without being granted specific and official membership in some other nation-state.

How, then, does the social ecologist go about impressing the good sense of scientific discovery or intuitive pleas about natural systems upon people who may be inclined to ignore all such knowledge, just as a person suspecting a carcinoma might reject examination for fear that the results will be depressing? How to impress on people that reality—the natural order of things—is important at all, when we live in a world of slippery, spooky rights which tumble over one another at the prodding of any passion, greed, or interest?

I hope that social ecologists will find ways to reach people without proclaiming rights, or they will just be making more noise in an already crowded atmosphere in which everyone's rights are jostling everyone else's.

Perhaps social ecologists must resign themselves to living on the basis of their own discoveries (being exemplary), sharing their information directly with people they know (being good neighbors) and with people they do not know (being publicists and educators), and working toward social organizations in which people confront directly their own responsibility for making decisions regarding the natural world.

So long as people derive rights from institutions of power, there will be little enthusiasm for the merely objective knowledge of living systems and consequences attendant upon exercising human will in them. The natural system will continue to be seen as subordinate to the rights of the institution.

Where environmentalists may see bad laws as the tools by which their personal concept of proper rights is denied, or good laws as a way of establishing those proper rights, the social ecologist should see law itself as a problem. Law is merely specific interest made enforceable. Law proceeds from institutions and contending interests. It can no more be balanced and unbiased than the observations of science can be free of the effect of the observer. Living systems, on the other hand, are information that is material. Humans are a part of these systems and are endowed with the particular sort of consciousness that makes them capable of being concerned about the consequences of their actions.

We are faced, in social ecology, therefore, with an unenviable but inevitable responsibility. We must make it as clear as possible that the natural world in which we live presents us with no model for a declaration of rights. It presents us with the certainty that every action has consequences—no rightness or wrongness, just consequences. It is we, and not nature, who deal in taxonomies of right and wrong. But what a grave responsibility this is!

And yet, we should do more than study and reveal consequences. Should we ever become deeply involved in pressing nature, and our fellow humans, into the mold of our own privilege or preference, we will have stepped from the study of ecology to the practice of law, force, and power.

What humans do is part of nature, and not apart from it. What we do often seems hideous, and, indeed, some feel the entire race is beyond redemption. Of course, should the race end, the rest of the natural world will proceed without it. There is a sad possibility here: if humans have become a pestilence, there seems little doubt that we will prove it ultimately in the form of a nuclear or biological war that would simply end the human cycle. Some life would probably remain, and even if none did, the barren planet could be re-seeded with life from elsewhere. Failing even that, the earth would just join other dead rocks whirling in a universe of such mysterious dimensions that even the dead rocks may be a part of the multi-galactic ecology.

My own feeling is far more optimistic. Perhaps we are as inimical to most life as the most deadly virus. But we have a not altogether bad record for self-correction. This depends on complete information, however, and we must see the consequences not as isolated incidents but as a part of the whole, so that eventually we will see the entirety of life itself. This is the information sought by the social ecologist, and this, not any theory of rights, holds bright promise for our future.

If we become bound in any way to rights, we may once again constrict our study and help restrict all study to matters compartmentally contained within the laws and powers of institutions of force. The ecological view has helped break through those compartments to the good and common sense of whole and related systems. Those whole and related systems, including the zones of our human residency, do not have rights. They simply are.

Not content with such simple observations, we have, in the past, tried to mold gods out of thin air and heavy dread, to erect great political structures on concepts of right or wrong, to plunge into wars, to fall into false pride, to consider ourselves as separate from the natural order, to proclaim dominion over even that which we do not understand or cannot see.

The ecological view does not restrain the human mind. No view or power short of extinction could do that. Some human mind is always poised on the edge of mystery, poking and probing for a way past the dimness or darkness. We really must live with that. Efforts to stifle human curiosity seem to me inhuman. But reckless refusal to understand the consequences of curiosity is sheer folly. We humans will ask every question.

It is urgent that we understand the changes created in our world by every answer. The ecological view, all rights and ideology aside, simply bids us to try, to the extent that we may, to know what the hell we are doing when we do it.

This is not our right. It is just something we can do.

Our Generation, Fall 1988